That
hat

The Reformed Faith of John Calvin

JOHN CALVIN
Anonymous 16th century portrait

The Reformed Faith *of* JOHN CALVIN

THE *Institutes* IN SUMMARY

DAVID J. ENGELSMA

REFORMED FREE PUBLISHING ASSOCIATION

© 2009 Reformed Free Publishing Association
All rights reserved
Printed in the United States of America

No part of this book may be used or reprinted
in any form without permission from the
publisher, except in the case of a brief quotation
used in connection with a critical article or review

All Scripture quotations by the author are taken
from the Authorized (King James) Version

Quotations from *Calvin: Institutes of the Christian Religion*, edited by John T. McNeill, translated by Ford Lewis Battles (Library of Christian Classics, volumes 20, 21), used by permission of Westminster John Knox Press

Reformed Free Publishing Association
1894 Georgetown Center Drive
Jenison, MI 49428
Website: www.rfpa.org
Email: mail@rfpa.org

ISBN: 978–1–936054–00–8
LCCN: 2009927138

*With gratitude to
Christ Jesus for the
life and labor of
his great servant,
John Calvin*

To Ruth

*Grant unto us, O Lord, to be occupied
in the mysteries of thy Heavenly wisdom,
with true progress in piety, to thy glory
and our own edification. Amen.*

—Prayer of John Calvin at the commencement of his lectures, from his *Commentary on the Book of the Prophet Daniel*

Contents

Preface — xiii

1 The Man and His Life: A Sketch — 1
  Birth, rearing, and conversion 1
  First pastorate in Geneva 2
  In Strasbourg 3
  Second pastorate in Geneva 4
  Influence and significance 8
  Noteworthy characteristics of Calvin's person and personal life 9

2 The Nature of the *Institutes* — 13
  Book of instruction 13
  Apology for the Reformed faith 17
  Confession of faith 18
  Purpose of the Institutes *18*
  Value of studying the Institutes *22*
  Influence of the Institutes *22*

3 The History of the Publishing of the *Institutes* — 24
  Introduction 24
  Editions in Calvin's lifetime 27
  Translations and abridgments 30

4 The Style and Structure of the *Institutes* — 32
  Style 32
  Structure 41

5 The Prefatory Address — 46
  Introduction 46
  Apologetic purpose 46

Defense of the Reformed faith 50
Duties of King Francis 56

BOOK ONE
The Knowledge of God the Creator

6   The Knowledge of God the Creator   61
Introduction 61
Knowledge of God apart from Scripture 62
Knowledge of God in Scripture 68
Testimony of the Holy Spirit 71

7   The Doctrine of the Trinity   75
Introduction 75
Calvin's doctrine: orthodox 77
Calvin's doctrine: simple and clear 78
Calvin's doctrine: biblical 79
Significance of the Trinity for Calvin 81
Condemnation of heresy 82
Respectful criticism of Calvin's doctrine of the Trinity 83

8   Creation, Human Nature as Created, and Providence   87
Introduction 87
Creation of the universe 89
Creation of angels and devils 92
Creation of man 98
What providence is 103
Defense of providence against error 112
Benefit of knowing the truth of providence 116

BOOK TWO
The Knowledge of God the Redeemer in Christ, First Disclosed to the Fathers under the Law, and Then to Us in the Gospel

9   The Condition of Fallen Man   119
Introduction 119

Original sin 121
Total depravity 128
Bondage of the will 131
Remnants of good in fallen man 133

10 The Person and Work of Jesus Christ   138
Introduction 138
The only savior 138
Christ and the law 140
Relation of the old and new covenants 158
The person and natures of the mediator 162
The incarnation 166
The offices of Christ 169
Christ's redemptive work as confessed by the Apostles' Creed 173

BOOK THREE
The Way in Which We Receive the Grace of Christ:
What Benefits Come to Us from It,
and What Effects Follow

11 Union with Christ   191
Introduction 191
Salvation as union with Christ 193
Faith as activity 194
The origin and foundation of faith 201
The object of faith 203
Repentance 203
The Roman Catholic doctrine and sacrament of penance 208

12 The Christian Life   211
Introduction 211
The pattern 212
Main elements of the Christian life 216

13 Justification   222
Introduction 222
Justification by faith 227

Justification by faith alone 231
Refutation of arguments against justification by faith alone 237
Necessity of justification by faith alone 242
Christian freedom 243

14 Prayer   247
Introduction 247
What prayer is 248
Rules for praying rightly 249
Jesus Christ, the only mediator of the prayers of the saints 253
Private and public prayers 255
The model prayer 256
Pastoral counsel concerning praying 263

15 Predestination   266
Introduction 266
Calvin's approach to the doctrine of predestination 269
What predestination is 271
Election is preeminent 275
Election and faith 278
Election and the call of the gospel 281
Defense of predestination against objections 284
Benefits of the knowledge of election 288
Preaching predestination wisely 289

16 The Final Resurrection: Calvin's Eschatology   290
Introduction 290
Nature of the resurrection body 290
Raised into union with God 291
Grounds of belief of the resurrection 292
Eschatological errors 293
Calvin's doctrine of the last things 294
The resurrection: our hope 294
Eternal punishment 295
Eternal bliss 296

BOOK FOUR
The External Means or Aids by Which God Invites Us into the Society of Christ and Holds Us Therein

17 The Doctrine of the Church   301
    Introduction 301
    What the church is 305
    The "visible church" 309
    The marks of the visible church 314
    Rome: the false church 321
    Church government 323
    The Roman Catholic hierarchy 327
    The papacy 331
    Church power 334
    The sacraments 350
    The sacrament of baptism 357
    Infant baptism 362
    The sacrament of the Lord's supper 370
    The papal mass 380
    Five false sacraments of Rome 382

18 Civil Government   386
    Introduction 386
    Civil government ordained of God 389
    The magistracy 391
    Civil laws 397
    The calling of the Christian toward civil government 398

Notes   405

Preface

The idea of this book sprang imperiously to mind when I was teaching a course on Calvin's *Institutes* at the Theological School of the Protestant Reformed Churches. There ought to be a one-volume summary—not an abridgment, but a summary—of Calvin's great work for the burdened seminarian, the busy pastor, the elder working on behalf of the church after he has put in a full day at his occupation, and the laity carrying out their time-consuming responsibilities at home, on the job, and in the church.

How many have not gazed wistfully at the two large volumes of John Calvin's *Institutes of the Christian Religion* on their shelves or at the bookstore, doubting that they would ever find or make time to read them.

The Reformed Faith of John Calvin is, as the subtitle expresses, a summary of Calvin's own teaching in his *Institutes* of all the doctrines of the Christian faith. The reader of this book will know the *Institutes* and the faith—the Reformed faith—that Calvin taught and defended in this classic work.

If, on occasion, a doctrine is not stated in Calvin's own words, I demonstrate the truthfulness of my summation of Calvin's teaching with quotations of Calvin. The book is replete with quotations of Calvin, usually (as it seemed to me) the most important or most vivid statements by Calvin concerning the doctrine being treated. The reader of this summary will hear, and learn from, Calvin himself.

At every point in the setting forth of Calvin's understanding of the Christian faith there is reference to the exact place in the *Institutes* (book, chapter, section, and page) where the quotation is found or the doctrine is treated. Thus, the interested reader can at once read further in the *Institutes* itself concerning a particular doctrine or practice. The doubtful reader can readily compare my summary with Calvin's own exposition.

The book is also more than a summary. At times, it offers explanation of Calvin's teaching. Often, it applies Calvin's doctrine or admonition to the church of the twenty-first century. On the rare occasion, it even gives a respectful criticism of Calvin's view.

The publisher and I offer this book especially to the Calvinistic community in commemoration of the five hundredth anniversary of the birth of Calvin in 1509, in gratitude to God for the priceless gift of the *Institutes* to Christ's church through his great servant, John Calvin, and in the conviction that the faith taught in the *Institutes* is the one, true faith of the gospel of Holy Scripture—the faith, therefore, not only for the church of the sixteenth century, but also for the church of our and every other day.

As always, I am grateful beyond telling to my wife, Ruth, who has patiently borne with yet another time-consuming writing project. John Calvin has been criticized by hopeless romantics and fervent feminists for the tribute he paid to his wife upon her death: "She never interfered with my work." That was high praise for a minister's wife. Even higher is the acknowledgment that, in addition, she has always encouraged the work. This is my tribute to my wife. It is only right that I dedicate this book to her.

—David J. Engelsma
July 10, 2009

CHAPTER 1

The Man and His Life: A Sketch

Birth, rearing, and conversion

It is not my intention to give a full description of the life of John Calvin. My purpose with this book is not the *life* of Calvin, but the *doctrine* of Calvin. Nevertheless, a sketch of Calvin's life is helpful for the study of his doctrine. The background of this remarkable man's life reminds us that there was a close connection between the man himself and the word of God, which he taught.

John Calvin was born in Noyon in northern France on July 10, 1509. When Martin Luther posted the ninety-five theses on the church door at Wittenberg, Calvin was eight years old, twenty-six years younger than Luther. Although they were contemporaries, Calvin and Luther never met or corresponded. On a couple of occasions, Calvin addressed letters to Martin Luther by means of Philip Melanchthon. Because Luther was in a foul mood over the debate on the presence of the body and blood of Jesus Christ in the Lord's supper, Melanchthon never delivered Calvin's letters to Luther.

Calvin had an excellent education in theology, law, and classical languages in some of the best schools and universities in France.

At some point in the early 1530s (the French biographer Bernard Cottret gives the date as 1532–1533[1]), when Calvin was about twenty-four years old, he underwent a "sudden conversion" from Roman Catholicism to the evangelical faith of Protestantism. "Since I was too obstinately devoted to the superstitions of Popery to be easily extricated from so profound an abyss of mire, God by a sudden conversion subdued and brought my mind to a teachable frame."[2]

1

Forced to flee France by the threat of persecution, Calvin left for Basel, Switzerland, in 1534.

Exiled from France for the rest of his life and carrying on his work of reformation outside of France, Calvin always had a heart for France and the Reformed church in France.

In 1535 and 1536 Calvin wrote and published the first edition of his *Institutes*. The first edition of this book immediately established his reputation in the entire European world as a leader in the Reformation and as an outstanding theologian.

Calvin intended to spend his whole life as a quiet scholar, studying and writing books. This intention was related to what he confesses as his shy, timid, retiring personality. "Being of a disposition somewhat unpolished and bashful, which led me always to love the shade and retirement, I then began to seek some secluded corner where I might be withdrawn from the public view." Calvin adds, "God...brought me forth to public notice."[3] His prominence on the world scene and his influence on the Reformation were not his choosing; they were contrary to his intention and his personality. God, however, intended otherwise. Later, reflecting on his very public and very stormy ministry, Calvin remarked, "God...thrust me into the game."[4]

First pastorate in Geneva

After his flight from France, Calvin traveled in Switzerland and Italy. On a trip to Strasbourg, Germany, Calvin was forced to detour through Geneva, Switzerland, where he hoped to spend the night unobserved. However, his presence was noted, and the fiery, redheaded preacher William Farel constrained Calvin to remain in Geneva and to help in the work of reformation that had already begun in the city. A reluctant Calvin pleaded his desire to be a quiet scholar. Farel replied that if Calvin refused to assist in the work of the Lord, the curse of God would fall upon him. In the threatened curse, Calvin perceived the will of God, to which then and always he was submissive. He remained in Geneva, taking up the work in August 1536.

Calvin worked there as a preacher, teacher, and organizer of the church until 1538, when the civil authorities of the city expelled both him and Farel from Geneva. The issues concerned liturgy and discipline. Of special importance to Calvin and Farel was the right of the church to excommunicate unworthy members from the Lord's supper, a right contested by the civil authorities of Geneva. Already at that early stage of his ministry, Calvin was contending for the autonomy of the church.

In Strasbourg

After his banishment from Geneva and a brief stay in Basel, Calvin accepted the invitation from his friend Martin Bucer, a prominent reformer in his own right, to come to Strasbourg to minister to a congregation of refugees who had fled persecution in France. Calvin took up his pastoral work in Strasbourg in 1538 and continued there until 1541.

This was an extraordinarily significant period in Calvin's life. During this time he revised the first Latin edition (1536) of his *Institutes*, expanded it from six chapters to seventeen, and published a second edition.

Calvin wrote commentaries on Scripture, notably his commentary on the epistle to the Romans. All the reformers viewed Paul's epistle to the Romans as the outstanding book of the Bible and as a systematic presentation of the doctrines that make up the heart of the gospel of sovereign grace, which was also the heart of the Reformation. His work with the epistle to the Romans was influential for Calvin's developing doctrine of predestination, as is evident from succeeding editions of the *Institutes*.

With Calvin banished from Geneva, the Roman Catholics saw an opportunity to reestablish themselves there. Cardinal James Sadolet wrote a persuasive letter to the leaders in Geneva to win them back to the Roman Catholic Church and to restore the bishops to Geneva. The leaders in Geneva did not want the Roman Catholics back; neither could they answer Sadolet. They asked Calvin to respond for them. The fact that Calvin complied with this request shows something of his graciousness. Even though these men had recently cast him out of the inheritance of the Lord and virtually deposed him from office, Calvin, like Jephthah, came to the help of the rulers of Geneva in their hour of need. Calvin loved Christ's church, regardless that it had treated him shabbily. Calvin wrote the brilliant "Reply by John Calvin to Letter by Cardinal Sadolet to the Senate and People of Geneva," answering the cardinal's arguments, contending that Geneva must maintain the Reformation, and explaining why the reformation of the church was necessary.[5] No doubt, Calvin directed the pamphlet as much to Geneva as to the cardinal.

Calvin was influenced by Martin Bucer during his stay in Strasbourg, especially with regard to church liturgy, church government, particularly the offices in the church, and predestination.

While living in Strasbourg, Calvin attended important theological conferences, at which the emperor pressured leaders of the Reformation and the Roman Catholic Church to come to doctrinal agreement in order to reunite the divided church. Theological conferences were held in Frankfort (1539), Hagenau (1540), Worms (1540), and Ratisbon (1541). At these conferences Calvin played merely an advisory role. He met the Roman Catholic leaders and rubbed shoulders with virtually all the leaders of the Reformation. An exception was Martin Luther, whom the Roman Catholic leaders would not allow to attend the conferences. Calvin struck up a friendship with Philip Melanchthon, and in spite of their theological differences, they were genuine, lifelong friends. By this friendship Calvin influenced Melanchthon to move away from Luther's view of the Lord's supper toward a more spiritual conception of the presence of Christ.

In 1540 Calvin married Idelette de Bure, the poor widow of an Anabaptist who had been converted to the Reformed faith by means of Calvin. She bore Calvin a son who died in infancy. About the death of his little son, Calvin said that it was "a severe blow," but our Father "knows what is best for his children."[6] To Rome's heartless reproach that God gave him no children, Calvin replied that he had "myriads of children in the whole Christian world."[7] After Idelette's death in 1549, Calvin remained a widower until his own death fifteen years later. He stated that he had "willingly chosen to lead a solitary life."[8]

Second pastorate in Geneva

By 1541 the authorities in Geneva had discovered that they needed Calvin desperately. They invited him back. Knowing full well the struggles and hardships that would confront him in Geneva, Calvin dreaded the prospect of a second pastorate in the Swiss city. Writing to William Farel in 1540, when pressure was already beginning to be brought to bear on him to return, Calvin declared, "Rather would I submit to death a hundred times than to that cross, on which one had to perish daily a thousand times over."[9]

In a letter to Farel, as Calvin was about to leave for Geneva, he explained his decision to take up again his labors in the church in that city: "When I remember that I am not my own, I offer up my heart, presented as a sacrifice to the Lord... I submit my will and my affections, subdued and held fast, to the obedience of God."[10]

The words "I offer up my heart, presented as a sacrifice to the Lord," have come to be regarded as the hallmark of Calvin's and the genuine Calvinist's life.

At the time he returned to Geneva, Calvin was thirty-two. He would spend the next twenty-three years in that city, until his death in 1564 at the age of only fifty-five.

His work was prodigious. He preached regularly several times a week, often daily. He gave theological and exegetical lectures. He wrote tracts on various theological and ecclesiastical subjects and commentaries on most of the books of the Bible. His correspondence with men and women everywhere in Europe was voluminous. He led consistory meetings and the meetings of the company of pastors in and around Geneva. He was active in pastoral care and discipline of the members of the Genevan church. All the while, he was continually revising and expanding the *Institutes*.

A contemporary of Calvin, who himself lived in Geneva, described the amazing work and wonderful devotion of the reformer:

> Calvin for his part did not spare himself at all, working far beyond what his powers and regard for his health could stand. He preached commonly every day for one week in two. Every week he lectured three times in theology. [In fact, the lecturing was also normally in alternate weeks, when he was not preaching.] He was at the *Consistoire* on the appointed day and made all the remonstrances. Every Friday at the Bible Study, which we call the *Congrégation,* what he added after the leader had made

his *declaration* was almost a lecture. He never failed in visiting the sick, in private warning and counsel, and the rest of the numberless matters arising out of the ordinary exercise of his ministry. But besides these ordinary tasks, he had great care for believers in France, both in teaching them and exhorting and counselling them and consoling them by letters when they were being persecuted, and also in interceding for them, or getting another to intercede when he thought he saw an opening. Yet all that did not prevent him from going on working at his special study and composing many splendid and very useful books.[11]

Calvin was sincere when he spoke of offering up his heart as a sacrifice to God.

François Wendel speaks of Calvin's "tireless and truly astonishing industry."[12]

By no means the least time-consuming, burdensome, and fruitful labor were Calvin's doctrinal controversies. Calvin was forced to contend with many false teachers over numerous theological issues. Some of the heretics surfaced from the company of pastors in Geneva. Others came to Geneva in order to oppose Calvin's teachings and thus to disturb the church. Others attacked Calvin's doctrine from afar.

There is something extraordinary about the number of false teachers and the wide range of false doctrines with which Calvin had to deal. God providentially raised up the heretics so that by his controversies with them Calvin might clarify and develop the truth. The Reformed churches are the beneficiaries of these agonizing struggles of Calvin.

Calvin defended the doctrine of the Trinity over against Michael Servetus, Giovanni Valentino Gentile, and Pierre Caroli. Against Jerome Bolsec, Calvin defended the doctrine of predestination. Sebastian Castellio's attack on the inspiration of Scripture, particularly the Song of Solomon (which Castellio dismissed as nothing but a lascivious celebration of erotic love), occasioned Calvin's defense of the doctrine of Scripture. The assault by the ferocious Lutheran Joachim Westphal on the Reformed doctrine of the Lord's supper required Calvin to give a spirited defense of this doctrine. Against the grievous errors of the Anabaptists, Calvin defended infant baptism and the doctrine of the covenant, including the essential oneness of the Old Testament covenant with Israel and the New Testament covenant with the church. Throughout his ministry Calvin did battle with the Roman Catholic Church and its theologians over the bondage of the will of fallen humans and over predestination.

One controversy of great importance, which strangely gets little attention today, was Calvin's sharp and sustained polemic against confessing Reformed Christians in France whom Calvin referred to as "Nicodemites." In order to escape persecution, these people participated in the public worship of the Roman Catholic Church. They excused themselves by claiming that in their heart they rejected the religion of Rome. They appealed to Nicodemus, whom they alleged was secretly a disciple of Jesus, although maintaining his position among Jesus' enemies.

Calvin uncompromisingly condemned the thinking and practice of the Nicodemites. Under no circumstances may a Reformed Christian worship with the Roman Catholic Church. Regardless of the consequences, whether heavy fines, imprisonment, or even death, the Reformed believer is called of God to worship as a member of a true, instituted church of Christ. Calvin did not hesitate to advise Reformed believers in France to emigrate to lands where worship in a true church was possible, if necessary leaving possessions and obdurate family behind.

For Calvin, the right worship of God in a true church is the supreme duty of man. It is not an option. It is not preferable. It is not desirable. It is necessary.[13]

In Article 28 of the Belgic Confession, the Reformed churches have made Calvin's assertion of the necessity of membership in a true church confessionally binding on all those who profess to be Reformed believers.

> It is the duty of all believers, according to the Word of God, to separate themselves from those who do not belong to the Church, and to join themselves to this congregation, wheresoever God hath established it, even though the magistrates and edicts of princes be against it; yea, though they should suffer death or bodily punishment.[14]

Complicating his ministry and vexing the reformer was his ongoing struggle with the civil magistrates in Geneva over the church's right to govern itself without interference from the magistrates. The cause of disagreement was especially the matter of excommunication. Toward the end of his ministry, Calvin was able to achieve a more-or-less self-governing church.

For many years Calvin had in mind to establish an "academy" in Geneva—a combination of Reformed seminary and Reformed college. His vision became reality in 1559. At Calvin's urging, Theodore Beza, not Calvin, was appointed rector. The academy, declares Wendel, "can be said without the least exaggeration to have been his [Calvin's] crowning work."[15]

Calvin died in Geneva in 1564, six weeks short of his fifty-fifth birthday.

Theodore Beza, Calvin's faithful disciple and successor in the church of Geneva, wrote regarding Calvin's death, "On that day, then, at the same time with the setting sun, this splendid luminary was withdrawn from us."[16]

Calvin had given instruction that his grave was not to be marked by any stone. His purpose was to prevent pilgrimages to his tomb in honor of the man John Calvin. He was well aware of his importance to Christ's church as a specially gifted, specially called servant of Christ. He did not suffer from false modesty, but he died as he lived, determined that to God alone would be the glory.

Influence and significance

Émile Doumergue, author of seven volumes that are the most complete treatment of the life and work of John Calvin,[17] has written regarding Calvin's role in the Reformation, "Luther created Protestantism; Calvin saved it."[18]

Doumergue is only partly right. Not only did Calvin "save" the Protestantism that Luther "created," but he also significantly developed it, giving it a more perfect form.

Calvin has had enormous, worldwide influence in the multitude of Reformed and Presbyterian churches. Fundamental to the existence, theology, and life of all of them have been the Reformed creeds. And the thumbprint of John Calvin is plainly visible on virtually every question and answer, every article, and every chapter of these creeds. This thumbprint is due mainly to the influence of Calvin's *Institutes*. Correctly, John McNeill wrote, "The *Institutes* became for three centuries the essential textbook of theology in the Reformed churches."[19]

In the lives of their members, these Reformed and Presbyterian churches have powerfully affected the societies and nations in which Christ has placed them. Thus they have influenced the history of the world. McNeill noted the influence of the Reformed faith, and Calvin through it, upon Western civilization: "All modern Western history would have been unrecognizably different without the perpetual play of Calvin's influence."[20]

Noteworthy characteristics of Calvin's person and personal life

God made Calvin the man he was, naturally and spiritually, to qualify him for the great work God had ordained for him.

Utterly to be repudiated is William Bouwsma's psychological analysis of Calvin, the theologian and reformer of the church. Bouwsma explains away Calvin's theology, particularly his concern for order, as the result of his anxieties, due in an important respect to his conflicted relationship with his father. Calvin's doctrine of the church, for example, derives significantly from "his experience with his own father... [Calvin] could not simply repudiate that part of himself which came from this bad father, whose teachings had been, in any event, a powerful force for order. It is scarcely remarkable that Calvin, made so anxious by disorder, was unable to purge himself of attitudes that were, in him, sometimes more rigid than those of the papal church." Bouwsma's conclusion is that Calvin's doctrine of the church established him as "the tyrant of Geneva."[21]

By means of such analysis, one can effectively nullify the theology of anyone, including the apostle Paul. Calvin could better have fallen into the hands of his Roman Catholic foes, who at least took his teachings seriously, than into the hands of a William Bouwsma.

It is a commentary on the sorry state of Calvin studies in the twenty-first century that scholars appeal to Bouwsma as an authority.

The best that can be said of Bouwsma's psychologizing deconstruction of Calvin's teachings and reforming labors is that it is annoying.

God blessed the man Calvin with extraordinary natural gifts, especially a brilliant mind and a resolute will.

His brilliant mind enabled him to grasp the full truth of the gospel, to perceive the harmonious relationships of all aspects of the gospel, to teach the truth clearly and systematically, and to expose errors as contrary to the gospel.

Calvin was able in his preaching to translate the original Hebrew of the Old Testament and the original Greek of the New Testament on the spot. On the pulpit he worked not with a translation but with the original languages of the Bible.

He had a vast store of biblical texts and passages from the church fathers in his mind and a marvelous ability to recall them as needed. Calvin demonstrated this gift in his controversy with Jerome Bolsec. At a meeting of the pastors of Geneva, Bolsec assailed the doctrine of predestination, unaware that Calvin had entered the gathering. After Bolsec had finished speaking, Calvin, without any preparation and from memory, refuted Bolsec's arguments and defended the doctrine of predestination, giving abundant proof from Scripture and providing copious quotations from the church fathers, especially Augustine.

Calvin's resolute will enabled him to endure abuse and opposition both from within and from outside the church. Members of his own church named their dogs Calvin, loudly belched and farted as he was preaching, fired their guns outside his home, and threatened his life. The Anabaptists and the Roman Catholics exhausted their storehouse of ridicule and reproach in hatred of him. However, Calvin never compromised his confession of the truth or wavered in his stand on behalf of it.

The firmness of his will regarding the maintenance of the truth stood him in good stead during the Bolsec controversy over predestination. Even though almost all his colleagues, including the influential Heinrich Bullinger, refused to support Calvin in his defense of sovereign reprobation and indeed undercut Calvin's stand, thus lining up with Bolsec, Calvin stood fast in that hour of crisis for the Reformation's gospel of salvation by sovereign, particular grace.

Only an amazingly strong will explains Calvin's carrying on with his work despite bodily pain and physical ailments that would have sent most men into early retirement. Health was not one of the natural gifts God gave to John Calvin. One rather gets the impression that a sickly body was Calvin's "thorn in the flesh."

Among the natural gifts that served the reformer well was a solid, thorough liberal arts education in the best schools available in his day. Well educated themselves, and convinced of the benefit of good schooling, all the reformers insisted on good, Christian schools, especially for ministers, but also for all the children.

No description of the personal characteristics of Calvin, fitting him for his unique ministry, can overlook his self-discipline. He lived as in a spiritual arena, "agonizing" (in the original, biblical sense) in his strenuous effort to run the race of the ministry to which God had called him and to reach the goal God had set before him. He was abstemious in eating, drinking, sleeping, and indulging in recreation. For years he ate only one meal a day, partly because of a weak stomach, but partly also because eating interfered with his work. He slept very little. I doubt that he ever took a day off for relaxation and leisure.

This self-denial had nothing whatever to do with earning his salvation, or with a morbid renunciation of earthly necessities and comforts. It had everything to do with Calvin's devotion to the God of his salvation and with his love for God's church. He did truly offer up his heart as a sacrifice of thanksgiving to God. Offering his heart, he gave God all else in addition.

How shameful, in light of Calvin's self-discipline, is squandering of their gifts by capable ministers because, lacking self-discipline, they indulge themselves too much in earthly pursuits and pleasures.

And what an example to every Reformed minister is the consecrated life of John Calvin!

Even the unbelieving biographer Bernard Cottret was captivated by the personal characteristics of Calvin.

> The portraits of Calvin...leave an indefinable impression of moral strength and physical weakness: the grave, studious forehead so often throbbing with migraine; a burning gaze; sweetness stamped with severity; smooth cheeks contrasting with a

carefully tapered beard, rounded off above the neck...A nervous man as well as a thinker, his head covered by a cap of elegant simplicity...the refined face, the diaphanous skin, and the circled eyes indicate long vigils. He hardly had a body. Sleeping little, eating similarly, prey to violent headaches, Calvin did not hesitate to dictate certain of his works while lying in bed at the end of a life of austere labor...His slender, almost elegant body housed a will of iron; he was an intellectual, a writer, a craftsman in language and thought, immersed in a project of reform that involved both church and city. He was a churchman more than a statesman, but a churchman as one is a statesman.[22]

CHAPTER 2

The Nature of the *Institutes*

Book of instruction

The *Institutes* is a book of instruction in the whole of the Christian faith, as this faith is contained in Holy Scripture. The *Institutes* teaches all of the doctrines of the Christian religion in a comprehensive, systematic way, making plain throughout by quotations from, or allusions to, Scripture that its teaching is biblical.

Benjamin B. Warfield describes the *Institutes* this way: "What he [Calvin] professe[s] to give us in his 'Institutes' is thus, to put it simply, just a Christian man's reading of the Scriptures of God."[1] Warfield is right; this is why Christian laymen can and should read the *Institutes*.

With reference to the first edition of the *Institutes*, Calvin himself describes it as "a small treatise containing a summary of the principal truths of the Christian religion."[2] The Latin of a "small treatise" is *breve enchiridion*, "brief handbook." *Enchiridion* is the title of Augustine's comprehensive work on Christian doctrine, which is the first systematic theology. In the 1559 edition Calvin describes his *Institutes* as "a short textbook."[3] The French is *petit livret*, "small booklet [handbook]." In his "Subject Matter of the Present Work" in the French edition of 1560, Calvin analyzes the *Institutes* as "a sum of Christian doctrine."[4] Hence Karl Barth writes about Calvin and his *Institutes*, "At the beginning of the history of the Reformed church . . . stood a schoolmaster with his textbook."[5]

Barth reminds us that, in fact, the *Institutes* is a book of instruction in the *Reformed* faith. We must not conceive this too narrowly. Calvin was indebted to Luther and brought into his *Institutes* doctrines taught by Luther, for example, justification by faith alone. In addition, the *Institutes* contains the teachings of the church fathers, especially Augustine, and the teachings of the ecumenical creeds of Nicea and Chalcedon.[6] Nevertheless, the *Institutes* is a comprehensive, systematic handbook of the Reformed faith, indeed the very first such complete Reformed theology, the first Reformed dogmatics or systematic theology. In addition, the *Institutes* is foundational to all subsequent Reformed dogmatics—the fountainhead of distinctive Reformed theology. The *Institutes*, therefore, is of stupendous significance for all Reformed churches.

Viewing the *Institutes* as the first Reformed dogmatics, a complete Reformed theology, may not lead us to suppose that the Reformed faith is merely one species of the genus Christianity, alongside Roman Catholicism and Anabaptism. This does not do justice to Calvin's thinking about the *Institutes* or, indeed, to the Reformed faith. Calvin did not intend to present the Reformed faith as one species alongside others, but he intended to present *Christianity* itself in its outline and in its leading doctrines. The *Institutes* sets forth what we now call "Reformed theology" as Christianity—the one faith revealed in the Bible and the one gospel of Jesus Christ. The content of the *Institutes*, therefore, is Christianity in distinction from Roman Catholicism and Anabaptism, which are not Christianity but perversions of Christianity. Regarding Lutheranism, Calvin would have said that the Christianity of the *Institutes* is a purer, sounder, and more developed form than that of Lutheranism.

That this is the nature of the *Institutes*—a book setting forth in a systematic way the entire Reformed faith as the pure, sound expression of genuine, biblical Christianity—is evident from its title. The short title of the original, Latin version of 1536 is *Christianae religionis institutio*. Calvin gave the significantly expanded 1539 edition the title *Institutio Christianae religionis*, moving *Institutio* from the end of the title to the beginning.

The key word is *Institutio*, which means "instruction." The corresponding subtitle of the 1536 Dutch edition is *Onderwijs in de Chris-*

telijke Religie (*Instruction in the Christian Religion*), according to van't Spijker's 1992 translation of the 1536 edition.[7] *Institutio* also can be translated as "education." *Institutio* also carries with it the idea of a "compendium," a "summary" or *summa*, the "main topics" of the Christian religion, and this is the idea of Calvin's *Institutes* as well.

Notice that the title in the original Latin edition is singular: *Institutio*. Calvin did not give his work the plural title *Institutiones*. English translations used the singular *Institution* until 1813, when John Allen employed the plural *Institutes* in his translation, and the plural title has prevailed ever since. It would have been preferable to retain the singular. Not only was this Calvin's choice, but also the singular brings out the nature of the book as "instruction." It is one unified instruction concerning the whole of the Christian religion. Although usage requires the plural, *Institutes*, one should understand the reference to be to a single instruction.

The title of the 1536 edition contains something else that is important for understanding the nature of the book. The full title is *Institutes of the Christian religion, embracing almost the whole sum of piety and whatever is necessary to know of the doctrine of salvation. A work most worthy to be read by all persons zealous for piety, and recently published*. Although this long subtitle was likely added by the publisher,[8] the vital word, which accurately describes the content of the book, is *piety*. The subtitle uses *piety* twice: once as a description of the doctrine of Scripture and once as the desire of those who read the *Institutes*.

Calvin described *piety* (Latin: *pietas*) as "that reverence joined with love of God which the knowledge of his benefits induces. [It is present when] men recognize that they owe everything to God, that they are nourished by his fatherly care, that he is the Author of their every good."[9]

Piety is essentially the same as the biblical word *godliness* (εὐσέβεια): "But godliness with contentment is great gain" (1 Tim. 6:6). Piety, or godliness, is reverence and love of God. It is the Old Testament phrase "fear of Jehovah" (יִרְאַת יְהוָה): "The fear of the LORD is the instruction of wisdom" (Prov. 15:33).[10]

Alexandre Ganoczy writes concerning the meaning of *piety* for John Calvin:

> If we are not mistaken, we can now affirm that piety is the fundamental virtue of Calvin's spirituality. It springs from a personal knowledge of the living God and Christ. It constitutes a special attitude of the soul that believes in God, not with a theoretical and passive "historical faith," but with a faith that is truly trusting. Its principal characteristic is its childlike trust which is animated by feelings of love for and fear of the heavenly Father. It is surely not an accumulation of prayers, good works, or satisfactions that one offers to God in a servile and mercenary spirit; rather, it is a free and spontaneous desire to live according to God's will. Piety is also a distinctive sign to distinguish the faithful and the unfaithful, the evangelical and the papists. The first, with few exceptions, live according to a piety which the second, in general, do not possess.[11]

Piety is an honorable word in the Reformed vocabulary. Pietism is an evil that has corrupted the Reformed faith and life; piety is of the essence of the Reformed faith and life. As a book of piety that aims at the piety of the reader, the *Institutes* is instruction in the doctrines of Scripture as these doctrines reveal God as Father in Jesus Christ to believers and their children; as these doctrines are known by believing minds; and as these doctrines have their end, or goal, in the love and reverence of believers for God.

Insofar as the introduction to the McNeill/Battles edition of the *Institutes* plays piety off against theology in its description of the *Institutes*, it is mistaken: "He [Calvin] calls his book not a *summa theologiae* but a *summa pietatis* [not a summary of theology but a summary of piety]."[12] Also Ganoczy's description of the piety of Calvin, quoted above, suffers from the failure to imbed piety in orthodox theology. For Calvin, right, orthodox theology is fundamental to genuine piety. The *Institutes* is a summary of piety because it is a book of sound doctrine.

Nevertheless, Calvin does not present the Reformed faith, nor may it ever be presented, whether in sermons, catechisms, or books, as simply a number of scientific assertions, which one is to consider and assent to only intellectually. Rather, as the pure Christian religion, as the very gospel of inspired Scripture, it is the doctrinal revelation of the God of grace and glory in Jesus Christ, which is to be embraced by a believing heart and whose purpose is that the elect believer loves and reverences this great God.

Abraham Kuyper's remarks in his "Introduction" to a Dutch edition of the *Institutes* are pertinent. Kuyper declared that the Huguenots, the Reformed, the Calvinists, or however one names the confessors of the purest confession, were not "emotionalists" (Dutch: *gevoelslieden*).[13] Rather, they honored the life of the mind. It was for these people that Calvin wrote the *Institutes*.

Then Kuyper added, "Nevertheless, they were emphatically not *intellectualists*. Calvin's healthy, warm, high mysticism [Dutch: *mystiek*] contradicts those unjust accusations in a conclusive manner."[14] Evidently attributing this in large part to Calvin, particularly to his *Institutes*, Kuyper judged that "the Reformed confession has then entirely escaped the curse of intellectualism, but at the same time is very sharply on its guard not to go under in the waters of the incomprehensibilities of feeling."[15]

It is significant that Augustine began *The Enchiridion on Faith, Hope and Love* by setting forth, and insisting on, *piety*. For Laurentius, who had asked Augustine for a "handbook of Christian doctrine," Augustine desired "wisdom."[16] Augustine states, "The true wisdom of man is piety," and piety is "the fear of God." Piety "refers specially to the worship of God." The *Enchiridion*, which may well be the first systematic theology of the post-apostolic church, is instruction as to "the proper mode of worshipping God."[17]

In nature and purpose, Calvin's *Institutes* is a vastly expanded form of Augustine's *Enchiridion*. And Calvin would have been pleased by this description.

Apology for the Reformed faith

In addition to being instruction, the *Institutes* is an apology for the faith of the Reformation: *a defense of Reformed Christianity*. Positively, the *Institutes* demonstrates that the Reformed faith is pure, sound, biblical Christianity, against the charge that the Reformed faith is dangerous heresy.

Negatively, the *Institutes* sharply distinguishes Reformed Christianity, especially from Roman Catholicism and from Anabaptism

("Catabaptism" in Calvin's phraseology). In this connection the *Institutes* refutes and condemns these two errors.

Defense of the faith of the Reformation against Rome and Anabaptism was demanded by the occasion for Calvin's writing his *Institutes* and was basic to his original purpose. Long after the specific need for the limited defense of the faith that was the purpose of the original *Institutes* had passed, in its subsequent editions the *Institutes* continued to defend the Reformed faith, increasingly on a broader front.

Karl Barth aptly remarks, "He [Calvin] originally planned it [the *Institutes*] as a redoubt with two main fronts but gradually built it up into a fortress with guns trained in every direction. Reformed Protestantism was militant from the first."[18]

Opposition to a militant defense of the Reformed faith, which is widespread in Reformed churches in the twenty-first century, pits itself against the Reformed tradition generally and against the *Institutes* in particular.

As a defense of the Reformed faith, the *Institutes* will be helpful both to strengthen Reformed Christians in the faith against assaults and to remind them that they *should defend* the Reformed faith.

Confession of faith

We should also recognize the *Institutes* as a kind of *confession of faith*. As such it was originally presented to King Francis I of France, in the service of its apologetical purpose.

Already then, and down through the ages, the *Institutes* served as a confession of faith to Reformed believers: this is our faith; this is our understanding of Scripture. Although it is much too lengthy to function as a creed in the technical sense, it has framed, and embodied itself in, the official Reformed creeds. All of them are influenced heavily by the *Institutes*.

Purpose of the Institutes

We must let Calvin himself inform us of his purpose with writing the *Institutes*, first from his autobiographical preface to his commentary on the Psalms:

The Nature of the *Institutes*

Leaving my native country, France, I in fact retired into Germany, expressly for the purpose of being able there to enjoy in some obscure corner the repose which I had always desired, and which had been so long denied me. But lo! whilst I lay hidden at Basle, and known only to a few people, many faithful and holy persons were burnt alive in France; and the report of these burnings having reached foreign nations, they excited the strongest disapprobation among a great part of the Germans, whose indignation was kindled against the authors of such tyranny. In order to allay this indignation, certain wicked and lying pamphlets were circulated, stating, that none were treated with such cruelty but Anabaptists and seditious persons, who, by their perverse ravings and false opinions, were overthrowing not only religion but also all civil order. Observing that the object which these instruments of the court aimed at by their disguises, was not only that the disgrace of shedding so much innocent blood might remain buried under the false charges and calumnies which they brought against the holy martyrs after their death, but also, that afterwards they might be able to proceed to the utmost extremity in murdering the poor saints without exciting compassion towards them in the breasts of any, it appeared to me, that unless I opposed them to the utmost of my ability, my silence could not be vindicated from the charge of cowardice and treachery. This was the consideration which induced me to publish my Institute of the Christian Religion. My objects were, first, to prove that these reports [that none were treated with cruelty but Anabaptists and seditious persons, who were overthrowing not only religion but also all civil order] were false and calumnious, and thus to vindicate my brethren ... next that as the same cruelties might very soon after be exercised against many unhappy individuals, foreign nations might be touched with at least some compassion towards them and solicitude about them. When it [the *Institutes*] was then published, it was not that copious and laboured work which it now is, but only a small treatise containing a summary of the principal truths of the Christian religion; and it was published ... that men might know what was the faith held by those whom I saw basely and wickedly defamed by those flagitious and perfidious flatterers.[19]

About his purpose with the *Institutes*, John Calvin also says,

> Moreover, it has been my purpose in this labor to prepare and instruct candidates in sacred theology for the reading of the divine Word, in order that they may be able both to have easy access to it and to advance in it without stumbling. For I believe I have so embraced the sum of religion in all its parts, and have arranged it in such an order, that if anyone rightly grasps it, it will not be difficult for him to determine what he ought especially to seek in Scripture, and to what end he ought to relate its contents... The godly reader [can]... approach Scripture armed with a knowledge of the present work, as a necessary tool.[20]

In light of Calvin's information, the following were his distinct purposes with the *Institutes*.

First, Calvin wanted to defend the faith of the persecuted Reformed saints in France and, if possible, to protect them from persecution. This was a prominent purpose, as Calvin stated in his preface to his *Commentary on the Book of Psalms* and in his prefatory address to King Francis, with which every edition of the *Institutes* begins.

With regard to this purpose, the occasion for the publishing of the *Institutes* in 1536 is important. King Francis and the Roman Catholic Church were persecuting the Reformed saints in France and defending this persecution to the Protestant princes in Germany, whose political support Francis needed, as suppression of revolutionary, seditious Anabaptists. The Anabaptist debacle at Münster climaxed in 1535. By publishing his *Institutes*, Calvin was determined to convince Francis, if possible, that the Reformed were different from the Anabaptists. The Reformed faith does not teach revolution against the government. At the same time, Calvin intended to distinguish the Reformed faith from Anabaptism in the minds of all. Calvin also hoped, by thus distinguishing the Reformed faith and church from Anabaptism, to prevent the persecution of other Reformed believers in the future.

Second, Calvin also wanted to give the Reformed, especially those Reformed Christians in France, an expression and confession of their faith. The fact is that Calvin had written the *Institutes* before the persecution broke out in France early in 1535, and before he wrote the prefatory address to King Francis. In the prefatory address Calvin speaks of his original intent

> to transmit certain rudiments by which those who are touched with any zeal for religion might be shaped to true godliness. And I undertook this labor especially for our French countrymen, very many of whom I knew to be hungering and thirsting for Christ; but I saw very few who had been duly imbued with even a slight knowledge of him. The book itself witnesses that this was my intention, adapted as it is to a simple and, you may say, elementary form of teaching.[21]

In the 1536 *Institutes*, regarding this purpose to instruct the believers in France, Calvin writes that he had in mind "the simpler folk, for whom we above all are writing."[22]

Always, Calvin's fundamental purpose with the *Institutes* was teaching the truth, thus confirming faith, extending the kingdom of Christ, and building up the church. This is certainly Calvin's emphasis in publishing the definitive edition of 1559. In his "John Calvin to the Reader," there is no mention of an apologetic purpose. Rather, Calvin wants "to prepare and instruct candidates in sacred theology for the reading of the divine Word, in order that they may be able both to have easy access to it and to advance in it without stumbling."[23] He adds that "knowledge of this present work" is a "necessary tool" for understanding Scripture rightly.[24] The *Institutes* "can be a key to open a way for all children of God into a good and right understanding of Holy Scripture."[25]

Calvin has a high estimation of his book. It is a sound guide for Reformed Christians, especially aspiring ministers, in their study of Scripture.

Heiko Oberman rightly says that Calvin intended the *Institutes* to be "a textbook for future preachers."[26]

It is worthy of note that Calvin did not recommend an unprepossessed, neutral approach to Scripture by each individual on his own. The Reformed approach, rather, is guided by a sound, comprehensive statement of the main teachings of the Bible. Still today, the Reformed student of Holy Scripture should read and study Scripture in the light of the Reformed creeds, all of which owe much to Calvin's *Institutes*.

Value of studying the Institutes

The value of the study of the *Institutes*, especially for the budding theologian, will be that he learns the Reformed faith both with regard to its distinctive doctrines and with regard to its system and unity—the harmonious relation of all the doctrines. This is the faith that must be the content of his preaching and teaching.

He will learn the necessity and nature of a vigorous defense of the Reformed faith against all the false doctrines that threaten it. Some of the errors are the same today as in Calvin's time, for example, the rejection of infant baptism with the concomitant denial of the oneness of the old covenant and the new covenant (dispensationalism). In these cases, Calvin's defense of sound doctrine serves the Reformed minister well yet today. Other errors are new. In these cases, new defenses of the faith are called for. But the *Institutes* demands the defense of the truth and provides a rich and detailed model.

The seminarian will also learn piety. Reading the *Institutes*, he will breathe in piety for himself personally, by the working of the Spirit. He will also be trained to teach the doctrines of Scripture in such a way that the fruit of them is the piety of his congregation.

In all of this valuable learning, the student of the *Institutes* will be rooted and grounded in Holy Scripture. The *Institutes* is a most biblical book.

Influence of the Institutes

The influence of the *Institutes* has been enormous, both in the sixteenth century and down the ages to the present time. This has been recognized by foe and friend alike. Will Durant has written this about the influence of the *Institutes* upon the Reformation and upon the subsequent history of the church: "[It is] the most eloquent, fervent, lucid, logical, influential, and terrible work in all the literature of the religious revolution."[27]

John McNeill judged that the *Institutes* is "one of the few books that have profoundly affected the course of history."[28] Through the *Institutes* Calvin is "one of the makers of the modern mind."[29] "The *Institutes* became for three centuries the essential textbook of theology in the Reformed churches."[30]

Benjamin B. Warfield declared:

> As the first adequate statement of the positive programme of the Reformation movement, the "Institutes" lies at the foundation of the whole development of Protestant theology, and has left an impress on evangelical thought which is ineffaceable. After three centuries and a half, it retains its unquestioned preëminence as the greatest and most influential of all dogmatic treatises.[31]

Warfield then quoted the Protestant liberal Albrecht Ritschl: "There is the masterpiece of Protestant theology."[32]

Scottish theologian William Cunningham said, "The 'Institutio' of Calvin is the most important work in the history of theological science ... and has exerted directly or indirectly the greatest and most beneficial influence upon the opinions of intelligent men on theological subjects."[33]

The most important influence of the *Institutes*, in the providence of God, has been upon the Reformation itself and upon the Reformed and Presbyterian churches. The *Institutes* completed and established the sixteenth-century Reformation of the church. Especially by its strong and pervasive influence on the Reformed confessions, it was used by Christ to form, found, and defend Reformed and Presbyterian churches throughout the world. By the confession and lives of the members of these churches, the *Institutes* has powerfully affected Western civilization.

CHAPTER 3

The History of the Publishing of the *Institutes*

Introduction

The *Institutes* as we have it in its final form, whether in the Allen, Beveridge, or Battles translation, is not the *Institutes* as Calvin originally wrote and published it. What we are familiar with is a much expanded and developed edition of the book.

The *Institutes* has a history. It had a history in Calvin's own lifetime.

This history spans some twenty-four years between the publication of the first edition in 1536 and that of the final, definitive edition in 1559, which was published in French a year later. Calvin began writing the *Institutes* shortly after his sudden conversion, probably between April and May of 1534.[1] He gave the *Institutes* its definitive form in 1559, five years before his death on May 27, 1564. He likely translated at least part of the Latin edition of 1559 into the 1560 French edition.

Writing, revising, expanding, developing, editing, and translating the *Institutes* was the life's work of Calvin. François Wendel remarks that Calvin was "endlessly remodelling the *Christian Institutes*."[2]

In his other labors, especially the writing of his commentaries, Calvin continually kept the *Institutes* in view. His ongoing work of exegeting Scripture and writing his commentaries affected the development of the *Institutes*. He incorporated the exegesis in various ways into the later editions. This points out an important relation between his *Institutes* and his commentaries. Rather than delineate the doctrines in detail in the commentaries, as was the custom, for example, of Bucer, Calvin only explains the text in his commentaries, referring the reader to the *Institutes* for the doctrinal deliverances. Thus Calvin kept his commentaries brief. "If, after this road has, as it were, been paved [the writing of the *Institutes*], I shall publish any interpretations of Scripture, I shall always condense them, because I shall have no need to undertake long doctrinal discussions, and to digress into commonplaces."[3]

Over the years in its successive editions, the *Institutes* shows significant change in size and form. From what Calvin called the "little book (*libellus*)"[4] of only six chapters of the 1536 edition, the *Institutes* became the four books and eighty chapters of the final, 1559 edition. The *Institutes* of 1559 was five times larger than the original. The full title of the 1559 edition acknowledged the greatly expanded size and the change of format, stating about the 1559 edition, "It can almost be regarded as a new work."[5]

The *Institutes* changed in content over the years, not with regard to the basic doctrine, but with regard to the topics, as well as to the thoroughness of the treatment.

The *Institutes* also changed in structure and arrangement. Calvin arranged the material of the 1536 *Institutes* along the lines of a Reformation catechism: law; the Apostles' Creed; prayer; the sacraments; and Christian freedom, including both spiritual and political power. He structured the 1559 edition according to a trinitarian order.

Regarding the changes in the *Institutes* from the 1536 edition to the 1559 edition, Benjamin Warfield states, "The changes it had undergone since its composition were immense—quintupling its size, revolutionizing its arrangement, changing its very purpose and proposed audience."[6]

The successive editions reflected Calvin's theological development over the years by means of his continued reading in the church fathers, his exposition of Scripture in producing his commentaries and lecturing to his students, and importantly his controversies with various heretics, for example, Caroli over the Trinity, Andreas Osiander over justification, and Westphal over the Lord's supper. Battles proposes that Calvin's controversy with various errors was fundamental to his development of the *Institutes*.[7]

In a statement to Albertus Pighius, Calvin freely acknowledged his constant improvement of his publications:

> It is indeed possible that we use different ways of speaking, that almost every one of us has his own manner of speaking which is different from that of others. But why could we not be al-

lowed something that has been the common practice of everyone in every generation? This too I recognise without reluctance, that when our works are reprinted we improve what was rather coarse, we soften what was too harshly expressed, we clarify obscure points, we explain more fully and at greater length what was too compressed, we also strengthen our argument with new reasons, and finally, where we fear the danger of causing offence, we also tone down and soften our language. For what would be the point of living if neither age nor practice nor constant exercise nor reading nor meditation were of any benefit to us? And what would be the point of making progress if it did not result in some profit reaching others also? On the contrary, if Pighius does not know it, I should like it to be absolutely clear to him that we strive night and day to shape our faithfully transmitted teachings into a form which we also judge will be the best.[8]

Nevertheless, with regard to the fundamental theology of the *Institutes*, it remained essentially the same throughout the history of the various editions. The development was organic: growth, not revision. This is remarkable. What Calvin believed already in 1536, he believed in 1559.

Karl Barth says about the various editions of the *Institutes*: "One new version after another, in which it remained the same, but was always totally fresh."[9]

J. D. Benoit says:

> Calvin never stopped revising, reshaping, and developing his book to such an extent that we can say that the *Institutio* is a work of his whole life. And this development was organic, if one can put it thus; it meant the maturing and expansion of thought within the framework which already existed. It was not a case of new chapters being added on one after another like extending a wall ... It was rather the growth of a living entity.[10]

Warfield continues his description of the development of the *Institutes*, quoted earlier: "And yet through all these changes it remained in a true sense the same book, and bore in its bosom precisely the same message."[11]

That the *Institutes* of 1559 is doctrinally the same as that of 1536 is evident from a comparison of the treatment of predestination in the two editions. The explanation of the doctrine is the same, as is Calvin's insistence on the importance of the doctrine. The differences of the treatment of the doctrine in the 1559 *Institutes* are the lengthier and more thorough explanation; the placement of the doctrine at the conclusion of the treatment of the doctrine of salvation, as the source of salvation, rather than in the context of the doctrine of the church, as was the case in the 1536 *Institutes*; and the polemical defense of the doctrine.[12]

When one considers that the author of the 1536 *Institutes* was twenty-six years old when he wrote it[13] and only recently converted, the young theologian's early grasp of the gospel is amazing.

Editions in Calvin's lifetime

The 1536 *Christianae religionis institutio* had been written by 1535, when Calvin wrote the prefatory address to King Francis. He published this first edition of the *Institutes* in Basel, Switzerland, in March of 1536. Benjamin B. Warfield suggests that Calvin wrote it in 1534, perhaps in Angoulême in southern France, where he was living with his friend Louis duTillet under the pseudonym Charles d'Espeville after he had fled France in the fall of 1533.[14] Calvin wrote the book in Latin, and it is the only edition that has not been translated into and published in French. That Calvin wrote in Latin indicates that he intended to reach the learned in France and elsewhere in Europe in the interest of reform. There is reason to believe that Calvin planned to publish a French translation soon afterward.

This first edition contains six chapters: four on the subjects of the law, the Apostles' Creed, the Lord's prayer, and the sacraments of the Lord's supper and baptism; a polemical chapter repudiating Rome's additional five sacraments; and a chapter on Christian liberty, which includes ecclesiastical power and civil government. The size is about the size of the New Testament through Ephesians. The book was very popular and soon sold out.

Ford Lewis Battles translated the 1536 *Institutes* into English, and

Eerdmans published his translation in 1975. A revised edition of this Battles translation, published in 1986, contains the following significant appendices: "The Placards of 1534"; "Martin Bucer on the Lord's Prayer"; "The Academic Discourse Delivered by Nicholas Cop... on 1 November 1533," in which Calvin had a hand; and "John Calvin's Latin Preface to Olivétan's French Bible (1535)." In his preface to Olivétan's Bible, Calvin speaks of "that mad passion to write something which continually produces for us so many swarms of books with no measure, no delight, no shame."[15]

Calvin wrote the second edition of the *Institutes* in Latin in 1538 while living in Basel. He published it in Strasbourg in 1539 while living with Martin Bucer after being expelled from Geneva. This edition of seventeen chapters is three times larger than the 1536 edition. Calvin expanded some sections significantly, particularly the section on predestination. In the 1539 edition, Calvin defends predestination against attacks upon it. There is also definite development of the doctrine of the Trinity, reflecting Calvin's controversy with Pierre Caroli in 1537. There is new material, including a chapter on the unity of the Old and New Testaments, arising out of his controversy with the Anabaptists, and two chapters on repentance and faith. Calvin enhanced the work with quotations from the church fathers and church councils. Perhaps to indicate the changes, Calvin changed the title to *Institutio Christianae religionis* (putting *Institutio* first).

Calvin translated this edition into French and published it in 1541. The French translation made the work popular, in distinction from the Latin version that addressed the educated.

Indicating the impact of the *Institutes* already at that early date is the fact that the French *parlement*, under the influence of the Roman Catholic Church, condemned both the Latin and French editions of the *Institutes*. Anyone possessing a copy of the book had to be reported to the authorities. Piles of the *Institutes* were ceremoniously burned before Notre Dame in Paris. The decree of the civil authorities suppressing heretical books mentioned only one title: the *Institutes*.[16] Rome has always known its foe.

Despite Satan's bonfires, the work of Christ through Calvin continued, and flourished. A third Latin edition was published in 1543. It had twenty-one chapters, which included new material on monasticism and angels. Calvin expanded his treatment of the Apostles' Creed, the church, and the offices in the church. The French translation was published in 1545.

The fourth Latin edition of 1550 was much the same as the 1543 edition, although there was expansion, including new exposition of the human conscience, new quotations from the church fathers, and new references to church councils. (Calvin kept reading.) Calvin made a notable improvement in the 1550 edition by dividing the contents into chapters with numbered paragraphs. This edition was printed in French in 1551 and reprinted in 1553, 1554, and 1557. The French edition added exposition of the resurrection of the body.

The *Institutes* received its final and definitive form in 1559 in Latin. The French translation appeared in 1560. Some scholars question whether Calvin himself translated the whole book into French, but no one questions the faithfulness of the translation. The 1559 edition is significantly changed from the earlier editions. In addition to a new trinitarian structure, the 1559 *Institutes* is eighty percent larger than the preceding edition. Some of the new material is due to Calvin's theological controversies, for example, the expanded treatment of the Lord's supper, occasioned by the conflict with Westphal.

The 1559 edition consists of eighty chapters in four books. Significant alterations of the method of treating the material include the separation of the doctrines of predestination and providence; the explanation of the doctrine of the church in book four, whereas it had appeared in the exposition of the Apostles' Creed in connection with faith; and the placement of the well-known treatment on the Christian life in book three as the work of the Spirit.

Of the 1559 edition Calvin said, "Although I did not regret the labor spent [on previous editions], I was never satisfied until the work had been arranged in the order now set forth."[17] How important he viewed this final recasting of his *Institutes* is evident from the fact that, although convinced he was dying, he forced himself to labor on the book, dictating while lying in bed wracked with pain and fever. He gave clear testimony to the great zeal that moved him "to carry out this task for God's church."[18]

Translations and abridgments

The first translation of the 1559 edition into another language (other than the French translation of 1560) was a Dutch translation published on December 5, 1560, during the time of the ferocious persecution of Reformed believers and their children by Spain and the Roman Catholic Church, shortly before the outbreak of the great struggle of the Dutch for political and religious freedom, and one year before the publication of the Belgic Confession. A new Dutch translation by Wilhelmus Corsmannus was published in 1650 and reprinted in 1889 with an introduction by Abraham Kuyper. A Dutch translation of the 1536 edition of the *Institutes* by William van't Spyker was published in 1992.

Thomas Norton translated the *Institutes* into English for the first time in 1561. Norton was theologically connected. He was a son-in-law of Archbishop Cranmer, and his mother-in-law was the niece of Andreas Osiander, the theologian with whom Calvin carried on a controversy over justification.[19] The first and second editions of Norton's translation were plagued with errors. Norton ruefully admitted that these editions came from the publisher full of errors because of "the evill manner of my scribbling hand."[20] The errors were finally corrected in the third edition.

The second English translation was by John Allen in 1813. The third English translation was by Henry Beveridge in 1845 under the auspices of the Calvin Translation Society founded in 1843. In 1960, Ford Lewis Battles translated a fourth English edition, which was edited by John T. McNeill.

According to T. H. L. Parker, Norton's English translation is still the best and most faithful to the original. Beveridge's translation of 1845 is more accurate than Allen's 1813 translation. Battles' 1960 translation is guilty of "blatant errors of translation."[21]

There have also been several abridgments. The first was an abridgment in Latin by Edmund Bunney published in 1576.[22] It was translated into English in 1580. A good abridgment in Latin by William Delaune was published in 1583. This was translated into English in 1585.[23] Delaune refers to his abridgment as "a nosegay from the pleasant garden of divinity."[24]

Two recent abridgments of the *Institutes* in English are *John Calvin's*

"*Instruction in Christianity,*" translated and abbreviated by Joseph Pitt Wiles, edited and abridged by David Otis Fuller, and published by Eerdmans in 1947; and *Calvin's Institutes: Abridged Edition*, edited by Donald K. McKim and published by Westminster John Knox Press in 2001.

There is reason to believe that Calvin did not intend, or expect, the constant expansion of his original, 1536 *Institutes* in the successive editions. He never expected the warm and widespread reception of the book. In his remarks to the reader at the beginning of the 1559 edition, Calvin wrote,

> In the first edition of this work of ours I did not in the least expect that success which, out of his infinite goodness, the Lord has given. Thus, for the most part I treated the subject summarily... But when I realized that it was received by almost all godly men with a favor for which I never would have ventured to wish, much less to hope, I deeply felt that I was much more favored than I deserved. Consequently I thought that I should be showing extreme ingratitude not to try at least, to the best of my slender ability, to respond to this warm appreciation for me, an appreciation that demanded my further diligence. Not only did I attempt this in the second edition, but each time the work has been reprinted since then, it has been enriched with some additions. Although I did not regret the labor spent, I was never satisfied until the work had been arranged in the order now set forth. Now I trust that I have provided something that all of you will approve.[25]

The *Institutes* unfolded in the providence of God, not with Calvin's intention.

The history of the publication of the *Institutes*, therefore, culminating in the marvelous edition of 1559, was the purpose and working of God.

CHAPTER 4

The Style and Structure of the *Institutes*

No analysis of the *Institutes* may ignore its style and structure—its form. Not only do the style and structure enhance the content, but they also contribute to the effectiveness of the message.

Style

Calvin wrote the *Institutes* in two languages, Latin and French. The first edition was the only edition that Calvin did not immediately translate into French. Latin was the language of the learned and the scholars; French was the language of the people. By publishing the various editions in Latin, Calvin indicated that he intended to reach the theologians, the ministers, the humanist scholars, and the rulers in the church. By publishing the *Institutes* in French, Calvin indicated that he also intended to reach the common people, the members of the church.

Especially the latter is noteworthy. Calvin did not write only for the scholars and theologians. He took seriously the Reformation teaching of the priesthood of all believers.

However, Calvin did not write only to the common people; he also confronted the leading theological, ecclesiastical, and humanist scholars of his day with the Reformed faith. Calvin was not ashamed of the Reformed faith. In fact, it was Calvin's sincere purpose to gain some of these scholars to the faith of the Reformation. In the preface to the 1541 French edition of the *Institutes*, Calvin wrote, "First I wrote it [the 1536 *Institutes*] in Latin... that it might be serviceable to all studious persons, of what nation soever they might be."[1]

In both the Latin and the French, Calvin wrote outstandingly well. His Latin was pure, classic Latin. It impressed the scholars of his day, and it still impresses Latin scholars today. Capable Latin scholars remark on the elegance of Calvin's Latin. This is due in part to the fact that as a young man he received good instruction from an outstanding teacher of the classical languages. He studied at the College de la Marche in Paris and learned Latin from Mathurin Cordier. John McNeill suggests that it was from Cordier that Calvin, then a teenage boy, "discovered the delights of good learning and acquired that unfailing sense of style and diction that marks all his writings."[2] This points out the influence that a good high school teacher can have upon a capable student, which will bear fruit, particularly in the work of a minister in the church.

Later, when Calvin was in his second pastorate in Geneva, he invited his old Latin teacher to head up the academy in Geneva.

Benjamin Warfield gives expression to the universal judgment of the Latin of the *Institutes* when he writes, "Wings were given to it [the Latin original of the *Institutes*] by the nobility of its form and the unwonted elegance of its language. For Calvin's Latin is as fine in its way as his French; and the Latin 'Institutes,' too, deserves to be called a classic."[3]

By his French translation of 1541, Calvin became a creator of the modern French language. As Luther formed the German language by his translation of the Bible, so Calvin formed the French language by his *Institutes*. Scholars recognize that the *Institutes* was the first book in French that can be called a "classic": the first book on a grand theme in pure, elegant, majestic French.[4] Jean-Daniel Benoit observed that the 1541 French edition of the *Institutes* was the "first time that French [was] used to handle the lofty subjects of philosophy and morality."[5]

John McNeill describes the French edition of 1541 as follows:

> The French version...is a landmark in the history of French prose. This is commonly affirmed on two grounds. The first is the fact that no similarly elaborate and serious work of thought had ever appeared in that language. The other reason is its literary distinction. By almost unanimous verdict of the scholars, the 1541 *Institution de la religion chrestienne* is a French classic, and through it Calvin, with no rival except Rabelais, stands in

the van of the fathers and creators of the French literary tradition.[6]

As is evident in every English translation of the *Institutes*, Calvin's style of writing is marked by clarity. Clarity is not to be confused with superficiality. As the truth itself is profound, Calvin is profound. But Calvin exercises the gift of expressing the truth clearly. The *Institutes* does not suffer from ambiguity. Neither is it unintelligible by virtue of the admission of sheer contradiction into theology, deceitfully called paradox. The Reformed theology of John Calvin is logical. Calvin reasons from premises to conclusions. He draws out the implications of a doctrine. In his theology the fundamental rule of discourse obtains, namely, the rule, or law, of noncontradiction. All the individual doctrines are harmoniously related to each other and form a unified whole. The Reformed faith of John Calvin can be, and is, summarized in the systematic, coherent Reformed creeds, specifically, the Three Forms of Unity and the Westminster Standards. Every reader of the *Institutes* can observe this aspect of Calvin's clarity for himself.

Contributing to the clarity of the *Institutes* is Calvin's theological method of beginning his discussion of a doctrine or an issue with a definition. He then proceeds to explain and defend the doctrine, or to explore the issue, in harmony with the definition. This method makes for clarity and precludes confusion.

Not only is this method of treating his subjects evident throughout the *Institutes*, but Calvin also expressly states that this is his method. In the 1536 *Institutes*, having criticized the "Scholastic Sophists" for their failure to work with a definition of the topic, Calvin says, "Now, for my part, when there is a dispute concerning anything, I am stupid enough to refer everything back to the definition itself, *which is the hinge and foundation of the whole debate.*"[7]

Much of contemporary, twenty-first-century theology, especially theological controversy, is hopelessly muddled by the failure clearly to indicate the subject or to identify the issue by a definition. The result is doctrinal confusion and ignorance.

As for those theologians who glory in their paradoxical murkiness, they have a different spirit than Calvin. Calvin is zealous to teach the people—the common people, God's people—so that they understand God's clear gospel.

His style in both Latin and French is marked by brevity. This does not mean that the writing is short. In fact, the *Institutes* in the final form is not a little book. It is a long, bulky book. But brevity means that Calvin's writing is characterized by *his not wasting any words.* Warfield puts it this way: "clear, sharp, [and] precise."[8] Calvin had command of the languages. He uses just the right words to express the thought he intends to teach and then moves on.

His is an elegant style. The historian John Mosheim says this about Calvin's style: "His *Institutes* are written in a perspicuous and elegant style, and have nothing abstruse and difficult to be comprehended in the arguments or mode of reasoning."[9]

Calvin's elegance, however, did not prevent him from condemning errors and heretics with what many refer to as "vituperation." Vituperation is harsh censure. The *Institutes* is full of harsh censure of heretics and false doctrine. It is customary in our tolerant age to criticize this aspect of Calvin's (and Martin Luther's) writings, to deplore such name-calling as is found throughout the *Institutes,* and then to excuse it somewhat by appealing to the uncivilized, rather barbarous time in which Calvin lived, or by noting that everyone did it.

Battles is representative. He inveighs against the harsh censure of the Roman Catholic Church that characterizes Calvin's writings in the *Institutes*: "the too abundant invective"[10] and "unnecessary vituperation."[11] This criticism has to do with what Calvin said concerning Rome's doctrine of the mass and the five additional sacraments that Rome adds to the sacraments instituted by Christ. Again:

> On occasion, Calvin shows a typically humanist mastery of the language of disparagement and *vituperation.* His horror of abuses led him at times to use *epithets* of abuse, and he sometimes resorts to this in assailing the legitimate views of an opponent. This is a *deplorable feature* by which in parts Calvin's work is marred for the *sensitive reader,* but it is not so prevalent as some critics have charged; and in his case invective is not a substitute for argument but a misconceived attempt to enhance its force.[12]

This is typical of the reaction of contemporary scholars to Calvin's harsh condemnation of false doctrines, false teachers, and false churches.

Battles' mention of the grating of Calvin's harsh language on "sensitive" readers is worth noting. Those today who object to Calvin's harsh language like to present themselves as loving, sensitive souls, but often these same people can stomach television programs and movies containing violence, sexual filth, and the taking of God's name in vain. If the people who deplore Calvin's harsh language are theologians, they are often the same theologians who can tolerate with equanimity the defaming of God's name by false doctrine. That fundamental doctrines of the Christian faith are denied bothers them not at all, but their "sensitive" souls are troubled when Calvin refers to enemies of the gospel as "dogs" and "hogs."

No Reformed Christian should object to Calvin's harsh language. The fact is that this kind of condemnation of error is thoroughly biblical, including referring to enemies of the faith as "dogs" and "hogs." In Philippians 3:2, Paul calls those who teach works-righteousness "dogs." In 2 Peter 2:22, the apostle calls those who preach and practice antinomianism "hogs"—swine who return to their muck and mire. I note also that the Heidelberg Catechism is sharp and vituperative in its condemnation of the Roman Catholic mass when it calls it "a denial of the one sacrifice and passion of Jesus Christ [and an accursed idolatry]."[13]

The vehement condemnation of error by Luther, Calvin, and many of their colleagues arose from their piety. Particularly in the case of Calvin, his severe condemnation of error had its source in his godliness, his love of and reverence for God, and his corresponding abhorrence of all those who showed themselves to be enemies of God. Calvin was a "sensitive" soul, but the sensitive soul of Calvin was sensitive to a diminishing of God's honor. Of this sensitivity, there is a notable lack in the twenty-first century, especially among Protestant theologians.

Calvin's sharp condemnation of doctrinal errors, and of those who taught them, is an aspect of the reformer's polemical style. Calvin thought that polemics are necessary in the teaching of the truth of the gospel. In his commentary on Luke 12:51, "Suppose ye that I am come to give peace on earth? I tell you, Nay; but rather division," Calvin remarks, "We cannot *confess* Christ without encountering the resistance and hatred of many. Christ therefore warns his followers to prepare for battle, for they must necessarily fight for the testimony of truth."[14]

Significantly, the printer's mark, or colophon, for all Calvin's writings was a sword. That device accurately symbolized his writing in the *Institutes*, indeed all his teaching, including his sermons.

So prominent are polemics in the *Institutes* that Calvin's antithetical writing style becomes part of the structure of the book. Antithetical style means that Calvin not only sets forth the truth positively, but also immediately contrasts the truth with the error or errors that oppose the truth. The error or errors he then refutes and condemns. A major reason for the expansion of the *Institutes* over the years was Calvin's controversies with various heretics. This method of teaching greatly contributes to the clarity of Calvin's teaching. The truth stands out more sharply against the background of the lie.

J. I. Packer has rightly observed that Calvin was a fighter and that his *Institutes* is a "fighting book."[15]

But it is not only his supporters who have recognized the prominence and importance of a vigorous defense of the faith in Calvin's writings, particularly the *Institutes*. Even the secular author James Anthony Froude called attention to this characteristic of Calvin's ministry, attributing it to his zeal for the truth.

> The Reformers required a position more sharply defined, and a sterner leader [than Martin Luther], and that leader they found in John Calvin.
>
> There is no occasion to say much of Calvin's personal history. His name is now associated only with gloom and austerity. Suppose it is true that he rarely laughed. He had none of Luther's genial and sunny humor. Could they have exchanged conditions, Luther's temper might have been somewhat grimmer, but he would never have been entirely like Calvin. Nevertheless, for hard times hard men are needed, and intellects which can pierce to the roots where truth and lies part company. It fares ill with the soldiers of religion when "the accursed thing" is in their camp. And this is to be said of Calvin, that so far as the state of knowledge permitted, no eye could have detected more keenly the unsound spots in the received creed of

the Church, nor was there a reformer in Europe so resolute to excise, tear out, and destroy what was distinctly seen to be false,—so resolute to establish what was true in its place, and make truth to the last fibre of it the rule of practical life.[16]

Reformed ministers and theologians have much to learn from this aspect of Calvin's style, particularly in the *Institutes*. The spirit of the age encourages, indeed insists on, friendliness, tolerance, and being positive. It discourages, indeed damns and threatens, controversy, condemnation, and negativity. Many Reformed theologians have caved in to, if they have not embraced, this spirit. The colophon of most contemporary sermons, theological articles, and religious books might well be a feather duster, rather than a sword.

The truth is at stake! As Calvin knew, if the truth is not defended it cannot endure. Tolerance of the lie betrays a lack of love for the truth. Justifying his strong defense of predestination in his treatise "On the Eternal Predestination of God" to the civil authorities of Geneva against the attacks on predestination by Pighius and Bolsec, Calvin wrote, "Iniquity, unless it be resolutely met, makes its creeping way (as saith Paul) 'like a canker' (2 Tim. 2:17)."[17]

In his polemics Calvin allowed himself the use of satire. His writings, including the *Institutes*, are liberally sprinkled with irony and sarcasm. One example was Calvin's description of Ami Perrin, leader of the Libertine faction in Geneva, with which Calvin struggled for a time, as "*Caesar comicus*," a comic Caesar. Perrin's formidable wife, Francesca Favre, was an example of the aristocratic, forward, truculent woman in the church with whom every pastor is familiar. She was one of Amos' "kine [cows] of Bashan" (Amos 4:1). Calvin referred to her as "Penthesilea," after the mythological queen of the Amazons who fought the Greeks before Troy and, significantly, was killed by the Greek hero Achilles.

The outstanding instance of Calvin's use of irony and sarcasm in defense of the faith is the entirety of his treatise "An Admonition, Showing the Advantages Which Christendom Might Derive from an Inventory of Relics."[18] With reference to Rome's absurd multiplication of relics, Calvin remarks that if it were not for the fact that Rome teaches that Mary's body is no longer on earth, the Roman Catholic

Church would have collected so many bones of Mary as holy relics as to give "her a body of such a size as would suffice to fill a thousand sarcophaguses."[19] To compensate for the absence of Mary's bones, various Roman Catholic churches all over the world have collected her milk in such vast quantities, observes Calvin, that "had the breasts of the most Holy Virgin yielded a more copious supply than is given by a cow, or had she continued to nurse during her whole lifetime, she scarcely could have furnished the quantity which is exhibited."[20]

Calvin employs satire strategically also in the *Institutes*, as is pointed out in this summary. About this aspect of Calvin's polemical style, church historian Philip Schaff remarks, "Calvin wielded the sharp sword of irony, wit, scorn, and contempt in defense of truth, but never from personal hatred and revenge."[21]

Some who acknowledge the necessity of refuting error are critical of this aspect of Calvin's defense of the faith. But the criticism is mistaken. Not only have all the great defenders of the faith satirized enemies of the truth, but also Scripture does the same. The prophet ridicules the idolater (Isa. 44:9–20). Elijah mocks the prophets of Baal (1 Kings 18:27). Paul ironically expresses the desire that the proponents of circumcision go all the way and emasculate themselves (Gal. 5:12). False doctrine is foolish and ought to be held up to ridicule. God himself laughs at his enemies and has them in derision (Ps. 2:4).

No doubt, Calvin's superb style of writing was a natural gift with which he was peculiarly graced by the Holy Spirit, so that he could be the effective servant of the word of God that he was.

Calvin developed the gift by wide, lifelong, energetic reading. Calvin was a reader. He read in the profane classical literature; he read Plato and Cicero, as is evident from his quotations of them in the *Institutes*. He knew the church fathers thoroughly. And he diligently read Holy Scripture.

Calvin also developed his style of writing by practice. He wrote much, and he wrote constantly. Writing forces one to be clear, precise, and exact, as is stated in the well-known proverb of Francis Bacon: "Reading maketh a full man; conference, a ready man, and writing, an exact man."

Regarding his development not only of the form of his writing, but also of the content, by means of writing much, Calvin concludes his

"John Calvin to the Reader" with an intriguing and useful quotation from Augustine: "I count myself one of the number of those who *write as they learn and learn as they write.*"[22]

There is a spiritual factor contributing to Calvin's good style of writing. Calvin burned, in his zeal for God's glory and his ardor for the salvation of the church, to communicate the word of God with clarity and power. Gripped himself by the word of God, he was determined to make human words the forceful vehicle of the divine word.

The great French biographer of Calvin, Émile Doumergue, had this in view when he called Calvin, *"l'homme de la parole"* ("the man of the word").[23] This for Doumergue was the essence of Calvin. By this description of Calvin, Doumergue meant that Calvin was not only a man full of zeal for the word of God, but also a man who gave himself to words, and especially to writing words in the service of the word of God. By the written word Calvin influenced church and nations.

Specifically regarding Calvin's clarity, Calvin himself explains this important, indeed essential, quality of a preacher and a religious writer: "Nobody teaches clearly a thing of which he has not been persuaded."[24] Conviction produces clarity.

There is something here for Reformed preachers in the twenty-first century. They must read widely and continually and exert themselves in writing. When other men are golfing or watching television, ministers ought to be in their studies reading and writing. In addition, they must read and write as men who are themselves seized and gripped by the word of God and as men who are convinced in our nonverbal, and even antiverbal, age that the glory of God and the kingdom of Jesus Christ are still promoted by the word. God's glory and the welfare of the church are promoted not by pictures, drama, and ritual, but by words—human words in the service of the word of God in Scripture. This has become a challenge for Reformed preachers and churches. Will we give up on the word? Churches have given up on the word of God, and the word of God has given up on them, when instead of the Sunday evening sermon, they show C. S. Lewis' "The Lion, the Witch, and the Wardrobe."

In the twenty-first century, as in the sixteenth, the true church is preserved and enlarged by the word.

The significance of Calvin's ability in the two influential languages of his day and his felicitous style was that the employment of these two languages enabled the witness to the Reformed faith to spread among the learned throughout Europe and among the common people in France and wherever French was spoken. Thus the two languages served to promote the Reformation and to establish the Reformed church.

Calvin's style supported and enhanced his message. The clarity was especially important to the people. The purity and majesty of the Latin commended the message to the scholars.

The Reformed preacher may not discount the importance of good style, whether in preaching or in writing. He hinders the effectiveness of his ministry if he supposes that, since his message is the truth, it does not matter how he speaks or writes it.

Good grammar is required. It is fundamental in preaching and in writing to be clear. Ministers should study brevity. This means that a minister may preach for fifty or sixty minutes, but not because he has rambled, said the same thing in five different ways, or was not careful to use just the right word to express just the right thought, so that he has to come back and rehash to make his point clear.

Taking heed to style also includes being as vivid, forceful, and elegant as one's own gifts permit him to be.

Style is not the main thing, but it is important. We can learn from Calvin's *Institutes* that style enhances the message and serves the effectiveness of the message. When the message is the Reformed faith, it is worthy of the very best style.

Structure

Even though something has been said about this already, it will be helpful, before getting into the content of the *Institutes*, to take note of the structure of this carefully laid-out work of theological piety, or pious theology. Calvin changed the structure of the 1559 *Institutes* radically from that of the original, 1536 edition, indeed from that of all the preceding editions.

The structure of the 1536 *Institutes* was that of a typical Protestant catechism of that day, although not in question and answer format. The 1536 *Institutes* treated the topics of the law, the Apostles' Creed, the model prayer, and the sacraments, in this order. Calvin added two chapters: one on the five false sacraments of the Roman Catholic Church and another on Christian freedom, church power, and civil government.

In the 1559 *Institutes* Calvin adopted a different structure altogether—a trinitarian structure after the pattern of the Apostles' Creed. There are four books, which Calvin entitled: "The Knowledge of God the Creator"; "The Knowledge of God the Redeemer in Christ"; "The Way in Which We Receive the Grace of Christ [Holy Spirit]"; and "The External Means or Aids by Which God Invites Us into the Society of Christ [the Church]."[25]

What this fourfold division of all the main teachings of Holy Scripture amounts to is "God the Creator"—the first part of the Apostles' Creed; "God the Redeemer"—the second part of the Apostles' Creed; and "God the Sanctifier"—the third part of the Apostle's Creed. Book four is further treatment of the third part of the Apostles' Creed, concerning the Spirit's work upon and in the church. The final chapter, on civil government, is added to the exposition of the work of the Spirit, and more directly to the doctrine of the church, inasmuch as Calvin thought that civil government is called of God to cooperate with the church on behalf of the gospel and to support the true church.

The entirety of the Christian faith is set forth within this trinitarian framework. All the doctrines of Scripture find their place in connection with the three persons of the Trinity. This system of dogmatics is Calvin's alternative to the later Reformed tradition of dividing the content of theology into six loci, or main topics.

The significance of the structure of the 1559 *Institutes* is, first, that this foundational statement of the Reformed faith is remarkable for "order and symmetry."[26] Order and symmetry contribute to the effectiveness of the book. Certainly, the order of the *Institutes* is a testimony to Calvin's orderly mind and to the determination of his will that the Reformed faith and life be well ordered. Calvin loved order in every aspect of theology and the church. He expressed his detestation of disorder by recurring variations on the line, "Else we live pell-mell like rats in the straw."

However, this insistence on order was no personal psychological obsession, even "hang-up," on the part of Calvin, as the psychologizing historians and biographers suggest. Rather, it was simple obedience to the word of God, which commands that all things in the church "be done decently and in order" (1 Cor. 14:40).

Indeed, Calvin's orderly theological mind, and therefore the orderly structure of the *Institutes*, reflects the order of the word of God and, thus, the order of the mind of God. God is not a God of disorder and confusion. Such a God could neither know himself or be known by us.

A second significance of the structure of the 1559 *Institutes* is that patterning the Reformed faith after the Apostles' Creed recommends this faith as the authentic contemporary representation and development of the ancient faith of the church. The Reformed faith, as the pure, sound, full faith of the Protestant Reformation, is not a novelty, as its foes charged. The reformers insisted that the Reformation *reformed* the church according to the apostolic doctrine. Responding to the charge of Cardinal Sadolet that the Reformation "tore up and destroyed" all that the church had approved for fifteen hundred years, Calvin wrote, "Our agreement with antiquity is far closer than yours, but... all we have attempted has been to renew that ancient form of the Church, which, at first sullied and distorted by illiterate men of indifferent character, was afterwards flagitiously mangled and almost destroyed by the Roman Pontiff and his faction."[27]

Third, Calvin's use of the trinitarian framework makes the doctrine of the Trinity preeminent in his exposition of the faith of the church. The truth of God triune is central, not only in the content of the book, but also in its form.

A brief overview of the main subjects treated in each of the four books is beneficial. Book one treats the knowledge of God and its importance; the knowledge of God from the creation; the knowledge of God from Scripture; the doctrine of the Trinity; the creation of man and his nature as created; and providence, which in the 1559 *Institutes* is separated from predestination for the first time.

Book two treats the fall of man, total depravity, and the bondage of the will as a unit; redemption alone in Christ the mediator; the law of God, in various respects; the relation of the Old and New Testaments; and Christology proper, that is, the person, natures, and offices of Jesus Christ.

Book three, on the saving of the elect sinner, begins with the Holy

Spirit as "the bond by which Christ effectually unites us to himself."[28] Book three continues with the related truths of faith, regeneration, and repentance; the Christian life (sanctification); justification; Christian freedom; prayer, including an exposition of the model prayer; predestination, which in the 1559 *Institutes* is separated from providence and treated as the source of the salvation of the elect sinner; and the resurrection of the body—the climax of the work of salvation.

Book four treats the true church; the offices, government, and discipline of the church; the papacy; vows; the sacraments; the mass; the five false sacraments of the Roman Catholic Church; and civil government.

Certain observations of a general nature concerning the content of the *Institutes*, thus arranged, are in order at the outset of this summary.

The *Institutes* is God-centered. The content, as well as the trinitarian structure, proclaims the message that was the hallmark not only of the Calvinistic branch of the Reformation, but also of the whole of the Reformation—of the Reformation as such: "to God alone be the glory." The *Institutes* is God-centered in such a way that it breathes a reverential love of God. Battles correctly states, "[The *Institutes* is] suffused with an awed sense of God's ineffable majesty, sovereign power, and immediate presence with us men."[29]

But the *Institutes* is God-centered, not apart from, but in Jesus Christ. Battles calls attention to this characteristic of Calvin's explanation of Christian doctrine: "The focal point of the *Institutes* is not found in God's sovereignty, or in predestination, or in insistence on obedience to God's Word itself, *apart from constant reference to Jesus Christ, whom the written Word makes known.*"[30]

Such is the prominence of Christ in Calvin's exposition and defense of Christian doctrine that some have proposed viewing the four books of the *Institutes* as the treatment of "Christ the Creator, Christ the Redeemer, Christ the Inspirer, and Christ the King."[31]

In the *Institutes* Calvin practices what he preached concerning the interpretation of Scripture: "We must read Scripture with the intention of finding Christ therein. Whoever departs from this focus could toil and study a whole life-time and never attain knowledge of the truth. Or could we be wise without the wisdom of God?"[32]

The *Institutes* is God-centered in Jesus Christ because it is thoroughly biblical. Not only is there constant, explicit appeal to and quotation of Scripture, but also biblical thoughts, allusions, and partial quotations are woven into the text as part of the ongoing exposition. Calvin's knowledge of the Bible was marvelous. His use of it was masterful.

Battles comments on Calvin's use of Scripture: "Calvin more often quotes Scripture *ad sensum* than *ad litteram* and... even when he is quoting directly very often no known Scriptural version is followed verbatim."[33] No doubt, this is in keeping with Calvin's practice of preaching and teaching directly from the original languages of Scripture, giving his own translation.

So basic is the epistle to the Romans to the content of the *Institutes* that Battles, with pardonable exaggeration, calls the *Institutes* "an extended commentary on Romans."[34]

Whether there is one particular doctrine that stands out in, is central to, and controls the *Institutes* is a question that has mightily engaged the scholars. The search for one such doctrine is mistaken, and futile.

Rather, with Alexander Smellie, the reader should take note of a number of outstanding doctrines in the *Institutes*, as in the Scriptures of which the *Institutes* is the exposition. Smellie mentions the following emphases of Calvin: the centrality of God; reverence for Scripture; the depravity of the natural man; Christ Jesus as the only savior; and predestination, which, as the explanation of the salvation of some and of the damnation of the others, affirms that salvation is by the sovereign grace of God alone.[35]

To this list certainly must be added the union of the elect church with Christ and, thus, with the ever-blessed God. And inasmuch as this union is, in fact, the essence of the covenant of grace, the truth of the covenant is dominant in Calvin, regardless that he does not explicitly put the covenant on the foreground.

CHAPTER 5

The Prefatory Address

Introduction

Prefixed to the original, 1536 edition of the *Institutes* is the "Prefatory Address to King Francis I of France." It remained virtually unchanged throughout all subsequent editions.

The prefatory address is unanimously and widely regarded as a masterpiece of such literature. Alexander Smellie says that it is "one of the greatest letters ever composed."[1] Another reputable judge of such writing, comparing it to similar writings, both religious and secular, ranks it with two other addresses as the three greatest addresses ever written.

Apologetic purpose

The prefatory address confronts us at once with the apologetic purpose and nature of the *Institutes*, especially the first edition. Calvin's purpose is to defend the Reformed faith and the Reformed citizens in France to the king of France. Calvin begins:

> I perceived that the fury of certain wicked persons has prevailed so far in your realm that there is no place in it for sound doctrine. Consequently, it seemed to me that I should be doing something worth-while if I both gave instruction to them [my countrymen] and made confession before you [your Majesty] with the same work. From this you may learn the nature of the doctrine against which those madmen burn with rage who today disturb your realm with fire and sword. And indeed I

shall not fear to confess that here is contained almost the sum of that very doctrine which they shout must be punished by prison, exile, proscription, and fire, and be exterminated on land and sea. Indeed, I know with what horrible reports they have filled your ears and mind, to render our cause as hateful as possible to you.[2]

Thus Calvin indicates the dire condition of the Reformed Christians in France that occasioned his address to King Francis. Open persecution against Reformed Protestants had broken out in early 1535. It was a persecution by the state, but persecution encouraged by the powerful Roman Catholic Church.

The immediate occasion of the persecution was the affair of the placards on October 18, 1534, an act of radicalism instigated by the preacher Antoine Marcourt of Neuchâtel. Radicals among the Protestants posted placards throughout Paris that violently denounced the Roman Catholic mass. These radicals thrust a placard into the king's bedchamber. When King Francis awoke in the morning, he was confronted with a condemnation of the mass, to which he was committed heart and soul. Besides, the intrusion into the king's bedchamber was an affront to the royal dignity and even a threat to the king's life. The infuriated Francis unleashed persecution. Alexandre Ganoczy writes that this radical act "compromised the cause of the reformists more than any preceding incident."[3]

Although persecuting Reformed Protestants in France, King Francis was desirous of a political treaty with the German Lutheran princes. Therefore, he represented the persecution as the French government's punishment of Anabaptist revolutionaries. The memory of the Peasants' Revolt was still fresh in Germany. About this time, the Anabaptist debacle at Münster was playing out.

Calvin's prefatory address is a defense of Reformed Christians in France against the suspicion and charge that they were seditious Anabaptists. It was a real concern of the Reformed churches at that time to distinguish the Reformed churches from the Anabaptists. This comes out in Article 36 of the Belgic Confession of Faith:

> We detest the error of the Anabaptists and other seditious people, and in general all those who reject the higher powers and

magistrates, and would subvert justice, introduce community of goods, and confound that decency and good order which God hath established among men.[4]

A radical fringe troubled Protestantism from the very outset of the sixteenth-century Reformation. Another expression of this radicalism was the iconoclasm—the physical destruction of images and paintings by rampaging mobs, in the name of Christ on behalf of a thoroughgoing Reformation—that attached itself to the spread of the gospel throughout Europe.

Also today there are threats to Reformed Christianity—genuine Protestantism—from an ultra-conservative radicalism. This radicalism takes form in the tax-protest movement, the refusal to pay taxes to an ungodly state; in the bombing of abortion clinics; and in the stockpiling of and practicing with guns in order to defend Christ's kingdom against the imminent assault by an antichristian nation, if not to overthrow the antichristian nation.

Calvin's prefatory address, as well as the repudiation of sedition and of the confounding of decency and good order by Article 36 of the Belgic Confession, stands Reformed churches in good stead today, with regard to distinguishing themselves from a radicalism that revolts against the authority of the state.

By his defense of Reformed Christians, Calvin desired also to stop the persecution of French Christians and to keep Francis from future persecution of the Reformed church.

Did Calvin sincerely suppose that he might convince Francis by this address? There is reason to think that Calvin supposed that he might convince Francis. In his earlier years Francis had showed himself a humanist. In the beginning of the Reformation, there was a certain friendliness on the part of humanist scholars toward the Reformation, not because they shared the theology of the Reformation, but because they appreciated the learning of the Reformation and desired a reform of the immoral lives of the Roman Catholic clergy. Erasmus of Rotterdam was an outstanding example of these humanists.

Also because of the political situation in Europe at that time, there was reason to think that Francis had leanings toward ending persecution. He needed the support of the Protestant leaders in certain military ventures.

Not long before Calvin wrote his prefatory address, Francis had asked leading reformers to come to Paris to advise him concerning the religious situation.

Calvin might indeed have thought that it was possible that a well-reasoned defense of the Reformed faith might sway Francis to put an end to the persecution and allow the Reformed people to organize Reformed churches and practice the Reformed religion.

Nevertheless, Calvin was no fool. At the end of the prefatory address, Calvin recognizes the likelihood that Francis will give the Reformation no hearing. In this case, Calvin reminds the lordly monarch, one of the great kings of his day, of the coming deliverance of the church and the punishment of her tormentors by the Lord Jesus Christ:

> Suppose, however, the whisperings of the malevolent so fill your ears that the accused have no chance to speak for themselves, but those savage furies, while you connive at them, ever rage against us with imprisonings, scourgings, rackings, maimings, and burnings [cf. Heb. 11:36, 37]. Then we will be reduced to the last extremity even as sheep destined for the slaughter [Isa. 53:7, 8; Acts 8:33]. Yet this will so happen that "in our patience we may possess our souls" [Luke 21:19]; and may await the strong hand of the Lord, which will surely appear in due season, coming forth armed to deliver the poor from their affliction and also to punish their despisers, who now exult with such great assurance.[5]

This is a strong warning to the king of France that as he is lord over the poor citizens whom he is allowing to be maimed, racked, burned, and killed, he also has a Lord to whom he will answer in the final judgment.

There is no evidence that Francis ever read the prefatory address. This, however, did not render the prefatory address to Francis useless as an apologetic piece, as Calvin well knew. Long after Francis was dead, Calvin continued to include the prefatory address as the first part of his *Institutes*. At all times and in all circumstances, it serves to distinguish the Reformed faith not only from Anabaptism, but also from Roman Catholicism.

Defense of the Reformed faith

In the first place, then, the prefatory address defends the Reformed church against the suspicion and charge of Anabaptism. It is worth noting that Calvin does not speak of Anabaptism, but of *Catabaptism*. *Anabaptism* refers to rebaptism because this movement rejects infant baptism and insists that adults be rebaptized. The first part of the word *Catabaptism* comes from the Greek preposition *kata* (against). *Catabaptism* describes the movement as opposed to infant baptism and, therefore, to the sacrament of baptism rightly understood and practiced. The implication of Calvin's name for the movement is that it is the Reformed who truly honor baptism, so that Reformed Christians are the genuine "Baptists." It would be right, today, to refer to those who reject infant baptism as "Catabaptists." Usage, unfortunately, prevents this.

Calvin insists that the charge against the Reformed Christians that they are disorderly and revolutionary Anabaptists is unjust. Passages of Scripture expressing the Reformed commitment to order in society are 1 Corinthians 14:33, Galatians 2:17, and 1 John 3:8. These texts teach that God is not the author of confusion but of peace. Calvin insists that the Anabaptists are the authors of confusion, but that Reformed people are not characterized by disorder. In this connection Calvin remarks to King Francis, "We are, I suppose, contriving the overthrow of kingdoms—we, from whom not one seditious word was ever heard; we, whose life when we lived under you was always acknowledged to be quiet and simple; we, who do not cease to pray for the full prosperity of yourself and your kingdom, although we are now fugitives from home."[6]

Calvin affirms that the Reformed faith is nonrevolutionary. He will demonstrate this fundamental characteristic of the Reformed faith more fully in the chapter on civil government. In a way the last chapter of the *Institutes*, on civil government, is a conclusion to the prefatory address to King Francis. It establishes that the Reformed faith is nonrevolutionary and calls Reformed believers to submit to civil rulers even though they are persecuting tyrants (like Francis I of France).

In the second place, the prefatory address defends the Reformed faith against the false charges brought against it by the Roman Catholic Church and sharply distinguishes the Reformed faith from the Roman Catholic religion. Francis was Roman Catholic, and Rome was behind the persecution, provoking the king with slanderous charges against the Reformed Christians in France. In a succinct way in the prefatory address, Calvin denies and disproves these charges. By far the greater part of the prefatory address is taken up with Rome's charges and, therefore, with a defense of the Reformed faith against Roman Catholic error.

There is in the defense against Rome a clear statement of the gospel, including the gospel's importance in the present doctrinal controversy. Calvin writes that the gospel is the word of salvation by grace alone:

> For what is more consonant with faith than to recognize that we are naked of all virtue, in order to be clothed with God? That we are empty of all good, to be filled by him? That we are slaves of sin, to be freed by him? Blind, to be illumined by him? Lame, to be made straight by him? Weak, to be sustained by him? To take away from us all occasion for glorying, that he alone may stand forth gloriously and we glory in him [cf. 1 Cor. 1:31; 2 Cor. 10:17]? When we say these and like things our adversaries interrupt and complain that in this way we shall subvert some blind light of nature, imaginary preparations, free will, and works that merit eternal salvation, even with their supererogations [doctrine of the treasury of merits]. For they cannot bear that the whole praise and glory of all goodness, virtue, righteousness, and wisdom should rest with God. But we do not read of anyone being blamed for drinking too deeply of the fountain of living water [John 4:14]. On the contrary, those have been harshly rebuked who "have dug for themselves cisterns, broken cisterns that can hold no water" [Jer. 2:13]. Besides, what is better and closer to faith than to feel assured that God will be a propitious Father where Christ is recognized as brother and propitiator?[7]

The importance of the issue of the doctrinal controversy in France is nothing less than "how God's glory may be kept safe on earth." "A very great question is at stake: how God's glory may be kept safe on earth, how God's truth may retain its place of honor, how Christ's Kingdom may be kept in good repair among us. Worthy indeed is this matter of your hearing, worthy of your cognizance, worthy of your royal throne!"[8]

The first Roman Catholic charge against the Reformation that Calvin refutes, to the Roman Catholic king, is the charge that the gospel of salvation by grace alone is new and can display no miracles to confirm itself. Calvin acknowledges that the gospel of the Reformation is indeed new to the Roman Catholic clergy. However, it is not new in the church of Christ. Appealing to Romans 4:25, Calvin declares that the doctrine of justification by faith alone—the heart of the Reformation gospel—is "ancient." "But he who knows that this preaching of Paul is ancient, that 'Jesus Christ died for our sins and rose again for our justification'... will find nothing new among us."[9]

Because it is not a new gospel, but the old gospel of the Scriptures, which has already been confirmed by all the miracles of Christ and of the apostles, the gospel of the Reformation neither needs, nor allows for, new miracles. "We... are retaining that very gospel whose truth all the miracles that Jesus Christ and his disciples ever wrought serve to confirm."[10] The only gospel that needs new miracles is a new gospel.

Calvin reminds the king that God himself, in Deuteronomy 13:1–5, has warned his people against a credulous, uncritical acceptance of every purported "sign or... wonder." Alleged wonders must be tested. The test is whether they "seal the truth." And the "mark of true doctrine" is, according to Christ in John 7:18 and John 8:50, that a doctrine "does not tend to seek men's glory but God's."[11]

For Calvin, alleged and even seeming miracles do not determine one's confession and church membership. "Doctrine... is superior to [church] miracles." And the infallible and clear hallmark of sound doctrine is that it glorifies God rather than man.[12]

With appeal to Matthew 24:24 and 2 Thessalonians 2:9, Calvin notes that Satan will perform extraordinary, dazzling deeds in the last days, on behalf of the lie, deceiving many nominal Christians.

Calvin's defense of the absence of miracles from the Reformation and his devastating indictment of the miraculous in the Roman Catholic Church are the defense and indictment by genuine Protestantism in the twenty-first century against the charge and claim on the part of the charismatic movement. The gospel of genuine Protestantism is the doctrine that the apostles confirmed by their "signs, and wonders, and mighty deeds" (2 Cor. 12:12). The gospel needs no additional miraculous confirmation. Evidently, the gospel of the charismatic movement is a novelty, needing new confirmation. In addition, teaching salvation and its baptism in the Spirit dependent on the will of man, the charismatic gospel is a doctrine that glorifies man, rather than God. Not one of its "signs and wonders," therefore, is of God.

A second charge against the Reformation by the Roman Catholic Church, refuted by Calvin to King Francis, is that the early church fathers opposed the doctrines taught by the Reformation. "They unjustly set the ancient fathers against us."[13] Calvin responds that he is able to prove the truth of the Reformation gospel from the fathers. Nevertheless, the church fathers are not the final authority in the church. Christ, speaking in the Scriptures, is the Lord of the church. "He who does not observe this distinction will have nothing certain in religion, inasmuch as these holy men [the church fathers] were ignorant of many things, often disagreed among themselves, and sometimes even contradicted themselves."[14]

Calvin notes in this connection that Roman Catholic theologians have a curious penchant for combing the church fathers to find their "faults and errors," which the theologians then advocate as authoritative doctrine. Meanwhile, they deliberately ignore "the wise and excellent things" in these fathers, including all the statements of salvation by grace, which support the Reformation. One could say that the Roman theologians' "only care is to gather dung amid gold."[15]

The same perversity characterizes much of Calvin scholarship in Reformed and Presbyterian churches in the twenty-first century. Ignoring Calvin's massive, powerful, clear confession of eternal, sovereign predestination, election and reprobation, the scholars trumpet their discovery of a few stray statements, usually in Calvin's commentaries, that seem to teach a desire of God to save all as proving that Calvin, in fact, was a theologian who taught that God loves all without exception and sincerely desires to save all.

Similarly, Presbyterian and Reformed theologians bend every effort to find isolated expressions in Calvin's commentaries that permit them to set aside Calvin's explicit, full defense of justification by faith alone, apart from all human works, in his *Institutes* and to present Calvin as the sixteenth-century proponent of the heresy of justification by faith and works that now surfaces in Reformed churches. Thus, contrary to his avowed agreement with Luther on the doctrine, Calvin is made to differ with Luther on the fundamental doctrine of justification.

Those do the same who scour Calvin's sermons and commentaries for the careless statement that will allow them to appeal to Calvin in support of their radically "un-Calvinistic" doctrine that true faith is not assurance of salvation, that is, that true faith is doubt.

These hunt for "dung amid gold" in Calvin.

Demonstrating his thorough knowledge of the church fathers, Calvin turns the tables on his Roman Catholic opponents. He pits the church fathers against prominent Roman Catholic beliefs and practices, including luxurious ceremonies; abstinence from meat during Lent; monkery; images; transubstantiation; the lack of discipline regarding participation in the Eucharist; withholding the cup from the laity; decreeing ecclesiastical laws without scriptural basis; forbidding the clergy to marry; and engaging in theological squabbles over trifles.[16]

A third charge of Rome was that the Reformed faith contradicts "custom" and, with this, the opinion of the majority.[17] Calvin responds that seldom have "the better things pleased the majority."[18] He adds, "In the Kingdom of God his eternal truth must alone be listened to and observed, a truth that cannot be dictated to by length of time, by long-standing custom, or by the conspiracy of men."[19] In Article 7, the Belgic Confession of Faith echoes Calvin's teaching concerning the only rule of faith in the church: "nor ought we to compare custom, or the great multitude, or antiquity."[20] Effectively, Calvin appeals to lonely Noah, who condemned the whole world.

The fundamental Roman Catholic charge, in Calvin's day as in our own, is that the Reformation opposes the church, that is, the ancient and imposing institution identified with the Roman Catholic Church. Calvin remarks, "Our controversy turns on these hinges: first, they contend that the form of the church is always apparent and observable. Secondly, they set this form [of the church] in the see of the Roman Church and its hierarchy."[21]

Calvin's refutation of the charge consists, first, of a rejection of Rome's doctrine that the church is essentially a visible organization: "We, on the contrary, affirm that the church can exist without any visible appearance."[22] Calvin appeals to the seven thousand in the days of Elijah. The Belgic Confession also takes issue with the Roman Catholic doctrine of the church as essentially an imposing institution:

> And this holy Church is preserved or supported by God against the rage of the whole world; though she sometimes (for a while) appear[s] very small, and, in the eyes of men, to be reduced to nothing: as during the perilous reign of Ahab, when nevertheless *the Lord reserved unto him seven thousand men, who had not bowed their knees to Baal.*[23]

Basic to the argument of both Calvin and the Belgic Confession is the belief that the church of Christ is essentially a spiritual body made up of elect believers and their genuine children.

Regarding its institutional form, the church (the true church) is not identified by antiquity, splendor, or size. "It has quite another mark: namely, the pure preaching of God's Word and the lawful administration of the sacraments."[24]

Then Calvin points to Scripture to prove that an institution with the name *church* can err, and err greatly. Aaron, who was high priest of the Old Testament church, made a golden image for the nation of Israel (Ex. 32:4). Calvin contends that institutions with the name *church* can be false churches. The Sanhedrin condemned Jesus Christ (John 11:47–57).

As a good student of church history, Calvin nails down his refutation by pointing out that Pope Eugenius IV was deposed by the Council of Basel, replaced by another pope, and then restored. Where was the church in all of this conflict and confusion? Rome cannot maintain its doctrine of the church in its own history.

Finally, there is the charge that the Reformation causes tumult, uproar, and division in church and society. Calvin's refutation runs along these lines: Satan has long been lolling about (one can visualize Satan stretched out on a couch, resting, with his head in his hand) because the church is apostate. Why should he bestir himself when everything is going famously for him in what we now call the Roman Catholic Church? The gospel is not being preached; discipline is not being exercised; people, priests, monks, and popes are living like the devil. But as soon as Satan sees that the Reformation has recovered the gospel and that the true church is being reformed, he bestirs himself, inciting rulers such as Charles V, Henry VIII, and Francis I to persecute the church and arousing heretics and schismatics to create internal disturbances in the church. It is not at all surprising that there are tumults and uproars, but the fault does not lie with the Reformation. "The blame for these evils is unjustly laid upon it [the preaching of Reformed doctrine], when this ought to have been imputed to Satan's malice."[25]

Scripture supports Calvin's analysis of the troubles that have followed the Reformation. Calvin points to Ahab's accusation that Elijah was guilty of troubling Israel: "Art thou he that troubleth Israel?" (1 Kings 18:17). Charges of sedition were lodged against the apostles for "turn[ing] the world upside down" (Acts 17:6). The gospel always provokes a hostile reaction from the world without and occasions opposition from heretics within. Tumult and trouble by no means mark a church as false, any more than mere earthly peace proves a church to be true. There is the peace of the graveyard.

Calvin is not content to refute the charges made by Rome against the Reformed Christians in France. Addressing the Roman Catholic king, he passes a damning indictment upon the Roman Catholic Church and its clergy. Calvin speaks of the "lazy, wine-cask bellies of monks in these stews and brothels."[26] Of the priests he observes, "Their God is their belly... their kitchen their religion!"[27] Concerning Roman Catholic doctrine, which is the main thing in the great controversy of the Reformation, Calvin advises the king, "If you will devote a little of your leisure to the reading of our words, you will unmistakably recognize that this, this very doctrine itself whereby they claim to be the church, is a deadly butchery of souls, a firebrand, a ruin, and a destruction of the church."[28]

Duties of King Francis

Calvin charges King Francis with his duties as a magistrate, called by God.

First, in simple justice Francis must give the accused Reformed Protestants in France a hearing and not condemn them on the testimony of their enemies:

> It is sheer violence that bloody sentences are meted out against this doctrine without a hearing; it is fraud that it is undeservedly charged with treason and villainy. So that no one may think we are wrongly complaining of these things, you can be our witness, most noble King, with how many lying slanders it is daily traduced in your presence... But with what right has it been condemned?... This case... has been handled... with no order of law and with violent heat rather than judicial gravity.[29]

Here is the trained lawyer pleading for justice on behalf of oppressed citizens, who are also God's dear children.

Second, it is the duty of Francis—and Calvin calls on him to do his duty—to deliver and promote the Reformed church as the true church according to the standard of the word of God.

> Indeed, this consideration makes a true king: to recognize himself a minister of God in governing his kingdom. Now, that king who in ruling over his realm does not serve God's glory exercises not kingly rule but brigandage. Furthermore, he is deceived who looks for enduring prosperity in his kingdom when it is not ruled by God's scepter, that, his Holy Word; for the heavenly oracle that proclaims that "where prophecy fails the people are scattered" [Prov. 29:18] cannot lie. And contempt for our lowliness ought not to dissuade you from this endeavor.[30]

Here Calvin's view of the magistracy surfaces, which is that the magistrate must not only keep civil order and punish those who outwardly break the laws of society, but must also promote the true church with the sword. Unspoken is the implied mandate that Francis should convert himself to the Reformed faith and then harry the Roman Catholic Church, as he formerly harried the Reformed church.

BOOK ONE

The Knowledge of God the Creator

CHAPTER 6

The Knowledge of God the Creator

Introduction

The opening line of the *Institutes* is fundamental to the entire work and to the Reformed, Protestant faith that is the content of the work: "Nearly all the wisdom we possess, that is to say, true and sound wisdom, consists of two parts: the knowledge of God and of ourselves."[1] The opening line of the 1536 edition was virtually the same: "Nearly the whole of sacred doctrine consists of these two parts: knowledge of God and of ourselves."[2]

In this line Calvin affirms that the foundation and core of all truth and wisdom is knowledge of God, right knowledge of God. He also asserts the mutuality of our knowledge of God and of ourselves. To know God is to know ourselves the way we should know ourselves, and we cannot know ourselves without immediately directing our attention to the knowledge of God.

The significance of this opening statement is, first, that the content of the *Institutes* is the knowledge of God: the highest end of man. Second, all the doctrines of the Christian religion, which is fundamentally the right knowledge of God, are set forth as known, and to be known, by the believing heart and mind. The knowledge of God consists of propositions, statements, doctrinal truths, and apart from these there is no right knowledge of God. But Calvin does not teach these biblical propositions as abstract, scientific, theological theory. Rather, he teaches them as truths known, that is, embraced and loved, by the believer. Third, the doctrines of the faith, all of which are about God, are set forth in the *Institutes* in their significance for man.

Calvin begins with the knowledge of God and proceeds "afterward" to treat the knowledge of man. This for Calvin is "the order of right teaching."[3] One would not expect anything else from this God-centered man.

This order of the knowledge of God first and then the knowledge of man is not only a temporal order, but also a logical and theological order, an order of priority: always God is first and always man is second; man always and only in the light of God.

At the outset of his treatment of the knowledge of God, Calvin lays down the fundamental truth that "properly speaking, God is [not] known where there is no religion or piety."[4] Calvin describes piety, and the knowledge of God characterized by piety, in such a way as to make plain that the only person who "properly" knows God is the elect, believing child of God, that is, one who knows God in Jesus Christ. Before he considers the knowledge of God that the unregenerated have from the creation, Calvin has denied the possibility of their having "proper," that is, true, knowledge of God.

Knowledge of God apart from Scripture

This having been established, Calvin affirms that there is a certain knowledge of God the creator that every human being has. There is a knowledge of God apart from Holy Scripture. "Men one and all perceive that there is a God and that he is their Maker... Yet there is... no nation so barbarous, no people so savage, that they have not a deep-seated conviction that there is a God."[5]

The explanation of this knowledge is God's revelation of himself to all: "God himself has implanted in all men a certain understanding of his divine majesty."[6]

For Calvin, all knowledge of God is due to revelation: *an act of God, making himself known to human beings.* No man can know God in any sense, proper or improper, apart from God's own act of making himself known to that person. Man cannot climb up to God to find out about him; God must come down to make himself known to human beings.

God's revelation of himself to people who do not have Scripture, or the preaching of the gospel, is twofold.

First, there is what Calvin calls *divinitatis sensum*,[7] a sense of divinity, a sense of deity, or a sense of the existence of God that he has implanted in the heart and mind of every human being already in the womb, so that every human being comes into the world with this sense of divinity. We might call this an innate knowledge of God. "This conviction, namely, that there is some God, is naturally inborn in all, and is fixed deep within, as it were in the very marrow."[8]

Second, God makes himself known to every human being through creation, or what we would call "nature." Included in this creation is the human being's own body and soul. There is a knowledge of God that every human being inescapably receives from creation, because, by means of all the various creatures, God actively makes himself known as the creator of the universe. "[God] revealed himself and daily discloses himself in the whole workmanship of the universe. As a consequence, men cannot open their eyes without being compelled to see him."[9] In a favorite phrase, Calvin speaks of "a dazzling theater ... [of] the glory of God."[10]

Included in this theater of God's glory, revealing God to all men, is God's government of the world. "In administering human society he so tempers his providence that, although kindly and beneficent toward all in numberless ways, he still by open and daily indications declares his clemency to the godly and his severity to the wicked and criminal."[11]

Although this knowledge of God from creation is not *proper* knowledge, it is *real* knowledge. The revelation of God in creation is not dim, obscure, and very difficult to discover. Rather, it is dazzlingly bright and unmistakably clear: "so clear and so prominent that even unlettered and stupid folk cannot plead the excuse of ignorance."[12]

Furthermore, God impresses this revelation of himself on the mind of every human. Not only is the truth of God clearly displayed in creation, but there is also an activity of God powerfully and indelibly impressing this truth upon the mind of every spectator in the theater, so that he knows the truth that God is. There is no atheist, nor agnostic. Whoever says, "There is no God," or, "I do not know whether God exists," lies.

Shrewdly, Calvin observes that the reprobate themselves, under "necessity," often give evidence that they know God. Although ordinarily they deny him or "wittily joke about God," "if any occasion for despair presses upon them, it goads them to seek him and impels their perfunctory prayers."[13] All of the passengers on a plunging airplane pray.

In his doctrine of a knowledge of God on the part of all men from creation and providence, Calvin has his eye mainly on Romans 1:18–32: "They knew God" (v. 21).

This knowledge, however, is always immediately smothered, corrupted, and perverted, so that it never is, nor can become, *proper* knowledge of God. Man's sense of deity never goes anywhere positively: "All degenerate from the true knowledge of him"[14]; "One and all, we forsake the one true God for prodigious trifles."[15] It is "not only the common folk and dull-witted men" who are guilty of thus changing the truth of God into a lie (Rom. 1:25), but also the "whole tribe of philosophers" have done the same, manifesting "their stupidity and silliness." Even "Plato, the most religious of all and the most circumspect,... vanishes in his round globe."[16] Calvin is not impressed with the philosophers.

The conclusion is that "if men were taught only by nature, they would hold to nothing certain or solid or clear-cut, but would be so tied to confused principles as to worship an unknown god."[17] Calvin is referring to Acts 17:23 and the worship by the philosophers in Athens of the unknown god.

The fault is not in the revelation, but in fallen man's wicked nature and perverse will. The sun can be shining brightly in the heavens, but a blind man cannot see it.

In an important statement in the opening section on the necessity of Scripture, Calvin says that the purpose of God with his revelation in creation is to render all guilty: "God, to involve the human race in the same guilt, sets forth to all without exception his presence portrayed in his creatures."[18]

There is, therefore, no "natural theology," nor the possibility of "natural theology." Although he does not use these theological phrases, Calvin's position is that there is "general revelation" but not any "natural theology." Warfield is correct when he says that the issue of natural theology comes up in Calvin's doctrine of the knowledge of God and when he asserts that Calvin denies natural theology:

The Knowledge of God the Creator

> [Calvin] does deny that any theology worthy of the name can be derived from this natural revelation by the "natural man," that is, by the man the eyes of whose mind and heart are not opened by the Spirit of God—who is not under the influence of the testimony of the Spirit; and in this sense he denies the possibility of a "Natural Theology."[19]

By natural theology is meant a sound, true knowledge of God derived from the revelation in creation alone and known by man's mind without the illumination of grace. Proponents of natural theology usually acknowledge that, although this knowledge of God is a sound, true knowledge of God, it is not adequate for salvation. However, this knowledge of God is supposed to be a stepping-stone toward the saving knowledge of God by special revelation. Either, as Rome teaches, the sinner earns from God the higher knowledge by natural theology or, as Arminian Protestants hold, natural theology is a positive "point of contact" for the gospel, enabling the unregenerated sinner to respond positively to the gospel and, thus, gain the saving knowledge of God. The Canons of Dordt refer to this latter error, and condemn it, in the fifth error appended to the third and fourth heads of doctrine:

> The true doctrine having been explained, the Synod *rejects* the errors of those... who teach that the corrupt and natural man can so well use the common grace (by which they understand the light of nature), or the gifts still left him after the fall, that he can gradually gain by their good use a greater, namely, the evangelical or saving grace and salvation itself.[20]

Natural theology increasingly finds favor among contemporary Presbyterian and Reformed theologians. Explaining the right knowledge of God that pagans have from creation as a work of God's "common grace," some vigorously defend natural theology as important for apologetics (the defense of the faith) and evangelism.[21]

Others go so far as to contend that natural theology is not only the necessary point of contact for the gospel but also a knowledge of God that can save men, altogether apart from the gospel of Scripture.[22]

On the basis especially of Romans 1:18–25 and Romans 2:14, 15,

Calvin acknowledges, indeed insists, that from creation or nature all men know God, specifically "his eternal power and Godhead" (Rom. 1:20) and his will demanding righteousness and forbidding unrighteousness. Thus Calvin affirms the truth that is basic to the teaching of what are called "the rational proofs for the existence of God," that is, proofs for the existence of God from nature and from man's own consciousness, apart from any knowledge of Scripture.[23] The truth basic to these proofs is that all men know from the creation that God is and that he must be served.

But Calvin denies emphatically the *use* to which these proofs are put by many theologians and Christian philosophers. The knowledge of God that men have from creation is not a positive "point of contact" for the gospel. Much less can it function as a stepping-stone to the advanced knowledge of God in the gospel. It certainly is not, and can never be, a saving knowledge of God. The sole use of the knowledge of God that men have from nature, apart from the gospel, is to render men without excuse before God. God's one purpose with general revelation is that "they are without excuse" (Rom. 1:20).

The reason that the knowledge of God from creation cannot function positively with regard to the saving knowledge of God, that is, the explanation of the absolute impossibility of natural theology, is that the totally depraved and rebellious sinner "hold[s] the truth in unrighteousness" (v. 18) and "change[s] the truth of God into a lie" (v. 25). This is all that the depraved sinner *can* do.

Only the gospel of Christ is "the power of God unto salvation to every one that believeth" (v. 16).

> It is therefore in vain that so many burning lamps shine for us in the workmanship of the universe to show forth the glory of its Author... Where Paul teaches that what is to be known of God is made plain from the creation of the universe [Rom. 1:19], he does not signify such a manifestation as men's discernment can comprehend; but, rather, shows it not to go farther than to render them inexcusable.[24]

Calvin's rejection of natural theology is confessional with Reformed churches: "So far is this light of nature from being sufficient to bring him [man] to a saving knowledge of God, and to true conversion, that he is incapable of using it aright even in things natural and civil"[25]; "What... the light of nature... could [not] do... God performs by the operation of his Holy Spirit."[26]

Rejection of natural theology does not imply a denial of general revelation, that is, God's making himself known to the unregenerate through the creation, including man himself as a creature of God, and through God's works in providence. With appeal to Romans 1:18–25 and Romans 2:14–16, Calvin teaches general revelation. Every man recognizes the creator in creation, so that he knows God. This is due not only to the objective testimony "out there," but also to a work of the Spirit within the ungodly: "manifest in them; for God hath showed it unto them" (Rom. 1:19); "which shew the work of the law written in their hearts" (Rom. 2:15).

The importance of this knowledge of God from creation is not inconsiderable. It renders all men inexcusable before God; indeed, this and this only is God's purpose with general revelation.

General revelation never leads to natural theology, nor can it lead to natural theology, because there is no revelation of Christ and grace in general revelation, and because the unregenerate is totally depraved and a rebel. Instantly, the ungodly holds under and perverts the knowledge of God in idolatry.

This is the biblical doctrine as it is the Reformed tradition.

Karl Barth denied general revelation in the interest of his stress on revelation only in Christ. This was the subject of his famous book responding to Emil Brunner.[27] But Barth had the honesty to admit that on reaching heaven and after greeting Mozart, the first thing he would do is ask Paul what the apostle could possibly have meant by Romans 1:18–25.

To deny general revelation is to excuse the ungodly and thus to jeopardize the justice of God when he judges.

In its resistance to natural theology, the Reformed faith does not neglect to teach that the regenerated Christian is enabled to see rightly the wisdom and power of God in all of creation. Indeed, he is duty-bound to do so.

For Calvin, then, there is no sound religion or worship based on the knowledge of God from creation. The "sense of deity" and "seed of religion" in every human result in a powerful drive to worship. All humans worship a god. The question, therefore, is not: Will you worship God, or will you not worship at all? But the question for every human being is: Will you worship the true God, or will you worship a god of your own making?

Calvin condemns all worship arising from general revelation as the worship of "demons in place of God," "falsehood and lying," "vain error," and "open idolatries." "There was no pure and approved religion, founded upon common understanding alone." Calvin appeals, in support of his condemnation of all pagan worship, to Paul's indictment of the Athenians' worship of "the unknown God" in Acts 17:23: "To worship an unknown god... by chance is no light fault."[28]

This sharp, biblically based condemnation of pagan worship contrasts with the approval of pagan worship by the universalistic, tolerant theology of the twentieth and twenty-first centuries. C. S. Lewis, who is highly regarded by evangelicals, gave expression to this tolerant, universalistic, and syncretistic approval of pagan worship in the last volume of his popular Narnia series, *The Last Battle*. Lewis had the lion Aslan, the representative of Jesus Christ, say to Emeth, a lifelong worshiper of the idol Tash and hater of Aslan, "Child, all the service thou hast done to Tash, I account as service done to me."[29]

For Calvin, only the worship of God that arises out of God's revelation of himself through Scripture in a regenerated heart is pleasing to God. At this point already Calvin asserts the important regulative principle of worship: God must be worshiped only as he prescribes in his word. "The Holy Spirit rejects as base all cults contrived through the will of men."[30]

Knowledge of God in Scripture

For the right knowledge of God, as for pure worship, Scripture is necessary. Scripture is God's revelation of himself in the written word. Calvin refers to Scripture as the "spectacles" that "bleary-eyed men" put on in order to see the true God.[31] Immediately, Calvin declares that God gives this knowledge only to his elect:

> He added the light of his Word by which to become known unto salvation; and he regarded as worthy of this privilege those

whom he pleased to gather more closely and intimately to himself... This, therefore, is a special gift, where God, to instruct the church... opens his own most hallowed lips. Not only does he teach the elect to look upon a god, but also shows himself as the God upon whom they are to look.³²

Benjamin B. Warfield calls attention to this:

> Therefore it is that Calvin represents the provision for the knowledge of God both in the objective revelation in the Word and in the subjective testimony of the Spirit as destined by God not for men at large, but specifically for His people, His elect, those "to whom He determined to make His instructions effectual."³³

God's gracious saving revelation of himself in Scripture is particular.

There is not a lengthy, thorough doctrine of Scripture at this point in the *Institutes*. Calvin affirms the necessity, sufficiency, and authority of Scripture and quickly moves on to the testimony of the Holy Spirit. He does not say much about the origin and inspiration of Scripture, but what he does say in the section on the testimony of the Holy Spirit is conclusive concerning Calvin's regard for Scripture: "Hence the Scriptures obtain full authority among believers only when men regard them as having sprung from heaven, as if there the living words of God were heard."³⁴ Concerning the origin of Scripture, Calvin also writes, "God is its Author."³⁵

Calvin has more to say on the inspiration of Scripture in book four, chapter eight, in connection with the power of the church, where he argues that the power of the church is strictly limited by and to the word of God, Holy Scripture. He is opposing the Roman Catholic teaching. He declares that the church does not have power apart from the Holy Scriptures: "No other word is to be held as the Word of God, and given place as such in the church, than what is contained first in the Law and the Prophets, then in the writings of the apostles; and the only authorized way of teaching in the church is by the prescription and standard of his Word."³⁶

Here, Calvin declares that the apostles wrote "with Christ's Spirit as precursor in a certain measure dictating the words [Latin: *verba quodammodo dictante Christi Spiritu*]."³⁷ This is an important statement indicating Calvin's doctrine of Scripture.

In a footnote, editor John McNeill tries to weaken the word "dictating," denying that Calvin meant the "verbal inspiration" of Scripture. He says that Calvin refers to "the authoritative message of Scripture."³⁸ But Calvin does not talk about Scripture's general message in this paragraph. He rather refers to *words*: "dictating the words." The adverb *quodammodo*, translated by Battles as "in a certain measure," is not, as the editor suggests, a weakening qualification, but a descriptive qualification meaning "in a way." The Spirit dictated the words of Scripture "in a [certain] way." The Battles translation, "in a certain measure," is erroneous. Henry Beveridge's translation is "in a manner dictated words to them."³⁹ John Allen's translation is "under the guidance and dictation of the Spirit of Christ."⁴⁰

Calvin calls the apostles "sure and genuine *scribes* of the Holy Spirit" in their writing of the New Testament Scripture.⁴¹ The Latin word translated "scribes" is *amanuenses*. Beveridge translates, "sure and authentic amanuenses of the Holy Spirit."⁴² Again, the Battles/McNeill edition of the *Institutes* feels compelled to insert a mitigating footnote denying that Calvin was teaching "verbal inerrancy" and asserting that Calvin was merely safeguarding "the teaching" of Scripture.⁴³ In fact, this commentary on Calvin rather promotes contemporary theology's rejection of verbal inspiration than does justice to Calvin's own doctrine.

On Calvin's view of the Spirit's dictating the words of Scripture "in a [certain] way," the apostles' "writings are therefore to be considered oracles of God."⁴⁴

Calvin also teaches, and defends, the doctrine of the divine inspiration of Scripture in its entirety in his commentary on 2 Timothy 3:16: "All scripture is given by inspiration of God." The entire Old Testament is "not a doctrine delivered according to the will and pleasure of men, but [was] dictated by the Holy Spirit." The sole "Author of the Scripture" is God. Therefore, "we owe to the Scripture the same reverence which we owe to God; because it has proceeded from him alone, and has nothing belonging to man mixed with it."⁴⁵

Calvin's doctrine of Scripture is the very highest. He confesses verbal inspiration, so that the Scriptures are the very word of God written and, therefore, authoritative, as only the infallible word of God is and can be authoritative.

Calvin recognizes that in Scripture God "lisp[s], . . . as nurses commonly do with infants," that is, "accommodate[s] the knowledge of him to our slight capacity." Calvin's specific reference is to the descriptions of God in Scripture that theology calls anthropomorphisms—descriptions of God and his acts in terms appropriate to humans, for example, God's "mouth, ears, eyes, hands, and feet."[46] But to affirm that, in his condescending grace, God talks baby talk to his children is by no means to admit that he lies or errs.

Even though Scripture is inspired and, therefore, inherently clear, not one human will receive it, believe it, and be saved by it apart from the testimony of the Holy Spirit.

Testimony of the Holy Spirit

As much as any doctrine can be, the doctrine of the testimony of the Holy Spirit is original with Calvin. It is a marvelous contribution by Calvin to Christian theology.

The testimony of the Holy Spirit establishes and confirms within the elect believer both the canon of Scripture and the authority of Scripture. That is, the Spirit testifies to the elect believer that all of the sixty-six books that make up the canon are rightly part of the inspired Scriptures and that this Scripture has the authority of God's own word. Without the testimony of the Spirit, therefore, no one would acknowledge Scripture as inspired or submit to the authority of Scripture.

Against Rome's claim that the reception of Scripture depends on the testimony of the church, that is, that Scripture depends on the church, Calvin teaches that the word of God cannot, and must not, rest on the witness of man. Referring to faith concerning Scripture, Calvin says, "Again, to what mockeries of the impious is our faith subjected, into what suspicion has it fallen among all men, if we believe that it has a precarious authority dependent solely upon the good pleasure of men!"[47]

Warfield was correct in noting that, in his explanation of the Spirit's testimony regarding Scripture, Calvin largely ignored that the Spirit's testimony also gives the elect believer right understanding of the content of Scripture. Reformed theology refers to this aspect of the testimony of the Spirit as "illumination." "The particular question which Calvin addresses himself to when he turns to the consideration of what he calls the testimony of the Spirit concerns the accrediting of Scripture, not the assimilation of its revelatory contents."[48] But Warfield rightly added that the illumination of the believer regarding the content of Scripture is implied by Calvin's doctrine that the Spirit testifies to the believer concerning Scripture's inspiration and authority.[49]

The testimony of the Spirit is something that "each believer experiences within himself."[50]

The Spirit testifies concerning Scripture to the believer by means of Scripture itself. Or, to say it differently, Scripture renders itself authentic and authoritative to the believer by the testimony of the Spirit speaking through Scripture. Scripture is self-authenticating. "Let this point therefore stand: that those whom the Holy Spirit has inwardly taught truly rest upon Scripture, and that Scripture indeed is self-authenticated."[51]

The Spirit's testimony does not take place apart from Scripture, nor does it add anything to the content of Scripture.

Calvin appeals for proof of the testimony of the Spirit to 1 Corinthians 2:9–16:

> But as it is written, Eye hath not seen, nor ear heard, neither have entered into the heart of man, the things which God hath prepared for them that love him. But God hath revealed them unto us by his Spirit: for the Spirit searcheth all things, yea, the deep things of God. For what man knoweth the things of a man, save the spirit of man which is in him? even so the things of God knoweth no man, but the Spirit of God. Now we have received, not the spirit of the world, but the spirit which is of God; that we might know the things that are freely given to us of God. Which things also we speak, not in the words which man's wisdom teacheth, but which the Holy Ghost teacheth; comparing spiritual things with spiritual. But the natural man receiveth not the things of the Spirit of God: for they are foolishness unto him: neither can he know them, because they are spiritually discerned. But he that is spiritual judgeth all things,

yet he himself is judged of no man. For who hath known the mind of the Lord, that he may instruct him? But we have the mind of Christ.

All of the truth the apostles preached and all of the truth the apostles wrote in the New Testament Scriptures came from the Holy Spirit. The Spirit made it known to them, and now as they teach this truth to the church, spiritual men understand the apostolic word because the Spirit works with that word and by that word testifying in their hearts of the authenticity, authority, and meaning of that word.

Reformed Christians confess the testimony of the Spirit in the Belgic Confession:

> We receive all these books, and these only, as holy and canonical, for the regulation, foundation, and confirmation of our faith; believing, without any doubt, all things contained in them, not so much because the Church receives and approves them as such, but more especially because the Holy Ghost witnesseth in our hearts that they are from God, whereof they carry the evidence in themselves. For the very blind are able to perceive that the things foretold in them are fulfilling.[52]

Calvin sharply condemns "evidentialist apologetics." This is the theory and practice of proving to unbelievers that Scripture is the word of God and, thus, that Christianity is true by means of rational, nonbiblical arguments. "They who strive to build up firm faith in Scripture through disputation are doing things backward."[53] Against those who "wish and demand rational proof," Calvin declares, "The testimony of the Spirit is more excellent than all reason."[54] In fact, "it is not right to subject it [Scripture] to proof and reasoning."[55] God's word may not depend upon a word, or argument, of man.

After Calvin has recognized some arguments that "fortify" the conviction that is worked by the testimony of the Holy Spirit, he concludes, "But those who wish to prove to unbelievers that Scripture is the Word of God are acting foolishly, for only by faith can this be known."[56] By this statement, Calvin expresses the relation between the testimony of the Spirit and faith. The Spirit's testimony to Scripture includes working faith in the elect. "The same Spirit ... who has spoken through the mouths of the prophets must penetrate into our hearts to persuade us that they faithfully proclaimed what had been divinely commanded."[57]

In connection with his consideration of the testimony of the Spirit to Scripture, Calvin opposes the "fanatics" who demean and reject Scripture as a "dead and killing letter" in the interest, as they say, of "exalting the teaching office of the Spirit."[58]

Against this perennial fanaticism, Calvin affirms the fundamental Reformed, indeed Christian, truth that God has bound together the Spirit and the written word of God. "By a kind of mutual bond the Lord has joined together the certainty of his Word and of his Spirit."[59] Explaining 2 Corinthians 3:8, "the ministration of the Spirit," Calvin teaches that "the Holy Spirit so inheres in his truth, which he expresses in Scripture, that only when its proper reverence and dignity are given to the Word does the Holy Spirit show forth his power."[60]

Therefore, to exalt the Spirit at the expense of Scripture by separating the Spirit's work from Scripture is "a heinous sacrilege." By this "sacrilege these rascals tear apart those things which the prophet [Isaiah, in chapter 59, verse 21] joined together with an inviolable bond."[61]

Rather than disparage Scripture, believers "are not unaware that the Word is the instrument by which the Lord dispenses the illumination of his Spirit to believers." Rather than fascinate themselves with a freewheeling spirit operating above, beyond, and apart from the simple, sober Scripture, believers "know no other Spirit than him who dwelt and spoke in the apostles, and by whose oracles they are continually recalled to the hearing of the Word."[62]

Calvin's sharp warning against the fanatical Anabaptists of his day applies to the mysticism of the charismatic movement in our day. Not only does the charismatic movement disparage Scripture by exalting the supposed extraordinary shenanigans of the Spirit over the preaching, hearing, and believing of the doctrine of Scripture, but also, by its teaching of ongoing "prophecies," the movement cuts the Spirit loose from the written word of God. This is fanaticism.

CHAPTER 7

The Doctrine of the Trinity

Introduction

Calvin's orthodox confession of the doctrine of the Trinity is not academic. He was compelled to oppose the main trinitarian heresies in Geneva. There are two main forms of trinitarian false doctrine: denial of the oneness of God and denial of the threeness of God. Arius is the outstanding representative of the former error, and Sabellius, of the latter.

In the 1536 *Institutes*, Calvin notes that there are basically two forms of false doctrine concerning the Trinity. "One has to resist the Arians on the one hand, the Sabellians on the other."[1] In his ministry Calvin resisted both errors.

He had to oppose the denial of God's oneness in the person and preaching of Giovanni Valentino Gentile, an Italian who came to Geneva as a teacher.[2] Gentile's errant trinitarian doctrine was condemned in 1558 by the governing council of the church. Although Calvin does not name him, he refers to him: "From this morass another similar monster has come forth."[3]

Calvin opposed a denial of the threeness of God in the person and teaching of the infamous Michael Servetus, a Spaniard who came to Geneva in 1553 and was condemned and executed there the same year. Calvin names him as a trinitarian heretic: "The impiety of Servetus was even more detestable, when he asserted that God was never revealed to Abraham and the other patriarchs, but that in his place an angel was worshiped... Again, Servetus yelps that God took on the person of an angel."[4] Calvin also refers to Servetus later when he describes Servetus' heresy more fully: "For Servetus the name 'Trinity' was so utterly hateful and detestable that he commonly labeled all those whom he called Trinitarians as atheists."[5]

Another reason that Calvin had a lively, personal interest in the doctrine of the Trinity was the trinitarian controversy that Pierre Caroli forced on him. Caroli was at that time a Protestant pastor in nearby Lausanne, Switzerland. He charged Calvin and Farel with heresy, specifically the heresy of Arianism. That was a damning charge.

The reason Caroli charged Calvin with this heresy was that Calvin did not include a section on the Trinity in his Confession of Faith of 1537. In addition, Caroli thought that Calvin's treatment of the doctrine of the Trinity in the 1536 edition of the *Institutes* was far too scanty, thus exposing Calvin as a trinitarian heretic.[6]

Caroli to the contrary notwithstanding, Calvin's treatment of the Trinity in the 1536 *Institutes* is thorough. Further, Calvin uses and defends the trinitarian terms. Calvin also gives extensive biblical proof for the Trinity. That Caroli should have attacked, and the Reformed community given credence to the attack, in spite of the 1536 *Institutes* is astounding.

Calvin was formally put on trial for trinitarian heresy. This jeopardized and seriously threatened his ministry at the outset. Then to compound his difficulties, at the synod in Lausanne where Caroli's charges were treated, Calvin hurt himself still more by refusing to subscribe to the Athanasian Creed, the great trinitarian creed, at Caroli's demand that he prove his orthodoxy by subscribing to it. Further, at that synod Calvin spoke somewhat disparagingly of the Nicene Creed.

Why Calvin did these things is puzzling. As he stated later, he was in agreement with both the Nicene and the Athanasian creeds. Calvin indicates a reason for his strange behavior, particularly why he refused to subscribe to the Athanasian Creed: "Really, I am not, indeed, such a stickler as to battle doggedly over mere words."[7] Then he warns "against forthwith so severely taking to task, like censors, those who do not wish to swear to the words conceived by us, provided they are not doing it out of either arrogance or frowardness or malicious craft."[8]

François Wendel remarks concerning Calvin's refusal to subscribe to the Athanasian Creed, under Caroli's demand, "Calvin was not good at putting up with contradiction, still less personal attack."[9]

The result was that the controversy raised by Caroli over Calvin's doctrine of the Trinity imperiled Calvin's ministry as no other single controversy did. In fact, the effect of Caroli's charge against Calvin lingered for some ten years, during which time Calvin was always having to be busy exonerating himself of the charge that he was weak, if not heretical, concerning the Trinity.[10]

As to the significance of the Caroli affair, Wendel observes, "It was the painful memory of Caroli's insinuations that led the reformer afterwards to insist so strongly upon the trinitarian dogma: perhaps it also played a part in his attitude towards Servetus."[11]

Calvin's doctrine: orthodox

Calvin taught the orthodoxy of the ancient Christian church as confessed in the Apostles' Creed, the Nicene Creed, and the Athanasian Creed. Calvin indicates his dependency on Augustine, especially his great book *On the Trinity*.[12] Calvin quotes from the church father Hilary.[13]

Calvin insists on the propriety, indeed the necessity, of using the church's accepted terms, such as *Trinity* and *person*, even though these terms are not found in Scripture. Theologians have the right, even the duty, to use nonbiblical, theological terms to make Scripture plain. The use of these terms is necessary especially in order to expose heretics, who are "slippery snakes":

> The novelty of words... becomes especially useful when the truth is to be asserted against false accusers, who evade it by their shifts. Of this today we have abundant experience in our great efforts to rout the enemies of pure and wholesome doctrine. With such crooked and sinuous twisting these slippery snakes glide away unless they are boldly pursued, caught, and crushed. Thus men of old, stirred up by various struggles over depraved dogmas, were compelled to set forth with consummate clarity what they felt, lest they leave any devious shift to the impious, who cloaked their errors in layers of verbiage.[14]

In fact, Calvin goes so far as to say that objection to these terms is wickedness: "What wickedness, then, it is to disapprove of words that explain nothing else than what is attested and sealed by Scripture!"[15] At the same time, Calvin says he is not such a stickler for the terms as long as all agree on the doctrines intended to be conveyed by the terms. "Really, I am not, indeed, such a stickler as to battle doggedly over mere words."[16]

Here Calvin recalls the terminological differences and difficulties between the Latin western and Greek eastern churches over the doctrine of the Trinity. The Latin West used the term *substance* to refer to the divine being of God; therefore, they said that God is *one* in substance. But the Greeks (Hilary) at one time used the term *substance* to refer to the persons, so that in the East the theologians said that God is *three* in substance. Then the theologians recognized that they were using the same term to refer to two different things, and they came to an agreement.

Calvin's doctrine: simple and clear

In keeping with his concern for these virtues in writing, his conception that the knowledge of God is piety, and his purpose to instruct the ordinary believer, Calvin's presentation of the doctrine of the Trinity is characterized by simplicity and clarity.

Calvin gives two definitions or concise statements of the doctrine. The first is, "Father and Son and Spirit are one God, yet the Son is not the Father, nor the Spirit the Son, but... they are differentiated by a peculiar quality."[17] The second is, "Under the name of God is understood a single, simple [undivided] essence, in which we comprehend three persons, or hypostases."[18] What this means for Calvin is that in the one essence, or being, of God are three distinct persons. These persons are different from each other by an incommunicable property, a property they do not share.

Being a master teacher, Calvin defines a *person*: "'Person,' therefore, I call a 'subsistence' in God's essence, which, while related to the others, is distinguished by incommunicable quality."[19] Significantly, Calvin sees the relation of each person to the others as part of the very definition of a person.

He proves his definition by appealing to John 1:1: "The Word was with God, and the Word was God." "For if the Word were simply God, and yet possessed no other characteristic mark, John would wrongly have said that the Word was always with God."[20] Calvin also appeals to Hebrews 1:3, which says that Jesus Christ is "the express image [χαρακτὴρ τῆς ὑποστάσεως αυτοῦ] of [God's] person."

The incommunicable quality of each of the persons, by which each is different from the other persons, is the property indicated by the name of each person. The incommunicable property of the Father is that he generates the Son and breathes forth the Spirit. The incommunicable property of the Son is that he is begotten of the Father and breathes forth the Spirit. The incommunicable property of the Holy Spirit is that he is breathed forth by the Father and Son.

There are three persons in the Trinity, and Calvin recognizes them. He quickly warns, however, that the personal distinctions do not divide the essence of God. "The words 'Father,' 'Son,' and 'Spirit' imply a real distinction—let no one think that these titles, whereby God is variously designated from his works, are empty—but a distinction, not a division."[21] Following Augustine and reflecting the trinitarian doctrine of the western church, Calvin shows himself to be a vehement defender and an ardent proponent of the divine oneness. The oneness of essence is the main thing and the thing that has to be emphasized and defended. Having quoted with "vast delight" Gregory of Nazianzus' statement of both the oneness and the threeness of the Trinity, Calvin immediately stresses the oneness: "Let us not, then, be led to imagine a trinity of persons that keeps our thoughts distracted and does not at once lead them back to that unity."[22]

Calvin's brevity and simplicity in his treatment of the Trinity are reflected in Question and Answer 25 of the Heidelberg Catechism, which is a very brief, simple, clear statement of the Trinity:

> Since there is but one Divine Being, why speakest thou of three, Father, Son, and Holy Ghost?
> Because God has so revealed himself in his Word that these three distinct Persons are the one, true, eternal God.[23]

Calvin's doctrine: biblical

In his doctrine of the Trinity, Calvin is deliberately and rigorously biblical. He warns against all speculation, all theorizing that goes beyond the limits of Scripture, especially with regard to this doctrine. He affirms as a virtue of his treatment of the Trinity that he has avoided "troublesome and perplexed disputations."[24]

He specifically refuses to enter into the question whether the eternal generation of the Son involves an ongoing generation of the second person. Does the Father's generation of the Son mean that "the Father always begets," or that the Father accomplished the begetting in the eternal past? Although Calvin refuses to consider the question at any length, he renders a judgment: "It is foolish to imagine a continuous act of begetting, since it is clear that three persons have subsisted in God from eternity."[25]

In sections seven through fifteen of chapter thirteen of book one, he proves the deity of the Son and the Spirit from both the Old and New Testaments. Noteworthy is Calvin's powerful appeal to 1 Corinthians 12:11, "But all these worketh that one and the selfsame Spirit, dividing to every man severally as he will," to prove the divine power and personality of the Spirit. That the Spirit works, dividing as he will, proves that the Spirit "resides hypostatically in God" (resides as a person in the Godhead).[26] Those who are opposed to the doctrine of the Trinity always especially challenge the personality of the Spirit.

To prove the unity of the one essence, Calvin points to Ephesians 4:5, which speaks of one baptism, and to the baptism formula in Matthew 28:19, which refers to one's being "baptized into the name of the one God who has shown himself with complete clarity in the Father, the Son, and the Spirit. Hence it is quite clear that in God's essence reside three persons in whom one God is known."[27]

Calvin's determination to be biblical is related to his one great interest with the doctrine of the Trinity, namely, that it provides the church "what is useful to know"[28] and what is edifying. Speculation is not useful and does not edify. Calvin is "zealous for the edification of the church."[29]

One implication of Calvin's concern to be biblical in his trinitarian doctrine and his determination to avoid speculation is his rejection of the notion that the Trinity can be illustrated from "comparisons from human affairs."[30] That is, we must avoid all attempts to prove the doctrine of the Trinity from various phenomena, supposedly manifesting a combination of threeness and oneness, that we see in the creation.

Calvin refers to what theologians call "vestiges of the Trinity." Although Calvin does not name him, he has particularly in mind Augustine, who in the last part of *On the Trinity* illustrated and even proved the Trinity from the sun and from water. Especially was Augustine enamored with what he called the three parts of the soul of man—understanding, memory, and will. Although Calvin does not name Augustine in this connection in the *Institutes*, in his commentary on Genesis 1:26, 27 he names Augustine as one of those who erred in proving the Trinity from phenomena in nature. "But Augustine, beyond all others, speculates with excessive refinement, for the purpose of fabricating a Trinity in man. For in laying hold of the three faculties of the soul enumerated by Aristotle, the intellect, the memory, and the will, he afterwards out of one Trinity derives many."[31]

That the Trinity is a heavenly mystery that must be taught and understood from Scripture alone is a fundamental truth. There is no proof, or even illustration, in creation of the uniquely wonderful reality of the "three in one" of the blessed Trinity of God.

From Scripture, a certain order in the Trinity should be known. "The Father is the beginning, . . . fountain and wellspring" of the Godhead. The Son is the "ordered disposition of all." The Spirit is the "power and efficacy of that activity."[32]

It is worthy of note that there is not a word in Calvin's treatment of the Trinity in his *Institutes*, or, for that matter, in his commentaries, about the *family* nature of the Trinity, about the obvious biblical revelation of the "three in one" as fellowship in love.

Significance of the Trinity for Calvin

With the early church, Calvin regards the doctrine of the Trinity as fundamental to the gospel. That Calvin regards the doctrine of the Trinity as fundamental is evident from his exposition, as from his vigorous condemnation of all who deny the Trinity. How important he thinks the doctrine of the Trinity to be comes out in the final trinitarian structure of the 1559 *Institutes*.

Specifically, the significance and the importance of the doctrine of the Trinity for Calvin are, first, that the doctrine distinguishes the true God from all idols. In fact, this is Calvin's approach to the doctrine in the 1559 *Institutes*. The section prior to his treatment of the Trinity has to do with the idols. From a condemnation of idols and idolatry, Calvin turns to the worship of the true God by setting forth the doctrine of the Trinity. He writes, "God also designates himself by another special mark to distinguish himself more precisely from all idols." The one true God is triune. Such is the importance of the Trinity that "unless we grasp these [three persons], only the bare and empty name of God flits around in our brains, to the exclusion of the true God."[33]

Second, the importance of the doctrine of the Trinity is that upon this doctrine depend the deity of Jesus Christ and the deity of the Spirit of Jesus Christ. For Calvin, it is absolutely necessary for salvation that Jesus Christ be very God and that the Holy Spirit be very God. Calvin's thinking is this: If the one who died on the cross is not God, his sacrifice does not have the worth and value to pay for our sins. Likewise, if the Spirit who dwells within us is not God, he cannot raise us from our spiritual death, sanctify us, and raise our body from the grave.

Condemnation of heresy

This conviction of the importance of the Trinity explains Calvin's vehement denunciation of trinitarian heretics. Calvin's exposure and condemnation of trinitarian heretics and heresies take up a large part of the section devoted to the Trinity.[34] Calvin's procedure is typical. He first sets forth the truth positively, and then he exposes and condemns the errors that are opposed to the truth. "Now the truth which has been peaceably shown must be maintained against all the calumnies of the wicked."[35]

Calvin's language in condemning the heretics is strong. Those who deny the Trinity in one way or another are "slippery snakes,"[36] "dogs,"[37] "frenzied persons,"[38] and "monster[s]."[39] With both basic kinds of trinitarian heretics—those who deny the threeness of God and those who deny the oneness of God—Calvin had personal contact in controversy. Michael Servetus was a Sabellian. The ancient heretic Sabellius denied that God is truly three. He taught that the Son and the Spirit are only distinct manifestations of the one person of the Godhead, the Father. "Sabellius says that Father, Son, and Spirit signify no distinctions in God. Say they are three, and he will scream that you are naming three Gods."[40] This was the heretical doctrine of Servetus: "He would hold the persons [of the Godhead] to be certain external ideas which do not truly subsist in God's essence, but represent God to us in one manifestation or another."[41]

Against Servetus, Calvin teaches the real distinctions of the persons subsisting in the being of God.

Giovanni Valentino Gentile was an Arian, a tritheist; he denied the real oneness of God. Gentile taught that God formed a Son and a Spirit and then gave part of his essence to this Son and Spirit so that they are gods too—smaller gods than the Father, but gods nevertheless, so that in reality God is three gods. "[Gentile taught] that the Father, who is truly and properly the sole God, in forming the Son and the Spirit, infused into them his own deity."[42] Arius also denied the name "God" to Jesus but taught that God *made* Jesus divine. Against Gentile, Calvin teaches that the three persons share the one divine essence.

The contemporary spiritual representative of the heresy of Arius and Gentile is the sect of the Jehovah's Witnesses, which teaches the very same heresy that Gentile taught in Geneva.

In this connection Calvin teaches what has come to be known as the aseity of the eternal Son: the Son receives his *person* from the Father in his begetting of the Son, but the Son has his *essence*, his divine being, of himself; he does not receive it from the Father. "Therefore we say that deity in an absolute sense exists of itself; whence likewise we confess that the Son since he is God, exists of himself, but not in respect of his Person; indeed, since he is the Son, we say that he exists from the Father. Thus his essence is without beginning; while the beginning of his person is God himself."[43] Calvin's commendable purpose in this teaching is to guard against any subordination of the Son to the Father and to defend the truth that the Son is equally God with the first person.

Benjamin B. Warfield praises Calvin highly for this teaching. Among other things, Warfield thinks that by this doctrine Calvin shut the door to all subordination of the Son to the Father and deserves to be ranked with the greatest trinitarian theologians of the church.[44]

Respectful criticism of Calvin's doctrine of the Trinity

In spite of Warfield's warm praise of the doctrine, one may question Calvin's doctrine of the aseity of the eternal Son. It is, at the very least, doubtful whether Calvin does justice to the Greek word in the gospel of John and the first epistle of John that expresses the relation between the first and second persons of the Trinity, the word translated "only begotten" by the Authorized Version (μονογενής; see John 1:14, 18; John 3:16; 1 John 4:9). Neither the word itself nor the rest of Scripture suggests that the eternal begetting of the Son is restricted only to his person. Just as the begetting of a son by a human father involves generating both person and nature, so also the Father begets both the person and the essence of the Son.

Since this essence is the very essence of the Father—the one essence of the Godhead—it is exactly the begetting of the Son as to his essence, or being, that explains and establishes that the Son, who becomes flesh in Jesus, is "of one substance [essence] with the Father," as the Nicene Creed confessed.[45] The begetting of the essence of the Son from the essence of the Father does not imply the subordination of the Son to the Father, but the full equality of essence, or being. Only, the Son possesses the divine essence as Son.

The word at Nicea that preserved orthodox Christianity was *homoousios* ("of one substance"). Behind this word and its doctrine, explaining the one and the same divine essence of the Son, was the biblical word *monogenees* ("only begotten").

That Calvin's doctrine of the aseity of the Son is questionable is indicated by the fact that Calvin always had difficulty with the expression in the Nicaeno-Constantinopolitan Creed, "very God [out] of very God" (θεὸν ἀληθινὸν ἐκ θεοῦ ἀληθινοῦ).[46] That Jesus Christ, the eternal Son of the Father, is "God of God" certainly strongly suggests that he has his Godhead, being as well as person, from the Father. With this, Calvin was uncomfortable.

A weightier criticism of Calvin's doctrine of the Trinity is that, with the tradition of the church of the West, Calvin did not do justice to the threeness of God. He did not develop the truth of the three persons, nor did he apply this truth either to the life of God himself or to the life of God with his people, the covenant of grace.

The life of God triune is eternal, delightful fellowship among the persons. The life of the triune God is specifically *family* fellowship: the communion of Father and Son in the Holy Ghost. "The only begotten Son...is in the bosom of the Father" (John 1:18).

This blessed triune life of God is the source, by gracious divine decree, of the fellowship of God with the church in Jesus Christ by the Holy Spirit, which fellowship is the church's salvation. "That which we have seen and heard declare we unto you, that ye also may have fellowship with us: and truly our fellowship is with the Father, and with his Son Jesus Christ" (1 John 1:3).

Indeed, the covenant, Christian, earthly family of godly husband and godly wife and usually regenerated children owes its existence to, and is patterned after, the triune, family life of God. "Thy wife shall be as a fruitful vine by the sides of thine house; thy children like olive plants round about thy table" (Ps. 128:3).

Calvin's orthodox doctrine of the Trinity needs development in the Reformed tradition, particularly with regard to the threeness of God. This development takes place in those churches that know the covenant of grace as essentially fellowship with God in Jesus Christ, as is clearly expressed by the covenant formula: "I ... will be their God, and they shall be my people" (Jer. 31:33).[47]

Calvin's failure to develop the doctrine of the Trinity was due, in part, to his fear of empty and even dangerous "speculation" concerning the Trinity. Calvin voices this fear at the end of his treatment of the doctrine:

> Finally, I trust that the whole sum of this doctrine has been faithfully explained, if my readers will impose a limit upon their curiosity, and not seek out for themselves more eagerly than is proper troublesome and perplexed disputations. For I suspect that those who intemperately delight in speculation will not be at all satisfied. Certainly I have not shrewdly omitted anything that I might think to be against me: but while I am zealous for the edification of the church, I felt that I would be better advised not to touch upon many things that would profit but little, and would burden my readers with useless trouble. For what is the point in disputing whether the Father always begets? Indeed, it is foolish to imagine a continuous act of begetting, since it is clear that three persons have subsisted in God from eternity.[48]

He refers specifically to the issue of the eternal generation of the Son, whether this generation is "a continuous act of begetting."

Fear of speculation concerning the Trinity is commendable. But there is also the danger of failing to do justice to Scripture's abundant revelation of the Trinity and of the implications of this fundamental truth for the salvation of the covenant of grace.

The same fear that kept Calvin from developing the doctrine of the Trinity caused him to deny that a number of passages in the Old Testament to which the church has appealed in proof of the Trinity are, in fact, trinitarian. Characteristic are Calvin's comments on Micah 5:2, "Out of thee [Bethlehem] shall he come forth unto me that is to be ruler in Israel; whose goings forth have been from of old, from everlasting." Calvin's explanation is "that God had from the beginning determined to give his people an eternal King."[49] Calvin is reluctant to understand the text as teaching Christ's eternal existence as the second person of the Trinity:

> Some, I know, pertinaciously maintain, that the Prophet speaks here of the eternal existence of Christ; and as for myself, I willingly own that the divinity of Christ is here proved to us; but as this will never be allowed by the Jews, I prefer taking the words simply as they are,—that Christ will not come forth unexpectedly from Bethlehem, as though God had previously determined nothing respecting him. *His goings forth* then *are from the beginning.*"[50]

Calvin was overly cautious concerning the doctrine of the Trinity.

CHAPTER 8

Creation, Human Nature as Created, and Providence

Introduction

For Calvin, the importance of the doctrine of creation is that, in the light of the truth of creation, believers may know the true God, and know him truly, in the universe he has made. Here we must distinguish carefully between the knowledge of God that unbelievers have from the creation and the knowledge of God that Calvin purposes to give believers by confessing the biblical doctrine that God made the heavens and the earth.

Calvin holds that all men know God from the creation, although without the "inner revelation of God through faith" they all will "smother" that knowledge of God.[1] Calvin's purpose, however, in setting forth the doctrine of creation on the basis of "Moses" (Genesis) is to give believers what they need in order to know God from his works in the creation and to preserve believers in their knowledge, guarding them against turning away from the true God to idols. This is the same as the purpose of God in inspiring the account of creation in the opening chapters of Genesis: "Therefore it was his will that the history of Creation be made manifest, in order that the faith of the church, resting upon this, might seek no other God but him who was put forth by Moses as the Maker and Founder of the universe."[2]

In this context Calvin uses a powerful figure: "Eyes, when dimmed with age or weakness or by some other defect, unless aided by spectacles, discern nothing distinctly."[3] There is a serious problem with our eyes because of sin. When God gives Scripture to the believers, he is putting glasses on them so that they might know him rightly.

The urgent purpose of the right knowledge of God in creation, that is, the origin of the universe, is to enable believers to know God in his wonderful works. "Moses' history [is] as a mirror in which his [God's] living likeness glows."[4]

Calvin is in dead earnest about this. He wants believers to see "God's inestimable wisdom, power, justice, and goodness" shining forth in every creature, as well as in the universe as a whole.[5] The knowledge of God is the important thing.

Calvin thinks it is the duty of every Christian "not merely [to] run over them [the works of God] cursorily, and, so to speak, with a fleeting glance; but... [to] ponder them at length, turn them over in [his] mind seriously and faithfully, and recollect them repeatedly."[6] Alas, how little we do this. Nevertheless, every believer must live his everyday life in the world conscious of God in creation. When he sees the splendor and order of the stars, he is conscious of "the greatness of the Artificer" of these beautiful and orderly bodies.[7] When he moves around on the earth, he marvels at God's upholding "so great a mass."[8] When he observes the wisdom apparent in his own soul and body, he dwells on the wisdom of God.

Calvin writes that the benefit of the "liberal arts" and natural sciences, that is, a liberal arts education, is not so much the pleasure of the artists and students, or even the advantage of the human race, as it is the enabling of those who engage in these things to explore God's wonderful works more deeply.[9]

For Calvin, the believer on the operating table, contemplating his impending, intricate surgery, before falling unconscious will think more of the wisdom of God in the skill of the surgeon than of his own restoration to health. Calvin does, in fact, refer to the great Greek physician Galen and observes that we ought to contemplate the wisdom of the creator in a great physician like him.[10]

The age of the earth, which Calvin thinks is not yet six thousand years in his day, has as its main purpose to confront Christians with "God's eternity."[11] The young earth calls attention to the contrasting eternity of God. In his later treatment of predestination, Calvin acknowledges that profane men "will not refrain from guffaws when they are informed that but little more than five thousand years have passed since the creation of the universe."[12] It is not enough, then, to contend

Creation, Human Nature as Created, and Providence

for a young earth, but Reformed ministers must always be putting the congregation in mind of the eternity of God. Those who teach that the world is billions of years old weaken the contrast between the short age of the earth and the eternity of God and thus detract from the consciousness of God's eternity. In a way what is implied by the contemporary teaching that the earth is billions of years old is that the earth is virtually eternal, so that believers of an old earth are not confronted by the contrast between the short age of the world and the eternity of God.

By virtue of creation's being brought into existence by God's creative act, this world is, in Calvin's lovely phrase, the theater of God's glory.[13] Repeatedly Calvin describes our world this way. This, then, is at stake in the contemporary struggle for the biblical truth of creation. Shall this creation be regarded as the theater of God's glory, or shall it be regarded as the accidental outcome of the blind forces of natural powers over billions of years?

In his exposition and defense of creation, Calvin bases himself on the opening chapters of Genesis, which he receives as inspired history: "Moses was a sure witness and herald of the one God, the Creator."[14] How literally Calvin took Genesis 1, particularly the six days of Genesis 1, is shown in a later passage in the *Institutes* when Calvin is treating the related doctrine of providence. Calvin argues that the various creatures do not exert a natural power, but that God works as he wills through every creature as his means. Calvin proves this by appealing to the creation of the sun *after* the creation of plants, which, of course, is contrary to the natural order of sunlight before plants. Calvin's point is that God can sustain plant life by means of the sun or without the sun as he pleases.[15] This shows that Calvin does not interpret Genesis 1 figuratively, nor would he have been an advocate of what is called the "framework hypothesis." Calvin takes Genesis 1 as history, as it demands to be taken, and interprets Genesis 1 literally, as it demands to be interpreted.

We can subsume what Calvin says about creation under two headings: creation and providence.

Creation of the universe

Calvin's treatment of God's creation of the universe, as recorded in Genesis 1, is not quite as brief as it might seem from the fact that, after only two sections on this subject, Calvin moves quickly to the doctrine of angels and devils. For, first, Calvin returns to the subject of the creation of the world in connection with the practical application of the truth of creation to our worshipful knowledge of the creator from this, his work.[16] Indeed, section twenty is the fullest description of the work of creation in chapter fourteen. Second, Calvin has earlier said some important things about God's creation of the world in connection with the knowledge of God from creation.[17] Nevertheless, his treatment is brief, as Calvin himself acknowledges, referring the reader to Genesis 1 and 2, as well as to some of the church fathers.[18] No doubt, when Calvin refers the readers of the *Institutes* to Genesis 1 and 2, he expects that they will read his commentary on Genesis 1 and 2, which Calvin had completed five years before the 1559 edition of the *Institutes*.

The fundamental elements of Calvin's doctrine of creation include the following.

First, for Calvin, creation was the act of the true God of bringing the world and every creature into existence *ex nihilo*, that is, "out of nothing," by his word and Spirit in six days. "God by the power of his Word and Spirit created heaven and earth out of nothing."[19]

Second, Calvin clarifies what the origin of the world really was by rejecting two popular, erroneous theories. The first is a theory of origins that attributes the world to "nature": "They [the teachers of this popular error] set God aside, the while using 'nature,' which for them is the artificer of all things."[20] This is the error of materialism, or naturalism, according to which matter is eternal and develops by blind chance. The second popular error rejected by Calvin is the teaching that the universe is an emanation of the being of God. Servetus resurrected this old heresy of the Manichees, applying it particularly to man's soul: "They [the Manichees] thought the soul to be a derivative of God's substance, as if some portion of immeasurable divinity had flowed into man."[21]

Calvin's condemnation of these two popular errors in his day is highly relevant to our own struggle for the truth of creation today. Attributing everything to nature is basically the theory of atheistic, Darwinian evolution or naturalism, the theory that matter is all there is, that matter is eternal, and that matter has developed into the present form of the world. The second popular error, that this world emanated from the being of God and is really a part of the being of God, is a form of pantheism and appears in our day in process theology and new age philosophy.

A third fundamental element of Calvin's doctrine of creation is his teaching that the effect of the creative act of God is a world of beauty and order. Calvin has been charged with being indifferent to beauty. This is not true. He may have expressed his appreciation of the beauty found in creation differently than other theologians expressed it, but in his treatment of the doctrine of creation, Calvin emphasizes the beauty of creation and calls believers to see the beauty in creation as a reflection of the creator. "Let us not be ashamed to take pious delight in the works of God open and manifest in this most beautiful theater."[22]

Calvin certainly does stress the order of the creation. Order is a basic recurring theme in Calvin. He insists upon order in the physical world, order in the church, order in the home, and order in one's personal life. The emphasis upon order is by no means due to a grave psychological weakness in Calvin, as some have charged. Rather, Calvin's emphasis on order, specifically in the creation, is Calvin's recognition of the importance of order to God the creator. God is a God of order, and order characterizes all his works.

Calvin thinks the order in creation is especially evident in the heavenly bodies, "the starry host of heaven in such wonderful order," which regulates our lives by "days and nights, months, years, and seasons."[23] Although especially evident in the heavenly bodies, order is evident anywhere: "God...endowed each kind with its own nature, assigned functions, appointed places and stations."[24]

One of the powerful influences of the *Institutes* is the inclusion of its teaching in the Reformed confessions. Here is such an instance. The Belgic Confession incorporated Calvin's insistence on the order of creation in its teaching on creation: "The Father...[gave] unto every creature its being, shape, form, and several offices to serve its Creator."[25]

A fourth fundamental element of Calvin's doctrine of creation has to do with the purpose of the creator in creating. Calvin sees God's purpose especially in his preparing the world for the man Adam in the work of the six days that led up to the creation of Adam. Before creating Adam and Eve, God prepared a home for man. This indicates that God's purpose in creation was the good of mankind. Indeed, Calvin speaks of "God's fatherly love for mankind" in this.[26]

Although Calvin does not further identify the "mankind" for whom God had "fatherly love" when he created the world, "mankind" must be understood Christologically. That is, God made the world in the beginning for Jesus Christ: "All things were created...for him" (Col. 1:16). Therefore, God made all things in the beginning for Christ's church, the new human race. This is the apostle's teaching in 1 Timothy 4:3: "God...created [all earthly things] to be received with thanksgiving of them which believe and know the truth."

Accordingly, God's children are "to petition him for whatever we desire; and we are to recognize as a blessing from him, and thankfully to acknowledge, every benefit that falls to our share."[27]

Fifth, even though Calvin teaches that God's purpose in creating was the good of mankind, Calvin does not end in man in his doctrine of creation. The ultimate purpose of knowing the truth of creation is the believer's glorifying the creator. The believer is to "recognize God's powers in the creation of the universe."[28] Calvin concludes his treatment of the creation of the world with this exhortation: "Let us study to love and serve him with all our heart."[29]

Creation of angels and devils

Calvin quickly moves from the creation of the world to a treatment of the creation of angels and devils. It might strike us as peculiar that the greater part of the discussion of creation in the *Institutes* is taken up with the creation of angels (both "elect" and "reprobate," as Calvin observes from 1 Timothy 5:21). Of twenty-two sections devoted to creation, seventeen sections (3–19) are about angels and devils.

In this respect too, Guido de Brès followed Calvin in Article 12 of the Belgic Confession, where two-thirds of the article on creation is devoted to the creation of the spirit world.

Whatever we may think about it, Calvin certainly is timely in our age. The fiction of J. R. R. Tolkien, C. S. Lewis, Frank Peretti, and others expresses and encourages a fascination, if not an obsession, with regard to angels and devils. It is good to be reminded what a sober, sound

Creation, Human Nature as Created, and Providence

theologian believed about angels and devils, and what a Reformed believer should believe about the spirit world.

Calvin's interest in angels and devils is largely due to errors that are a danger to the faith of the saints. Calvin's purpose, then, is polemical.

There is the danger of virtually, and even actually, deifying the spirits. The Manichees did this with their doctrine of two eternal principles: a good God and a bad god, "God and the devil."[30] Some in Calvin's day were doing the same thing by ascribing independency to the devil. This is dualism. Dualism surfaces in Reformed churches today, as is evident from the bold denial that God governs evil events in human history. All evil events are attributed to the devil.

Against this error Calvin fights in his treatment of angels and devils. He strikes at the heart of the heresy when he says, "Now where is God's omnipotence, if such sovereignty is conceded to the devil that he carries out whatever he wishes, against God's will and resistance?"[31]

Although Calvin certainly does justice to the spiritual warfare between God and the devil, he renounces dualism when he insists, "[Satan] can do nothing unless God wills and assents to it . . . Therefore Satan is clearly under God's power, and is so ruled by his bidding as to be compelled to render him service."[32] This is stronger than saying that Satan is subject to God's control; this makes Satan a *servant* of God. Against the error of deifying the spirits and making a god out of the devil, Calvin teaches that all of the spirits are mere creatures. How important, then, is the truth of the creation of the angels. What is created cannot be God, or even a "god" against God.

A second error that Calvin refutes is that the devils are naturally evil, that is, evil from the beginning of their existence. This would make God responsible for their wickedness. The truth of creation guards against this blasphemous error: God made all good, including the spirits that now are evil; the devils (and Calvin notes that this also is true of man) are not evil by nature, but by their fall. "The depravity and malice both of man and of the devil . . . do not spring from nature, but rather from the corruption of nature."[33] Concerning Satan himself, Calvin writes,

> This malice, which we attribute to his [Satan's] nature, came not from his creation but from his perversion. For, whatever he

has that is to be condemned he has derived from his revolt and fall. For this reason ... Christ declares that "when Satan lies, he speaks according to his own nature" and states the reason, because "he abode not in the truth" [John 8:44].³⁴

Calvin's insistence regarding the devils that evil in the world is due to a fall from original goodness, not to nature, bears on Reformed orthodoxy's controversy with theistic evolution. Theistic evolution is a theory concerning the origin of all things. Teaching that the present form of the universe evolved naturally over billions of years, theistic evolution maintains that the presence of evil in the world, specifically death in the realm of all living things including humanity, and sin in the human race are part of the natural process of evolution from the beginning. Thus evil in the world is attributed to the creator, who, according to theistic evolution, began the process and superintended it. By implication the presence of devils in the world is also the fault of God, if indeed theistic evolution has any place for devils at all. But to make God responsible for evil, including demons, is, as Calvin avers, blasphemous.

Yet a third concern of the reformer, ever jealous of the prerogatives of God, is that even believers can come to depend too heavily on angels as "ministers and dispensers of all good things" and thus glorify the means—angels—rather than the savior God. Calvin describes this as "superstition."³⁵ Astutely, against this error he says, "Not only is Christ to be preferred before all angels but ... he is the author of all good things that they have [Col. 1:16, 20]."³⁶ Calvin mentions various ranks of angels that God made for Christ, and God's purpose of gathering all things into one in Jesus Christ. No doubt, Calvin has in mind the warning of Colossians 2:18: "Let no man beguile you of your reward in a voluntary humility and worshipping of angels." One of the natural effects of the popular stories today that exaggerate the place and power of angels in the life of the Christian is that impressionable readers begin to put their trust in angels. Calvin warns against this.

Calvin teaches that God created angels sometime during the six days of Genesis 1, but he disavows any interest in speculating *when* during the six days. Calvin was not a speculative theologian. Where Scripture is silent, Calvin is also silent.

Calvin teaches that God created angels especially to be God's servants in the saving of the elect. For the work of angels, Hebrews 1:14 is an important text for Calvin: "Are they not all ministering spirits, sent forth to minister for them who shall be heirs of salvation?"

Angels are real, invisible, personal spirits. They are not merely unsubstantial ideas or "the impulses that God inspires in men or those examples of his power which he puts forth."[37] Angels serve us in ways mostly unknown to us. Calvin is dubious about the popular notion of individual guardian angels and reminds us, "We ought to hold as a fact that the care of each one of us is not the task of one angel only, but all with one consent watch over our salvation... For if the fact that all the heavenly host are keeping watch for his safety will not satisfy a man, I do not see what benefit he could derive from knowing that one angel has been given to him as his especial guardian."[38] Angels are merely instruments of God and Christ. We must trust God and Christ and honor them, not the angelic instruments.

Throughout, Calvin warns against unbiblical speculation about angels; he is strictly biblical, and he wants the Reformed churches to be biblical also. Sarcastically, Calvin comments on *Celestial Hierarchy* by Dionysius, a popular book of his day on angels: "If you read that book, you would think a man fallen from heaven recounted, not what he had learned, but what he had seen with his own eyes."[39] We ought to be warned, for we live in an age of such fantastic speculation about angels and devils.

Scripture limits as well its revelation about Satan and the devils, refusing to satisfy our curiosity. Calvin notes that God does not satisfy our "curiosity" by telling us much at all of Satan's fall.[40] The purpose of Scripture's revelation regarding devils is that we may be armed to resist these numerous, determined, crafty, powerful foes. Calvin's insistence on Scripture's practical purpose with its revelation concerning the devils reminds the Reformed minister of the word of God of his duty. He must warn the church and each member of the church about the reality of devils and about their unceasing, determined efforts to destroy the church and the saint.

Calvin begins his section on devils this way: "All that Scripture teaches concerning devils aims at arousing us to take precaution against their stratagems and contrivances."[41] The first rule of warfare, whether spiritual or earthly, is to know the enemy. Especially those passages of Scripture that teach the punishment of devils, for example, Matthew 8:29, Matthew 25:41, and 2 Peter 2:4, would be "meaningless... if devils were nonexistent." Calvin wants the children of God to know the reality of devils, lest "thinking themselves without an enemy, [they] become more slack and heedless about resisting."[42]

Three motives "ought to fire us to an unceasing struggle against him [Satan]." First, "if we have God's glory at heart, as we should have, we ought with all our strength to contend against him who is trying to extinguish it." This is quintessentially Calvin: he does not start with the church or with one's personal salvation, but with zeal for the glory of God. If Satan trips up someone, especially publicly, Satan brings great shame to him as a Christian, but far worse is his dishonoring of God. Our second motivation is concern for Christ's kingdom, which Satan plots to ruin. Third, "if we care about our salvation at all, we ought to have neither peace nor truce with him who continually lays traps to destroy it."[43]

In the context of denying that God made Satan and the devils evil, which, of course, would make God culpable, Calvin insists that they were good angels by creation, who then willingly rebelled and fell by their own will: "They were when first created angels of God, but by degeneration they ruined themselves, and became the instruments of ruin for others."[44] Calvin appeals to 2 Peter 2:4: "God spared not the angels that sinned, but cast them down to hell, and delivered them into chains of darkness, to be reserved unto judgment." Then, characteristically, Calvin indicates the sovereignty of God in the fall of the angels by appealing to 1 Timothy 5:21, which calls the angels who stood "elect angels." This, says Calvin, implies that those who fell were "reprobate angels" and that their fall was according to God's purpose.[45]

This sovereignty of God with regard to the fall of the angels is emphatically and sharply stated by Calvin. He teaches, first, that Satan can do only what God wills. In support of this, Calvin refers to a number of biblical events and passages, beginning with Job. The history of Job proves that Satan must ask permission before he can touch Job and that God sets limits to Satan's activity (Job 1:12; Job 2:6). Accordingly, Calvin indicates that such is God's control that Satan renders God service, "and so he obeys his Creator, whether he will or not, because he is compelled to yield him service wherever God impels him."[46] Of course, the meaning is not obedience as willing service from the heart, but rather carrying out God's will in spite of Satan's hostility to God. Satan obeys, not God's precept, but his decree.

The preeminent service of God that Satan and the devils render is that "they exercise believers in combat, ambush them, invade their peace, beset them in combat, and also often weary them, rout them, terrify them, and sometimes wound them."[47] God directs the unholy host against believers to teach them warfare; to mature them in combat.

This assault upon believers by Satan and his demons includes the spiritual, psychological distresses of the people of God. Calvin is saying that when the believer has his peace of soul invaded, becomes weary in the Christian life, and is terrified and wounded, he must not immediately reach for pills or liquor, or call a psychiatrist, but he should consider rather that the infernal hosts of Satan are coming against him and that fundamentally God is sending these spirits to exercise him in combat. He ought to be aware of this spiritual struggle and vigorously fight with the spiritual weapons he has at his disposal: justification by faith alone, God's providential care and love, and the confidence that God's strength is made perfect in the believer's weakness (2 Cor. 12:9).

We live in an age when this aspect of psychological distress is in danger of being ignored. Paragraph 1.14.18 of the *Institutes* is worth reading and rereading: the preeminent service rendered by the devils is to exercise believers in combat. God's purpose is not that devils overcome the believers, but that believers are strengthened in the battle. Because of the divine sovereignty over devils, Satan can never conquer or destroy one elect member of the church. "Because that promise to crush Satan's head [Gen. 3:15] pertains to Christ and all his members in common, I deny that believers can ever be conquered or overwhelmed by him [Satan]."[48]

The general reason that Satan cannot conquer the elect is God's sovereignty, but the particular reasons are also significant. First, demons can never overcome even one believer because of the promise, which "pertains to Christ and all his members" (Gen. 3:15). Second, "Christ, by dying, conquered Satan . . . and triumphed over all his forces, to the end that they might not harm the church."[49] These, then, are invincible shields behind which believers take refuge in personal combat with Satan: the promise of the gospel and the death of Christ.

The clear implication of Calvin's appeal to these reasons is that the promise of God is for believers alone and that the death of Christ is for the elect church alone.

Creation of man

The treatment of the creation of man, as the "noblest and most remarkable"[50] revelation of the creator, is what Calvin aims at from the outset of his exposition of creation. The lengthy treatment of angels is a parenthetical insertion, as Calvin indicates in its opening line: "Before I begin more fully to discuss man's nature, I ought to insert something concerning angels."[51]

The purpose of our study of man as created must be that we have a "clear and complete knowledge of God." We cannot have this knowledge of God "unless it is accompanied by a corresponding knowledge of ourselves."[52] Here we are reminded of the important assertion of Calvin at the beginning of the *Institutes*—a grand theme running throughout the book—"True and sound wisdom consists of two parts: the knowledge of God and of ourselves."[53] The necessary knowledge of ourselves is twofold: knowledge of what we were by creation and knowledge of what we now are by the fall.

In this connection it is Calvin's deepest concern that we not attribute our present, sinful condition to the creator, as we must if we deny or ignore man's original creation as perfectly good. This is a real danger, since man desires to excuse himself in this way. Some boldly "impute to [God] the fault" for their present evils and defects; others, more carefully, "blame their depravity on nature," which is also to "insult God."[54]

The concern of Calvin that man not blame God for his depravity is found in the Heidelberg Catechism when it asks the question, "Did God create man thus wicked and perverse?" and answers, "No; but God created man good, and after his own image."[55]

The grievous error of blaming God for man's depravity is introduced into Reformed churches today by the theory of theistic evolution, as the Reformed scholar Jan Lever freely acknowledges. What the Christian church has called sin is merely the weakness, or savagery, inherent in the evolutionary process from the beginning. Since God originated the evolutionary process, according to the proponents of theistic evolution, with this weakness or savagery "built" into the process, God is to blame for the evils of humanity.⁵⁶

Theologically, the heresy of absolving man of the guilt of his depravity and making God responsible is the error of denying original sin, particularly the error of denying that man's corruption of nature is an evil for which man is responsible. This denial of original sin, closely linked to an evolutionary theory of origins, takes form today in the teaching that, although homosexual acts may be sinful, homosexual tendencies of nature are not sinful. The argument of churches and theologians who take this position is, "God made certain men and women with a homosexual 'disposition,'" that is, a homosexual nature. The sinner is excused. God is blamed.

Christ, however, does not restrict the sin of adultery to the act but condemns the adulterous "disposition," or nature, as well (Matt. 5:27, 28).

Ultimately, the denial of original sin, particularly the denial of the sinfulness of man's depraved nature, is due to the denial of an original good creation and of a historical fall of Adam, and of the race in him. Calvin teaches both the creation of man as good and the historical fall of Adam.

Concerning man as created, Calvin teaches that man's origin is from "earth and clay," which humbled Adam even in paradise. "Adam could rightly glory in the great liberality of his Maker."⁵⁷ Man was made body and soul. The soul is a real created essence, or substance, distinct from the body. Calvin argues this against the naturalism of his day that was intent on reducing man to his physical makeup, thus denying an everlasting existence for man. A contemporary proponent of this naturalism was the philosopher Ludwig Feuerbach, who famously wrote, "Man is what he eats" (German: *"Der Mensch ist was er isst"*).⁵⁸

In this connection and for this reason, Calvin contends for an "immortal" soul.⁵⁹ He means by "immortal" the spiritual nature of a real substance making the soul indestructible so that it exists everlastingly. The Belgic Confession follows Calvin here: "The wicked ... being immortal, shall be tormented in that everlasting fire."⁶⁰

One may take issue with Calvin's use of the word "immortal" to describe the soul of man. *Immortal*, strictly speaking, means "incapable of dying." But the soul of man as created by God could, and did, die. The soul of Adam died spiritually at the moment of his disobedience, becoming totally depraved. The soul of every unregenerated sinner is spiritually dead in sin (Eph. 2:1–3). God will kill the soul of every reprobate sinner in hell, inflicting upon the soul, as well as upon the body, eternal death (Matt. 10:28; Rev. 20:14, 15). The soul of man was created mortal, that is, capable of dying.

By his resurrection, the man Jesus Christ first entered into immortal human life, body and soul. He is the one "that liveth, and . . . [is] alive for evermore," having the keys of the grave and of death (Rev. 1:18). True immortality of the soul, as of the body, is the gift of grace only to those who are united to the risen Christ by faith in him. For them "Jesus Christ . . . hath abolished death, and hath brought life and immortality to light through the gospel" (2 Tim. 1:10).

If we differ with Calvin over the *word* he chose to describe the soul of man as created by God on the sixth day of the creation week, let us take pains to teach Calvin's *doctrine* of the soul, namely, that it is a real spiritual substance, indestructible and therefore existing everlastingly either in heaven or in hell. By virtue of his creation by God, man is far more than he eats.

The soul is virtually the same as "spirit" in Scripture, although Calvin allows for a distinction between *soul* and *spirit* when the two terms are used together. "Sometimes it [the soul] is called 'spirit.' For even when these terms are joined together, they differ from one another in meaning; yet when the word 'spirit' is used by itself, it means the same thing as soul."[61]

Calvin holds that "the human soul consists of two faculties, understanding and will." For him the understanding is the primary faculty; it is "the leader and governor of the soul."[62]

The soul is "the proper seat" of the image of God in which Adam was made, although the image extended to Adam's entire being.[63]

An important question in theology always is: What is this image of God in which Adam was created? And in connection with this: Does man retain the image after the fall, or part of the image, or has man lost the entire image?

Of fundamental importance to Calvin's doctrine of the image of God is Calvin's method of determining what the image of God in man is. Calvin insists that the content of the image of God with which Adam was created must be determined from two New Testament passages that describe the salvation of the elect sinner as a restoration of the image in Jesus Christ. In Colossians 3:10 and Ephesians 4:24 the restored image is described as knowledge, righteousness, and holiness. On the basis of these passages, Calvin determines that "God's image is the perfect excellence of human nature which shone in Adam before his defection."[64] Calvin becomes more specific: "true piety, righteousness, purity, and intelligence."[65] Calvin, therefore, defines the image as the spiritual perfections that Adam possessed by virtue of his creation by God.

Calvin expressly rejects the theory that the image consisted of the "dominion" that God gave Adam and Eve (Gen. 1:28), a theory picked up today by the Christian reconstructionists and others. Calvin faults the dominion theory for locating the image of God "outside" of man rather than "within" him.[66]

This leads to the controversial question whether man lost the image of God in the fall. About this there is disagreement in Reformed and Presbyterian circles, to say nothing of broader Christianity. Many Reformed theologians teach that, although he lost much of the image, Adam retained part of the image of God. They appeal to Calvin in support of this teaching. The danger of this doctrine, of course, is that it implies that fallen, unregenerated humans yet remain truly good and still retain some ability for performing what is truly good, if not the ability of a "free will," upon which salvation itself depends. Thus are denied the doctrine of total depravity and the gospel of salvation by grace.

Already in connection with man's creation in the image of God, Calvin makes a full and typical statement about the effect of Adam's disobedience on the possession and loss of the image: "God's image ... was subsequently so vitiated and almost blotted out that nothing remains after the ruin except what is confused, mutilated, and disease-ridden."[67] He repeats this statement numerous times in slightly different words throughout his writings. Equally strong statements amounting to the affirmation of the complete loss and utter perversion of the image of God by the fall of Adam are found in Calvin's defense of the doctrine of the bondage of the will against the Roman Catholic Pighius. With specific reference to "the image of God" in which "Adam was created," Calvin writes, "Paul teaches that this needs to be restored from day to day in the faithful, and that not by their own power but by the power of the Holy Spirit. It follows therefore that it [the image of God] has been erased and corrupted."[68]

A right reading of Calvin will conclude that Calvin teaches that, with regard to the *content* of the image of God, the image is completely lost. Fallen man has no piety, no righteousness, no holiness, no proper knowledge of God, no goodness anymore. Calvin certainly teaches that fallen man still remains man, showing that he was originally made in the image of God. Indeed, this will be true of the damned in hell. Fallen man is still capable of bearing the image if God is gracious, but this capability, which is man's humanity, is no spiritual neutrality, much less a residue of goodness. Rather, fallen, unregenerated human beings are clothed with spiritual impiety, unrighteousness, unholiness, and ignorance. Man is now characterized by the opposite of the spiritual excellence that once he had at creation.

The truth of the image includes that Adam had both a sound "mind" that led him to God and a "free will."[69] The controversy over free will was the occasion for Calvin to devote the last section on the creation of man to a careful treatment of free will. Calvin affirms that Adam had a "free will," that is, a will that was capable of choosing to remain in the state of rectitude and bliss in paradise. However, Calvin is quick to caution that he is not affirming the autonomy of Adam over against God's predestinating decree, but only that the "nature" of Adam's will was such that it could choose God and the good.[70] It could also choose against God and the good, and Calvin expressively designates Adam's free will as "mediocre."[71]

Calvin can understand that the philosophers hold that man still has a free will, since they are ignorant of the fall. Professing Christians who teach that man still has a free will are "playing the fool."[72]

God cannot be blamed for creating Adam with a will that, although good, could choose the evil, since he was under no necessity to create man otherwise. Calvin contents himself with saying that God's reason for this "lies hidden in his plan."[73] We may and should go further and confess that the reason is that God purposed Jesus Christ in the original creation (see Col. 1:15–20). The whole creation was made for Jesus Christ, and the apostle calls him "the image of the invisible God." The glory of God for the sake of which he gave Adam "a mediocre and even transitory will" is his glory in Jesus Christ as redeemer of the church, who so restores the image that we receive a will that cannot choose against God.[74]

We should now face the question whether Calvin indicates what he thinks concerning the possibility of Adam's attaining a higher life by the proper exercise of his free will in paradise. One statement seems to teach this: "In this integrity man by free will had the power, if he so willed, to attain eternal life."[75] Similarly, he proposes in his commentary on Genesis 2:16, 17, the command not to eat of the tree of the knowledge of good and evil, that had Adam not fallen, "his earthly life truly would have been temporal; yet he would have passed into heaven without death, and without injury."[76] But Calvin also speaks of Adam's remaining in his original earthly estate, had he not disobeyed: "Adam could have stood if he wished."[77]

Calvin simply does not address the issue that has become controversial in the Reformed tradition, in connection with the truth of God's covenant with Adam—the issue, namely, whether Adam by his obedience could have "attained" the eternal life that the incarnate Son of God has earned for the church by his lifelong obedience and atoning death.

What providence is

Calvin correctly sees providence as the necessary implication of creation, a further aspect of God's work of creation. Providence is the necessary relation to the world and its history by the creator after he had made the world. Calvin teaches that if God made the world, he will not abandon it, but he will care for it, uphold it, and govern it. So much is this the case, that Calvin states that a failure to confess providence simply indicates that one does not truly believe the doctrine of creation: "Nobody seriously believes the universe was made by God without being persuaded that he takes care of his works."[78] In short, providence is an aspect of the full truth of creation.

This connection of creation and providence is expressed creedally for the Reformed churches in the Heidelberg Catechism. Answering the question what it means that God is the "Maker of Heaven and

Earth," as confessed in the Apostles' Creed, the catechism speaks of creation and providence in one breath: "[God the Father]... who of nothing made heaven and earth, with all that in them is,... *likewise upholds and governs the same by his eternal counsel and providence.*"⁷⁹ Creation, which is the answer to the question, includes providence. The catechism then devotes a separate question and answer to the doctrine of providence—Question and Answer 27—*as part of its explanation of creation.*⁸⁰

This connection between creation and providence explains certain serious, glaring heresies now surfacing in evangelical and Reformed churches: the outright denial that God governs evil occurrences in history, particularly those that strike church members, and the teaching that God is an "open God." By an "open God" is meant not only that God is ignorant of the future, but also that God does not control history. God waits for human beings to make their decisions, which will then determine how God must react to make things turn out well in the end.

These errors are a form of a denial of providence. The explanation of this denial of providence, in part, is that for a long time already these evangelical and Reformed churches have denied the biblical doctrine of creation. Deny creation, and a denial of providence must follow. It is misleading when theologians contend that the people of God need not be disturbed by the denial of the creation account in Genesis 1 and 2, because the novel, figurative explanations they propose do not affect salvation and the Christian life. When we battle for the truth of creation, as we do when we insist uncompromisingly on six historical days in Genesis 1, each containing one evening and one morning, we must keep in mind that at stake is not only the biblical doctrine of creation, but also the biblical doctrine of providence.

For Calvin, providence is God's living, active relation to the world and to each creature, in which God sustains and governs the world and his creatures by his almighty power and according to his wise plan or decree.

Although Calvin does not, as far as I know, use the term, providence affirms God's immanence, that is, God's presence in the creation, God's nearness to his creation and to every creature in the creation. God is also transcendent; he is exalted high above the creation and is essentially different from the creation, but at the same time he is immanent. We think of Acts 17, where in his sermon to the Greeks on Mars Hill, Paul preached that God, who "made the world and all things therein" (v. 24), is "not far from every one of us" (v. 27), for "in him we live, and move, and have our being" (v. 28).

The charge is sometimes made against Calvin that he only taught a transcendent God, a God far away in his exalted majesty. This charge is false, indeed absurd, and those who make it show that they have not read the *Institutes* on providence. Whether Calvin used the term *immanence* or not, his powerful doctrine of providence is the teaching of a God who, having made the earth, does not withdraw from it, as does the god of deism. Rather, he is intimately present with all his being in the creation he has made. He is so near the world and every creature that moment to moment they are kept in existence by God and governed by him. Providence in this aspect Calvin calls God's "hand," God's almighty power by which he is actively at work.[81]

An essential aspect of providence is the "plan," or decree, according to which God governs all things. "All events are governed by God's secret plan."[82] "Creatures... are governed by God's secret plan in such a way that nothing happens except what is knowingly and willingly decreed by him."[83] Shorthand for the providence of God is "his hand and plan." God's hand is at work upholding and governing everything, and it works just as does the hand of an intelligent human, namely, according to a wise plan.

Consequently, the truth of providence is the death of the notion of a universe and its history "tumbling" about at the whims of chance and fortune.[84] It is also the death of the contemporary theory that history is governed by the autonomous decisions of men to which God reacts, albeit with superior wisdom. The issue in providence and history as in predestination, that is, in accounting for history as in accounting for salvation, is God's free will or man's free will, God's sovereignty or man's sovereignty. In his doctrine of providence, Calvin comes down on the side of God's free will in history.

There is good reason that the editions of the *Institutes* leading up to the 1559 edition treated providence and predestination together. In the 1559 edition, for the first time, Calvin separates his treatment of providence and predestination, treating providence in the first book of the

Institutes as part of the doctrine of God and predestination in book three as the source and explanation of the Spirit's salvation of the sinner. Earlier Calvin treated providence and predestination together because both of them have to do with the same issue: Who or what is sovereign in the history of the world, and who or what is sovereign in the salvation of sinners?

Viewing providence as both "hand and plan," Calvin gives a basic description of providence in the following words: "We make God the ruler and governor of all things, who in accordance with his wisdom has from the farthest limit of eternity decreed what he was going to do, and now by his might carries out what he has decreed."[85]

Calvin thinks it necessary to explicate this truth of providence further to guard it against misunderstanding. Calvin repudiates an explanation of providence as merely a vague, general movement of all things by God. Calvin sharply affirms that providence is direct action by God upon each creature individually.

To drive his point home, Calvin says, "It is certain that not one drop of rain falls without God's sure command."[86] More than once Calvin appeals to Jesus' word "that not even a tiny and insignificant sparrow falls to the ground without the Father's will [Matt. 10:29]."[87] Also in a very earthy example of God's providence, Calvin—the pastor, speaking to real situations in his congregation—observes that "some mothers have full and abundant breasts, but others' are almost dry, as God wills to feed one [child] more liberally, but another more meagerly."[88]

This raises the perennial question (and charge): Does not such a doctrine of providence, extending to the wicked deeds of devils and ungodly people, make God responsible for these sinful deeds? In his preface to the Psalms commentary, where Calvin opens up his life more than he does in any other place, he says that the fiercest attacks leveled against him during his ministry were attacks on his doctrine of predestination and his doctrine of providence. The charges were that "I represent God as the author of sin" and deny the responsibility of man.[89]

Calvin treats this matter of God's providential government of the sinful deeds of devils and men especially in chapter eighteen of book one of the *Institutes*. This chapter is new in the final 1559 edition. There can be no doubt that Calvin in the last edition adds a chapter defending God's providential government of the wickedness of demons and sinful men because of his recent controversy over this aspect of providence with one who denied God's providential government of sin. Calvin's struggle with this person also occasioned Calvin's publishing a great treatise, "A Defence of the Secret Providence of God," in 1558. Calvin refers to this denier of providence as "a certain worthless person."[90]

Calvin affirms that providence, in the active, individual sense of God's government of his creation, extends to the ungodly. Calvin does not pull back from a strong, comprehensive doctrine of providence, regardless of opposition to it and regardless of slanderous charges made against him. With appeal to David's explanation of Shimei's cursing of him—a grievous sin—("the LORD hath said unto him, Curse David," 2 Sam. 16:10) and Job's explanation of his troubles, which included sins on the part of Satan and on the part of ungodly men ("The LORD hath taken away," Job 1:21), Calvin boldly states that God "is the doer" of the sinful deeds of Satan and wicked men, without being responsible for them.[91] "That God does whatever he wills [Ps. 115:3], certainly pertains to all the actions of men."[92]

What Calvin means by affirming that God "does" these wicked deeds, he makes clear. God has decreed the sinful deeds in his counsel of providence. God also works by his "secret," mysterious, almighty power within and upon "Satan himself and all the wicked" to "bend or draw" them "to his will." In this government of sin, God works in such a way that Satan and the wicked themselves act wickedly, for evil ends, whereas God works, through their wickedness, "to carry out his [righteous] judgments."[93]

Calvin rejects the popular attempt to relieve God of responsibility for evil and to maintain the responsibility of the sinner by explaining God's providential government of sin as "bare permission." Calvin rejects "the figment of bare permission."[94] Against the attempt to solve the problem of divine sovereignty and human responsibility by speaking of "permission," Calvin asserts that God's providence is "the determinative principle for all human plans and work," equally for "the reprobate" as for "the elect."[95] Calvin is contemptuous of those who reduce the providence of God with regard to sin to mere "permission": "They babble and talk absurdly who . . . substitute bare permission—as if God sat in a watchtower awaiting chance events, and his judgments thus depended upon human will."[96]

The adversaries of Calvin's doctrine of providence charged him with teaching "two contrary wills" in God. They contended that "if nothing happens apart from God's will," as Calvin taught, "there are in him [God] two contrary wills, because by his secret plan he decrees what he has openly forbidden by his law."[97]

Because this charge is an objection to Calvin's doctrine that God wills the sinful acts of Satan and wicked men in the sense of decreeing them in his eternal counsel, Calvin points out that "this cavil [namely, that there are two contradictory wills in God] is not hurled against me but against the Holy Spirit."[98] It was not Calvin but the Holy Spirit who inspired Job to confess that "as it pleased God, so was it done" to Job.[99] It was not Calvin but the Holy Spirit who inspired Luke to write that all the evil done to Jesus Christ "God's hand and plan had decreed [Acts 4:28]."[100]

Calvin denies the charge that he teaches two contradictory wills in God. Calvin insists on the unity and simplicity of the will of God. The one will appears "manifold" to us, partly because of "our mental incapacity"[101] (the Beveridge translation has "imbecility"[102]) and partly because of the incomprehensibility of God. At the same time, Calvin points out the important fact that God's decree and his command are "utterly different."[103] To confuse them, as they do who suppose that God's decree that Absalom commit adultery with David's wives contradicts God's command that Absalom not commit adultery, is biblically and theologically irresponsible. "His [God's] will [of decree] is wrongly confused with his precept."[104]

Calvin's doctrine of the will of God is important, and timely. As God is one, so there is one will in God. To posit two contradictory wills in God is serious error, as Calvin's foes understood well when they charged his doctrine of providence with exactly this absurdity. But God's one will can, and must, be distinguished in two aspects: the will of his decree—what he purposes be done—and the will of his precept—what he commands men to do. Inasmuch as the will of God's precept only sets forth man's duty, not what God purposes to do, the command does not contradict the decree, even though the decree purposes something other than is commanded. God commanded Pilate to judge justly in trying Jesus Christ. He decreed that Pilate would judge unjustly. "Yet God's will is not therefore at war with itself, nor does it change, nor does it pretend not to will what he wills."[105]

Maintaining the fundamental truth that God has one will depends squarely on the sharp, clear distinction between the will of the decree and the will of the command. To confuse, or even obliterate, this distinction by presenting God's precept as expressing his purpose, desire, or wish is to become guilty of the error of two contradictory wills in God—the error falsely charged against Calvin by his enemies and the error Calvin so vigorously repudiated. In this case, God both purposed that Pilate condemn Jesus in the decree and purposed, or wished, that Pilate not condemn Jesus in the precept.

Two important considerations bear on the matter of providence and sin. First, the wicked are not coerced to do evil contrary to their nature, specifically their will. Second, when a wicked man sins according to God's decree and government, that wicked man has a different purpose from the purpose of God with the sinful deed. "The Jews intended to destroy Christ."[106] God, who "wittingly and willingly determined what the Jews carried out," purposed "redemption."[107]

Calvin appeals to the magnificent statement by Augustine in his *Enchiridion*:

> In a wonderful and ineffable manner nothing is done without God's will, not even that which is against his will. For it would not be done if he did not permit it; yet he does not unwillingly permit it, but willingly; nor would he, being good, allow evil to be done, unless being also almighty he could make good even out of evil.[108]

We must maintain Calvin's bold apology for divine sovereignty in providence in the face of charges both from without and from within the churches. There may be no weakening of this sovereignty, for example, by contenting ourselves with "bare permission" regarding the evil deeds of human beings and Satan.

Nevertheless, providence for Calvin is not about bare sovereignty. Evident in Calvin's treatment of providence, and fundamental to his doctrine of providence, is that God's relation to the world is that of a loving, heavenly Father who cares for the world he made. That is, he has an attitude of favor toward the world and purposes good for the world. Calvin's description of providence is that "[God] sustains, nourishes, and cares for, everything he has made."[109] Referring to the godly man, Calvin describes providence this way: "His Heavenly Father so holds all things in his power, so rules by his authority and will, so governs by his wisdom, that nothing can befall except he determine it."[110] His heavenly Father so governs all things that everything comes to the believing man for his good and in the favor of God. This idea is picked up by the Heidelberg Catechism, which makes providence the work of "God the Father," indeed, of "the eternal Father of our Lord Jesus Christ."[111]

Reformed preachers must not overlook this in their preaching of providence. If they present providence only as a matter of bare sovereignty, they are missing something that lies at the heart of the Reformed, biblical truth of providence. The God of providence is not simply a sovereign God; he is the eternal Father of our Lord Jesus Christ. As the eternal Father of the Lord Jesus Christ, he upholds all things. God cares for his world; God sustains his world; God is directing his world to a glorious end. The reference is not only to elect humanity, but also to the earth and heavens, plants and animals.

There can be some question how Calvin understood this fatherly care of creation. There are expressions in Calvin that leave the impression that there is a certain favorable care of God for every creature, including reprobate men, so that the good gifts of providence are blessings for reprobate men. For example, Calvin writes, "[God] so tempers his providence that, although kindly and beneficent toward all in numberless ways, he still by open and daily indications declares his clemency to the godly and his severity to the wicked and criminal. For there are no doubts about what sort of vengeance he takes on wicked deeds."[112] Another example is this statement concerning the "end" of providence: "God may reveal his concern for the whole human race, but especially his vigilance in ruling the church."[113]

However, there are also statements in Calvin opposing the notion of providential favor to the ungodly. In fact, Calvin's preponderant teaching is fatherly goodness to believers. Good gifts to the wicked are not expressions of grace. Rather, they are a curse and render the wicked more guilty. An instance of this doctrine in Calvin is this statement:

> In short, if all things flow unto us according to our wish, but we are uncertain of God's love or hatred, our happiness will be ac-

cursed and therefore miserable. But if in fatherly fashion God's countenance beams upon us, even our miseries will be blessed. For they will be turned into aids to salvation.[114]

Similar is Calvin's prayer at the end of his lecture on Zechariah 1:12–16:

> Nor let us in the meantime envy the evanescent happiness of thy enemies; but patiently wait, while thou showest that the chief object of desire is to have thee propitious to us, and that accursed is every good thing which the ungodly receive while they provoke thee and make thee angry, until Christ shall at length reveal to us the real happiness and glory of thy Church, when he shall appear at the last day for our salvation.[115]

Regardless how Calvin understood God's fatherhood in providence, the right understanding is that God does indeed love, preserve, and purpose the good of his universe. However, he loves, preserves, and purposes a good of the universe as this universe was eternally conceived by God in Jesus Christ, created for Jesus Christ, and destined to be renewed in Jesus Christ as the peaceful and secure home for Jesus Christ and his body, the elect church. The favor of God is upon the creation organically, not upon each creature individually (certainly Satan is excluded). And the divine blessing of providence is *in Christ* and, therefore, upon the elect only who are in Christ. The curse and judgment of providence, which Calvin also recognizes, are for all those outside of Christ.

That God conceived and made the universe for "his dear Son," Jesus Christ, is the explicit teaching of Colossians 1:16: "All things were created by him, and for him." The universe created for Jesus Christ and destined to be reconciled to Jesus Christ (v. 20) is the "world" (κόσμος) that God loves, according to John 3:16: "God so loved the world." Its renewal as "a new heaven and a new earth" (Rev. 21:1) is the good for which the present creation groans:

> For the earnest expectation of the creature waiteth for the manifestation of the sons of God. For the creature was made subject to vanity, not willingly, but by reason of him who hath sub-

jected the same in hope, because the creature itself also shall be delivered from the bondage of corruption into the glorious liberty of the children of God. For we know that the whole creation groaneth and travaileth in pain together until now (Rom. 8:19–22).

That God's loving, fatherly care in creation and providence is particularly directed to men and women who believe in Jesus Christ is taught by 1 Timothy 4:3. With regard to the use and enjoyment of the earthly ordinance of marriage and of earthly things ("meats"), the apostle declares that "God hath created [these things] to be received with thanksgiving of them which believe and know the truth."

Defense of providence against error

Having carefully explained the doctrine of providence, Calvin gives a spirited defense of it.

Calvin defends providence against the ascription of all events to chance or fortune. He says concerning fortune's ruling the world and men that it would tumble "all things at random up and down."[116]

Defending providence, Calvin condemns deism, the philosophical theory that God, having once created all things, afterward withdraws from the world and allows it to run on, and eventually run out, on its own. God plays the role merely of interested, or disinterested, spectator.

> To make God a momentary Creator, who once for all finished his work, would be cold and barren, and we must differ from profane men especially in that we see the presence of divine power shining as much in the continuing state of the universe as in its inception.[117]

Providence is God's "hand," not merely his eye.

Calvin also defends providence against the charge that providence, as held by Calvin, is the same as stoical "fate"[118] or "determinism." This is a common description of the creedal, Reformed doctrine of providence still today, especially by Christian philosophers. Calvin denies the false and malicious charge, as we today deny the identification of providence with determinism. Providence is not a form of determinism. Providence and determinism are qualitatively different. The difference is not that in the one case (determinism) everything is determined, whereas in the other case (providence) nothing is determined. But the difference is that in the philosophical teaching of stoical fate, everything is determined by impersonal necessity, by the way things are in themselves; whereas in providence everything is determined by a wise and good God. Calvin's rejoinder to stoical fate is:

> We do not, with the Stoics, contrive a necessity out of the perpetual connection and intimately related series of causes, which is contained in nature; but we make God the ruler and governor of all things, who in accordance with his wisdom has from the farthest limit of eternity decreed what he was going to do, and now by his might carries out what he has decreed.[119]

Calvin also sharply distinguishes the biblical doctrine of providence from philosophical determinism, or "fate," in his little book *Concerning Scandals*. Although the subject he treats is predestination, Calvin makes an important statement about providence (indicating how closely related the two truths are in the mind of Calvin):

> They [the "madmen" who oppose God's predestination and providence] gain nothing by artfully discrediting the providence of God by giving it the name of fate. For we do not talk foolishly about an intricacy of connected causes with the Stoics, or subject the government of the world to the stars, or invent a necessity in the very nature of things; but that, of course, is what profane men call "fate." The predestination of God is, therefore, quite a different thing from fate. But let us be done with a battle over words. "If," they say, "the necessity of things is fixed by the eternal decree of God, it is useless to teach what the nature of everybody's duty is. For teaching will not alter in the slightest what has been determined already." Yet they ought to ponder once again that teaching has also been ordained by God himself for the purpose of serving his secret purposes. Will not teaching, like an outstretched hand, lead those whom he

has preordained to life by his eternal adoption to the place which he has appointed? For what else is effectual calling but the fulfillment of the election that was previously hidden? He takes the reprobate to task with various rebukes, and, it seems, without any success. But since he renders them inexcusable in this way, teaching appears to have some force in their case also. Foolish men do not perceive how the works of God harmonize with each other in a beautiful order. As a result, they rashly set up a conflict between teaching, which is nothing else but the handmaid of his eternal will, and that will itself.[120]

In this connection Calvin recognizes, and stresses, the importance of, and exhorts proper observance of, "means" and "secondary causes."[121] Although God governs everything, he governs by means. God governs our health and life, but he uses means: our eating and drinking and our working to provide for ourselves. "God's providence does not always meet us in its naked form, but God in a sense clothes with the means employed."[122] The danger is that we lose sight of providence because of the means.

Calvin also defends providence against those who charge that "the plan of God does not stand firm and sure, but is subject to change in response to the disposition of things below" with appeal to passages in Scripture that speak of God's repenting (Gen. 6:6; 1 Sam. 15:11; Jer. 18:8) or of some "abrogations of his decrees" (Jonah 3:4, 10; Isa. 38:1, 5; 2 Kings 20:1, 5; 2 Chron. 32:24).[123] Calvin explains the biblical "repentance" of God as a "mode of speaking that describe[s] God for us in human terms," that is, in anthropomorphisms. In fact, "neither God's plan nor his will is reversed, nor his volition altered; but what he had from eternity foreseen, approved, and decreed, he pursues in uninterrupted tenor, however sudden the variation may appear in men's eyes."[124]

Calvin's defense of God's unchanging plan of providence is timely in the twenty-first century in view of the vicious attack on the doctrine of providence by contemporary proponents of Arminian theology. Developing the fundamental Arminian doctrine of the free will of fallen man to its logical conclusion, these theologians deny that God governs all events in history, or even *knows* all events before they occur. Men are

Creation, Human Nature as Created, and Providence 115

sovereignly free in their decisions and in determining the events that follow from their decisions. God learns about men's decisions after they make them. God can only react to men's actions and then make the best of them.

Defending this view of God's relation to human decisions and action, Clark H. Pinnock charges that the Reformed doctrine of providence is "determinism": "A theological shift is underway among evangelicals as well as other Christians away from determinism as regards the rule and salvation of God and in the direction of an orientation more favorable to a dynamic personal relationship between God, the world, and God's human creatures."[125]

Richard Rice appeals to the statements in Scripture concerning God's repenting in support of the doctrine "that the future is genuinely open to God," that is, unplanned and even unknown on God's part.

> The Bible speaks of God as repenting, as grieving, and as rejoicing. The concept of absolute divine foreknowledge requires us to interpret such descriptions as so many anthropomorphisms and robs them of their evocative power. But on the view that the future is genuinely open to God, statements like these can retain their natural meaning. They indicate that God appreciates and responds to the events in our lives as they happen.[126]

One reflects on what this basically Arminian doctrine of God's relation especially to the sinful decisions and deeds of men would do to such a passage of Scripture as Acts 4:27, 28: "For of a truth against thy holy child Jesus, whom thou hast anointed, both Herod and Pontius Pilate, with the Gentiles and the people of Israel, were gathered together, for to do whatsoever they sovereignly decided to do, things that thou, O Lord, never dreamed of, and in response to which thou hast scrambled, successfully, we hope, in order somehow to have them serve the redemption of the church. And now, O Lord, we, thy church in the world, have our fingers crossed, that the ungodly do not again take thee by surprise, and the next time with a plot against Christ and his church for which thou are not able to come up with a remedy."

Calvin's grand defense of the sovereignty of God in providence refutes these contemporary foes, as effectively as it refuted the foes in Calvin's day. And it exposes the contemporary foes, as it exposed those in Calvin's day, as "madmen" and enemies of the Christian faith, contrary to their claims to be "evangelical Christians."

Benefit of knowing the truth of providence

Calvin proclaims the benefit for believers of the knowledge of the truth of providence. The benefit is threefold: "Gratitude of mind for the favorable outcome of things, patience in adversity, and also incredible freedom from worry about the future all necessarily follow upon this knowledge."[127] What a lovely description of a precious benefit, particularly the phrase, "incredible freedom from worry about the future"!

To Calvin, the benefit to the believer of the knowledge of providence is great, indeed, essential for life. From the knowledge of providence comes "the immeasurable felicity of the godly mind."[128] "The highest blessedness lies in the knowledge of it [providence]."[129] On the other hand, "ignorance of providence [including the "open theism" of the twenty-first century] is the ultimate of all miseries."[130]

Calvin carefully guards against various misunderstandings of the believer's knowledge of providence, which would prevent the believer from profiting from the doctrine as he should. The misunderstandings include supposing that the believer can figure out God's purpose in every event in his life; that providence makes the prudent use of means and of prayer superfluous; and that providence excuses sin.

The doctrine of providence is no less dear to Calvin than the doctrine of predestination. "The principal purpose of Biblical history is to teach that the Lord watches over the ways of the saints with such great diligence that they do not even stumble over a stone."[131]

Such is the benefit of knowing the providence of God that it must be taught in its full truth as extending to all events, including evils and sins.

Calvin condemns those who "find fault that things are put forth publicly [by John Calvin!], which if God had not judged useful for men to know, he would never have bidden his prophets and apostles to teach."[132]

BOOK TWO

The Knowledge of God the Redeemer in Christ,
First Disclosed to the Fathers under the Law,
and Then to Us in the Gospel

CHAPTER 9

The Condition of Fallen Man

Introduction

With the reality of the spiritual condition of fallen man, John Calvin begins book two of the *Institutes of the Christian Religion*. The heading of book two is "The Knowledge of God the Redeemer in Christ, First Disclosed to the Fathers under the Law, and Then to Us in the Gospel." Recalling the opening lines of the *Institutes*, concerning knowledge of God and knowledge of ourselves, Calvin declares that we cannot know God as redeemer if we do not know ourselves as fallen and depraved. The danger, however, is exactly that men know themselves as good, able, and excellent. Calvin refers to this deliberate self-deception as "blind self-love."[1]

Therefore, the subject of the right knowledge of our spiritual condition as fallen is fundamental. Calvin expressly states this with specific reference to the bondage of the will of the fallen sinner: the truth of the bondage of the will and of the depravity of fallen man is "fundamental in religion."[2] Such is the seriousness of the error of knowing oneself as naturally good, able, and excellent, rather than depraved, incapable, and vile, that "any mixture of the power of free will that men strive to mingle with God's grace is nothing but a corruption of grace."[3] Calvin asserts that any notion of good in oneself by nature is from the devil; the notion is fatal.[4] That man has the best knowledge of himself who most thoroughly knows his depravity.

This approach to the treatment of the condition of man by nature is that of the Heidelberg Catechism:

> How many things are necessary for thee to know, that thou in this comfort, mayest live and die happily?
>
> Three things: First, the greatness of my *sin* and *misery*. Second, how I am *redeemed* from all my sins and misery. Third, how I am to be *thankful* to God for such redemption.[5]

The requisite manner of this right self-knowledge, according to Calvin, is the light of "God's truth."[6] "God's truth" is, first, the revelation in Scripture of our good creation in Adam. Only in light of our creation in the beginning as good will we view ourselves as fallen from our former high position.

> God would not have us forget our original nobility, which he had bestowed upon our father Adam... That recognition [of our first condition in Adam], however, far from encouraging pride in us, discourages us and casts us into humility. For what is that origin? It is that from which we have fallen. What is that end of our creation? It is that from which we have been completely estranged, so that sick of our miserable lot we groan, and in groaning we sigh for that lost worthiness.[7]

Denial of God's creation of man as good, therefore, which is the implication of every evolutionary theory of man's origin, theistic as well as atheistic, is necessarily the annulment of man's knowledge of himself as sinful. What the Christian church (to say nothing of the Bible!) has regarded as the sinfulness of man is merely the innate savagery of his animal ancestry, a "congenital weakness."[8] If man has not fallen from the original high estate described in Genesis 1 and 2, there is no original sin. That this is indeed the implication of theistic evolution's account of the origin of man is acknowledged by the Reformed writer Jan Lever and by the evangelical Henri Blocher.[9]

Second, "God's truth," which is necessary for our right knowledge of ourselves, is the divine standard that requires perfection of us. We must examine ourselves "according to the standard of divine judgment."[10]

The purpose of Calvin's admittedly dark analysis of man's spiritual condition—the "Calvinistic" doctrine of total depravity—is to open up the way to belief of the gospel of Jesus Christ, which is the only source and means of the salvation of the sinner. Immediately following the description of man's depravity and hopelessness, Calvin declares, "We must, for this reason, come to Paul's statement: 'Since in the wisdom of God the world did not know God through wisdom, it pleased God through the folly of preaching to save those who believe' [1 Cor. 1:21]."[11] Calvin makes the same observation in his commentary on Romans 5:20:

> Our condemnation is not set before us in the law, that we may abide in it; but that having fully known our misery, we may be led to Christ, who is sent to be a physician to the sick, a deliverer to the captives, a comforter to the afflicted, a defender to the oppressed (Isa. 61:1).[12]

Then occurs a damning indictment of the notion that there can be salvation outside of Christ in the gospel:

> Thus, all the more vile is the stupidity of those persons who open heaven to all the impious and unbelieving without the grace of him whom Scripture commonly teaches to be the only door whereby we enter into salvation.[13]

The reference, no doubt, is to Desiderius Erasmus and Ulrich Zwingli. Today, Calvin's condemnation falls upon multitudes of Protestant theologians.

Original sin

Calvin teaches that all men come into the world depraved of nature. At conception and birth, every human is sinful, is corrupt. Calvin teaches original sin, which he defines thus:

> Original sin, therefore seems to be a hereditary depravity and corruption of our nature, diffused into all parts of the soul, which first makes us liable to God's wrath, then also brings forth in us those works which Scripture calls "works of the flesh" [Gal. 5:19]. And that is properly what Paul often calls sin.[14]

This depravity is not only lack of original righteousness. It is also an active source of all evil, positively: "a burning furnace giv[ing] forth flames and sparks... so fertile and fruitful of every evil that it cannot be idle."[15]

For this corruption of nature with which each man is born without his will, man is guilty before God. The reason is that this is not how God made man. God made man upright and holy. Further, God's standard, by which alone we know our misery, as Calvin has insisted before, requires a sinless, righteous nature.

This depraved nature is inherited from our parents. We are corrupt not only *at* conception and birth, but also *by means of* conception and birth. At this point, Calvin refutes "the profane fiction" of Pelagius:

> That Adam sinned only to his own loss without harming his posterity. Through this subtlety Satan attempted to cover up the disease and thus to render it incurable. But when it was shown by the clear testimony of Scripture that sin was transmitted from the first man to all his posterity [Rom. 5:12], Pelagius quibbled that it was transmitted through imitation, not propagation.[16]

Against the Pelagian heresy, Calvin appeals to Psalm 51:5: "Surely there is no doubt that David confesses himself to have been 'begotten in iniquities, and conceived by his mother in sin.'"[17]

The source and explanation of original sin is the transgression of Adam. In this connection, Calvin proposes a distinctive and intriguing analysis of the basic nature of Adam's sin. The traditional view has been that Adam's sin was primarily pride, attended by ambition. Calvin agrees that pride was the "beginning of all evils" but suggests a "fuller definition." Calvin sees Adam's sin as primarily unfaithfulness, rooted in distrust of God's word. "Hold[ing] God's Word in contempt," Adam "turned aside to falsehood." "Unfaithfulness, then, was the root of the Fall."[18]

This view of the sin of Adam has distinctly covenantal overtones. Indeed, in thus describing Adam's sin as the unfaithfulness of disobedience, Calvin has his eye on Romans 5:12–21. Adam was in covenant with his creator, so that his sin was covenant transgression. Calvin's understanding of Adam's sin also stresses the importance of the word of God, which Adam disobeyed. Calvin's description of the sin suggests that it was idolatrous in that Adam trusted the word of another. According to the Heidelberg Catechism, idolatry is "instead of the one true God who has revealed himself in his Word, or along with the same, to conceive or have something else on which to place our trust."[19]

For Calvin, the transgression of Adam is the cause and source of original sin in all men inasmuch as Adam was the root of the race. Adam's sin ruined us all. "Adam, by sinning, not only took upon himself misfortune and ruin but also plunged our nature into like destruction."[20] The reformer says the same when contending with Pighius' teaching that man has some freedom of nature to do the good. Calvin remarks that this teaching "betrays the fact that he [Pighius] does not hold to the first axiom of our faith, that we and all our power to act well perished in Adam."[21]

Adam's sin ruined the whole human race in this way, that the effect of Adam's deed corrupted his own nature. He then, as the progenitor of the race, passed on this corruption through physical generation. "He infected all his posterity with that corruption into which he had fallen ... Adam so corrupted himself that infection spread from him to all his descendants."[22]

The Belgic Confession uses this language of infection when it describes and defends original sin: "Through the disobedience of Adam, original sin is extended to all mankind; which is a corruption of the whole nature, and an hereditary disease, wherewith infants themselves are infected even in their mother's womb, and which produceth in man all sorts of sin, being in him as a root thereof."[23]

Calvin's doctrine of original sin, therefore, consists of the teaching of original depravity, which depravity is due to Adam's being the root of the race. Reformed theology speaks of this relation of Adam to the race as his "organic headship."

Manifesting his wisdom, Calvin declines to enter into an "anxious discussion" of *how* Adam's sinfulness, especially sinfulness of the soul, can be transmitted to his posterity by physical generation.[24]

The question necessarily comes up, whether there is in Calvin's doctrine of original sin any teaching of original guilt, that is, the liability of the entire race to punishment for Adam's disobedience because of

Adam's being the legal representative, or federal head, of the human race. Original guilt is certainly not Calvin's emphasis in his discussion of original sin. Nor is this clearly affirmed. It certainly is not developed in Calvin.

Yet there are some intimations, admittedly faint, of the doctrine of original guilt. Calvin explains the controversy over original sin among the church fathers from this, that "nothing is farther from the usual view than for all to be made guilty by the guilt of one, and thus for sin to be made common."[25] Contending that it is just that we are condemned for our corrupt nature, Calvin says:

> This is not liability for another's transgression. For, since it is said that we became subject to God's judgment through Adam's sin, we are to understand it not as if we, guiltless and undeserving, bore the guilt of his offense but in the sense that, since we through his transgression have become entangled in the curse, he is said to have made us guilty.[26]

Calvin comes the closest to a clear statement of original guilt in his refutation of an objection against his doctrine of the bondage of the will. The objection is that if the will of man is enslaved to sin by nature, man sins of necessity, but to sin of necessity is not sin. Calvin responds that the sinner's inability to choose the good derives "from the fact that Adam willingly bound himself over to the devil's tyranny... The first man fell away from his Maker." Calvin adds, "If all men are deservedly held guilty of this rebellion, let them not think themselves excused by the very necessity in which they have the more evident cause of their condemnation."[27]

Calvin says something similar in his *Defence of the Secret Providence of God*. He responds to his adversary's attack on reprobation by pointing out that the adversary overlooks the fall of the human race in Adam: "All men," says Calvin, "are hateful to God in fallen Adam."[28] Calvin continues:

> Whence arises this miserable condition of us all, that we are subject not only to temporal evils, but to eternal death? Does it not arise from the solemn fact that, by the Fall and fault of one man, God was pleased to cast us all under the common guilt?[29]

Against the interpretation of Calvin that has him teaching the doctrine of original guilt, albeit in embryonic form, stands Calvin's commentary on Romans 5:12–17. There he explains our relation to Adam in terms of Adam's *extending his corruption* to us, which corruption constitutes our only guilt in the matter of Adam's sin. He explicitly rejects the doctrine of original guilt in the sense of our responsibility for Adam's deed of disobedience:

> There are indeed some who contend, that we are so lost through Adam's sin, as though we perished through no fault of our own, but only, because he had sinned for us. But Paul distinctly affirms, that sin extends to all who suffer its punishment: and this he afterwards more fully declares, when subsequently he assigns a reason why all the posterity of Adam are subject to the dominion of death; and it is even this—because we have all, he says, sinned. But to sin in this case, is to become corrupt and vicious; for the natural depravity which we bring from our mother's womb, though it brings not forth immediately its own fruits, is yet sin before God, and deserves his vengeance: and this is that sin which they call original.[30]

Commenting on verse 17, which compares death's reigning by Adam and our reigning in life by Jesus Christ, Calvin calls attention to a "difference between Christ and Adam":

> By Adam's sin we are not condemned through imputation alone, as though we were punished only for the sin of another; but we suffer his punishment, because we also ourselves are guilty; for as our nature is vitiated in him, it is regarded by God as having committed sin. But through the righteousness of Christ we are restored in a different way to salvation.[31]

For Calvin, our sinning in Adam, as taught in Romans 5:12, is strictly that "we are all imbued with natural corruption, and so are become sinful and wicked."[32] The race becomes guilty for Adam's transgression only by sharing in Adam's depraved nature. Adam sinned. The punishment for Adam was, in part, the immediate corruption of his nature. But this is the nature of all his posterity (Christ excepted). All of

Adam's posterity are held responsible for the corrupted nature. Not sheer legal representation by a covenant head, but involvement in a corporate nature, renders the race guilty before God. Therefore, I am not responsible for Adam's disobedience of eating the forbidden fruit. But I am responsible for the sinful nature with which God punished Adam for his act of disobedience.

Calvin's commentary on "the offence of one" in Romans 5:15 confirms this understanding of Calvin's doctrine of original sin: "[Adam's] sin is the cause of our sin... our sin I call that which is implanted in us, and with which we are born."[33]

Calvin's view of original sin leaves him with a huge problem: *By what right did God inflict the punishment of a corrupt nature on Adam's posterity?* That the corruption of human nature was divine punishment on Adam, Calvin acknowledges. But it was as well punishment of Adam's posterity. This, Calvin does not like to acknowledge. Rather, he likes to regard the depraved nature only as the *guilt* of Adam's posterity. The question that exposes the weakness—*serious* weakness—of Calvin's doctrine here is this: If I am not guilty for Adam's act of disobedience, with what right does God punish me—not *Adam*, but *me*—with a totally depraved nature?

Calvin's explanation of the origin of the sin of the human race also has an important implication for the headship of Adam. Adam was head of the race, to be sure. But for Calvin, his headship consisted only of his depraving the human nature of which all partake. His was not the headship of legal representation. Adam did not stand in such a covenantal relation to all men that, altogether apart from the consequent corrupting of the nature, all are responsible before God for Adam's act of disobedience.

In view of the apostle's comparison between Adam and Christ in Romans 5:12–21 ("as the offence of one... even so by the righteousness of one," v. 18), Calvin's explanation of the headship of Adam would mean that Christ's headship also consists only of his being the source of righteousness to his people by actually infusing it into them. If Adam's headship was not legal representation, neither is Christ's headship legal representation. But this destroys the fundamental gospel-truth of justification as the imputation of Christ's obedience.

Calvin recognizes the danger. Therefore, in his commentary on Romans 5:17, he proposes a "difference between Christ and Adam." "By Adam's sin we are not condemned through imputation alone," but "through the righteousness of Christ we are restored in a different way to salvation."[34] The trouble is that Paul does not teach such a "difference between Christ and Adam." Paul rather declares, "As by the offence of one judgment came upon all men to condemnation; even so by the righteousness of one the free gift came upon all men unto justification of life" (v. 18). If our guilt in Adam is not by imputation of a deed of disobedience, neither is our righteousness in Christ by imputation of a deed of obedience. This is the theology of Rome, dishonoring the God of grace. It is also the heresy that increasingly finds favor with Protestant theologians.

The "difference between Christ and Adam" that Calvin injects into Romans 5:12–21 does not exist. Verse 18 teaches that the transgression of one man—Adam, according to verse 14—was the condemnation of all men. In verse 19, the apostle states that the disobedience of the one man rendered many people sinners. The verb translated "made" by the Authorized Version does not mean "made" in the sense of causing people actually to become sinful. Rather, it means "constituted" in the sense of a legal standing of guilt before God the judge. One could translate: "By one man's disobedience many were *declared* sinners."[35] Even so, the righteousness of one—Jesus Christ—was the justification of all whom he represented, and his obedience constitutes many people righteous.[36]

The comparison between the two covenant heads of the human race in history consists exactly of this, that both are legal representatives of others, Adam of the entire human race, Christ only excepted, and Christ of the new human race of the elect church. Because Adam was covenant (federal) head of the race, his act of disobedience was imputed to the race as their guilt. Because Christ is covenant (federal) head of the elect church, his obedience is imputed to the church as our righteousness.

The Canons of Dordt go beyond Calvin in formulating the doctrine of original sin. Like Calvin, the Canons teach that the posterity of Adam have "derived corruption from their original parent . . . by the propagation of a vicious nature."[37] Unlike Calvin, the Canons, as originally adopted by the Synod of Dordt, add that all the posterity of

Adam have this corrupt nature "in consequence of a just judgment of God."[38] The depravity of nature of the human race is not simply our guilt. It is also divine punishment upon us all for our guilt in the disobedience of Adam in the garden.

In his doctrine of original sin, Calvin tells us that he is opposing three main errors. The first is men's natural approval of themselves. The second error is Pelagianism. The third is the error of ascribing man's natural corruption to God himself, as though he created man so. Of course, Calvin is not contending with the error of theistic evolution. Nevertheless, the third error that Calvin opposes has a modern expression in this theory of origins. If man has descended from the primates, even though this has happened under God's superintending providence, man is "wicked" and subject to death from the very beginning of his existence. Since his origin as evil and subject to death is God's own "creation" of him in this way, God himself is responsible for man's evil condition. Following Calvin, the Heidelberg Catechism in Question and Answer 6 condemns the theory of theistic evolution, which would not appear as a threat to the Reformed churches until hundreds of years after the writing of the catechism:

> Did God create man thus wicked and perverse?
> No; but God created man good, and after his own image—that is, in righteousness and true holiness; that he might rightly know God his Creator, heartily love him, and live with him in eternal blessedness, to praise and glorify him.[39]

Having established original depravity, Calvin concerns himself with the extent of this depravity.

Total depravity

Calvin teaches that, apart from the regenerating grace of Christ, the depravity of fallen man is total. The whole nature is completely corrupted by the infection of sin, so that there is in fallen man no capability of doing any good and so that he performs what is evil. It is "indisputable that free will [which Calvin accepts here for the sake of argument, meaning by "free will" only a will that is not under "compulsion"] is not sufficient to enable man to do good works, unless he be helped by grace, indeed by special grace, which only the elect receive through regeneration."[40] Calvin goes on to deny the doctrine that man "still has some power, though meager and weak," which "with the help of grace also does its part."[41] This is the context in which occurs the line that is well-known in the controversy over the "well-meant offer of the gospel": "For I do not tarry over those fanatics who babble that grace is equally and indiscriminately distributed."[42] Henry Beveridge translates this line differently: "For I stay not to consider the extravagance of those who say that grace is offered equally and promiscuously to all."[43]

Summing up his doctrine at the conclusion of the treatment of the depravity of man, Calvin says this:

> Therefore let us hold this as an undoubted truth which no siege engines can shake: the mind of man has been so completely estranged from God's righteousness that it conceives, desires, and undertakes, only that which is impious, perverted, foul, impure, and infamous. The heart is so steeped in the poison of sin, that it can breathe out nothing but a loathsome stench. But if some men occasionally make a show of good, their minds nevertheless ever remain enveloped in hypocrisy and deceitful craft, and their hearts bound by inner perversity.[44]

This statement of man's total depravity fills out the terse judgment that Calvin had passed upon man's fallen nature at the outset of his treatment: "The whole man is of himself nothing but concupiscence."[45]

Another way for Calvin to express man's total depravity is to assert that fallen man has lost the image of God in which he was created. Calvin holds that the image is "obliterated."[46] Mere "traces" remain, which distinguish man from the brutes.[47] It is doubtful that any clearer, sharper statement of the loss of the image can be found in the writings of Calvin than that in the first chapter of the original, 1536 edition of the *Institutes*. This statement also reveals Calvin's view of the image itself in which Adam was created, as well as Calvin's assessment of the apparent good that is done by unregenerated men and women.

In order for us to come to a sure knowledge of ourselves, we must first grasp the fact that Adam, parent of us all, was created in the image and likeness of God [Gen. 1:26, 27]. That is, he was endowed with wisdom, righteousness, holiness, and was so clinging by these gifts of grace to God that he could have lived forever in Him, if he had stood fast in the uprightness God had given him. But when Adam slipped into sin, this image and likeness of God was cancelled and effaced, that is, he lost all the benefits of divine grace, by which he could have been led back into the way of life [Gen. 3]. Moreover, he was far removed from God and became a complete stranger. From this it follows that man was stripped and deprived of all wisdom, righteousness, power, life, which—as has already been said—could be held only in God. As a consequence, nothing was left to him save ignorance, iniquity, impotence, death, and judgment [Rom. 5:12–21]. These are indeed the "fruits of sin" [Gal. 5:19–21]. This calamity fell not only upon Adam himself, but also flowed down into us, who are his seed and offspring. Consequently, all of us born of Adam are ignorant and bereft of God, perverse, corrupt, and lacking every good. Here is a heart especially inclined to all sorts of evil, stuffed with depraved desires, addicted to them, and obstinate toward God [Jer. 17:9]. But if we outwardly display anything good, still the mind stays in its inner state of filth and crooked perversity. The prime matter or rather the matter of concern for all rests in the judgment of God, who judges not according to appearance, nor highly esteems outward splendor, but gazes upon the secrets of the heart [1 Sam. 16:7; Jer. 17:10]. Therefore, however much of a dazzling appearance of holiness man may have on his own, it is nothing but hypocrisy and even an abomination in God's sight, since the thoughts of the mind, ever depraved and corrupted, lurk beneath.[48]

For Calvin, the image of God in which Adam was created was the spiritual perfections that qualified and adorned his whole nature. By his transgression, Adam lost the image entirely. Indeed, the creator "stripped" Adam of the image. Nothing of it remains, except "traces." These "traces" are not any part of the content of the image itself, some residue of "goodness." Rather, they are merely evidences that man once had the image—an aggravation of man's misery. The "traces" amount to man's humanity, which he retained, and could not but retain, after the fall. The "traces" consist of man's body with its natural skills, his soul with its thinking and willing, and his enduring conscious relation to God, now a relation on man's part of hostility and dread.

Because of the loss of the image, whatever appearance of goodness fallen man displays is appearance only. Even the occasional "dazzling" appearance of goodness is never genuine. It is "hypocrisy." Especially the "dazzling" appearance of holiness, which greatly impresses theologians and church synods so that they pronounce it truly good by virtue of natural theology or common grace, is abomination. For it pretends to be real goodness, when in fact the heart of the pretender is far from God. And, unlike the theologians and synods, "God... gazes upon the secrets of the heart."

Bondage of the will

Calvin maintains total depravity by contending for the bondage of the human will. Much of the section on man's original sin is devoted to the bondage of the will. Then as now, denial of man's depravity takes the form of affirming free will. In addition to the important treatment of the bondage of the will in the *Institutes*, in 1543 Calvin wrote *The Bondage and Liberation of the Will*, a treatise on the subject, as a response to the Dutch Roman Catholic theologian Albertus Pighius, who was defending free will as the fundamental teaching of the Roman Catholic gospel.

In developing the truth of the bondage of the will, Calvin shows himself a good teacher by distinguishing carefully. He notes, and insists on, the importance of maintaining the distinction between *compulsion* and *necessity* regarding a denial of the freedom of the will. The will of the sinner does not choose evil under compulsion, that is, against its own inclination. On the contrary, the will of the sinner chooses evil willingly. But it does choose evil necessarily, inasmuch as it is under the ruling power of sin in the nature of man. The will of the unregenerated sinner is like a horse that is ridden by Satan. It is controlled by Satan.[49]

According to Calvin the will is enslaved, is in bondage to sin: "Because of the bondage of sin by which the will is held bound, it cannot move toward good, much less apply itself thereto."[50] Calvin defines the bound will as "one which because of its corruptness is held captive under the authority of evil desires, so that it can choose nothing but evil, even if it does so of its own accord and gladly, without being driven by any external impulse."[51]

With the bondage of the will, Calvin teaches the corruption also of man's reason, which logically precedes the activity of the will, so that the mind cannot bring the good, as good, to the will's attention.

The specific inability of man by virtue of his enslaved will is his incapability to come to Christ, to choose salvation when it is presented in the gospel, or to believe.

Calvin's demonstration and proof of the bondage of the will in the *Institutes* are overwhelming. He adduces many texts, including John 3:6, Romans 3, Romans 8, Ephesians 4:22–32, and Jeremiah 7:9.

Of decisive importance for the controversy over the bondage of the will is Calvin's rejection of the appeal by the defenders of a free will to Romans 7. The testimony of Romans 7:19, "The good that I would I do not: but the evil which I would not, that I do," says Calvin rightly, is that of a "regenerated" person.[52] The importance of the right interpretation of Romans 7 for the truth of the bondage of the will and, therefore, for the gospel of salvation by grace alone cannot be stressed too strongly. It was not accidental that James Arminius first disclosed his heresy in his exposition of Romans 7. Arminius taught that verses 13–25 describe the spiritual condition of the unregenerated man. Unregenerated men therefore have a free will, a will that can choose and does choose the good. The doctrine of free will is fundamental to the Arminian heresy. If an unregenerated man is speaking in the chapter, as a number of evangelical and Reformed theologians are contending today, fallen man has a free will, the heresy of Pelagius and Arminius is vindicated, and the gospel of grace is overthrown.[53]

Certain of Calvin's arguments on behalf of the bondage of the will are worthy of note. If God in conversion must give us a heart of flesh, the stony heart was incapable of willing the good (Ezek. 36). God works in us to will (Phil. 2:13). Good willing arises from faith, and faith is the gift of God (Eph. 2:8). God works all in all in us (1 Cor. 12:6).

Free will is the exclusive "privilege of the elect."

> It is obviously the privilege of the elect that, regenerated through the Spirit of God, they are moved and governed by his leading. For this reason, Augustine justly derides those who claim for themselves any part of the act of willing, just as he reprehends others who think that what is the special testimony of free election is indiscriminately given to all. "Nature," he says, "is common to all, not grace." The view that what God bestows upon whomever he wills is generally extended to all, Augustine calls a brittle glasslike subtlety of wit, which glitters with mere vanity. Elsewhere he says: "How have you come? By believing. Fear lest while you are claiming for yourself that you have found the just way, you perish from the just way. I have come, you say, of my own free choice; I have come of my own will. Why are you puffed up? Do you wish to know that this also has been given you? Hear him calling, 'No one comes to me unless my Father draws him' [John 6:44]." Any one may incontrovertibly conclude from John's words that the hearts of the pious are so effectively governed by God that they follow Him with unwavering intention. "No one begotten of God can sin," he says, "for God's seed abides in him" [1 John 3:9]. For the intermediate movement the Sophists dream up, which men are free either to accept or refuse, we see obviously excluded when it is asserted that constancy is efficacious for perseverance.[54]

The end of this lengthy quotation has Calvin insisting that the grace of God that gives freedom of the will to the elect is efficacious. It does not merely make coming to Christ possible, but effectually draws to Christ. With this insistence, Calvin had begun section ten:

> He does not move the will in such a manner as has been taught and believed for many ages—that it is afterward in our choice either to obey or resist the motion—but by disposing it efficaciously. Therefore, one must deny that oft-repeated statement of Chrysostom: "Whom he draws he draws willing."[55]

Remnants of good in fallen man

We are compelled to recognize that, however inconsistently, unclearly, and relatively infrequently, Calvin does teach some remnants of good in fallen man by virtue of what he calls a "general grace" of God. There are in fallen men, writes Calvin, certain gifts and abilities regarding earthly life, including "civic fair dealing and order"[56] and "the arts, both liberal and manual," that are to be ascribed to "the peculiar grace of God,"[57] or as Calvin calls it elsewhere, "the general grace of God," "God's kindness," and "God's special grace."[58]

Also, there is a certain "purity" and "virtue" in some unbelievers that is due to "God's grace," which does not "cleanse" corrupt human nature but "restrain[s] it inwardly."[59]

These are the materials in Calvin that Abraham Kuyper and Herman Bavinck seized in order to construct their far more elaborate and optimistic theory of a common grace of God that must produce a good culture and even Christianize society.[60]

Calvin's "general grace" is not a grace that is saving, or that desires to save, or that enables one to come to Christ for salvation. Calvin definitely limits his general grace to earthly things and to earthly life.

Significantly, the biblical Calvin offers no proof from Scripture for his notion of a general grace of God to the reprobate ungodly.

Often, in the very same passages that teach this general grace there are expressions indicating that the phenomena that Calvin describes in terms of general grace should rather be described in terms of God's providence. Indeed, Calvin himself suggests that, although he speaks of grace, he has providence in mind. This is true of that passage in the *Institutes* that is the most troublesome. Calvin is impressed by "persons who, guided by nature, have striven toward virtue throughout life." These persons show "some purity in their nature."[61] Seemingly, they give the lie to the Bible's and Calvin's doctrine of total depravity. Calvin then accounts for what he judges to be the honorable conduct of these unregenerated persons:

> But here it ought to occur to us that amid this corruption of nature there is some place for God's grace; not such grace as to cleanse it, but to restrain it inwardly. For if the Lord gave loose rein to the mind of each man to run riot in his lusts, there would doubtless be no one who would not show that, in fact, every evil thing for which Paul condemns all nature is most truly to be met in himself.[62]

Having listed the sins that Romans 3:10–18 finds in the unregenerated, Calvin continues:

> If every soul is subject to such abominations as the apostle boldly declares, we surely see what would happen if the Lord were to permit human lust to wander according to its own inclination. No mad beast would rage as unrestrainedly; no river, however swift and violent, burst so madly into flood. In his elect the Lord cures these diseases in a way that we shall soon explain. Others he merely restrains by throwing a bridle over them only that they may not break loose, inasmuch as he foresees their control to be expedient to preserve all that is.[63]

By mentioning a "bridle," Calvin already goes in the direction of explaining his restraining "grace" as providence. That, in reality, he has providence in mind as the power by which God restrains sinners and controls the power of sin is made explicit in the concluding sentence of the paragraph: "Thus God *by his providence* bridles perversity of nature, that it may not break forth into action; but he does not purge it within."[64]

This having been said in mitigation of Calvin's doctrine of a general grace of God upon and in the unregenerated, we must disagree with Calvin on this matter. The natural gifts of the ungodly are to be explained from man's remaining human after the fall and from the providential operations and gifts of the Spirit that uphold and govern natural life. The natural gifts are not to be explained from any grace of God.

Calvin's theorizing about a restraining grace that accounts for good deeds by the noble heathen is unbiblical and contrary to Calvin's own theology. Calvin has just appealed to God's searing judgment upon all mankind by nature in Roman 3:10–18. Then, with his eye on Camillus and other noble pagans, Calvin asserts a general, restraining grace and says regarding the Romans 3 passage, "We surely see what *would* happen *if* the Lord were to permit human lust to wander according to its own inclination."[65]

But Romans 3:10–18 does not teach what *would* happen, apart from *general, restraining grace*. Romans 3:10–18 teaches what *does* happen, what is true of all, apart from *the gospel* and its *regenerating grace*.

Calvin has forgotten what he had written on good works against Pighius: "Since the worth of good works depends not on the act itself but on perfect love for God, a work will not be righteous and pure unless it proceeds from a perfect love for God."[66]

Enthusiastically picking up on Calvin's erroneous teaching of a general grace of God for the reprobate ungodly, some in the later Reformed tradition have developed a theory of common grace that effectively overthrows the biblical doctrine of total depravity that Calvin so powerfully taught and so vehemently defended. By virtue of common grace, fallen man retains much good. In many Reformed churches today, total depravity, although acknowledged, is defined as man's being corrupt in every part of his being. Common grace has forged a doctrine of partial depravity. This is, in fact, the rejection of total depravity by those who claim to confess it.

Reformed theologian Anthony Hoekema maintains that what Reformed theology has traditionally called "total depravity" means only that "the corruption of original sin extends to every aspect of human nature: to one's reason and will as well as to one's appetites and impulses." It "does not mean that the unregenerate person by nature is unable to do good in any sense of the word. Because of God's common grace...the development of sin in history and society is restrained. The unregenerate person can still do certain kinds of good and can exercise certain kinds of virtue." Recognizing that it is a mistake, if not absurd, to call a depravity that is merely partial "total," Hoekema proposes a new adjective to describe the depravity of the unregenerated man: "pervasive."[67] Although Hoekema does not notice, this results in a change in the historic acronym describing the Reformed confession of the doctrines of grace: PULIP. Hoekema's doctrine, which is probably the prevailing opinion in Reformed circles today, is open rejection of the confessionally Reformed doctrine of man's total, that is, complete, depravity by nature. So open a rejection is it that this new doctrine changes the name of the traditional, confessional doctrine. It is a doctrine of *partial* depravity. And common grace is the cause.

The enemies of Calvinism see through this posturing. Clark Pinnock has written:

> The depth of human sinfulness was another matter that soon demanded my attention. Calvinists, like Augustine himself, if the reader will excuse the anachronism, wanting to leave no room at all to permit any recognition of human freedom in the salvation event, so defined human depravity as total that it would be impossible to imagine any sinner calling upon God to save him. Thus they prevented anyone from thinking about salvation in the Arminian way. Leaving aside the fact that Augustinians themselves often and suspiciously qualify their notion of "total" depravity very considerably and invent the notion of common grace to tone it down, I knew I had to consider how to understand the free will of the sinner in relation to God.[68]

Pinnock points out what is at stake in "toning down" the doctrine of total depravity.

The Reformed churches must maintain, or recover, Calvin's doctrine that fallen human nature is nothing but concupiscence and that the heart of the natural man breathes forth "nothing but a loathsome stench."[69] This humbles the sinner. This magnifies the grace of God in the salvation of the elect sinner. And this, under the blessing of the Spirit of Christ, opens the way to faith's seeking the righteousness of God in the cross of Jesus Christ alone.

CHAPTER 10

The Person and Work of Jesus Christ

Introduction

From the "undoubted truth" about fallen man, "which no siege engines can shake,"[1] namely his total depravity, it follows that "fallen man ought to seek redemption in Christ." This is Calvin's own heading of the chapter in which he begins his treatment of the person and work of the redeemer, Jesus Christ.[2]

Strikingly, Calvin introduces the redeemer in these words: "God ... appeared as Redeemer in the person of his only-begotten Son."[3] The saving knowledge of Jesus Christ, therefore, is in fact knowledge of God the Son.

This identification of the redeemer indicates several truths. First, it indicates the trinitarian structure of the *Institutes*. Book two of the *Institutes*, of which Calvin's doctrine of Christ is the main part, treats the second person of the Holy Trinity. Second, it indicates the God-centered nature of Calvin's theology, that is, of the Reformed faith. Third, it indicates that Calvin's doctrine of the person of Christ is that of the Nicene Creed (AD 325/381) and of the Creed of Chalcedon (AD 451).

The only savior

With appeal to such texts as John 10:9, "I am the door: by me if any man enter in, he shall be saved," Calvin begins his doctrine of Christ by establishing that Jesus Christ is the only savior. Apart from faith in him, no one can be saved.

The teaching of those "who open heaven to all the impious and unbelieving without the grace of him whom Scripture commonly teaches to be the only door whereby we enter into salvation" is "vile ... stupidity."[4] Very likely, Calvin has Erasmus and Zwingli in mind, both of whom taught the salvation of the nobler heathen.

Calvin condemns "all pagan religions as false." "No worship," Calvin asserts, "has ever pleased God except that which looked to Christ."[5] Calvin's judgment of the religion of the "Turks," that is, Islam, is of contemporary interest: "The Turks, although they proclaim at the top of their lungs that the Creator of heaven and earth is God, still, while repudiating Christ, substitute an idol in place of the true God."[6]

The reason pagans cannot be saved and are unable to worship God rightly is that they have no knowledge of God as loving Father from creation: "We cannot by contemplating the universe infer that he is Father."[7] The cause of this ignorance is threefold. First, after man's fall, creation confronts us with "God's curse." Second, sin blinds our minds in that we do not even "perceive what is true" in creation.[8] Third, creation does not reveal the "Mediator" by whom alone it is possible "truly to taste God's mercy."[9]

Knowledge of the mediator and redeemer, upon which salvation and right worship depend, is possible only from "the preaching of the cross." Calvin quotes 1 Corinthians 1:21: "Since in the wisdom of God the world did not know God through wisdom, it pleased God through the folly of preaching to save those who believe."[10] It is noteworthy that Calvin refers not to Scripture, but to the preaching of the gospel. This expresses the Reformation's and Scripture's high view of the office of the ministry of the word.

Of particular concern to Calvin is the truth that Christ was the only way to the Father for the Jews under the old covenant. From the outset of his explanation of the doctrine of Christ, Calvin insists on the unity of the old and new covenants and the essential oneness of Israel and the New Testament church. Old Testament Israel was "the church." The unity of the covenants and the oneness of the two peoples is Jesus Christ himself. "The blessed and happy state of the church always had its foundations in the person of Christ."[11] Although Calvin will return to the relation of the old and new covenants later in book two, where he will demonstrate their essential oneness, in his brief preliminary statement he makes plain that the issue between the Reformed faith, indeed the Protestantism of the Reformation (which regards Israel and church as one covenant people), and dispensationalism (which regards the two peoples and covenants as essentially different) is nothing less than the preeminence and oneness of Jesus Christ himself.

In this connection, Calvin describes the covenant people of God in the time of the old covenant as those included in Jesus Christ, who is the seed of Abraham and the head of the covenant. Calvin explicitly appeals to Galatians 3:16: "And to thy seed, which is Christ." In support of his contention "that not all who sprang from Abraham according to the flesh were reckoned among his offspring," Calvin refers to Romans 9:10–13, God's election of Jacob and reprobation of Esau.[12]

That the godly under the old covenant knew that "the original adoption of the chosen people depended upon the Mediator's grace" is evident from a text such as Psalm 80:17: "Let thy hand be upon the man of thy right hand, upon the son of man whom thou madest strong for thyself."[13]

"Under the law Christ was always set before the holy fathers as the end to which they should direct their faith."[14]

Christ and the law

Calvin's full, thorough treatment of the law of God is subsumed under the knowledge of God in Jesus Christ. The law is strictly subservient to God's purpose of the redemption of the elect church in Jesus Christ. Thus, Calvin and the genuine Calvinism that followed him ward off both of the heresies that always threaten the gospel: works-righteousness, which suspends salvation on the sinner's obedience to law, and antinomianism, which releases the justified sinner from the obligation to obey the law (as the expression of Spirit-worked gratitude). For Calvin and Calvinism, with regard to the elect believer law is an aspect of gospel.

Deliberately, Calvin begins his explanation of the law by alluding to Galatians 3:16, 17: "The law was added about four hundred years after the death of Abraham."[15] The law was given by God to serve the gracious promise of the covenant and to send the chosen people to Christ. Calvin tells us that by "law," verse 17 has in mind the entire "form of religion" revealed by God through Moses, not only the ten commandments. "And Moses was not made a lawgiver to wipe out the blessing promised to the race of Abraham."[16]

So much is it true that Christ is the end of the law that if the ceremonies and precepts of the law are separated from Christ, their end, they are mere "vanity."[17] Calvin specifies the sacrifices of the old covenant.

The ten commandments also end in Christ. The believer is to view them as fulfilled by Christ and as having their demanded righteousness realized in the believer's life by imputation and regeneration. "Righteousness is taught in vain by the commandments until Christ confers it by free imputation and by the Spirit of regeneration."[18]

Regarding Paul's contrasting law and gospel as two opposite principles, Calvin's explanation is that this is due to "perverse teachers who pretended that we merit righteousness by the works of the law."[19] When Paul contrasts law and gospel, he is taking "the bare law in a narrow sense."[20] In fact, law in its right, God-intended sense is not opposed to grace. Law and gospel are opposed only when law is erroneously construed by heretics as a way of salvation for sinners. Calvin refers to the error of teaching that sinners "merit" righteousness by their obedience to the law. Included as well are the error of teaching that sinners accomplish their own salvation by obedience to the law and the error of teaching that one's salvation depends upon his obedience to the law. The law does not, and cannot, save. So far from saving sinners, the moral law of the ten commandments exposes men's guilt, convincing them "of their own condemnation."[21]

The law does, indeed, promise eternal life to those who obey it. But the obedience demanded by the law is "complete obedience," which no one is able to render.[22] "Observance of the law is impossible."[23] That Calvin applies this "impossibility" to believers is evident from the fact that Calvin bases his indictment on Romans 7:24, "O wretched man that I am," which Calvin rightly understands as the confession of the believing child of God. Echoing the apostle in Romans 8:3, Calvin speaks of "the feebleness of the law."[24]

In one respect the explanation of the impossibility of salvation by the law is the sinful nature that remains in the regenerated child of God. Calvin calls this corrupt nature with its sinful thoughts, desires, and passions "concupiscence." Calvin appeals, among other texts, to Psalm 143:2, which Calvin renders as "Every man living will be unrighteous before thee." The reformer appeals as well to the experience of every one of us: "Who will contradict this [the fact of concupiscence]?"[25]

But then Calvin goes down to bedrock in his explanation of the impossibility of salvation by the law. "I call 'impossible'... what God's ordination and decree prevents from ever being."[26] Calvin does not here identify "ordination and decree," but there can be no doubt that he refers to God's eternal decree that salvation shall be by faith alone in Jesus Christ, so that salvation may be of grace alone, to the glory of God alone.

Here is wisdom and finality. In the never-ending controversy between law (as "bare law in a narrow sense") and gospel, against heretical teachers of righteousness and salvation by the law of every subtle shade and stripe, let the defender of salvation by grace alone confess, "God has ordained and decreed salvation by grace alone." End of debate!

Having established that the purpose of the law is Christ, Calvin proposes three uses of the "moral law," that is, the ten commandments.

The first use is to show man his unrighteousness: "It warns, informs, convicts, and lastly condemns, every man of his own unrighteousness."[27] Especially the tenth commandment, the prohibition of sinful desire, functions to discover to the sinner that he is "teeming with a multitude of vices."[28] In this respect, "the law is like a mirror."[29] This use of the law functions in the interests of grace. "Thereby the grace of God, which nourishes us without the support of the law, becomes sweeter."[30] Calvin appeals to Romans 3:19 and Romans 11:32. The law brings us to Christ. "In Christ his [God's] face shines, full of grace and gentleness, even upon us poor and unworthy sinners."[31] This is the first use of the law for "the children of God."[32] "This first function of the law is exercised also in the reprobate."[33] Rather than flee to Christ, they are "struck dumb by the first terror and lie in despair."[34]

The second use of the law is the restraint of sinners by fear of punishment. Reformed theology commonly speaks of this use of the law as the maintenance of order in society. Calvin refers to a "constrained and forced righteousness... necessary for the public community of men."[35]

Because the popular, modern theory of common grace misstates this use of the law as an inner working of the Holy Spirit in unregenerated persons, delivering them from total depravity and making them somewhat good, Calvin's terminology is important: "by fear of punishment to restrain certain men."[36] Against the common grace philosophy of Abraham Kuyper, Herman Bavinck, and their contemporary disciples, Calvin adds, "not because their inner mind is stirred or affected, but because, being bridled... they keep their hands from outward activity, and hold inside the depravity that otherwise they would wantonly have indulged."[37] Calvin appeals to 1 Timothy 1:9, 10.

There is special application of this use of the law, Calvin thinks, to elect children of God prior to their regeneration: "The bridle of the law restrained them in some fear and reverence toward God until, regenerated by the Spirit, they began wholeheartedly to love him."[38]

The third use of the law is, for Calvin, the "principal use."[39] This is the use of the law by the Spirit regarding the believer's life of sanctification. The use of the law in sanctification is twofold. The law gives the holy child of God more thorough instruction in God's will for him. Also, the law rouses the child of God, who does aspire to do God's will but who is hindered by his "listless flesh," to more energetic obedience. Regarding the latter, Calvin uses the example of a whip on the back of "an idle and balky ass."[40]

Calvin sums up the third use of the law this way: "[a] rule to live rightly and justly."[41] Calvin adduces Psalms 19 and 119 as teaching the third use of the law.[42] Even with regard to its important third use, the law functions, and is to be used, in such a way that in it the believer "apprehend[s] the Mediator, without whom there is no delight or sweetness."[43] What this means is that the believer is not to lay hold exclusively upon the precept, for example, "Thou shalt have no other gods before me." But he is also to lay hold upon "the accompanying promise of grace."[44] Calvin does not further explain. But "the promise of grace" in this context can only consist of the promise that, with regard to righteousness before God the judge, God will impute to the believer the perfect obedience of Christ to the first commandment in the believer's stead; of the promise that God will forgive all the believer's imperfections in obeying the first commandment; of the promise that God will work in the believer by the Spirit of Christ the keeping of the first commandment; and of the promise that God will accept the imperfect obedience of the believer for Christ's sake. This accompanying promise alone "sweetens" the law in its third use. Otherwise, even regarding the third use the law is "bitter."[45]

The pastoral Calvin encourages believers who are tempted to be discouraged by their imperfect obedience. "The law is not now acting toward us as a rigorous enforcement officer." Rather, exhorting us to perfection, the law holds before us "the goal toward which throughout life we are to strive."[46]

One who regards the third use of the law as the main one is the sworn foe of antinomianism. Antinomianism is the false doctrine that denies that the law is, and must be, the rule of the Christian's holy life. In Calvin's words, it is the teaching that "bid[s] farewell to the two Tables of the Law." Calvin condemns the heresy: "Banish this wicked thought from our minds!"[47]

The abrogation of the law taught by such passages as Romans 7:6, "But now we are delivered from the law," refers to the law's "power to bind [believers'] consciences with a curse."[48] The law continues to have "power to exhort believers."[49] "Through Christ the teaching of the law remains inviolable."[50] Thus, the law "forms us and prepares us for every good work," as the apostle teaches in 2 Timothy 3:16, 17.[51]

Calvin is a theologian of holiness, and he insists on the law's fundamental function in Christ's saving work of making his people holy.

In contrast to the moral law, the ceremonial laws of the old covenant have been abrogated with regard to their use. Christ has abolished them so that believers no longer observe them, indeed, *may not* observe them. Still, the believer has the "effect" of the ceremonies in Christ, who is their "substance," as the apostle teaches in Colossians 2:17.[52]

This penetrating insight of Calvin into the meaning of the ceremonies of the old covenant, and by implication the relation of the old and new covenant, the Belgic Confession has made authoritative for Reformed churches:

> We believe that the ceremonies and figures of the law ceased at the coming of Christ, and that all the shadows are accomplished; so that the use of them must be abolished among

Christians: yet the truth and substance of them remain with us in Jesus Christ, in whom they have their completion. In the mean time we still use the testimonies taken out of the law and the prophets, to confirm us in the doctrine of the gospel, and to regulate our life in all honesty to the glory of God, according to his will."[53]

Calvin is now ready to explain the ten commandments—the endurring moral law of God—in detail. Before he gives this explanation, however, he makes several observations of a general nature concerning the moral law that will promote the believer's understanding of and obedience to the law.

First, Calvin relates the moral law to the "inward law, which . . . [is] written, even engraved upon the hearts of all."[54] By this "inward law," Calvin refers to Romans 2:15, which, in fact, does not teach that the *law* is written on men's hearts (the writing of the law on one's heart is the covenant blessing of salvation, according to Jeremiah 31:33), but that "the work of the law" is written on the hearts of all men. What Calvin calls the "inward law" expresses itself as man's conscience. The conscience witnesses to man what he "owe[s] God" and the "difference between good and evil."[55] This inward law is "natural law." Because "natural law" is obscure and because sinful men are rebellious, "the Lord has provided us with a written law to give us a clearer witness."[56]

Second, the law of the ten commandments confronts us with God's rights toward us as our Father and creator, and with our corresponding obligation. Our inability to perform our duty is no excuse for our failure, for our inability is our own fault. Calvin refers to the guilt of the human race for the disobedience of Adam, which Calvin has taught earlier.

The result in us is the law's humbling of us in the knowledge that we do not conform to the law's righteousness. Indeed, we are convicted that our powers to fulfill the law are "utterly nonexistent."[57] Then enters in the reality of "God's judgment" upon the disobedient—"the dread of death," "the awareness of eternal death."[58] In this way, the goal of the law with us is reached: each of us "betakes himself to God's mercy alone, as the only haven of safety."[59]

It is evident that Calvin sets forth the right understanding of the ten commandments by the regenerated child of God. It is also evident that Calvin sees the two great functions of the moral law—teaching the regenerated believer his guilt and guiding his holy life—as operating together throughout the life of the Christian. Having brought us to Christ for mercy, by the law God "imbue[s] our hearts with love of righteousness and with hatred of wickedness," so that we will obey the law. To this end, as stronger motivations, God has added "promises and threats."[60]

Third, Calvin warns sharply against a besetting sin of religious people: adding works of their own devising to the works required by the law. Calvin speaks of "the playfulness of the human mind... to dream up various rites."[61] "Playfulness," however, does not indicate that the evil is insignificant. "Any zeal for good works that wanders outside God's law is an intolerable profanation of divine and true righteousness."[62] Deuteronomy 12:32, which Calvin quotes, warns that adding to God's law is as wicked as taking from it.

There can be no doubt that Calvin has the Roman Catholic Church in mind. Rome bound, and still today binds, the consciences of its members with countless precepts that are neither expressed nor implied by the ten commandments. But Calvin deliberately does not name Rome. The evil is a temptation to all. Calvin's abrupt question is apt: "What about us?"[63]

The ten commandments are "the rule of perfect righteousness."[64]

Concerning the nature of the ten commandments, it is necessary to view them, and explain them in preaching, as demanding "inward and spiritual righteousness."[65] By no means are they satisfied with outward acts. The reason, says Calvin, is that God is "a spiritual lawgiver."[66] Calvin quotes, or refers to, Romans 7:14, Matthew 5, and 1 John 3:15.

It also belongs to the nature of the law that there is more, far more, to each commandment "than is expressed in words."[67] Calvin explains how the expositor of the law is to derive the full range of the "Lawgiver's pure and authentic meaning."[68] It is especially important to realize that a prohibition includes commanding the opposite virtue. That is, forbidding murder includes commanding that we seek the neighbor's welfare. In addition, Calvin calls attention to the fact that the commandments condemn various evils by means of "the most frightful and wicked element in every kind of transgression."[69] The necessity of this tactic is our insensitivity to sin. Only when they are included in the category of murder do such sins as anger and hatred seem grave to us.

No explanation of the ten commandments can ignore that God gave them on two tables of stone. For Calvin, the meaning is that the law, containing "the whole of righteousness," is "divided ... into two parts." The first part, or table, contains "those duties of religion which particularly concern the worship of his [God's] majesty; the second ... the duties of love that have to do with men."[70] Immediately, Calvin gives an impassioned, eloquent account of the primacy of the first table. "The worship of God [is] the beginning and foundation of righteousness." Therefore, "it is vain to cry up righteousness without religion."[71] Such is the "vanity" of all deeds of purported love for the neighbor apart from pure worship and sound doctrine that "when [the worship of God] is removed, whatever equity, continence, or temperance men practice among themselves is in God's sight empty and worthless."[72]

Ignoring this dependence of the second table upon the first, theological modernism's zeal for "social justice" is rendered "empty and worthless."

How the proponents of the theory of common grace, claiming to be Calvinists, can ascribe truly good works in the realm of society, that is, among men mutually, to unregenerated persons is bewildering. Surely, unregenerated persons do not worship God, and according to Calvin, whatever is done apart from the pure worship of God is "empty and worthless."

Calvin returns to the important relation of the first and second tables of the law after he has given his detailed explanation of each of the commandments. He repeats his assertion that obedience to the second table depends on "fear and reverence toward God as its foundation."[73]

The reason that Christ and the apostles often referred only to the second table, as, for example, in Matthew 19:16–19, is not that the second table is more important than the first, much less that obedience to the second table is possible apart from obedience to the first table. Rather, by obedience to the second table one "prove[s] himself righteous,"[74] that is, love for God, which is primary, shows itself by deeds of love to the neighbor. In this connection Calvin makes the striking observation that, whereas our obedience to the first table does not benefit God (who is infinitely blessed in himself), by our obedience to the second table we do actually benefit the neighbor.

No one, therefore, should suppose that Calvin disparages obedience to the second table. Although the first table is fundamental, such is the relation between the two tables, or parts, of the law that our life best conforms to the will of God "when it is in every respect most fruitful for our brethren."[75]

Biblical proof for dividing the law into two parts, love for God and love for the neighbor, is Christ's teaching in Luke 10:27 and Matthew 22:37–40. The right and obvious distribution of the ten commandments between the two tables is four and six. The first four commandments make up the first table, the last six, the second.

Calvin takes note of the Roman Catholic Church's different division of the decalogue. Combining the first two commandments against idolatry and against image worship, Rome makes the first table to consist of three commandments. In order to maintain the number ten, Rome "absurdly tear[s] in two the Tenth Commandment." The explanation of Rome's strange numbering of the ten commandments is that Rome, in order to escape the second commandment's condemnation of its image worship, seeks to "erase from the number the commandment concerning images, or at least hide it under the First."[76]

Calvin's detailed exposition of the ten commandments begins with an explanation of the all-important preface, "I am the LORD thy God, which have brought thee out of the land of Egypt, out of the house of bondage" (Ex. 20:2). Calvin insists that these words are "a sort of preface to the whole law."[77] By this preface, God claims obedience from his people from the fact of his "majesty." He also attracts the obedience of his people "with sweetness by declaring himself God of the church."[78] Jehovah God reminds his people of the benefit he has given them by redeeming them from Egypt. This great benefit puts them under the debt of gratitude. And this redemption derives from the covenant relation between God and them, expressed in the words, "I am the LORD thy God"—"God . . . by his covenant that he has made with Israel."[79] Calvin relates the covenant promise, "I will be their God, and they shall be my people," closely to eternal election. "It is as if he [God] had spoken as follows: 'I have chosen you as my people.'"[80]

For Calvin, the moral law is the authoritative rule of the life of the redeemed people of God. It is the law for covenant life. The motive of willing obedience is gratitude.

Lest the members of the church of the new covenant suppose that the preface of the law and the law itself pertain to national Israel—the Jews—and therefore have "nothing to do with us, we must regard the Egyptian bondage of Israel as a type of the spiritual captivity in which all of us are held bound, until our heavenly Vindicator, having freed us by the power of his arm, leads us into the Kingdom of freedom."[81]

The first commandment requires especially four things of the covenant people: adoration, trust, invocation, and gratitude. "All [must be] rendered wholly to himself."[82] In order to render this fourfold worship, right knowledge of God is necessary. The phrase "before me," which more literally should be translated "before my face,"[83] reminds us that God beholds our right worship of him, but also any idolatry. Calvin uses the vivid example of a "shameless woman who brings in an adulterer before her husband's very eyes only to vex his mind the more." Calvin warns against "the most secret thoughts of apostasy," since God's eyes "gaze upon the most secret recesses of our hearts."[84]

The second commandment, in distinction from the first, demands that the worship of the one true God be *right* worship. It "makes us conform to his lawful worship, that is, a spiritual worship established by himself."[85] The two parts of the second commandment are a prohibition against "represent[ing God] by any form" and a prohibition against "worship[ing] any images in the name of religion."[86]

In explaining the reference to God's jealousy, Calvin compares the covenant relation that underlies the second commandment to earthly marriage: "God . . . takes on the character of a husband to us."[87]

Calvin does justice to the covenant curse: "The Lord's righteous curse weighs not only upon the wicked man's head but also upon his whole family."[88] He also does justice to the covenant mercy: "This blessing promised in the covenant [is] that God's grace shall everlastingly abide in the families of the pious."[89] Regarding both curse and blessing, Calvin quickly adds that these are the rule. They do not preclude either the reforming of some children of unbelieving image worshipers in the sphere of the covenant or the "degeneration" of some offspring of believers. Indicating that for Calvin the covenant and its salvation are governed by election, he explains that "the Lawgiver desired here to frame no such perpetual rule as might detract from his election."[90]

Lacking in the last edition of the *Institutes* is the lengthy refutation of the Roman Catholic defense of the use of images in the worship of God, particularly the defense that images are "books of the uneducated."[91] That was part of Calvin's explanation of the second commandment in the 1536 *Institutes*. The first part of Calvin's refutation of Rome's defense of their images in the 1536 *Institutes* is surprising. Calvin advises Rome to clothe their statues of Mary so that they will not be immodest. "Indeed, brothels," writes Calvin, "show harlots clad more virtuously and modestly than the churches show those objects which they wish to be seen as images of virgins."[92] Not only is this a scathing indictment of Rome's lack of concern for chastity—in the very buildings where God is to be worshiped and in the very objects by which this worship is supposed to be carried out—but it is also a condemnation of Rome's penchant for having great artists decorate their church buildings, regardless that these artists were usually thoroughly godless, sensual men.

The second part of the refutation is familiar to everyone who knows the explanation of the second commandment in Answer 98 of the Heidelberg Catechism. God is pleased to instruct the people of God by "the [lively] preaching of his Word," not by the "trash"[93] of images.

Among the many images used by Rome for the teaching of the people, Calvin singles out "so many crosses—of wood, stone, even of silver and gold."[94]

"Hallow[ing] the majesty of his [God's] name," which is the purpose of the third commandment, is to be done in three ways: glorifying God by mind and tongue, honoring his word and "worshipful mysteries," and praising all his works.[95] It is evident that Calvin understands God's name to be God himself as he has revealed himself in his word and in his works.

Since the third commandment has "particular reference to the oath,"[96] Calvin devotes the greater part of his explanation to this matter. He defines an oath as "calling God as witness to confirm the truth of our word."[97] One takes the name of God in vain in swearing oaths when he swears falsely, that is, perjures himself; swears needlessly; or swears by another than God. With appeal to many passages of Scripture that teach a legitimate use of the oath, Calvin refutes the Anabaptist's repudiation of "all oaths without exception."[98] Calvin carefully exegetes the passage on which the Anabaptists base their position, Matthew 5:33–37. Oaths are permitted, even required, "either to vindicate the Lord's glory, or to further a brother's edification."[99]

In his warning against swearing falsely, Calvin makes a strong statement regarding the importance of God's name, which consists of "his truth." If God is "despoiled of his truth... he will then cease to be God."[100] This reverence for God's name explains Calvin's and the Reformed faith's (indeed, genuine Christianity's) regard for sound doctrine. The clear implication of Calvin's strong statement concerning the third commandment is that apathy regarding and corruption of sound doctrine are the profaning of God's name. Among those professing Christians and Christian churches that are guilty of such profanation, God ceases to be God.

Calvin's explanation and application of the fourth commandment are of special interest, because he is widely thought to have dismissed the commandment as wholly ceremonial and therefore abrogated with regard to the observance of a Sabbath day. Even though Calvin is not as clear on this aspect of the fourth commandment as he might have been, it is mistaken to suppose that Calvin rejected its requirement of the observance of a Sabbath day in the time of the new covenant and regarded the entire commandment as ceremonial.

He does think that "this commandment has a particular consideration distinct from the others."[101] The main force of the commandment was its "foreshadowing... [of] spiritual rest" to Old Testament Israel.[102] Therefore, "by the Lord Christ's coming the ceremonial part of this commandment was abolished."[103] This aspect of the fourth commandment is realized in the New Testament believer when he rests from his own works in order to "repose" in God.[104]

But this ceremonial aspect is not the whole of the fourth commandment. For this reason, Calvin can agree with the early fathers, who called this commandment a "foreshadowing," only in part. "The early fathers... say truly, but they touch upon only half the matter."[105] In addition to its foreshadowing of spiritual rest, the fourth commandment also requires a "stated day" for worship and hearing the word of God, and it gives a day of rest to servants.[106] These two aspects of the fourth commandment "ought not to be relegated to the ancient shadows, but are equally applicable to every age."[107]

The fourth commandment still sets apart one day in seven for the church to use for her public worship and teaching. "Meetings of the church are enjoined upon us by God's Word; and from our everyday experience we will know how we need them. But how can such meetings be held unless they have been established and have their stated days?"[108]

For the New Testament church, writes Calvin, this "stated day,"[109] established by the fourth commandment, is the "Lord's day"—the first day of the week.[110] This was the day of the Lord's resurrection, and "the purpose and fulfillment of that true rest, represented by the ancient Sabbath, lies in the Lord's resurrection."[111] Inasmuch as the church's remembering the Lord's day by gathering for public worship, at the heart of which is the preaching of the true rest of God in the crucified and risen Jesus Christ, is obedience to the fourth commandment, Calvin can boldly declare that "in the churches founded by him [Paul], the Sabbath was retained for this purpose."[112]

Calvin's sharp warning that Christians must "shun completely the superstitious observance of days"[113] and his vehement condemnation of "Sabbatarian superstition"[114] concern an observance of the first day of the week characterized by "a certain scrupulousness [that imagines] that by celebrating the day they were honoring mysteries once commended."[115]

It is noteworthy that Calvin is "compelled" to insist on the fourth commandment's establishing one day in the week for the special use of the church in her worship on account of "some restless spirits... stirring up tumult over the Lord's day."[116] These restless spirits within Calvin's purview wanted to do away with a day of rest, based on the fourth commandment, altogether. The same "restless spirits" (aptly named) appear in Reformed churches today. Whereas Calvin resisted them by affirming the fourth commandment's establishment of a day for worship and meditation on the word, Reformed churches in the twentieth and twenty-first centuries yield to the "restless spirits" and to the restless spirit of the age by abolishing the fourth commandment in its entirety. Churches yield to the "restless spirits" concerning the fourth commandment either by declaring the fourth commandment entirely ceremonial, and therefore abrogated, or by tolerating the disregard and profanation of the day by their members.

The Heidelberg Catechism perfectly captures Calvin's explanation of the fourth commandment. The fourth commandment does, indeed, require the believer and his children to "rest from [their] evil works, allow the Lord to work in [them] by his Spirit, and thus begin in this life the everlasting Sabbath," "all the days of [their] life."[117]

But it also sets one day in seven apart as "the day of rest" and requires the believer on this day "diligently [to] attend church, to learn the Word of God, to use the holy Sacraments, to call publicly upon the Lord, and to give Christian alms."[118]

The urgent admonition with which Calvin concludes his exposition of the fourth commandment needs to be heard by professing Christians in the twenty-first century. "To prevent religion from either perishing or declining among us, we should diligently frequent the sacred meetings, and make use of those external aids which can promote the worship of God."[119]

The scope of the fifth commandment is much wider than only the relation of children and parents. God mentions the authority of parents as the "superiority which is by nature most amiable and least invidious" in order to accustom his people to "look up to [all] those whom God has placed over us."[120] The "honor" commanded in the fifth commandment consists of three elements: "reverence, obedience, and gratefulness."[121]

The command to honor is not conditioned by the personal worthiness or unworthiness of the one in authority. All that matters is that the superiors "attained their position through God's providence."[122] Nevertheless, the command is not unconditional, whether regarding magistrates or parents. If the superiors "spur us to transgress the law," we have the right and duty to disobey them. All honoring of earthly authorities is strictly subject to our honoring of our "true Father."[123]

Regarding the promise "that thy days may be long upon the land which the LORD thy God giveth thee" (Ex. 20:12), Calvin teaches that the long earthly life of obedient children in the Old Testament was only an "evidence of God's favor," the "reality" of which was enjoyed after death.[124] That is, the promise that encourages obedience is eternal life. The implied curse upon "all stubborn and disobedient children" is inflicted by God even though they may live to an old age and prosper materially. For "they are bereft of God's blessing, and can only miserably pine away, being reserved for greater punishments to come."[125]

The divine prohibition of murder—the sixth commandment—applies to the soul, regarding hatred and anger, as well as to the body, regarding the actual, physical injuring of the neighbor.

The basis of the commandment is twofold: "Man is both the image of God, and our flesh."[126]

The positive command implied by the forbidding of murder is that we have and express concern for the safety of both the neighbor's body and soul.

Calvin alerts the reader that he will have more to say about the subject of the sixth commandment and its basis when he comes to treat the Christian life.

The purpose of the seventh commandment is that "all uncleanness must be far from us."[127] Because adultery, or "fornication," as Calvin describes the sin forbidden in the seventh commandment, begins in impure sexual desire—"lust"—the seventh commandment forbids lust.[128] Marriage is the divine, "necessary remedy to keep us from plunging into unbridled lust." "Any other [sexual] union apart from marriage is accursed" by God.[129] Most men, lacking the gift of continency (Calvin appeals to 1 Corinthians 7:9), ought to marry. Men are "doubly subject to women's society [in marriage]," that is, by virtue of God's having created the man as needing a wife and by virtue of the fall, which resulted in the arousing of lust.[130]

Calvin inveighs against Roman Catholic "celibacy." Rome's laws demanding celibacy of its clergy "contend against God and the nature ordained by him."[131] The gross, public scandals of the twenty-first century involving many Roman Catholic clergy give evidence that in this contention of Rome against God and human nature, God and human nature win. The recent public sexual scandals only bring to public attention what has been happening secretly down through the ages. In his exposition of the seventh commandment in the 1536 *Institutes*, Calvin alludes to the homosexual acts of the supposedly celibate Roman Catholic clergy: "something much more evil and filthy," that is, than fornication and adultery. These foul acts are the Lord's "frightful punishments" of Rome's "contempt" for God's gift of marriage.[132]

Not all things sexual are permitted within marriage. Married couples must not "pollute it with uncontrolled and dissolute lust."[133] Calvin refers darkly to "wallow[ing] in extreme lewdness" within marriage.[134] He quotes Ambrose approvingly that a husband by shameful practices can be "an adulterer toward his own wife."[135]

If the seventh commandment forbids lust and sexual uncleanness, it requires "modesty": "God loves modesty and purity."[136] God, therefore, does not "permit us to seduce the modesty of another with wanton dress and obscene gestures and foul speech."[137]

The eighth commandment requires the justice of "render[ing] to each man what belongs to him."[138] In addition to various obvious forms of stealing, Calvin affirms God's prohibition of, and judgment upon, "hard and inhuman laws with which the more powerful oppresses and crushes the weaker person"; the "shiftless steward" who "devours his master's substance"; and the master who "savagely harasses his household—all these are deemed theft in God's sight."[139]

In keeping with the principle of interpreting the negative commandments that he laid down at the outset, Calvin explains the forbidding of theft as requiring that the people of God give to the needy "with our abundance."[140] Then, in a surprising paragraph, Calvin calls for the payment of every kind of debt. This includes that "rulers take care of their own common people" and that "ministers of churches faithfully attend to the ministry of the Word, not adulterating the teaching of salvation [cf. 2 Cor. 2:17], but delivering it pure and undefiled to God's people."[141] Radically different is the thinking of the Reformed Christian from that of Western society in the twenty-first century. Life with others is not a matter of asserting and then fighting for one's "rights," but of recognizing and then paying one's "debts."

"Practice truth without deceit toward one another." This, says Calvin, is the essence of the ninth commandment. The basis of the commandment, as the motive for obeying, is that "God (who is truth) abhors a lie."[142]

The commandment especially lays claim to the tongue: "This commandment is lawfully observed when our tongue, in declaring the truth, serves both the good repute and the advantage of our neighbors."[143] It also governs our ears: "Eagerness to hear detractions... [is] alike forbidden."[144]

Calvin notes the depravity of our nature regarding evilspeaking and evil hearing: "We delight in a certain poisoned sweetness experienced in ferreting out and in disclosing the evils of others."[145] An astute observer of human behavior, Calvin exposes "caustic wit" as a form of evilspeaking. Although disguised as "joking," such "witticisms" often "grievously wound" the brother.[146] "Evilspeaking" must be distinguished from lawful reproof, judicial accusation and denunciations, and public correction.[147]

Although very brief, Calvin's explanation of the tenth commandment is profound. The tenth commandment is not only a prohibition of a determined desire to have something that is the neighbor's, to his loss. Neither is the desire condemned by the tenth commandment—coveting—the same as the "intent" to murder or commit adultery that is condemned in the preceding commandments. Whereas the commandments prohibiting murder and adultery do indeed forbid the desire of the heart, in the case of these commandments the forbidden desire is "deliberate consent of will where lust subjects the heart." "But covetousness can exist without such deliberation or consent when the mind is only pricked or tickled by empty and perverse objects."[148]

The uniqueness of the tenth commandment is that by it "God... commands a wonderful ardor of love, which he does not allow one particle of covetousness to hinder. He requires a marvelously tempered heart, and does not permit the tiniest pinprick to urge it against the law of love."[149]

Calvin freely acknowledges that he gained this insight into the tenth commandment from Augustine.

It was this understanding of the tenth commandment that caused the apostle Paul to exclaim, "I had not known sin, but by the law: for I had not known lust, except the law had said, thou shalt not covet" (Rom. 7:7). With this understanding of the tenth commandment, the believer has no difficulty with the apostle's teaching in Romans 7:7–25 of the total depravity of nature of the regenerated, believing, and sanctified child of God as long as he lives.

Casting a glance back over the moral law, which he has just explained, Calvin states, "The purpose of the whole law: the fulfillment of righteousness to form human life to the archetype of divine purity."[150] God's own "character" is depicted in the law, so that "if any man carries out in deeds whatever is enjoined there, he will express the image of God... in his own life."[151]

Calvin observes that the law nowhere commands us to love ourselves or seek our own advantage. The reason is that all of us naturally love ourselves, indeed love ourselves "excessive[ly]."[152] No law is needed for self-love. What is needed are commandments that require us to love God and the neighbor. Calvin warns, "No one lives in a worse or more evil manner than he who lives and strives for himself alone, and thinks about and seeks only his own advantage."[153]

To the question, "Who is the neighbor whom I am to love?" Calvin answers bluntly, "The whole human race without exception."[154]

Calvin takes issue with the Roman Catholic teaching of "counsels."[155] He refers to Rome's doctrine that certain commandments, particularly the commandment of Christ in Matthew 5 and Luke 6 that his disciples love their enemies, are not commandments for Christians at all but merely "counsels," which Christians are "free either to obey or not to obey." The reason, according to Rome, is that these commands are "too burdensome and heavy" for the ordinary Christian.[156] Calvin points out that Matthew 5 and Luke 6 make the commands Rome regards as "counsels" binding upon all Christians as children of God. In a shrewd observation, Calvin notes that if Christians are to love only those who love them, the command to love those who hate them being "too burdensome," they do not differ from the heathens, according to Jesus himself in Matthew 5 and Luke 6. God, writes Calvin, is a "Lawgiver"; he is not "a mere giver of counsel."[157]

With regard to the undoubted difficulty of obeying especially some of God's commands, Calvin quotes Augustine: "Let him [God] give what he commands, and command what he will."[158] In the context, Calvin excellently states the place of the law in the life of the Christian, who is saved by grace: "To be Christians under the law of grace does not mean to wander unbridled outside the law, but to be engrafted in Christ, by whose grace we are free of the curse of the law, and by whose Spirit we have the law engraved upon our hearts."[159]

Calvin denies Rome's doctrine of "venial sins."[160] This doctrine is the minimizing of the gravity of certain sins, for example, a sinful desire to which one does not give deliberate assent. Such sins, according to Rome, do not deserve eternal punishment. On the contrary, "all sin is mortal," that is, deserving of damnation. The reason is "who it is that commands."[161] Even a "little transgression" violates the divine majesty and is worthy of the "death penalty."[162] Calvin adduces Ezekiel 18:4, 20 and Romans 6:23.

Relation of the old and new covenants

Calvin's thorough treatment of the relation of law and gospel, in which he contends that the law stands in the service of the gospel for God's people and leads to Christ, requires that Calvin carefully explain the relation of the old and new covenants or testaments.

Consideration of this important subject was also necessitated by the false teaching of "that wonderful rascal Servetus and certain madmen of the Anabaptist sect."[163] These heretics were teaching that the old covenant and the new covenant are essentially different and that Israel and the New Testament church, therefore, are essentially different peoples because, according to them, the old covenant with Israel gave the Israelites only earthly prosperity. Basically the same controversy over the covenants continues unabated today between the Reformed faith and the inherent dispensationalism of the Baptist descendants of the Anabaptists of Calvin's day.

It should not be overlooked that Calvin's explanation of the fundamental biblical truth of the covenant of grace occurs as an aspect of his doctrine of the knowledge of God the redeemer, that is, Christology. Indeed, Calvin's doctrine of the covenant immediately precedes his treatment of the person and office of Jesus Christ.

The biblical and theological justification of this presentation of Christ is that he came into the world in fulfillment of the prophecies and promise of Old Testament Scripture and that he came on behalf of the covenant of God with his chosen people. Calvin suggests this connection between his doctrine of the person of Jesus Christ and his immediately preceding treatment of the covenant by deliberately setting forth his doctrine of Jesus Christ as the truth concerning the "Mediator." Jesus Christ is "Mediator" of the covenant.[164]

The significance of this treatment of the doctrine of Jesus Christ in the closest connection with the truth of the covenant is that Calvin establishes the fundamental importance of the covenant. Jesus Christ is the covenant savior and Lord; his ministry is on behalf of the covenant; and his salvation is the realization of the covenant and, in the covenant, the bestowal of the benefits of the covenant.

Calvin did not develop the doctrine of the covenant. He left this to his theological successors. But he raised it to its due prominence. This was development of dogma. Reformed theology has followed Calvin, both in treating the doctrine of the covenant in Christology and in recognizing the covenant as central biblical truth. Reflecting the Reformed consensus, Heinrich Heppe explains "the covenant of grace" in the chapter immediately preceding his treatment of "The Mediator of the Covenant of Grace or The Person of Christ." Heppe's opening line in the chapter on the person of Christ is, "Consideration of God's covenant of grace leads directly to the exposition of... the mystery of God's Son becoming man to be the Mediator of this Covenant."[165]

The precise subject, Calvin informs the reader, is "the covenant that the Lord made of old with the Israelites... and that which God has now made with us."[166] These "two [covenants] are actually one and the same."[167] This point, Calvin insists, is "very important."[168] The unity of the covenants consists of three main elements: in both covenants, God's people aspire to "immortality," not to "carnal prosperity"; in both covenants union with God and its salvation are "solely by the mercy of God," not by human "merits"; in both covenants the people "had and knew Christ as Mediator."[169]

Among many proofs that the covenant with Israel was the same "spiritual covenant" that God now makes with the New Testament believer are the words that Calvin describes as "the very formula of the covenant": "I will be your God, and you shall be my people."[170] Calvin understands this covenant formula as defining the covenant as spiritual fellowship between God and his people. It indicates a "presence of him [God]" to his people, a "union" that brings with it "everlasting salvation."[171]

In its conception of the covenant as a contract, agreement, and bargain, much of later Reformed theology departed from Calvin and ignored the covenant formula itself.

The substantial unity of the covenant by no means rules out, or even minimizes, the progressive revelation of "the covenant of his mercy" in the history of redemption. "The Lord held to this orderly plan in administering the covenant of his mercy: as the day of full revelation approached with the passing of time, the more he increased each day the brightness of its manifestation."[172] In fact, the distinction between Old Testament Scripture, the content of which is what Calvin calls "the whole law," and New Testament Scripture, the content of which is the gospel of "the grace manifested in Christ," is simply fullness and clarity of revelation. "Where the whole law is concerned, the gospel differs from it only in clarity of manifestation."[173]

Calvin is sharp in his criticism of the dispensational heresy—"this pestilential error."[174] This was the teaching in Calvin's day, as it is also today, that the covenant with Israel is essentially different from the covenant with the New Testament church, inasmuch as the covenant with Israel promises earthly benefits. Calvin accuses this dispensational teaching regarding the old covenant of reducing the Israelites to a "herd of swine...fattened by the Lord on this earth";[175] of viewing Moses as inducing "carnal folk to worship God by promising them fertile fields and an abundance of all things";[176] and of holding "a carnal covenant."[177]

If the blessing of the saints in the old covenant was earthly and material, Calvin argues, they were of all men most miserable. For their earthly lives were troubled, notably lacking in merely earthly happiness. Among the examples to which he points is Noah, about whom Calvin vividly observes that in the ark he was in a "grave" for ten months, "almost immersed in the dung of animals!"[178] No doubt, Calvin poignantly reflects on his own experience when he remarks concerning Abraham's childlessness that to find oneself childless is "the most unpleasant and bitter feature of old age."[179]

Editor McNeill is correct in his comment in a footnote on this passage in the *Institutes* that Calvin did not regard earthly "prosperity in this life as associated with election."[180] Much less did Calvin regard prosperity as a proof of election. But neither did Calvin countenance the carnal kingdom of postmillennialism, especially in its contemporary Christian reconstruction form, as the triumph of the gospel in history. Calvin saw the Christian life as suffering; he viewed the church in history as persecuted.

Both contemporary dispensationalists and postmillennialists do well to take heed to Calvin's explanation of the Old Testament's promises of blessedness under the figures of earthly prosperity, earthly peace, and earthly power. "The better to commend God's goodness, the prophets represented it for the people under the lineaments, so to speak, of temporal benefits. But they painted a portrait such as to lift up the minds of the people above the earth . . . to ponder happiness of the spiritual life to come."[181]

Summing up his argument for the unity of the covenant, Calvin states, "Let us, therefore, boldly establish a principle unassailable by any stratagems of the devil: the Old Testament or Covenant that the Lord had made with the Israelites had not been limited to earthly things, but contained a promise of spiritual and eternal life."[182] The "obtuseness" of the Jews "in awaiting the Messiah's earthly kingdom" is "monstrous."[183]

So also is the obtuseness of all today who go on proclaiming and expecting an earthly messianic kingdom.

There are differences between the two covenants, but they are differences of administration, not of "substance."[184]

One difference is that in the old covenant with Israel God displayed "the heavenly heritage" by means of "earthly benefits."[185] Chief among the earthly benefits was the land of Canaan. Canaan was a type of heaven *to the Jews themselves*, and they "looked [at Canaan], as in a mirror, upon the future inheritance."[186] Israel needed to see the heavenly inheritance in the form of an earthly country because, in comparison with the mature New Testament church, Israel was an immature child. With appeal to the crucial text, Galatians 4:1, 2, Calvin compares Israel and the New Testament church, not to two different persons (as does dispensationalism), but to the child that the man once was and to the man that the child has become. "The same church existed among them [Israelites], but as yet in its childhood."[187]

Another difference is that the Old Testament reveals the truth by means of "figures" and "shadow[s]," whereas "the New Testament reveals the very substance of truth as present." Calvin demonstrates the typology of the Old Testament in the light of Hebrews, where is "a fuller discussion of it . . . than anywhere else."[188]

A third difference between the covenants concerns the external "letter" of the Old Testament, considered as law, in contrast to the inner, Spirit-worked spirituality of the New Testament, considered as gospel.

Calvin explicates this contrast by careful exegesis of Jeremiah 31:31–34 and 2 Corinthians 3.[189]

The fourth main difference is that the old covenant was a covenant of "bondage," whereas the new covenant is one of "freedom."[190] Here Calvin draws on and explains Galatians 4. The Old Testament, considered strictly as law, that is, the demand to be perfectly righteous with its threat of curse, subjects all to that curse. Thus the Old Testament "produces fear in men's minds."[191] In contrast, the New Testament, which is gospel, delivers men from this bondage into the freedom of being right with God by the cross of Christ. "The New Testament...lifts them to trust and assurance."[192]

Although the saints in the Old Testament "shared the same freedom and joy" that we New Testament believers have, this was an early "fruit of the New Testament."[193] In addition, the people of God who lived in the time of the Old Testament were distressed by ceremonial laws, as we New Testament Christians are not.

A fifth difference is that the old covenant was confined to one nation, whereas the new covenant extends to all nations. In the Old Testament "Israel was...the Lord's darling son."[194] "The calling of the Gentiles...is a notable mark of the excellence of the New Testament over the Old."[195]

The person and natures of the mediator

Only after a lengthy treatment of the law and an equally lengthy treatment of the relation between the Old and New Testaments does Calvin come, at last, to his doctrine of the person and natures of Jesus Christ.

Indeed, Calvin began his consideration of the knowledge of God the redeemer in Christ—the second book of the *Institutes*—with a thorough account of the fall of the human race in Adam and the consequent total depravity of mankind.

Eleven long chapters and some two hundred and twenty pages intervene between the opening of book two of the *Institutes*, concerning the knowledge of God the redeemer in Christ, and Calvin's taking up the subject of Christology proper.

The significance of this arrangement is that Calvin views, and wants his Protestant and Reformed readers to view, the person and work of Jesus Christ against the background of their misery of sin; as God's gracious satisfaction of the demands of his law upon them in their stead and on their behalf; and as the fulfillment of the covenant of grace, promised in the Old Testament.

If one does not know Jesus Christ in these ways, he does not know him rightly.

"Our Mediator" is "both true God and true man." According to Calvin, the necessity that the mediator of the new covenant be both God and man is the "heavenly decree."[196]

That Calvin immediately grounds the necessity of Jesus' Godhead and manhood in the decree is significant. The significance is not that Calvin fails to appreciate that the misery of those whom Christ must redeem demands a savior who is both God and man. But Calvin will not allow any aspect of salvation to derive from what he calls a "simple ... or absolute necessity," apart from the eternal decree of God.[197] Calvin was a "decretal theologian," and his theology is a "decretal theology," through and through. The concerted contemporary effort to present Calvin as a "biblical theologian" in distinction from the "decretal theology" of the Canons of Dordt and of the Westminster Confession of Faith shatters on the theology of John Calvin in his *Institutes*.

"Stemm[ing] from a heavenly decree," our complete estrangement from God by our iniquities necessitated that the "Son of God ... become for us 'Immanuel, that is ... God with us' [Isa. 7:14; Matt. 1:23]."[198] This necessity is twofold. First, only one who is both God and man is able to transform spiritually dead sinners into living children of God. Second, only one who is both God and man could "pay the penalties for sin."[199]

Although Calvin warns against detracting from either Christ's "divinity or his humanity,"[200] he emphasizes the humanity of the savior. The reason is "our weakness" in daring to seek a mediator who is the Son of God. The manhood of the mediator assures us that "he is near us, indeed touches us, since he is our flesh."[201]

Calvin gives the lie to the prevailing contemporary notion that a strong doctrine of the deity of Jesus necessarily minimizes Jesus' manhood, to the injuring of the faith of distressed sinners.

The teaching that the Son of God would have become flesh even though Adam had not fallen, Calvin rejects as "vague speculations that captivate the frivolous and the seekers after novelty."[202] Calvin has in mind, and names, the erratic Lutheran theologian Andreas Osiander. In refuting Osiander's contention, Calvin has recourse to "God's eternal decree" by which "these two were joined together," namely, the becoming flesh of the Son of God and its purpose in the redemption of "condemned men."[203] Calvin appeals to Ephesians 1:4–7. Calvin also points to the plain testimony of the Bible that "God sent forth his Son ... to redeem those who were under the law [Gal. 4:4, 5]."[204]

In response to Osiander's foolish argument that the Bible nowhere expressly refutes his doctrine that the Son of God would have become flesh even if Adam had not sinned, Calvin notes that, on this argument, Osiander would have to allow the monstrous doctrine that "the Son of God could have taken upon himself the nature of an ass."[205] No passage of Scripture expressly refutes this absurd notion.

Evident in Calvin's sharp, impatient handling of Osiander is the reformer's deep-grained dislike of the determination to be novel in theology, as also of the effort "to appear witty."[206]

Exactly these grave weaknesses characterize the contemporary theologian James Jordan, who resurrects the error of Osiander concerning the incarnation of the Son of God and spreads it in Christian reconstruction and federal vision circles.[207]

A little later in his explanation of passages of Scripture that teach the incarnation, Calvin distinguishes himself from such innovative exegetes with their fantastic interpretations of Scripture by obliquely describing himself as "a sober expositor who examines such great mysteries as devoutly as they deserve."[208]

In the course of his controversy with Osiander, Calvin insists that by God's appointment in eternity Jesus Christ is head, not only of the elect church, but also of the elect angels. "In the original order of creation and the unfallen state of nature Christ was set over angels and men as their Head."[209] The biblical proof is Colossians 1:15, where Christ is said to be "the firstborn of every creature."

Calvin's Christology does not restrict Christ to the role of the savior of sinners. Rather, it sets forth Jesus Christ as first in the counsel of God and, therefore, preeminent in all things, as Colossians 1:13–22— the passage adduced by Calvin—teaches. This doctrine of Christ is the principle of the distinctively Reformed, indeed Christian, worldview. Radically different is this principle from that which controls the prevailing worldview in Reformed and evangelical churches today—the principle of "common grace."[210]

Because he has abundantly proved the deity of Christ in the first book of the *Institutes*, in the treatment of the Trinity (1.13.7–13), Calvin here concentrates on demonstrating the humanity of the mediator. This demonstration of Christ's human nature is polemical. Calvin contends against the ancient Christological heresies of the Manichees and the Marcionites. The former taught that Jesus' "human" nature was a strange "heavenly flesh," essentially different from our human nature; the latter, that "Christ's body [was] a mere appearance." Both denied the "genuineness of his human nature."[211] And both denied the genuineness of Jesus' human body because they regarded the earthly and natural as base and evil.

Although he mentions only the Manichees and the Marcionites, second- and third-century heretics, Calvin is not beating dead heretics. He has his orthodox eye on a heretic and his heretical movement of Calvin's own day—the heretical Anabaptist Menno Simons and Menno's Anabaptist followers. Menno and his followers are the modern disciples of the Manichees and the "new Marcionites."[212] Menno denied that Jesus took his (real) human nature from the flesh and blood of his mother, Mary. Menno taught that Jesus' human nature was a special creation of God and that Jesus lay in Mary's womb as a piece of fruit lies in a basket. Like the old heretics, Menno thought that human nature, as material substance, is inherently and hopelessly evil. Article 18 of the Belgic Confession has Menno Simons in view when it condemns "the heresy of the Anabaptists, who deny that Christ assumed human flesh of his mother."[213]

Against Marchion, Mani, and Menno, Calvin marshals a host of passages, including Galatians 4:4, Matthew 1:1, and Luke 3:38, affirming that Jesus is a genuine son of Mary, David, Abraham, and Adam. Especially conclusive for Calvin are Christ's description of himself as "Son of Man" and the second chapter of Hebrews, where Jesus' sharing in the flesh and blood of the children is taught as necessary for the children's salvation.[214]

In refuting Menno, Calvin must comment on the genealogy of

Christ in Matthew 1. Calvin declares that "Matthew does not list Mary's ancestors, but Joseph's."[215]

Calvin does not content himself with exposing Menno's theological errors. He also criticizes the Anabaptist's scientific ignorance. In defense of his denial that Jesus took his human nature from Mary, Menno argued that the woman contributes nothing to the conception of a child. As Calvin phrases Menno's argument, "Women are 'without seed.'" "Thus," replies the more scientific Calvin, "they [the Anabaptists] overturn the principles of nature."[216] Babies are "engendered from the mother's seed," and therefore, "Christ was begotten of Mary."[217] Jesus Christ was, and is, a genuine man.

Against the charge that physical descent from Adam through Mary would expose Christ to the pollution of sinful human nature, Calvin responds that Jesus "was sanctified by the Spirit that the generation might be pure and undefiled."[218]

The necessity of Jesus' genuine humanity, as also the necessity of Jesus' deity, is his qualification to be the savior of human sinners. Specifically, "the sins of the world had to be expiated in our flesh, as Paul clearly declares [Rom. 8:3]."[219]

Calvin is at pains to deny that the incarnation of the Son of God implies universalism—a heresy increasingly prevalent in our day. "When we say that Christ was made man that he might make us children of God, this expression does not extend to all men. For faith intervenes, to engraft us spiritually into the body of Christ."[220]

The conclusion of the consideration of the real humanity of the Son of God by means of a virgin birth is a wonder: "Here is something marvelous: the Son of God descended from heaven in such a way that, without leaving heaven, he willed to be borne in the virgin's womb, to go about the earth, and to hang upon the cross; yet he continuously filled the world even as he had done from the beginning!"[221]

The incarnation

The wonder that explains Jesus' being both God and man is the incarnation. Calvin defines the wonder: "He who was the Son of God became the Son of man—not by confusion of substance, but by unity of person."[222] The outstanding biblical statement of the doctrine, which

Calvin quotes, is John 1:14: "The Word was made flesh." Calvin observes that it is the gospel according to John that most clearly and fully sets forth the truth of the incarnation.

By the wonder of incarnation, which took place at the instant of the conception of Jesus in Mary's womb, the person of the eternal Son of God united to himself human nature, so that Jesus Christ, whose person is the eternal Son of God, the second person of the Trinity, is both God and man. With explicit acceptance of the "church's definition" of Chalcedon (AD 451), Calvin declares that the "Word begotten of the Father before all ages took human nature in a hypostatic union." By "hypostatic union" is meant "that which constitutes one person out of two natures."[223] If there is an earthly analogy or "parallel" to the incarnation, it is union in the one person of a human of two distinct substances, soul and body.[224]

The main errors regarding the incarnation are the teaching that "the Word was turned into flesh," so as no longer to be the Word, that is, eternal God, and the teaching that the Word "confusedly mingled with flesh," so as to be neither God nor man, but a third thing—a "God-man." Calvin repudiates both of these errors.[225]

Again in his explanation and defense of the incarnation, Calvin is fiercely polemical. Many contemporary Calvin scholars deliberately ignore the polemical Calvin. Their Calvin is a Calvin of piety, or a pastoral Calvin, or even a Calvin of sweetness. If they refer to Calvin the polemicist at all, it is to decry the fierceness of his attack on doctrinal errors and the violence of his condemnation of the heretics. Calvin would not recognize himself in their portraits of him. What is worse, these Calvin scholars do serious damage to Calvin's theology. Like the theology of the prophets, of the apostles, and of Jesus himself (to refer to our chief prophet's own teaching during his earthly ministry), the theology of Calvin is polemical theology.

Calvin defends the truth of the incarnation against the ancient heretics Nestorius and Eutyches. Nestorius "devised a double Christ," that is, made Christ two persons. Eutyches "commingle[d] the two natures in Christ," that is, taught a Christ who is neither God nor man, but a mixture of deity and humanity—a demigod, or a superman.[226]

A "no less deadly monster" in Calvin's own age is Michael Servetus.

The confused and contradictory doctrine of this heretic consists of the denial that Jesus is the eternal Son of God: "He reduces to nothing the eternal hypostasis of the Word."[227] Holding his error to the end, Servetus' dying words at the stake were, "Jesus Christ, thou Son of the eternal God, have mercy upon me!" "He could not be induced, says Farel, to confess that Christ was the *eternal* Son of God."[228]

Calvin's purpose in refuting Servetus, as well as Nestorius and Eutyches, is practical: "The crafty evasions of this foul dog utterly extinguished the hope of salvation... Only he can be our Redeemer who, begotten of the seed of Abraham and David, was truly made man according to the flesh."[229]

In contrast to his brief treatment of Nestorius and Eutyches, Calvin devotes no fewer than four sections of chapter fourteen of book two to a thorough examination and refutation of the errors of Servetus. The significance of this is that Calvin regarded contemporary error as a greater threat to the church than the errors of ancient times. The Reformed installation form for professors of theology binds this wisdom of Calvin upon the professor of theology: "Caution them [seminary students] in regard to the errors and heresies of the old, but especially of the new day."[230]

Confession of the union of two natures—divine and human—in the one divine person of Christ requires explanation of the "communicating of properties."[231] Calvin accepts this description of Scripture's sometimes attributing to Christ "what must be referred solely to his humanity, sometimes what belongs uniquely to his divinity; and sometimes what embraces both natures but fits neither alone."[232] Calvin explains the communication of properties this way: "Things that he [Christ] carried out" in one nature "are transferred improperly, although not without reason" to the other nature, by virtue of the one person: "for the sake of the union of both natures."[233]

Although his explanation of the communication of properties obviously differs sharply from that of Luther and the Lutherans, Calvin does not here enter into the controversy with the Lutherans. He reserves his controversy with the Lutherans over the ubiquity of Christ's human nature for his (Calvin's) treatment of the Lord's supper in book four of the *Institutes*.

With one incidental aspect of Calvin's treatment of the incarnation we may differ. Calvin asserts that the mediatorial kingship will end at Christ's coming again:

> Until he comes forth as judge of the world Christ will therefore reign... But when as partakers in heavenly glory we shall see God as he is, Christ, having then discharged the office of Mediator, will cease to be the ambassador of his Father, and will be satisfied with that glory which he enjoyed before the creation of the world.[234]

As the quotation indicates, Calvin thinks that Jesus Christ will one day cease being the mediator. Christ sits on the right hand of God "but for a time."[235] When Calvin comes to treat the kingly office of Christ, Calvin calls the conducting of the "Last Judgment... the last act of his reign."[236] The basis of this teaching in Calvin's mind is 1 Corinthians 15:24: "Then cometh the end, when he shall have delivered up the kingdom to God."

A number of Reformed and Presbyterian theologians have followed Calvin in limiting Christ's mediatorial kingship to the present age. The Reformed confessions, however, have not followed Calvin in this teaching. Both the Heidelberg Catechism and the Belgic Confession call Christ an "eternal king."[237]

These creeds are right. The glorified man, Jesus Christ, who is personally God, sits on the right hand of God forever, exercising his mediatorial kingship over his messianic kingdom—the church in the new world—everlastingly. That on the world's last day Christ will deliver up the kingdom to the triune God means not that Christ will abdicate, but that Christ will present it to God as God's own perfected kingdom, ruled by God and on God's behalf by God's own Son in human flesh.

The offices of Christ

The ministry of the incarnate Son of God, Calvin explains as Christ's exercise of his threefold office. It is worthy of note that Calvin views the authoritative position of Christ as the servant of Jehovah God as one, with three distinct aspects, or "parts": "The office enjoined upon Christ by the Father consists of three parts."[238]

In setting forth the saving work of Christ as the exercise of his threefold office, Calvin significantly develops theology. Although theologians before him had referred to Christ's offices, as Calvin notes particularly regarding the "papists," they neither subsumed the whole of Christ's saving work under these offices nor gave the offices the prominence they deserve. The importance of the office of Christ for Calvin is nothing less than this, that in the threefold office "faith may find a firm basis for salvation... and thus rest in him [Christ]."[239]

The three "parts" of the office are "prophet, king, and priest."[240] The title that expresses the office of the mediator of the covenant is "Christ," or "Messiah," which refers to Jesus' anointing, not by "holy oil," but by the Holy Spirit.[241] Scattered throughout Calvin's treatment of the three offices are references to various passages of Scripture that teach the anointing of the Messiah, or Christ, as his appointment to and qualification for office in the kingdom of God. These passages include Isaiah 61:1, 2 and John 3:34.

The "visible symbol of this sacred anointing was shown in Christ's baptism, when the Spirit hovered over him in the likeness of a dove [John 1:32; Luke 3:22]." The meaning of the symbol is that "the Spirit has chosen Christ as his seat, that from him might abundantly flow the heavenly riches of which we are in such need."[242]

Having proved the prophetic office of Christ from both the Old and New Testaments, Calvin describes the work of Christ as prophet: "to be herald and witness of the Father's grace."[243]

In the gospel of Christ, evidently as found in the New Testament Scripture, is the full and perfect revelation of God for the church and the believer. "The perfect doctrine he [Christ] has brought has made an end to all prophecies. All those, then, who, not content with the gospel, patch it with something extraneous to it, detract from Christ's authority."[244] Thus Calvin condemns both the extrabiblical dogmas of the Roman Catholic Church and the post-biblical prophecies of the charismatic movement.

It is the deep concern of Calvin, not only regarding the prophetic office of Christ, but also regarding his kingship and priesthood, that Christ shares his anointing and, thus, his offices with his body the church. "Hence they [believers] are justly called Christians."[245] Regarding the anointing of Christ to the prophetic office, Calvin writes, "He received anointing, not only for himself that he might carry out the office of teaching, but for his whole body that the power of the Spirit might be present in the continuing preaching of the gospel."[246]

Contemporary churches that allow preaching to be obscured by other ecclesiastical activities would do well to give heed to Calvin's commendation of the preaching of the gospel: in the preaching of the gospel is the power of the Spirit of Christ.

The very first thing Calvin mentions concerning the kingship of Christ is "that it is spiritual in nature." Significantly, Calvin makes the observation in the form of a "warning" to his readers, indicating his awareness of the danger of conceiving the kingship of Christ as earthly and carnal. So important is the spiritual nature of the royal office of Christ that it would be "pointless" to speak of the kingship of Christ without establishing its spiritual nature.[247]

Calvin is forceful, and perfectly clear, in rejecting every earthly conception of Christ's kingdom: "It is not earthly or carnal."[248] The citizens of Christ's kingdom, therefore, are not to expect the "triumph" of the kingdom, or of themselves as citizens, in this life. "While we must fight throughout life under the cross, our condition is harsh and wretched."[249] Only when our "warfare [is] ended," after this life for the believer and after the conclusion of earthly history for the church, will "we [be] called to triumph."[250] Accordingly, "the happiness" promised to the citizen of Christ's kingdom "does not consist in outward advantages... but belongs to the heavenly life!"[251]

Calvin is the sworn foe of the postmillennial dream of a carnal kingdom eventually achieving an earthly victory in history, as he is of the contemporary "health-and-wealth gospel." The trouble with those who promote these false doctrines, and thus corrupt the truth that Christ is a spiritual king over a spiritual kingdom, is, in Calvin's words, that they are "too much inclined to things earthly from indulging in foolish dreams of pomp."[252]

The biblical proof of the spiritual nature of the messianic kingship and kingdom, for Calvin, includes John 18:36, "My kingdom is not of this world"; Luke 17:20, 21, "The kingdom of God cometh not with observation... the kingdom of God is within you"; and Romans 14:17, "For the kingdom of God is not meat and drink; but righteousness and peace, and joy in the Holy Ghost."[253]

The eternal benefit of Christ's spiritual kingdom for us is twofold.

One aspect "pertains to the whole body of the church." The other "belongs to each individual member." Regarding the church, King Christ will be "the eternal protector and defender of his church" so that "the perpetuity of the church is secure" against her many enemies and in the midst of all her struggles.[254]

Regarding the member of the church, Christ's kingship assures him of "a better life... in the age to come."[255] In this life "Christ enriches his people with all things necessary for the eternal salvation of souls"—what Calvin calls "the gifts of the Spirit"—"and fortifies them with courage to stand unconquerable against all the assaults of spiritual enemies."[256] In this spiritual warfare, evidently, believers share the kingly office of Christ.

The calling of the believers in view of Christ's kingship is that they "should one and all resolve to obey."[257]

By no means does Christ's kingship imply a gracious attitude of the king toward all men or the salvation of all. Messianic grace and salvation are only "for the godly who submit willingly and obediently." With regard to the ungodly, Christ "carries a 'rod of iron to break them and dash them all in pieces like a potter's vessel' [Ps. 2:9]."[258] He will perfect the destruction of his enemies at the final judgment.

The essence of the priestly office of Christ is "by his holiness to reconcile us to God." The priest is the believers' "advocate... between them and God."[259]

"God's righteous curse" upon the sins of the guilty people "bars our access to him."[260] Therefore, "expiation" is required, to "appease his [God's] wrath."[261] Expiation is only by the sacrifice involving the shedding of blood, as the Old Testament teaches, particularly Leviticus 16. The real sacrifice is the death of Christ. On the basis of Hebrews 7–10, Calvin explains the death of Christ as expiating sacrifice: "He [Christ] blotted out our own guilt and made satisfaction for our sins."[262] And the death of Christ so understood is "the principal point on which... our whole salvation turns."[263]

In the offering of the sacrifice that "propitiate[s] God" and opens up the way to God for us, Christ is "both priest and sacrifice."[264]

Christ's priestly office does not end with the offering of the sacrifice. It continues in the risen Christ's intercession for his people: "He is an everlasting intercessor."[265]

In addition to the book of Hebrews, Calvin appeals to Psalm 110:4 in support of the priestly office of Christ: "Thou art a priest for ever after the order of Melchizedek."

Believers also share in the priestly office of their head and mediator. Christ "receive[s] us as his companions in this great office [Rev. 1:6]. For we... are priests in him." We exercise this priesthood of all believers (which truth Calvin confesses in agreement with Luther) by "offer[ing] ourselves and our all to God" and by bringing our "sacrifices of prayers and praise" to God in the heavenly sanctuary.[266]

Calvin concludes his treatment of the priestly office of Christ with a ringing denunciation of the Roman Catholic Church's "fabrication" concerning Christ's priesthood, particularly his sacrifice of himself. Rome is "not content with Christ's priesthood," presuming "to sacrifice him anew! The papists attempt this each day, considering the Mass as the sacrificing of Christ."[267]

The reformers understood correctly the nature of the mass in the Roman Catholic Church and condemned it as gross denial of the cross of Christ, which is, as Calvin says, "the principal point on which... our whole salvation turns." The decisions of Protestant, indeed Reformed, churches in the twenty-first century denying that the mass is conducted as a daily repetition of the sacrifice of Christ on the cross and declaring that the reformers (and the Reformation creeds!) were in error in their understanding of the mass are an insult to the reformers and to the Spirit of Christ, who guided them to reform the church. These decisions are also false.

Christ's redemptive work as confessed by the Apostles' Creed

Consideration of the threefold office of Christ, particularly the priestly aspect with its fundamental act of sacrifice, which Calvin again describes as "satisfaction,"[268] leads Calvin to a closer examination of "how Christ has fulfilled the function of redeemer to acquire salvation for us."[269]

In the course of this examination of the work of redemption, Calvin informs us that he follows the articles of the second part of the "so-called 'Apostles' Creed.'"[270] In approving the creed's statement concerning Christ's descension into hell, Calvin praises the Apostles' Creed highly: "We have in it a summary of our faith, full and complete in all details; and containing nothing in it except what has been derived from the pure Word of God."[271]

At the conclusion of his exposition of the Apostles' Creed regarding the work of Christ, Calvin expresses himself concerning the authorship of the creed. He notes that "the old writers certainly attribute it to the apostles." He has no doubt that early in the history of the New Testament church the creed "was received as a public confession by the consent of all." For Calvin, the question of authorship is unimportant. What is important is that the creed "contains nothing that is not vouched for by genuine testimonies of Scripture."[272]

Before Calvin proceeds with his further examination of Christ's redemptive work, he wrestles with a seeming "contradiction" in the biblical testimony concerning that work. On the one hand, according to Calvin, God was "our enemy until he was reconciled to us through Christ." On the other hand, God could not have given his Son for us "if he had not already embraced us with his free favor."[273]

Although Calvin informs us that he treats this issue "in passing," in fact it is an issue of great importance, and one over which contemporary theologians stumble. Calvin is concerned to harmonize the truth that the source of all of salvation, including the cross of Christ, is the eternal love of God for his chosen people, on the one hand, and the truth that the cross of Christ *as satisfaction of the justice of God* was necessary for the salvation of the chosen people in the love of God, on the other hand. Passages such as John 3:16 and Romans 5:8 teach the former truth; passages such as Romans 5:10 and Galatians 3:10, 13, the latter truth. Calvin quotes all of these passages.

Contemporary theologians err concerning these two truths either by affirming that the death of Christ changed God's hatred into love (thus denying that the eternal love of God is the source and cause of all salvation), or by denying that the cross of Christ was satisfaction of divine justice (thus denying that salvation in the love of God requires satisfaction).

Although Calvin affirms both of the truths, his harmonizing of them is unsatisfactory. Having phrased the two truths in such a way that they are, in fact, contradictory, Calvin uncharacteristically embraces the contradiction. On the one hand, Calvin declares, God on his part was "our enemy," was "hostile to us," and even "hated" us. On the other hand, and at the same time, "by his love God the Father goes before and anticipates our reconciliation in Christ. Indeed, 'because he first loved us' [1 John 4:19], he afterwards reconciles us to himself."[274]

Quoting Augustine, Calvin makes the contradiction stark: "He [God] loved us even when he hated us."[275]

Adding to the confusion (and contradiction is necessarily confusion), Calvin toys with solving his problem by having recourse to a distinction between our sinful self and our created self: God hates us as we are sinful; he loves us as we are still his creatures. "However much we may be sinners by our own fault, we nevertheless remain his creatures."[276] The implications of this explanation are unacceptable, if not absurd, and contrary to Calvin's own theology, to say nothing of Scripture. If the explanation of the love of God for sinners, and then a love that gives Christ for them, is the creaturehood of these sinners, God loves the reprobate wicked, not only in this life, but also in hell (where they remain God's creatures), and God loves Satan, for he too is a creature. And if the sins of the elect are a cause of God's hatred of them personally, God hates the elect even though Christ died for them and even though they are born again and sanctified, for the elect remain sinners as long as they live.

To his credit, Calvin is uneasy with his startling affirmation concerning God's being the enemy of his people and hating them. "Expressions of this sort have been accommodated to our capacity."[277] "God is, *so to speak*, hostile to us."[278] These statements are pedagogical. They are intended to make us "experience and feel something of what [we] owe to God's mercy."[279]

We certainly appreciate, and agree with, Calvin's concern that believers experience that by their sins they are exposed to the wrath and curse of God, ending in hell apart from the cross of Christ that satisfied God's justice and reconciled them to God. Calvin is surely right when he says that we cannot "seize upon life [in Christ] ardently enough or accept it with the gratefulness we owe, unless our minds are first struck and overwhelmed by fear of God's wrath and by dread of eternal death."[280] But this does not imply that God hates those for whom he gave his Son, or that they think so.

The reason for Calvin's uncharacteristic confusion, indeed theological error, here is that he overlooks that Scripture never teaches that God hates his elect people, is on his part an enemy toward them, or is reconciled, or needs to be reconciled, to them. He hates their sinful nature and sins, to be sure, but not them themselves. He loves them with an eternal love in Jesus Christ, and this, according to Romans 5:8 and John 3:16, is the reason he sent his Son to reconcile them to himself, not himself to them (2 Cor. 5:18–21).

Calvin and Augustine, whom Calvin is quoting, express the truth when they affirm, "He [God] loved us, even when we practiced enmity toward him."[281]

Calvin then pursues his stated subject, how Christ has redeemed us. Calvin points, first, to Christ's lifelong obedience: "by the whole course of his obedience."[282] Calvin appeals to Romans 5:19: "By the obedience of one shall many be made righteous." That Calvin definitely has reference to Christ's entire life of holiness and obedience to the law of God, in distinction from his passion and death, is evident. Calvin refers to "the whole life of Christ."[283] He mentions Jesus' baptism as one specific act of obedience that "abolished sin" and "acquired righteousness" for us.[284] And he sharply distinguishes this obedience of Christ's life from his death. When he comes to treat Christ's death as redemption, he quickly adds, "Yet the remainder of the obedience that he manifested in his life is not excluded."[285]

Calvin certainly teaches, and emphasizes as an essential part of Christ's redemption, what the later Reformed tradition calls Christ's "active obedience." By this the tradition has in mind exactly what Calvin intends by "the whole life of Christ," namely, the entire life of Christ consisting of perfect love for God and perfect love for God's people in obedience to the law. Christ's holy life was not simply his own individual life of sinlessness. It was redemptive. It was the fulfillment by the Messiah of the law's demands in the stead of and on behalf of his people, who do not and cannot fulfill the law's demands. Christ's "It is finished" (John 19:30) applied not only to the punishment that the law required for a guilty people, but also to the law's requirement of perfect obedience to all its commandments upon a totally depraved people. Christ not only suffered and died as the representative head of the elect church, but he also *lived* as the church's representative head. By his obedient life, Christ earned righteousness with

God for everyone for whom he lived and obeyed, so that none of them is obliged to perform a single deed of obedience to the law as part of their righteousness with God. They are all obliged to obey all the commandments of God as their gratitude to God for their gracious salvation, but not a single act of obedience is demanded for righteousness.

It is this that the contemporary heresy in Reformed churches known as the federal vision finds objectionable in the doctrine of the active obedience of Christ. The men of the federal vision reject the doctrine of Christ's active obedience because they are determined that believers themselves accomplish part of their righteousness with God by their own active obedience to the law. The men of the federal vision have Calvin decidedly against them.[286]

"More exactly," Calvin's definition of redemption consists of "Christ's death." This death was Christ's payment of "the price of liberation in order to redeem us," as is the teaching, says Calvin, of Matthew 20:28, Romans 4:25, John 1:29, and other testimonies, which are "endless."[287]

Perceptively, Calvin insists on the obedience of Christ in his death. "Even in death itself his willing obedience is the important thing." The reason is that "a sacrifice not offered voluntarily would not have furthered righteousness."[288]

The pastoral and genuinely experiential Calvin directs his readers to the death of Christ for salvation and the assurance of salvation: "Trembling consciences find repose only in sacrifice and cleansing by which sins are expiated."[289]

Midway through the section in which Calvin explains that Christ redeemed us by his obedience, culminating in his voluntary laying down of his life for his sheep (2.16.5), Calvin allows his exposition of the redeeming work of Christ to be guided by the Apostles' Creed. Fittingly, since Calvin at this point in the *Institutes* is giving his thorough explanation of Christ's death, which is "the principal point on which ... our whole salvation turns," Calvin picks up his commentary on the Apostles' Creed with the words "suffered under Pontius Pilate." Calvin's commentary on these words in the creed and his commentary on the words that follow, "was crucified, dead and buried; he descended into hell," make plain with unmistakable clarity the fundamental nature of the death of Christ.

The words "suffered under Pontius Pilate" establish not only the historicity of Christ's death, but also that Christ "took the role of a guilty man and evildoer."[290] The legal process before the Roman judge signified that Christ freed us "both by transferring our condemnation to himself and by taking our guilt upon himself."[291] Pilate's earthly tribunal represented "God's heavenly judgment seat."[292]

Calvin finds in Isaiah 53, Mark 15:28, and Psalm 69:4 the substitutionary nature of Christ's death. The innocent Christ took the place of guilty sinners as their representative before the judgment seat of God in order to suffer their shame and punishment. Christ died "in the place of the sinner... He was burdened with another's sin." Calvin adds, "This is our acquittal: the guilt that held us liable for punishment has been transferred to the head of the Son of God."[293] Deliverance from the anxiety concerning "God's righteous vengeance" still hanging over us requires our remembering "this substitution."[294]

The "form of Christ's death"—"crucified"—signified that Christ removed the curse of God from those for whom he died. Hanging upon the cross, Christ "makes himself subject to the curse."[295] Christ took the curse due to others upon himself by the "imputation," or legal reckoning, to him of the sins of others by God the judge. Christ was "covered with them [the iniquities of others] by transferred imputation." By the imputation of our sins to Christ, they "cease to be imputed to us."[296]

Basic to this redeeming exchange—guilt imputed to the innocent Christ so that innocence might be imputed to guilty sinners—is the truth that Christ's death was satisfaction of offended divine justice. "Christ was offered to the Father in death as an expiatory sacrifice that when he discharged all satisfaction through his sacrifice, we might cease to be afraid of God's wrath."[297] The biblical passages that are decisive for believing the cross as deliverance from the curse are Isaiah 53, Deuteronomy 21:23, Galatians 3:13, 14, and 2 Corinthians 5:21.

In his explanation of the fifth petition of the model prayer, "Forgive us our debts," Calvin describes the cross—the judicial ground of the forgiveness of sins—as God's own act of satisfying himself as the substitute for his people. "[God exacts] no payment from us but mak[es] satisfaction to himself by his own mercy in Christ, who once for all gave himself as a ransom."[298] Into one brilliantly conceived phrase, Calvin manages to pack virtually everything that belongs to the nature of the death of Christ, as well as everything that contemporary theology finds objectionable in the doctrine of the cross.

Only because the death of Christ was substitutionary satisfaction of God's justice was it also Christ's triumph over the powers and principalities as proclaimed in Colossians 2:14, 15. In his death Christ was victor over Satan, his hosts, and all his powers because, and *only* because, his death was the bloody sacrifice offered to the just God in the stead of a guilty people.

The attempt by contemporary theology to explain the crucified Christ as *"Christus Victor"* (Christ the Conqueror), while rejecting substitutionary satisfaction, contradicts Calvin (as, indeed, the entire Reformation), is condemned by the passages of Scripture that were decisive for Calvin and the Reformation, and plunges the consciences of guilty minds into fear and despair. For "faith apprehends an acquittal in the condemnation of Christ, a blessing in his curse."[299]

Christus Victor expresses an explanation of the death of Christ as Christ's victory over Satan and the demonic powers, while denying that the death of Christ was penal satisfaction of the justice of God as the substitute for others (the "forensic" doctrine of the atonement). *Christus Victor* is associated with the Swedish theologian Gustaf Aulén, who promoted this doctrine of the death of Christ in a series of lectures in 1930, which were published in English translation in 1958.[300]

Calvin concludes his treatment of the death of Christ by noting that "Christ's shed blood served, not only as a satisfaction, but also as a laver... to wash away our corruption."[301] The cross cleansed from sin's pollution, as well as from sin's guilt.

In all his consideration of Christ's death, Calvin makes no issue of the extent of that redeeming death. That is, Calvin does not specifically address the issue whether Christ died only for the elect, or whether he died for all humans without exception. This omission affords the opportunity to some who profess to be Calvinists regarding other important doctrines to maintain that Calvin taught universal atonement.

By his clear, powerful description of the death of Christ as effectual substitutionary satisfaction of divine justice, on the basis of such texts as Isaiah 53, Mark 15:28, John 10:15, and Galatians 3:13, 14, Calvin teaches limited atonement, that is, the death of Christ only for the elect, unless he teaches that all men without exception will be saved (which heresy, of course, Calvin repudiates). No one can teach the nature of Christ's death as substitutionary satisfaction that effectually redeemed and obtained the acquittal of those whose sins were imputed to the crucified Christ, while holding that Christ died for multitudes who nevertheless must satisfy everlastingly in hell for their sins. In fact, those professing Calvinists who argue that Calvin taught universal atonement exactly *deny* that Christ's death was what Calvin says it is, namely, effectual substitutionary satisfaction.

Add to this that, as all must acknowledge, Calvin teaches that the source of the crucified Christ and his redemption is the election of some only and that the application to sinners of the benefits of the cross is by "irresistible grace," governed by election, and the conclusion is inescapable: Calvin teaches "limited atonement."

At the same time, we recognize that here, where he most directly and fully treats the death of Christ, and elsewhere, Calvin does not address the issue of the extent of the redemption of the cross. Also there are passages in his commentaries, especially his commentary on Romans 5:12–17, in which Calvin describes the atonement as universal.

The Canons of Dordt with their explicit declaration that Christ died for the elect and for "those only," therefore, represent development of the dogma of the death of Christ beyond Calvin.[302] In this development, the Canons express the doctrine that was implicit in Calvin's clear, firm confession of the nature of the death of Christ, regardless of ambiguous, careless, or even erroneous statements by Calvin here and there in his commentaries.

Calvin's explanation of Jesus' death and burial, following the Apostles' Creed, rigorously continues the theme of Christ's being our substitute. The meaning of Christ's death and burial is that "he in every respect took our place to pay the price of our redemption."[303] There are two outstanding benefits of Christ's death and burial for us. The first is that Christ's death and burial delivered us from physical death and its terror: "ensured that we would not die."[304] The second is deliverance from the ruling power of sin: "mortification of our flesh."[305] For the first benefit, Calvin appeals to Hebrews 2:14, 15, for the second, to Romans 6:4, 5.

Calvin reaffirms the "efficacy" of Christ's death: "There inheres in it an efficacy." It is not only an "example."[306]

Next in the Apostles' Creed is the controversial statement of Christ's descension into hell. Calvin freely acknowledges the late inclusion of the phrase "he descended into hell" in the creed. He also acknowledges that there have been many different explanations of Christ's descension into hell. Nevertheless, this part of the creed is "useful": "If it is left out, much of the benefit of Christ's death will be lost."[307] The Roman Catholic explanation, which has Christ going to the souls of the Old Testament saints in order to release them from their prison, Calvin dismisses as "nothing but a story."[308] The right explanation is that Christ suffered "in his soul the terrible torments of a condemned and forsaken man," not only "a bodily death."[309] Christ descended into hell in that he wrestled "hand to hand with the devil's power, with the dread of death, with the pains of hell."[310]

That Christ suffered the pangs of eternal death—and *feared* them—is evident from his extraordinary reactions to his suffering. "Drops of blood flowed from his face [Luke 22:44]." He needed an angel "to encourage him ... [Luke 24:43.]" He prayed that the cup pass from him (Matt. 26:39).[311]

Calvin is not frightened off from his strong statements concerning Christ's suffering of the torments of hell, including his struggles and fears, by adversaries who charge him with dishonoring the Son of God. Calvin speaks boldly of "Christ's weakness," although a weakness "pure and free of all vice and stain."[312] Those "quibblers," who foolishly think they honor Christ by denying the reality of his agonies of soul—denying his descension into hell!—are ignorant of the meaning of redemption from God's judgment.[313]

Acknowledging the reality and awfulness of Christ's suffering, including his human fear, "unbelievable bitterness of heart," and struggle with the will of God for him, is "wisdom: duly to feel how much our salvation cost the Son of God."[314]

Calvin exclaims, "[Christ's] goodness—never sufficiently praised."[315]

Christ's suffering in soul brings to mind "the error of Apollinaris," the ancient heretic who denied that Christ has a human soul. Reflection on Christ's expressing a human will, for example, in his prayer that the cup pass from him, is the occasion for Calvin's condemnation of the "Monothelites," ancient heretics who taught that Christ has only one will.[316]

The benefit for us of Christ's descension into hell is "that in death we may not now fear those things which our Prince has swallowed up."[317] The troubling of his soul with hellish agonies "drive[s] away fear and bring[s] peace and repose to our souls."[318]

The bodily resurrection of Jesus Christ, according to Calvin, was the completion of the work he accomplished by his death. "Through his death, sin was wiped out and death extinguished; through his resurrection, righteousness was restored and life raised up."[319] Such is the relation between Christ's death and resurrection that "whenever mention is made of his death alone, we are to understand at the same time what belongs to his resurrection. Also, the same synecdoche applies to the word 'resurrection.'"[320]

Since Calvin did not write in the twenty-first century, when heretical theologians busy themselves to deny Christ and destroy the church by casting doubt on the historicity and reality of the bodily resurrection of Christ, Calvin does not defend the reality of Christ's bodily resurrection. Nevertheless, he asserts it. The words "risen from the dead" express "the truth of his death and resurrection, as if it were said: he suffered the same death that other men naturally die; and received immortality in the same flesh that, in the mortal state, he had taken upon himself."[321]

The benefit of Christ's resurrection for the believer is, generally, assurance of victory over death. Specifically, the benefit is threefold: the restoration of righteousness (Rom. 4:25); spiritual resurrection into a new and holy life (Col. 3:1–5); and assurance of the believer's own bodily resurrection (1 Cor. 15:12–26). Calvin either refers to or quotes these biblical passages as teaching the benefit of Christ's resurrection.

"To the resurrection is quite appropriately joined the ascent into heaven." The ascension was Christ's bodily departure into heaven: "His body was raised up above all the heaven." With regard to his "physical presence," therefore, Christ is no longer with his church on earth, as he himself foretold in Matthew 26:11: "Me ye have not always."[322]

The purpose of Christ's departure in the body was that he might be present with the church in the world in a way that is "more useful to us ... an invisible but more desirable way." This, says Calvin, is Christ's presence in the Holy Spirit. Calvin appeals, rightly, to John 14:18, 19 and to John 16:7, 14. This "spiritual presence" of Christ consists of the diffusion of Christ's energy, power, and majesty.[323]

Thus at the ascension Christ "truly inaugurated his Kingdom."[324] The messianic kingdom and its glory will be visible to all only at Christ's coming in judgment. Until then, "his Kingdom lies hidden in the earth, so to speak, under the lowness of the flesh."[325] Calvin was no millennialist, whether pre- or post-, with a doctrine of a carnal kingdom triumphing in history so as to become visible to all.

The charge routinely raised against Calvin's doctrine of the kingdom of the risen and ascended Christ by the postmillennialists, that it is pessimistic (because it denies the earthly victory of a carnal kingdom in history), rings hollow in light of Calvin's extolling of Christ's power and rule throughout the present age. Christ ascended "to rule heaven and earth with a more immediate power."[326] In his sitting at God's right hand, "Christ was invested with lordship over heaven and earth, and solemnly entered into possession of the government committed to him."[327]

Explaining the creed's confession of Christ's sitting at the right hand of God the Father Almighty, Calvin applies to the exalted Christ such passages as Ephesians 1:20–22, 1 Corinthians 15:27, and Acts 2:30–36, which testify of Christ's sovereignty, might, rule, and majesty.

The trouble with postmillennialism (and a grievous trouble it is), especially the Christian reconstruction form of postmillennialism, is that it does not understand the *nature* of Christ's kingdom, kingdom-power, and kingdom-glory.

Calvin does understand the nature of the messianic kingdom. It is spiritual. Accordingly, as Calvin explains in detailing the benefits of Christ's ascension and sitting on God's right hand, the reign of King Jesus throughout the present age, until his coming in judgment on the world's last day, is his spiritual government and blessing of his church:

> [He] daily lavishes spiritual riches upon [his own people]. He therefore sits on high, transfusing us with his power, that he may quicken us to spiritual life, sanctify us by his Spirit, adorn his church with divers gifts of his grace, keep it safe from all harm by his protection, restrain the raging enemies of his cross

and of our salvation by the strength of his hand, and finally hold all power in heaven and on earth."[328]

Calvin concludes: "This is the true state of his Kingdom."[329]

Significantly, Calvin prefaces his description of the spiritual nature of Christ's reign with the words, "Faith comprehends his might."[330] Unbelief is oblivious to the spiritual might of King Jesus and ridicules it.

In the ascension and the sitting at God's right hand, which Calvin combines for this purpose, Calvin finds three main benefits. First, "in our Head" we who believe are already in heaven. Christ has opened for us "the way into the Heavenly Kingdom, which had been closed through Adam."[331] Second, Christ intercedes for us with the Father, thus preparing "a way and access for us to the Father's throne."[332] Third, Calvin declares that "faith comprehends his might, in which reposes our strength, power, wealth, and glorying against hell."[333]

Only at his return to conduct the final judgment will Christ "appear to all with the ineffable majesty of his Kingdom."[334] Like the ascension, Christ's coming in judgment will be a real, visible bodily change of place for Christ: "For he will come down from heaven in the same visible form in which he was seen to ascend."[335]

The final judgment will be Christ's kingly act of separating "the lambs from the goats, the elect from the reprobate." All humans must be judged: "No one—living or dead—shall escape his judgment."[336]

The comfort of the elect believer in the face of the coming judgment is not that he will avoid the judgment or be exempt from it. Rather, the comfort is that the judge will be his "Redeemer": "No mean assurance, this—that we shall be brought before no other judgment seat than that of our Redeemer, to whom we must look for our salvation!"[337]

The privilege of conducting the judgment will be a great honor for Christ: "By giving all judgment to the Son [John 5:22], the Father has honored him." But this honor, Calvin goes on to say, is "to the end that he may care for the consciences of his people, who tremble in dread of judgment."[338]

Having concluded his exposition of the Apostles' Creed, Calvin summarizes the teaching of the creed: "We see that our whole salvation and all its parts are comprehended in Christ." The exhortation that follows is this: "Let us drink our fill from this fountain, and from no other."[339]

Thus Calvin confesses the great theme of the sixteenth-century Reformation of the church: "Christ alone."

Confession of Christ as the only savior, however, is not Calvin's last word concerning the doctrine of Christ. Calvin closes his treatment of the saving work of Christ with an entire chapter—chapter seventeen of book two—devoted to a defense of the truth that Christ's redemptive work was meritorious. Calvin titles the chapter, "Christ Rightly and Properly Said to Have Merited God's Grace and Salvation for Us."

Defense of the meritorious nature of Christ's redemptive work is necessary, Calvin informs us, because certain men ("perversely subtle men") are denying that Christ merited salvation for his people. Their argument is that merit compromises the graciousness of salvation. "They think that it [merit] obscures God's grace."[340]

Calvin readily acknowledges that the merits of Christ are not the *cause* of the grace of God toward his elect people. On the contrary, Christ and his meritorious work are the *revelation* of the grace of God. Calvin quotes Augustine with approval: "The clearest light of predestination and grace is the Man Christ Jesus."[341]

Indeed, "it is absurd to set Christ's merit against God's mercy," as these "perversely subtle men" do, for Christ's merit is "subordinate to God's mercy," says Calvin. God has graciously ordained that his "free favor" would save us by means of, and on the basis of, Christ's meritorious work, and in no other way. "Christ's merit depends upon God's grace alone, which has ordained this manner of salvation."[342]

The "absurd" argument that Christ's merit conflicts with God's grace does not, and must not be allowed to, overthrow the truth that Christ's obedient life and atoning death were meritorious. Calvin emphatically confesses the meritorious nature of Christ's work on behalf of his people: "By his obedience...Christ truly acquired and merited grace for us with his Father."[343]

By "meriting," Calvin understands that fundamental aspect of Christ's obedience and death that consisted of acquiring salvation for guilty sinners by paying to God the price demanded by his righteousness and satisfying the justice of God on their behalf. "He acquired salvation for us by his righteousness, which is tantamount to deserving it."[344] Christ merited salvation for us by "his shedding of [his] blood" inasmuch as "God's judgment was satisfied by that price."[345]

The meritorious work itself was, generally, Christ's subjecting himself to the law—its demands and curse—in the stead of and on behalf of others: "Christ merited favor for us... by taking that burden [namely, of observing the law] upon himself."[346] For Calvin, the main element of this observance of the law by Christ is his payment of the price and suffering of the penalty demanded by the law through his suffering and death: "He paid the price to redeem us from the penalty of death."[347]

Basic to the meritorious character of Christ's obedience was that he observed the law, paid the price, and suffered the penalty, not for himself, as though he owed these things, but for others. "It was superfluous, even absurd, for Christ to be burdened with a curse, unless it was to acquire righteousness for others by paying what they owed."[348] One merits who does or gives something that is not required of him.

In this connection, Calvin's strong insistence that the meriting Christ is the eternal Son of God is important. Against "Lombard and the Schoolmen," that is, medieval, Romanizing theologians, who taught that "Christ merited... for himself," Calvin responds, "What need was there for God's only Son to come down in order to acquire something new for himself?"[349]

Mere man cannot merit, because mere man can never do or give more than God requires of him. But the Son of God in sinless human flesh could merit, and did merit.

From Calvin's piling up biblical passages that teach that Christ's death was expiation, propitiation, sacrifice, appeasement, satisfaction, payment of the ransom price, and suffering of the divine penalty, it is evident that Calvin sees clearly the seriousness of the denial of the meritorious nature of Christ's obedience, particularly his death. To deny merit is to deny that the death of Christ was the payment of the price to the justice of God.

Necessarily involved in the denial of Christ's merit as well is the denial of justification as (legal) imputation of Christ's righteousness to the believer. "For if we attain righteousness by a faith that reposes in him, we ought to seek the matter of our salvation [that is, Christ's merits] in him."[350]

Calvin's vigorous defense of the merits of Christ is timely for Reformed churches at the beginning of the twenty-first century. Once again, certain "perversely subtle men" attack the truth that Christ's obedience, suffering, and death were meritorious. Like the false teachers of Calvin's day, they absurdly argue that a meritorious obedience of Christ would compromise God's grace. And like the heretics with whom Calvin contended, these men intend their denial of Christ's merits to undermine the great truths of the gospel that Christ's death was the imputation to the substitute of the guilt of his elect church and that justification by faith alone is the imputation to the elect believer of the righteousness of his substitute. These are the men of the federal vision.[351]

BOOK THREE

The Way in Which We Receive the Grace of Christ: What Benefits Come to Us from It, and What Effects Follow

CHAPTER 11

Union with Christ

Introduction

The subject with which book three of the *Institutes* begins is soteriology, the doctrine of salvation, the saving of the elect sinner by the application to him of the benefits of salvation that have been obtained by the death of Jesus Christ. Book two concludes with the redemption accomplished by the death of Christ, which redemption is now stored up as it were in the risen and exalted Christ at God's right hand. Calvin opens book three with these words: "We must now examine this question. How do we receive those benefits which the Father bestowed on his only-begotten Son—not for Christ's own private use, but that he might enrich poor and needy men?"[1] Included in this salvation are the various works of the Spirit that make up the traditional Reformed *ordo salutis*, or order of salvation—regeneration, calling, faith, justification, sanctification, and glorification.

This section of the *Institutes* is as difficult to analyze as it is extraordinarily fascinating. It is fascinating as a fresh, biblical explanation of the utterly mysterious work of the Spirit in the heart and life of the elect sinner. For example, as Calvin describes it, the reality of "Christ in us" is so strongly urged as to leave the impression that the indwelling of Christ is *physical*. It is not, of course, and Calvin makes this plain, but Calvin is emphatic that Christ really lives in us: "Christ is not outside us but dwells within us. Not only does he cleave to us by an indivisible bond of fellowship, but with a wonderful communion, day by day, he grows more and more into one body with us, until he becomes completely one with us."[2]

Here is the key to understanding Calvin's doctrine of the Lord's supper, namely, the real spiritual presence of Christ in the supper so that by a believing use of the supper the believer has Christ in him more and more. Calvin's doctrine of the indwelling Christ, particularly by means of the supper, is reflected in the Heidelberg Catechism:

> What is it to eat the crucified body and drink the shed blood of Christ?
> It is not only to embrace with a believing heart all the sufferings and death of Christ, and thereby to obtain the forgiveness of sins and life eternal, but moreover, also, to be so united more and more to his sacred body by the Holy Ghost, who dwells both in Christ and in us, that although he is in heaven, and we on the earth, we are nevertheless flesh of his flesh and bone of his bones, and live and are governed forever by one Spirit, as members of the same body are by one soul.[3]

The difficulty of Calvin's doctrine of salvation is due in part to the difficulty of the subject itself. The biblical teaching of salvation is profound, and Calvin does full justice to the biblical presentation of this mysterious work of the Spirit of Christ in our salvation. Calvin's treatment of the work of salvation is also difficult because Calvin did not feel himself bound to develop soteriology along the lines of the later traditional *ordo salutis*. Calvin begins with *faith*. Faith is followed by repentance, which is not even mentioned in the traditional *ordo salutis*. And Calvin obviously understands regeneration differently than does the later Reformed tradition. Calvin identifies regeneration with repentance and views regeneration not as the act of a moment, but as a lifelong work of the Spirit within the elect sinner. "In a word, I interpret repentance as regeneration ... And indeed, this restoration does not take place in one moment or one day or one year; but ... throughout their lives."[4]

In setting forth Calvin's doctrine of salvation, I will follow Calvin and seek to understand Calvin. I will not force Calvin into the conceptions and structure of the traditional Reformed *ordo salutis*. It will be evident that, in the main, the later tradition faithfully confesses Calvin's doctrine, although sometimes in different terminology. At the same time, we will be open to the possibility that Calvin may *correct* the later orthodoxy.

Salvation as union with Christ

Calvin wants us to conceive of salvation as *union with Christ*, and such a union that Christ himself is *in* us: "As long as Christ remains outside of us, and we are separated from him, all that he has suffered and done for the salvation of the human race remains useless and of no value for us. Therefore, to share with us what he has received from the Father, he had to become ours and to dwell within us."[5]

Basically, this is the meaning of Christ's being our head and of the teaching of the Bible that we are ingrafted into Christ. Especially Paul speaks, again and again, of the saints being in Christ and of Christ being in the saints (Eph. 1:1; Eph. 3:17). Not only do we thus receive Christ's benefits, but also *Christ himself* with his benefits. Calvin would say, and did say, that the chief thing is that we receive *Christ*, and his benefits come along with him. This is the doctrine of salvation of the Heidelberg Catechism: "Are all men, then, saved by Christ, as they have perished by Adam? No; only such as by true faith are ingrafted into him, and receive all his benefits."[6]

Calvin then alludes to Ephesians 5:22–33 and describes this union of the child of God with Christ as "sacred wedlock."[7] This is what later Reformed theology has come to call the "mystical union."

According to Calvin, not only does the Holy Ghost create this union, but also the Holy Ghost *himself is the bond* that unites us to Christ. Calvin's exposition of the Spirit as the worker of salvation indicates that, although this Spirit is the third person of the Trinity, whose "eternal deity and essence" Calvin has discussed earlier in chapter thirteen of book one, the Spirit as the worker of salvation is this third person of the blessed Trinity as the Spirit of Jesus Christ. Of him, Calvin plainly says, "The Holy Spirit is the bond by which Christ effectually unites us to himself."[8] Surely, this is biblical, and every treatment in Reformed dogmatics and preaching of the doctrine of salvation, particularly of the order of salvation, must begin with the teaching of the Spirit of Christ as the personal bond between Christ and his people.

I suggest, as Calvin does not, that such a role of the Spirit in salvation is grounded in a similar relation of the Spirit in the being of God. In theological terminology, the rule is that the economic Trinity is the revelation of the ontological Trinity. That is, in the work of salvation, the triune God reveals himself as he is in himself. The Spirit is the bond who unites each elect believer to Jesus Christ, according to the reality in the Godhead. In the Godhead, the third person, the Spirit, is the personal bond of the friendship between the first person and the second person.

The Spirit functions as the bond of union with Christ by means of faith, which he works in the elect. Without denying that the Spirit is the bond, Calvin goes on to teach that *faith* is the bond of union between the believer and Christ. Referring to Christ's dwelling in us and our growing "into one body with him," Calvin says, "It is true that we obtain this [union with Christ] by faith." He immediately adds, with reference to faith, "Not all indiscriminately embrace that communion with Christ."[9]

It is plain that Calvin conceives faith not only as the activity of knowing and trusting in Jesus Christ, but also as union with Christ, although Calvin does not explicitly make this distinction. When later Reformed theology makes this distinction, it is true to Calvin. Faith is not exclusively an activity; faith is also, and more basically, union with Christ. For this reason, Calvin makes faith the beginning of the saving work of the Spirit. As a bond of union with Christ, faith precedes even the regeneration, or the rebirth, of the elect sinner. First one is, and must be, united to Christ by the bond of faith. Then through this bond, Christ and all his benefits come into the heart of the elect child of God.

Even though Calvin does not so describe it, we may note that on this view of salvation, namely, union with Christ, salvation is the realization of the covenant with the elect sinner personally. For the covenant of grace is union and communion with Christ.

Faith as activity

Faith is not only union with Christ, but faith is also an activity. As a good teacher, distinguishing well, Calvin gives a clear definition of faith: "Now we shall possess a right definition of faith if we call it *a firm and certain knowledge of God's benevolence toward us, founded upon the truth of the freely given promise in Christ, both revealed to our minds and sealed upon our hearts through the Holy Spirit.*"[10]

There are two main elements of faith as an activity, as Calvin points out and further explains in chapters fourteen through sixteen of book three.

The first main element of faith as an activity is knowledge. This knowledge is a knowledge of the illumined mind. The illumined mind is a mind that has been given the knowledge of God in Christ by the Holy Spirit. This knowledge comprehends the love of God in Jesus Christ for the one who thus believes. For Calvin, the knowledge of faith is more of the heart than of the mind.

Faith for Calvin is not a bare, objective, intellectual assent to the doctrine of the Christian faith set forth in the Bible. It is not the case that only when Calvin comes to the second element—trust or confidence—does faith take on the character of personal assurance of one's own salvation. That personal assurance is already an integral part of knowledge. "What is the knowledge of faith?" we ask Calvin. His answer is that, although faith certainly is a knowledge of the teachings of the word of God, it is not such a knowledge of the teachings of the word of God as leaves it an open question whether these truths apply personally to the one who believes. Rather, it is a knowledge that comprehends the love of God in Christ for him personally: "knowledge of God's benevolence toward us."

Away then with that pernicious notion that has infiltrated Reformed churches, that assurance is not of the essence of faith, so that one can make a certain external confession of being a believer for thirty, forty, or fifty years but never have the assurance of his own salvation. Whatever this notion may be, it is not the teaching of Calvin.

The second element of faith as an activity is "certainty," indeed, "full and fixed certainty" that God's love and salvation in Jesus Christ are personally for the one who believes.[11] "He alone is truly a believer who, convinced by a firm conviction that God is a kindly and well-disposed Father toward him, promises himself all things on the basis of his generosity; who, relying upon the promises of divine benevolence toward him, lays hold on an undoubted expectation of salvation."[12]

Since Calvin is at home in the psalms and is familiar with all of the moods of the soul found in them, he acknowledges the struggles that believers have with this certainty. There are doubts and fears; nevertheless, not unbelief, but the certainty of faith always prevails. He uses a vivid figure of a prisoner sitting in fetters in a dark jail cell. Deprived of the full view of the sun, the prisoner can see only a few rays shining into his cell through a narrow window. Calvin concludes: "However much we are shadowed on every side with great darkness, we are nevertheless illumined as much as need be for firm assurance when, to show forth his mercy, the light of God sheds even a little of its radiance."[13]

Calvin rails against "the half papist" doctrine that the Christian life is a continual alternation of faith and doubt.[14] Calvin does not excuse, secretly promote, glorify, or countenance *doubt* in the Christian experience.

The explanation of the sinner's confidence—not doubting—is *union with Christ*.

> We ought not to separate Christ from ourselves or ourselves from him. Rather we ought to hold fast bravely with both hands to that fellowship by which he has bound himself to us. So the apostle teaches us: "Now your body is dead because of sin; but the Spirit of Christ which dwells in you is life because of righteousness" [Rom. 8:10]. According to these men's [the half-papists'] trifles, he ought to have said: "Christ indeed has life in himself; but you, as you are sinners, remain subject to death and condemnation." But he speaks far otherwise, for he teaches that that condemnation which we of ourselves deserve has been swallowed up by the salvation that is in Christ. And to confirm this he uses the same reason I have brought forward: that Christ is not outside us but dwells within us. Not only does he cleave to us by an indivisible bond of fellowship, but with a wonderful communion, day by day, he grows more and more into one body with us, until he becomes completely one with us.[15]

For Calvin, assurance, certainty, or confidence of salvation, including perseverance unto eternal life, is not merely of the well-being of faith. It is also of the very *essence* of faith. A bold confidence of salvation in the face of many sins and troubles of all kinds is what true faith *is*. So important is this for Calvin that he says even about the element of knowledge that "the knowledge of faith consists in assurance rather than in comprehension."[16] Calvin does not deny that faith is knowledge and comprehension, to which biblical truth the *Institutes* itself is a testimony, but he says that even the knowledge of faith is assurance; and, if it comes down to it, faith is more assurance than comprehension. So essential is assurance to faith that "there is no right faith except when we dare with tranquil hearts to stand in God's sight."[17]

The Puritan doctrine that assurance of one's own salvation is not of the being of faith, but merely of faith's well-being, is a radical departure from Calvin, as indeed from the gospel of the sixteenth-century Reformation. Denying that true faith is confidence or assurance, leading Puritans taught, and their disciples teach today, that many, if not most, believers live in doubt of God's love for them and of their salvation for many years, and some for as long as they live. Doubt of one's own salvation is normal for believers. Assurance is extraordinary. The Puritan Thomas Brooks wrote:

> Now though this full assurance is earnestly desired, and highly prized, and the want of it much lamented, and the enjoyment of it much endeavoured after by all saints, yet it is only obtained by a few. Assurance is a mercy too good for most men's hearts, it is a crown too weighty for most men's heads. Assurance is *optimum maximum*, the best and greatest mercy; and therefore God will only give it to his best and dearest friends.
>
> Augustus in his solemn feasts, gave trifles to some, but gold to others. Honours and riches, etc, are trifles that God gives to the worst of men; but assurance is that "tried gold," Rev. 3:18, that God only gives to tried friends. Among those few that have a share or portion in the special love and favour of God, there are but a very few that have an assurance of his love.
>
> It is one mercy for God to love the soul, and another mercy for God to assure the soul of his love.[18]

"*The work of faith*," wrote the Puritan Thomas Goodwin, "*is a distinct thing, a different thing, from the work of assurance.*"[19]

That their doctrine of faith differs radically from Calvin's teaching was freely acknowledged by the Puritans themselves. Having rightly described Calvin's doctrine of true faith as teaching that the sealing with the Spirit, or assurance, is "the work of faith itself," that is, that assurance is of the essence of faith, Goodwin flatly declares that Calvin's teaching is "what it [the doctrine of assurance] is not."[20]

Reformed theologians who defend the Puritan doctrine candidly admit that the Puritan doctrine of faith was not that of Calvin. The Presbyterian William Cunningham readily acknowledges, "Calvin had undoubtedly taught... that saving faith necessarily includes or implies personal assurance."[21] However, declares this defender of the Puritan doctrine, "This view [that is, the view of Calvin] was certainly exaggerated and erroneous."[22]

Cunningham foolishly attempts to explain the reformers' doctrine of assurance, that is, that true faith *is* assurance of one's own salvation, by suggesting that God gave them, in their special circumstances, a different, better faith than he gives to other believers at other times. "God seems to have given to them [the reformers] the grace of assurance more fully and more generally than He does to believers in ordinary circumstances."[23]

Calvin, however, and all the other reformers were not describing their own, unique faith but the faith that God gives to all his children. When Calvin defined faith as assurance, he was defining the faith revealed in Scripture, not an extraordinary faith revealed in the sixteenth century, and then only in a few preachers of the gospel.

The response to Cunningham is Calvin's response to the Roman Catholic theologians who tried to escape Paul's doctrine in Romans 8:35–39 and other passages, that faith is certainty of salvation, by "prating that the apostle had his assurance from a special revelation," thus implying that assurance was the special possession of the apostle. Calvin's response is: "There [in Romans 8:35–39] he is discussing those benefits [particularly assurance of one's own salvation] which come to all believers in common from faith, not those things which he exclusively experiences."[24]

The practical consequences of the Puritan doctrine of faith are disastrous. Multitudes of professing believers in Jesus Christ live much, even all, of their life doubting their salvation. With regard to that most precious aspect of the blessedness of salvation that God wills for all his dear children—assurance—these multitudes of professing Reformed

Christians differ not one whit from the doubting hordes of Roman Catholics.

Calvin's and the Reformation's doctrine that faith is assurance is confessional for all Reformed churches and Christians subscribing to the Heidelberg Catechism.

> What is true faith?
> It is not only a certain knowledge whereby I hold for truth all that God has revealed to us in his Word, but also a hearty trust which the Holy Ghost works in me by the Gospel, that not only to others, but to me also, forgiveness of sins, everlasting righteousness and salvation, are freely given by God, merely of grace, only for the sake of Christ's merits.[25]

Where the truth concerning faith is confessed and taught, according to this question and answer of the catechism, believers and their children live and die in the confidence of God's love for them and of their salvation. This confidence is an essential element of the only comfort of those who believe in Jesus Christ. The Spirit of Christ bestows this confidence with the gift of faith.

Calvin contrasts true faith with spurious "faiths."

First, there is the "implicit faith" of Rome, that is, a commitment by the members of the Roman Catholic Church to whatever the church teaches, although they are ignorant of these teachings, indeed of the doctrines taught by Scripture. "Is this what believing means—to understand nothing, provided only that you submit your feeling obediently to the church?" Calvin responds, "Faith rests not on ignorance, but on knowledge."[26]

Then Calvin contrasts true faith with "unformed faith," that is, bare assent to doctrine. What he has in mind is roughly similar to what Reformed dogmatics calls historical faith—a purely intellectual knowledge of the teachings of the Bible that does not result in a holy life. Calvin insists that inasmuch as true faith "embraces Christ," it is always a faith that includes "the sanctification of the Spirit."[27]

This addresses the issue of the "lordship controversy" of our day. There are those professing evangelicals who hold that a believer can have Christ only as savior without having him as the lord of his life.

One can believe and be saved, therefore, even though he lives impenitently in sin. Since "true faith embraces Christ," every believer has Christ as lord, as well as savior. "Unformed faith" is merely a "shadow or image of faith."[28]

Third, in a lengthy treatment, Calvin distinguishes a certain spurious faith, found temporarily in reprobates, from true faith in the elect people of God. This is an extremely interesting and important section in Calvin's treatment of faith. He makes it plain that he has his eyes on Hebrews 6:4–6:

> For it is impossible for those who were once enlightened, and have tasted of the heavenly gift, and were made partakers of the Holy Ghost, and have tasted the good word of God, and the powers of the world to come, if they shall fall away, to renew them again unto repentance; seeing they crucify to themselves the Son of God afresh, and put him to an open shame.

In this connection, Calvin also mentions Luke 8:13, that part of the parable of the sower having to do with the seed that fell on a rock. About the people described in this part of the parable, Jesus says, "They on the rock are they, which . . . for a while believe." Calvin also has in mind the faith of Saul (1 Sam. 9–11).

The "faith" found temporarily in the reprobate ungodly is due to Christ's "steal[ing] into their minds"; a "lower working of the Spirit";[29] God's illumining their minds "with some rays of his grace."[30]

This language is reflected in the Canons of Dordt: "God . . . confers upon them [the unconverted] various gifts."[31] The Westminster Confession of Faith states, "Others, not elected . . . have some common operations of the Spirit."[32]

The "temporary faith" of some reprobate ungodly persons has certain similarities to the true faith of God's elect. For this reason, Jesus says that they "believe" for a while.

The differences between the faith found temporarily in some reprobates and the true faith that Christ gives to the elect, however, are fundamental. First, faith in the reprobate is not a work of grace in the heart: "These have no root" (Luke 8:13). Second, in the reprobate the feeling of salvation is superficial and confused. Third, faith in the reprobate does not last. Especially this characteristic distinguishes this faith from true faith. An outstanding characteristic of true faith is that it endures to the end. The truth of the perseverance of the saints surfaces here.

According to Calvin, the faith of the reprobate is qualitatively different from the faith of the elect. "Not that they [reprobates with temporary faith] are partakers of the same faith or regeneration with the children of God."[33] Temporary faith is a false faith.

That temporary faith in the reprobate is the same as true faith in the elect, except that it does not last, is an error condemned by the Synod of Dordt. The Arminians taught that faith in the reprobate is the same as true faith in the elect. They pressed this teaching in the service of their doctrine that the saints can fall away. One can possess true, saving faith and then lose it. The Canons reject this Arminian heresy: "The Synod *rejects* the errors of those...Who teach that the faith of those who believe for a time does not differ from justifying and saving faith except only in duration."[34] The Reformed creed teaches that the temporary faith of the reprobate is qualitatively different from the true faith of the child of God.

Calvin's and the Synod of Dordt's condemnation of the teaching that the temporary faith of reprobate, ungodly persons is essentially the same as true, saving faith falls as well on the twenty-first-century heresy that calls itself the federal vision. A basic tenet of this covenant theology is that all baptized children of godly parents alike are truly and savingly united to Christ. The union with Christ of many, however, is lost, so that they perish. Not only does this doctrine deny the biblical and Reformed truth of the perseverance of saints, including childish, covenant saints; inasmuch as union with Christ is faith, the doctrine also denies that the temporary faith of those who fall away is qualitatively different from the enduring faith of God's elect, covenant children.[35]

The origin and foundation of faith

Calvin teaches that faith is the gift of God to the elect sinner. Faith is not the sinner's own achievement; faith simply does not lie in man's own capability. The reason is that every human being is born totally depraved. The inability of the sinner to produce faith in himself holds both for faith as the bond of union with Christ and for faith as the activity of knowledge and confidence.

Since faith as union with Christ is the beginning of the work of salvation for Calvin, the saving of the sinner for Calvin is wholly and exclusively the work of God without the cooperation of the sinner.

With regard to faith as spiritual activity, Calvin says that it is a gift continually. Not only is the beginning of faith a gift; also the continuance of faith is a gift. God does not give a man the ability to believe and then leave it up to the man himself to believe, but God continues to maintain and increase faith in the man.

It is the Holy Spirit who gives faith. "Faith is the principal work of the Holy Spirit."[36] "Faith is a singular gift of God, both in that the mind of man is purged so as to be able to taste the truth of God and in that his heart is established therein. For the Spirit is not only the initiator of faith, but [also] increases it by degrees, until by it he leads us to the Kingdom of Heaven."[37] "In another place, when we had to discuss the corruption of nature, we showed more fully how unfit men are to believe... Let it suffice [now] that Paul calls faith itself, which the Spirit gives us but which we do not have by nature, 'the spirit of faith' [2 Cor. 4:13]."[38]

As the gift of the Spirit, faith is worked by, and always depends upon, the word of God. This word is not for Calvin the teaching of the Bible in general, but is specifically the good news of God's mercy in Christ to forgive guilty sinners. More specifically still, it is the *promise* of the forgiveness of sins by divine mercy: "We make the freely given promise of God the foundation of faith because upon it faith properly rests... faith properly begins with the promise, rests in it, and ends in it."[39] "Faith needs the Word as much as fruit needs the living root of a tree."[40]

This promise, from which faith arises like fruit from a "living root" and upon which faith depends, is an unconditional promise, according to Calvin: "For in God faith seeks life: a life that is... found... in the promise of mercy, and only in a freely given promise."[41] Faith springs out of the promise; faith depends upon the promise. The promise that is the "foundation of faith" is unconditional. It depends on nothing in the sinner, as a conditional promise would. A conditional promise would be worthless. "For a conditional promise that sends us back to our own works does not promise life unless we discern its presence in ourselves."[42] That is, a conditional promise would require the sinner to depend upon himself, rather than upon the promising God. This would be destructive of faith.

As much as Calvin stresses the necessity of the "Word" for faith, he insists that "without the illumination of the Holy Spirit, the Word can do nothing"; the Spirit must make the word effective in the heart.[43]

The object of faith

The object of faith is the word of God, but not the word in general, for example, commands and warnings. Rather, faith looks to the word of the mercy of God in Jesus Christ promising forgiveness. The thought is not that faith does not hold for truth everything that God says, including the commands and threats. But that which faith particularly looks to is the free promise of mercy.

In his discussion of the subject, "what strictly speaking, faith looks to in the Word," Calvin has this penetrating passage:

> God's word to Adam was, "You shall surely die" [Gen. 2:17] ... But these words are so far from being capable of establishing faith that they can of themselves do nothing but shake it ... Thus ... it is after we have learned that our salvation rests with God that we are attracted to seek him ... Accordingly, we need the promise of grace, which can testify to us that the Father is merciful; since we can approach him in no other way, and upon grace alone the heart of man can rest.[44]

Calvin adds, "The sole pledge of his love is Christ."[45]

Here is instruction for preaching: let the Reformed preacher preach the whole Scripture, and in every sermon let him proclaim the free promise of mercy in Christ.

If the preceding comes down to this, that the object of faith is Jesus Christ as the mercy of God, Calvin is not content with this but insists that the object of faith is God himself: "Borne up to heaven itself [by faith], we are admitted to the most hidden treasures of God and to the most hallowed precincts of his Kingdom."[46] Faith sees the face of God: "When first even the least drop of faith is instilled in our minds, we begin to contemplate God's face, peaceful and calm and gracious toward us."[47] This is the balm in Gilead that forgives the sins, soothes the troubles, allays the fears, and comforts the heart of the believer.

With God in Christ as the object of faith, it follows that salvation is faith's object: "Now, in the divine benevolence, which faith is said to look to, we understand the possession of salvation and eternal life is obtained."[48]

But this salvation, Calvin reminds us, is spiritual good, not earthly prosperity: "For faith does not certainly promise itself either length of years or honor or riches in this life, since the Lord willed that none of these things be appointed for us."[49]

Calvin concludes his lengthy treatment of faith by showing that love and hope arise from faith. "The teaching of the Schoolmen, that love is prior to faith and hope, is mere madness; for it is faith alone that first engenders love in us."[50] Although faith produces hope, faith is supported by hope: "Wherever this faith is alive, it must have along with it the hope of eternal salvation as its inseparable companion. Or rather, it engenders and brings forth hope from itself... Here we must keep our faith buttressed by patient hope."[51]

Repentance

We first should be clear what Calvin means by *repentance*. Calvin's use of the word can be confusing to twenty-first-century readers of the *Institutes*, whose understanding of repentance differs somewhat from Calvin's. He identifies repentance with regeneration: "I interpret repentance as regeneration, whose sole end is to restore in us the image of God."[52] He insists that repentance follows faith and then indicates that repentance is a lifelong activity, not the act of a moment.

Repentance in Calvin is what we have in mind with conversion. This is evident from the fact that Calvin defines conversion as basically a "turning"[53] and from the fact that he explains conversion as a mortifying of the old man and the quickening of the new man with reference to Ephesians 4:22–24 and Colossians 3:9, 10.[54]

However, by "conversion" or, in Calvin's common term, *repentance* is meant not a dramatic, one-time, dateable experience—at least not *only* this—but a lifelong, daily activity. By repentance Calvin has in mind the conversion described in the Heidelberg Catechism:

> In how many things does true repentance or conversion consist?
> In two things: the dying of the old man, and the quickening of the new.
> What is the dying of the old man?
> Heartfelt sorrow for sin; causing us to hate and turn from it always more and more.
> What is the quickening of the new man?
> Heartfelt joy in God; causing us to take delight in living according to the will of God in all good works.[55]

Repentance for Calvin, then, is more than sorrow over sin, although this is certainly included.

Why does Calvin identify repentance with regeneration? Calvin regards regeneration as the lifelong, ongoing renewal of the elect sinner springing from faith, rather than as the rebirth of the child of God in a never-repeated act of one instant.

Calvin intends by regeneration what the later tradition would describe as regeneration in the "broader sense." The later tradition did not entirely abandon Calvin's understanding of regeneration. In articles eleven through seventeen of heads three and four of the Canons of Dordt, the word *regeneration* is used exactly as Calvin uses it in the *Institutes*—not an instantaneous act, but an ongoing, lifelong renewal of the child of God by the Spirit of Christ. In this part of the Canons, the terms *regeneration* and *conversion* are used interchangeably, indicating that regeneration in the broader sense is in view.

Accordingly, repentance in Calvin's exposition includes sanctification, that is, the work of the Spirit making God's people holy and producing good works in them. This explains why Calvin enters into the following subjects: that regeneration leaves us with a sinful nature; that the regenerated man has the victory over his sinful nature; and that the regenerated man performs good works. All of this comes up in the discussion of regeneration, or repentance, because regeneration implies sanctification: a holy life is "the fruits of repentance."[56]

Calvin defines repentance as "the true turning of our life to God, a turning that arises from a pure and earnest fear of him; and it consists in the mortification of our flesh and of the old man, and in the vivification of the Spirit."[57]

Calvin sees "three heads" under which we must examine repentance, which he explains in turn.[58] The first head of repentance, or conversion, or even sanctification, is turning to God. This is a transformation of the soul itself, not merely a matter of outward works. The second main head of repentance is a fear of God. This is the cause of repentance in the consciousness of the sinner: "Repentance proceeds from an earnest fear of God."[59] Third, repentance is the mortifying of the old man and the vivifying, or making alive, of the new man (Eph. 4; Col. 3).

Concerning the origin of repentance, Calvin insists that, contrary to the opinion of some, repentance does not *precede* faith but *follows* faith and proceeds from faith. "Repentance not only constantly follows faith, but is also born of faith."[60] A little later, Calvin explains this: "A man cannot apply himself seriously to repentance without knowing himself to belong to God."[61] Also: "No one will ever reverence God but him [sic] who trusts that God is propitious to him."[62] In this connection Calvin sharply rebukes those—the "Anabaptists"—who prescribe for all converts that they must "practice penance" for a time before they are admitted to "the grace of the gospel."[63] This is the same as the notion that all who are truly saved must be able to speak of an experience of "conviction of sin," as they call it, for a period prior to the experience of salvation. Like the Anabaptists, the contemporary advocates of a prescribed period of deep sorrow over sin prior to admission "into communion of the grace of the gospel . . . marvelously exult in being considered spiritual."[64]

Arising as it does from faith, which is the gift of God, repentance is also a gift of God, not an act that man himself produces: "Repentance is a singular gift of God."[65] Calvin appeals to two texts: "Then hath God also to the Gentiles granted repentance unto life" (Acts 11:18); "If God peradventure will give them repentance to the acknowledging of the truth; and that they may recover themselves out of the snare of the devil" (2 Tim. 2:25, 26).

In this connection Calvin asserts that repentance is a gift given only to the elect, although all are exhorted to repentance. "Obviously God, renewing those he wills not to perish, shows the sign of his fatherly favor and, so to speak, draws them to himself with the rays of his calm and joyous countenance. On the other hand, he hardens and he thunders against the reprobate."[66]

Calvin is at pains at every point in soteriology to attribute every aspect of salvation to God and to view it as a gift of God to his chosen people.

In protecting the grace of salvation, particularly with regard to repentance, Calvin explains that, although repentance is necessary for forgiveness, repentance is not "the basis of our deserving pardon." Repentance is not a "condition" in this sense, but rather the *way* to pardon.

> For this reason, when God offers forgiveness of sins, he usually requires repentance of us in turn, implying that his mercy ought to be a cause for men to repent. He says, "Do judgment and righteousness, for salvation has come near." [Isa. 56:1]. Again, "A redeemer will come to Zion, and to those in Jacob who repent of their sins." [Isa. 59:20]. Again, "Seek the Lord while he can be found, call upon him while he is near; let the wicked man forsake his way and the unrighteousness of his thoughts; let him return to the Lord, and he will have mercy upon him." [Isa. 55:6, 7]. Likewise, "Turn again, and repent, that your sins may be blotted out." [Acts 3:19]. Yet we must note that this condition is not so laid down as if our repentance were the basis of our deserving pardon, but rather, because the Lord has determined to have pity on men to the end that they may repent, he indicates in what direction men should proceed if they wish to obtain grace. Accordingly, so long as we dwell in the prison house of our body we must continually contend with the defects of our corrupt nature.[67]

In another passage Calvin writes, "Repentance is not the cause of forgiveness of sins."[68]

Here Calvin refers specifically to the sinner's sorrow over, and turning from, his sins. This repentance is the required way to seek and find forgiveness from a merciful God. There is no forgiveness for an impenitent sinner. But this repentance is neither a condition unto forgiveness, that is, a work of the sinner making him worthy of forgiveness, nor the basis of the forgiveness. The sinner is unworthy of forgiveness. Confession of this total unworthiness is an aspect of genuine repentance. And the sole basis of forgiveness is the cross of Christ.

Calvin concludes his positive treatment of repentance with an examination of the unpardonable sin. He bases his examination largely on Hebrews 6:4–6; Hebrews 10:26–29; Matt. 12:31, 32; and the account of Esau's repentance in Hebrews 12:16, 17.

Calvin defines the unpardonable sin by describing those who are guilty of it: "They sin against the Holy Spirit who, with evil intention, resist God's truth, although by its brightness they are so touched that they cannot claim ignorance."[69] The unpardonable sin is "willful [apostasy]... from faith in the gospel"; attended by deliberate profanation of "Christ's blood."[70] It is a blasphemy of the Holy Spirit because these apostates "strive against the illumination that is the work of the Holy Spirit."[71]

With the concern of a pastor, Calvin observes that this sin is unpardonable, not because people who commit it repent and are refused forgiveness, but because God *will not give* them repentance. Calvin comforts those children of God who torture themselves with the possibility that they have committed the unpardonable sin. Everyone who repents of whatever sin he has committed, be it ever so heinous and vile, is forgiven, and everyone who does repent has not committed the unpardonable sin.

Those who commit the unpardonable sin are reprobates from eternity. No elect child of God will, or can, commit this sin and thus perish. The unpardonable sin is a "rebellion by which the reprobate forsake salvation." With appeal to 1 John 2:19 ("They went out from us, but they were not of us"), Calvin declares that those who fall away "were not of the elect."[72] Election assures that all who are "of us" abide in the faith of Christ.

The Roman Catholic doctrine and sacrament of penance

To his treatment of repentance, specifically with regard to heartfelt sorrow over sin and a turning to God for forgiveness, Calvin appends a searching critique of the Roman Catholic sacrament of penance. His interest is "what the Scholastic Sophists [that is, the Roman Catholic Church] have taught concerning repentance."[73]

Rome's doctrine and practice of "penance" are guilty of changing biblical "repentance" from an "inward renewal of the mind, which bears with it true correction of life" into mere "outward exercises."[74]

The Roman Catholic sacrament of penance, consisting of "compunction of heart, confession of mouth, and satisfaction of works," which is supposed to forgive sins and thus afford consciences peace with God, does the very opposite. It makes forgiveness utterly impossible and renders the conscience "tormented and vexed."[75] No Roman Catholic is, or ever can be, sure that he has sufficient compunction of heart for his sins. None can ever confess into the ear of the priest (a form of confession of sin, Calvin notes, that Scripture nowhere commands) all his known sins.

And since forgiveness depends upon the sinner's own works of satisfaction, no Roman Catholic can ever enjoy peace with God, for peace with God is given only to a faith that depends wholly and exclusively upon the satisfaction of Jesus Christ.

Basic to Rome's doctrine of penance is the teaching that the repentance of the sinner (which for Rome includes works of satisfaction) is the cause, basis, and condition of forgiveness. The truth of the gospel is "that repentance is not the cause of forgiveness of sins."[76]

Rome's sacrament of penance, which is fundamental to that church's gospel, worship, and discipline, tramples upon two precious purposes of God with his gospel of grace: "that Christ's honor be kept whole and undiminished [and] that consciences assured of pardon for sin may have peace with God."[77]

At stake in this controversy of the Reformed faith with the Roman Catholic Church's sacrament of penance, Calvin reminds both his Roman Catholic and Protestant readers, is "the most serious matter of all": "forgiveness of sins."[78]

Essential elements of the Roman Catholic sacrament of penance are the abominations of indulgences and purgatory. Indulgences are the merits of the saints that the pope distributes to the living and the dead as partial satisfaction to God for their sins. Such is the folly of the practice of indulgences that Calvin suggests that the Roman Catholics who teach and enforce indulgences "are fit to be treated by drugs for insanity rather than to be argued with."[79]

Because indulgences deny the sufficiency of the satisfaction for sin of the death of Christ and teach sinners to trust in human works for salvation, indulgences are "a profanation of the blood of Christ, a Satanic mockery, to lead the Christian people away from God's grace."[80]

Purgatory is the place, according to Rome, where almost all sinners who eventually will earn eternal life in heaven must finish paying for their sins by suffering exquisite torments. It too is a basic element of the Roman Catholic sacrament of penance. "Purgatory is a deadly fiction of Satan, which nullifies the cross of Christ, inflicts unbearable contempt upon God's mercy, and overturns and destroys our faith."[81]

The biblical gospel of the intermediate state of all elect believers exposes Rome's terrifying message of purgatory. "All godly men, no less than prophets, apostles, and martyrs, immediately after death enjoy blessed repose."[82] The reason is that Christ fully satisfied for all the guilt of all their sins, and they were forgiven by faith alone in the one sacrifice.

CHAPTER 12

The Christian Life

Introduction

The Christian life, as described in book three, chapters six through ten, links up with the preceding treatment of repentance, which Calvin calls regeneration and which we understand to be lifelong conversion, including the work of sanctification. Calvin calls attention to this connection with the opening line of his description of the Christian life: "The object of regeneration . . . is to manifest in the life of believers a harmony and agreement between God's righteousness and their obedience."[1] What we have, then, in the description of the Christian life is the fruit of repentance, the effect, or the manifestation, in the elect sinner of the work of sanctification.

If this is the case, Calvin treats sanctification before he treats justification. This is not the logical or theological order of salvation; rather, it is the order that fits Calvin's scheme of treating repentance in connection with faith. But the order of Calvin's treatment, as well as the marvelous content itself of his description of the Christian life, makes any charge that the Reformed faith minimizes holiness of life sheer absurdity. This charge is sometimes raised against the Reformed faith: "Calvin so emphasizes the sovereignty of God, particularly in predestination and in justification by faith alone, as to minimize holiness of life." One thing that one who makes this charge has never done is read the *Institutes*, the fountainhead of the Reformed faith. For not only is the description in the *Institutes* of the Christian life magnificent, but in it the treatment of sanctification precedes justification. The order of the treatment of sanctification and justification indicates that in Calvin's mind there is nothing inferior about the doctrine of sanctification.

What a grand, gripping, humbling, sobering, and moving description of the Christian this is! It is no wonder that this section of the *Institutes* was published separately in Latin and French in 1550, and that it is still in print today in English translation as *The Golden Booklet of the True Christian Life*.[2]

Reformed congregations must hear this biblical description of and calling to the Christian life in the preaching. The preaching of the Christian life is the preaching of doctrine in its necessary and glorious fruits and ends. Calvin expresses the right relation between doctrine and life: "We have given the first place to the doctrine in which our religion is contained, since our salvation begins with it. But it must enter our heart and pass into our daily living, and so transform us into itself that it may not be unfruitful for us."[3] And in preaching this Christian life, preachers should warn the people and themselves that "the gospel ... is a doctrine not of the *tongue* but of *life*."[4]

Such is the compressed wisdom, beauty, and power of this section of the *Institutes* that it simply defies any adequate summary. One can only do justice to it by reading the whole section in its entirety and then more than once.

The pattern

I call attention to the main lines of this classic pattern for the Christian life according to a Reformed understanding of it, and to a few of the more striking statements about the Christian life by our reformer.

What Calvin gives is the pattern of the Christian life, and therefore, "how the life of a Christian man is to be ordered."[5] Calvin knows God to be a God of order. As there must be order in the church by right church government and order in our homes, there must also be order in our personal lives. The Christian life is an orderly life.

Calvin draws this pattern of the Christian life from Holy Scripture. The pattern from Scripture describes how the Spirit works in everyone who is united to Christ by the bond of faith, but in such a way that he is called to be active in approximating this pattern, thus ordering his life. Therefore, Calvin begins by setting forth some powerful motivations. Calvin was a good pedagogue, a good teacher, and he knew that the Christian life is demanding; the Christian life is sacrificial; the Christian life is a matter of self-denial; the Christian life goes clean contrary to the corrupt nature that the believer retains. Christians need motivation to take up this task.

First, the motivation is that we are to strive to be holy as the God to whom we are united is holy. Second, our life ought to express Christ, the Christ who gave himself for us and pours out his benefits upon us. Third, every benefit God bestows upon us calls us to appropriate thankfulness.

In a line occurring at a crucial juncture in the argument, a line both surprising and difficult, Calvin says, "Even though the law of the Lord provides the finest and best-disposed method of ordering a man's life, it seemed good to the Heavenly Teacher to shape his people by an even more explicit plan to that rule which he had set forth in the law."[6]

Calvin's subject is plainly the objective standard, or rule, that forms the Christian life. As we live the Christian life, we need a guide or a rule. Clearly, Calvin holds up the law, the ten commandments, as "the finest and best-disposed method of ordering a man's life." This is the well-known third use of the law that is uniquely characteristic of Calvinism. The first use of the law is to keep outward order in society; the second use is to show the regenerated child of God his sin and misery; and the third use is a guide for a thankful life.

Regarding the third use of the law, Lutheranism after Luther differs from Calvinism. Lutheranism denies the third use of the law and charges that by teaching the third use Calvinism falls back into works-righteousness. Lutheranism so explains and emphasizes justification by faith alone as to deny that the law is a guide for the thankful life of the child of God.

Rejection of God's law as the rule of a holy life is also found among some who profess Calvinism. This error is antinomianism (literally, "against the law," that is, against the law as the authoritative standard of a holy life). Usually the antinomians who profess Calvinism argue that, not only is it unlawful—a sin against grace—to use the law as the rule of a holy life, but such a use of the law is also unnecessary. They contend that the Spirit works holiness of life in the believer spontaneously, by the gospel, so that there is no need for the law as a rule or standard.

This antinomian doctrine contradicts Calvin. It also contradicts the Reformed confessions. Question and Answer 91 of the Heidelberg Catechism, for instance, prescribes the law of God as the standard of the good works of the thankful Christian: "But what are good works? Those only which are done from true faith, *according to the law of God.*"[7] And Lord's Days 34–44 of the catechism give a detailed explanation of the ten commandments as the authoritative guide of a holy life.

An antinomian spirit may be present in churches that profess the third use of the law. One manifestation of the antinomian spirit is a church's toleration of public, impenitent disobedience to one or more of the ten commandments. Often such a church will justify its tolerance of disobedience by appeal to the mercy of God. In fact, the church is repudiating the law of God as the standard of the holy life of its members.

Or there are members of churches professing the third use of the law who, as soon as the minister of the word sharply preaches the duties and prohibitions of the commandments, respond with the accusation that he is a "law-preacher," not a preacher of the gospel of grace. In fact, such members are repudiating the law of God as the rule of a holy life. Sound preaching of the gospel *includes*, rather than *excludes*, preaching the ten commandments as the guide of the Christian life. And the commandments *command* and *prohibit*.

Calvin teaches that "the law of the Lord provides the finest and best-disposed method of ordering a man's life."[8]

Nevertheless, the phrase advocating the law as the rule of life is concessive: "*Even though* the law of the Lord provides the finest and best-disposed method of ordering a man's life." The force of the sentence is to promote another, "even more explicit plan" that will shape us to the Christian life God intends for his people.[9] This is intriguing. This "more explicit plan" is the doctrine found especially in the New Testament, particularly Romans 12:1, that the elect believer is not his own, but God's. Calvin correctly sees that implied in the injunction to believers that they must present their bodies as living sacrifices to God is the truth that believers belong to God.

This truth, then, even more than the law, must pattern our lives:

> If we, then, are not our own [cf. 1 Cor. 6:19] but the Lord's, it is clear what error we must flee, and whither we must direct all the acts of our life.
>
> We are not our own: let not our reason nor our will, therefore, sway our plans and deeds. We are not our own: let us therefore not set it as our goal to seek what is expedient for us according to the flesh. We are not our own: in so far as we can, let us therefore forget ourselves and all that is ours.
>
> Conversely, we are God's: let us therefore live for him and die for him. We are God's: let his wisdom and will therefore rule all our actions. We are God's: let all the parts of our life accordingly strive toward him as our only lawful goal... O, how much has that man profited who, having been taught that he is not his own, has taken away dominion and rule from his own reason that he may yield it to God! For, as consulting our self-interest is the pestilence that most effectively leads to our destruction, so the sole haven of salvation is to be wise in nothing and to will nothing through ourselves but to follow the leading of the Lord alone.
>
> Let this therefore be the first step, that a man depart from himself in order that he may apply the whole force of his ability in the service of the Lord.[10]

All that follows in the *Institutes* concerning the Christian life is implications and outworkings of this basic truth for the Christian life: we are not our own; we are God's. Are the ten commandments the guide for the life that more basically is patterned after the truth that we belong to God? Yes, they are. But the law is not the only pattern. Even more than the law, the pattern that must live in our consciousness, as we live the Christian life according to the truth, is, "I am not my own; I am God's." In any case, in all his description of the Christian life, Calvin does not use the law as the rule, but New Testament teachings concerning self-denial, bearing the cross, stewardship, etc.

What immediately strikes those who are familiar with the Heidelberg Catechism is that *Calvin's rule for the Christian life* is the very same as the believer's *only comfort* in life and death in Question and Answer 1 of the catechism. The very same truth that is the comfort of the gospel decisively forms and shapes the Christian life.

Main elements of the Christian life

What will characterize the Christian life that conforms to the law and more especially to the truth that by the redemption of the cross and the renewal of the Spirit we are "not our own, but the Lord's"?

First, the Christian life is characterized by the service of God. This is first, not the service of our fellow man, but the service of God.

> Let this therefore be the first step, that a man depart from himself in order that he may apply the whole force of his ability in the service of the Lord. I call "service" not only what lies in obedience to God's Word but what turns the mind of man, empty of its own carnal sense, wholly to the bidding of God's Spirit.[11]

Second, the Christian life will be characterized by self-denial. This, Calvin distinguishes as self-denial toward the neighbor and self-denial toward God. In Calvin's treatment of self-denial toward the neighbor, he lays bare with the sharp sword of the word our wickedness in seeking self and denying the neighbor.

Calvin grounds our love of the neighbor in the "image of God in all men."[12] Calvin warns that outward deeds of goodness toward the neighbor are not enough. We must have inward sympathetic love of the needy. Believers "first... must put themselves in the place of him whom they see in need of their assistance, and pity his ill fortune as if they themselves experienced and bore it, so that they may be impelled by a feeling of mercy and humaneness to go to his aid just as to their own."[13]

The Christian life of self denial is also self-denial toward God. This means that we simply "resign ourselves and all our possessions to the Lord's will," depend upon the Lord's blessing for the success of our earthly life, and bear adversities patiently.[14] In vivid detail Calvin describes the troubles of life and says that the believer can bear all of them without cursing God or resisting, because "he will know it [is] ordained of God... into whose power he once for all surrendered himself and his every possession."[15] Is this not, in fact, the secret of bearing adversity patiently without any resentment toward God, namely, that at the beginning of the Christian life by the grace of God we have surrendered ourselves and all that we have to God's power? This is living our belief and confession of divine sovereignty. How radically different this is from the thinking of the world and from some perverted forms of so-called Christianity: "assert yourself" and "stand for your rights."

The third characteristic of the Christian life is bearing the cross. "Each must bear his own cross [Matt. 16:24]."[16] This is an aspect of the Christian life that is largely ignored by the charismatics, with their emphasis on the enthusiasm of the baptism with the Spirit, and by all forms of "happy Christianity," which teaches that Christ wants to give all his followers a successful, trouble-free, and happy earthly life—a lie exposed by the Bible, the history of the church, and experience. Christ wills that his followers bear their crosses in this life. Cross-bearing is an aspect of self-denial, and self-denial is rooted in belonging to Jesus Christ.

Probably by this point in his reading of Calvin's description of the Christian life, the believer is stretched to his limit and waiting for Calvin to say "Amen" to the Christian life. Whereupon, Calvin says, "But it behooves the godly mind to climb still higher."[17] "Still higher"? Still higher! "Still higher" because, although Calvin has already foretold for us a Christian life with troubles, now he tells us that we must expect to share in *the sufferings of Christ*. This is cross-bearing! "For whomever the Lord has adopted and deemed worthy of his fellowship ought to prepare themselves for a hard, toilsome, and unquiet life, crammed with very many and various kinds of evil": "the bitterness of the cross," the bitterness of Christ's cross in our lives.[18]

Calvin does not think it necessary to explain that our cross is not atoning. Calvin certainly views our cross-bearing as our sharing in Christ's suffering at the hands of a hostile world and the false church. Calvin views the cross as imposed by God upon us to prove our sonship, not to pay for sin: we obey God in love especially when obedience is painful and costly. Chiefly, the cross is reproach and suffering for Christ's sake. "To suffer persecution for righteousness' sake is a singular comfort."[19]

But benefits for us spring from bearing the cross. It teaches us not to depend upon our own flesh. It teaches us to experience God's faithful help as we rest on God alone. Bearing the cross teaches us to manifest our endurance by grace. The word for this is *patience*. Cross-bearing teaches us in such a way as to guard us against wanton rebellion against God. Sometimes, the cross chastises us for our faults. Always, cross-bearing bestows honor upon us for it is suffering for righteousness' sake. Calvin says, "We see how many good things, interwoven, spring from the cross."[20]

Although Calvin grants that we are caused real sorrow by the cross (and sorrow is not sinful), nevertheless, in view of the benefits we can and should bear our cross cheerfully. Calvin concludes that the benefits enable and require us to be thankful for the cross with its bitterness. This is the explanation of the exhortation to the Christian to be thankful for all things, evil things as well as good things. The explanation is not that we enjoy the bitterness. We do not; we should not! But we are thankful for the cross in view of the benefits God brings us through the cross in our lives.

The fourth characteristic of every Christian life is contempt for this earthly life and hopeful meditation upon the future heavenly life, the life after death and especially after the Lord's second coming. This feature of the Christian life is related to the preceding characteristic of cross-bearing, inasmuch as tribulation (the cross) has this unavoidable, salutary effect on us: the greater the suffering imposed upon us, the more there is in us what Calvin calls a "contempt for the present life and... meditat[ion] upon the future life."[21]

In urging this as the pattern and character of the Christian life, Calvin uses vigorous language that is much too strong for our age, but language that Reformed saints in our age very much need to hear. If a minister would address the Reformed and Presbyterian church world today with Calvin's statements about contempt for the present life, not informing them that the statements were Calvin's, most of the people would scream at him, "World flight!" "Anabaptist!" Most of the Reformed church world would charge the minister with having a very poor worldview, or no worldview at all. Listen to Calvin, and imagine bringing this message to Amsterdam; Grand Rapids, Michigan; Sioux Center, Iowa; Vallecito, California; and Moscow, Idaho. "Let believers accustom themselves to a contempt of the present life."[22] We must "meditate upon the future life."[23] "The mind is never seriously aroused to desire and ponder the life to come unless it be previously imbued with contempt for the present life."[24] "Indeed, there is no middle ground between these two: either the world must become worthless to us or hold us bound by intemperate love of it."[25] Calvin exercises some sharp, spiritual, psychological examination of us all:

> There is not one of us, indeed, who does not wish to seem throughout his life to aspire and strive after heavenly immortality. For it is a shame for us to be no better than brute beasts, whose condition would be no whit inferior to our own if there were not left to us hope of eternity after death. But if you examine the plans, the efforts, the deeds, of anyone, there you will find nothing else but earth. Now our blockishness arises from the fact that our minds, stunned by the empty dazzlement of riches, power, and honors, become so deadened that they can see no farther. The heart also, occupied with avarice, ambition, and lust, is so weighed down that it cannot rise up higher. In fine, the whole soul, enmeshed in the allurements of the flesh, seeks its happiness on earth.[26]

Is not something of this "blockishness" true of us all? It is the reason we are shocked and saddened when the doctor announces to us that we have a terminal illness. We do not exclaim, "Ah, the goal. Now I will see and have what I have always been meditating upon." Therefore, Calvin uses vigorous language. The Christian life is contempt for the earth and all its dazzling nothingnesses and a meditation upon the heavenly life and its realities.

Calvin goes on to explain that he means that we view this life as preparation for the glory of the heavenly kingdom. Therefore, we must not make this life the end, the goal, or the main thing. Calvin warns that contempt is not "hatred" or "ingratitude" for this life.[27]

A worldview of contempt for this earthly life and meditation on the coming heavenly life implies that the believer does not fear death, but desires it. "Monstrous it is that many who boast themselves Christians are gripped by such a great fear of death, rather than a desire for it, that they tremble at the least mention of it, as of something utterly dire and disastrous."[28] "No one has made progress in the school of

Christ who does not joyfully await the day of death and final resurrection."[29]

It is evident that Calvin sees no golden age for the church in history:

> This is obvious: the entire company of believers, so long as they dwell on earth, must be "as sheep destined for the slaughter" [Rom. 8:36] to be conformed to Christ their Head. They would therefore have been desperately unhappy unless, with mind intent upon heaven, they had surmounted whatever is in this world, and passed beyond the present aspect of affairs [cf. 1 Cor. 15:19].[30]

Thus Calvin explodes the postmillennial dream.

Fifth, the Christian life is characterized by a right use of earthly benefits in order to live earthly life properly. Contempt for this life by no means rules out a proper use of earthly things. How must we use earthly things? "There is no doubt we ought to use...good things in so far as they help rather than hinder our course."[31] Calvin warns against two dangers. One is the unbiblical restriction that we use earthly things only as far as they are necessary. This is asceticism, to which Calvin is opposed. There is also an intemperate (immoderate) use that amounts to licentiousness and indulgence. Of the two dangers, Calvin fears indulgence more: "We wish men would follow a moderation closer to abstinence than to luxury."[32]

Although there is no "fixed formula" concerning the right use of earthly things, there are "two rules."[33] The first is a use of the world as not using it, according to 1 Corinthians 7:29–31, that is, use of the world that does not make too much of it, so as to divert us from the heavenly goal. The abuse of this world involves gluttony, luxury, pride, and the like:

> He who bids you use this world as if you used it not destroys not only the intemperance of gluttony...excessive indulgence...ambition, pride, arrogance, and overfastidiousness, but also all care and inclination that either diverts or hinders you from thought of the heavenly life.[34]

The second rule is that the Christian bear poverty "patiently." Calvin says, "If they keep this rule of moderation, they will make considerable progress in the Lord's school... To this end, then, let all those for whom the pursuit of piety is not a pretense strive to learn, by the Apostle's example, how to be filled and to hunger, to abound and to suffer want [Phil. 4:12]."[35]

"Besides, Scripture has a third rule with which to regulate the use of earthly things."[36] The third rule is that Christians must live their earthly lives in the consciousness that they are stewards who will give an account. "Thus, therefore, we must so arrange it that this saying may continually resound in our ears: 'Render account of your stewardship' [Luke 16:2]."[37]

The sixth characteristic of a Christian life is that we view and occupy our place in life as a divine "calling." Every work, every position is a sacred calling. Not only the clergy have a calling, a vocation, but also the work of a mother in the home and the labor of a husband in the factory are a calling. "No task will be so sordid and base, provided you obey your calling in it, that it will not shine and be reckoned very precious in God's sight."[38]

CHAPTER 13

Justification

Introduction

The importance of the doctrine of justification in Calvin's thinking is immediately evident. Justification was central in the Protestant Reformation launched by Luther and the main issue in the controversy that the Reformation waged with the Roman Catholic Church.

Was Calvin in agreement with Luther concerning not only the importance of justification, but also the nature of justification? Did Calvin agree with Luther as to what justification is? What was Calvin's doctrine of justification? Since the Reformed creeds are dependent upon Calvin's exposition of justification, for example, Questions and Answers 59–64 of the Heidelberg Catechism, does the Reformed faith as expressed in the confessions agree with Luther on the doctrine of justification?

Ultimately, of course, the question is: Was Calvin biblical in his teaching of justification?

Not only was justification central in the Reformation, not only was it the main issue between all the reformers and the Roman Catholic Church, but also the truth of justification is the heart of the gospel of grace.

Calvin's agreement with Luther on the doctrine of justification is questioned today by Presbyterian theologians who promote the covenant theology that calls itself the federal vision. In the interests of the federal vision's denial of justification by faith alone, they contend that, unlike Luther, Calvin had a place in the justification of the guilty sinner before God the judge for the good works of the sinner himself. If true, this would simply mean that Calvin taught justification by faith and works, aligning himself with the Roman Catholic Church against Luther and the entire sixteenth-century Reformation of the church—a notion that is absurd on the very face of it.

Contrasting Luther's doctrine of justification with that of the Reformed churches, Peter A. Lillback has written, ominously, "The Reformed hermeneutic discussed works in the context of justification because the covenant had two parts."[1] Under the heading, "Calvin's Disagreement with Luther Regarding God's Acceptance of the Believer's Good Works," Lillback deepened the alleged divide between Luther and Calvin regarding justification:

> Luther's understanding of justification by faith alone had no room for inherent righteousness, while Calvin's view required it as an inseparable but subordinate righteousness.
>
> The resulting difference is due to Luther's law/gospel hermeneutic versus Calvin's letter—spirit hermeneutic. Calvin's final statement on justification is in sharp contrast to Luther's comments which were immortalized in the *Formula of Concord*. Writing in the last year or so of his life, Calvin says in his commentary on Ezekiel 18:14–17,
>
>> When, therefore, we say that the faithful are esteemed just even in their deeds, this is not stated as a cause of their salvation, and we must diligently notice that the cause of salvation is excluded from this doctrine; for, when we discuss the cause, we must look nowhere else but to the mercy of God, and there we must stop. But although works tend in no way to the cause of justification, yet, when the elect sons of God were justified freely by faith, at the same time their works are esteemed righteous by the same gratuitous liberality. Thus it still remains true, that faith without works justifies, although this needs prudence and a sound interpretation; for this proposition, that faith without works justifies is true and yet false, according to the different senses which it bears. The proposition, that

faith without works justifies by itself, is false, because faith without works is void. But if the clause "without works" is joined with the word "justifies," the proposition will be true, since faith cannot justify when it is without works, because it is dead, and a mere fiction. He who is born of God is just, as John says. (1 John v. 18). Thus faith can be no more separated from works than the sun from his heat: yet faith justifies without works, because works form no reason for our justification; but faith alone reconciles us to God, and causes him to love us, not in ourselves, but in his only-begotten Son.

Calvin is insistent that works have a proper place in the discussion of justification by faith alone. Calvin avers that this terminology of "faith alone" is false if "a prudent and sound interpretation" is not given to it. On the other side is Luther's unbending commitment to the law/gospel distinction as quoted from his Galatians Commentary in the *Formula of Concord*.

> We certainly grant that we must teach about love and good works too. But it must be done at the time and place where it is necessary, namely, when we deal with good works apart from this matter of justification. At this point the main question with which we have to do is not whether a person should also do good works and love, but how a person may be justified before God and be saved. And then we answer with St. Paul that we are justified alone through faith in Christ, and not through the works of the law or through love—not in such a way as if we thereby utterly rejected works and love (as the adversaries falsely slander and accuse us) but so that we may not be diverted (as Satan would very much like) from the main issue with which we here have to do into another extraneous matter which does not belong in this article at all. Therefore, while and as long as we have to do with this article of justification, we reject and condemn works, since the very nature of this article cannot

admit any treatment or discussion of works. For this reason we summarily cut off every reference to the law and the works of the law in this conjunction.

The law had no place in Luther's discussion of justification. But in Calvin's mind, the believer's obedience was an "inseparable accident" to the justification doctrine.[2]

Lillback concluded that Calvin's doctrine of justification was "contrary to Luther['s]" in that Calvin allowed for "good works in relationship to justification." Calvin really sided with the "Schoolmen," that is, the Roman Catholic theologians, except that Calvin denied that the good works that enter into the justification of the sinner are meritorious.

> What is particularly important to remember at this point is that Calvin's development of the idea of the acceptance of men's works by God was expressed in terms of the covenant. The works were not seen as meritorious, but rather, God has promised to reward works with spiritual gifts, and this promise of the law is realized by the gracious gifts of the covenant. God in covenant has liberally forgiven the sin in men's works, and actually enabled those works by His Spirit. This idea he readily admits is the common doctrine of the Schoolmen, except they developed their idea of the covenant of acceptance in terms of merit, instead of justification righteousness and its subordinate righteousness of the Holy Spirit. Here one sees Calvin as the historical bridge between the medieval Schoolmen's covenant doctrine and that of the later Calvinistic federal theologians. Calvin simply excises the medieval doctrine of merit from the covenant of acceptance and replaces it with Reformation's justification by faith alone. Consequently, Calvin occupies a middle ground between the Schoolmen and Luther on the issue of the acceptance of good works in relationship to justification. Luther and Calvin are in full agreement against the scholastics regarding the issue of the unique instrumentality of faith and the non-meritorious character of all of human standing before God. On the other hand, Calvin, in agreement with the Schoolmen and contrary to Luther, accepts the fact that God can by

covenant receive the works of man. Calvin's doctrine of the acceptance of men's works by God is therefore an intermediate position between Luther and the medieval tradition.[3]

Calvin's exposition of justification in the *Institutes* is conclusive against the notions that Calvin differed from Luther and that Calvin's doctrine of justification occupied some nonexistent middle ground between Rome and Luther.

Although our main concern is the content of Calvin's doctrine of justification, it is interesting to notice where he places justification in the *Institutes*. He does not place it where one might expect it. Calvin's treatment of justification follows his treatment of the Christian life, that is, sanctification. His expressed reason for treating sanctification before justification is that "actual holiness of life ... is not separated from" justification.[4]

In a footnote, editor McNeill speaks of a "surprising order" and suggests that Calvin adopts this order to forestall a Roman Catholic objection to the Reformed doctrine of justification, namely, that the Reformed doctrine of justification disparages, or even denies, a life of holiness.[5] I suggest another, more substantial reason for Calvin's treatment of sanctification before justification. Calvin recognizes that in the work of salvation there is a sense in which sanctification, or newness of life, does precede justification. Regeneration in the narrow sense, or newness of life that comes about by union with Christ, makes us new creatures in Christ, and thus holy. And this does precede the activity of faith and conscious justification by faith. To put it very simply: we are united to Christ and in principle made new creatures in Christ before consciously believing in Christ and thus enjoying righteousness. Calvin himself makes this point later in his treatment of justification as he defends the truth of justification by faith alone against the Roman Catholic charge that the doctrine is detrimental to a life of good works.

> Although we may distinguish them, Christ contains both of them [justification and sanctification] inseparably in himself. Do you wish, then, to attain righteousness in Christ? You must first possess Christ; but you cannot possess him without being made partaker in his sanctification, because he cannot be di-

vided into pieces [1 Cor. 1:13]. Since, therefore, it is solely by expending himself that the Lord gives us these benefits to enjoy, he bestows both of them at the same time, the one never without the other. Thus it is clear how true it is that we are justified not without works yet not through works, since in our sharing in Christ, which justifies us, sanctification is just as much included as righteousness.[6]

Justification by faith

For Calvin, the doctrine of justification by faith has the same fundamental importance that it had for Luther. Calvin opens his treatment of justification by calling justification "the main hinge on which religion turns."[7] He does not come a whit behind Luther in emphasizing the importance of justification. Luther regarded the doctrine of justification by faith alone as the article, or truth, by which a church stands or falls. Both Luther and Calvin were right. This is the hinge on which religion turns. The confession and proclamation of this truth do demonstrate that a church is a standing church, or a true church of Jesus Christ. Corruption of this truth points out that the church that corrupts this truth is a falling church, a false church. The whole gospel is corrupted if the truth of justification is denied or debased.

Calvin expresses his conviction concerning the importance of the doctrine of justification by faith in his letter to the Roman Catholic Cardinal Sadolet:

> You, in the first place, touch upon justification by faith, the first and keenest subject of controversy between us. Is this a knotty and useless question? Wherever the knowledge of it is taken away, the glory of Christ is extinguished, religion abolished, the Church destroyed, and the hope of salvation utterly overthrown.[8]

Justification in Calvin's thinking is strictly a legal act of God as judge in which he forgives the believer's sins and reckons him righteous. Justification "means nothing else than to acquit of guilt him who was accursed."[9] But there is a positive aspect to the act of justification: the believer is "reckoned righteous in God's judgment."[10] Calvin combines the negative and the positive aspects in his definition of justification: "It consists in the remission of sins and the imputation of Christ's righteousness."[11] Compare Calvin's more full definition of justification: "But we define justification as follows: the sinner, received into communion with Christ, is reconciled to God by his grace, while, cleansed by Christ's blood, he obtains forgiveness of sins, and clothed with Christ's righteousness as if it were his own, he stands confident before the heavenly judgment seat."[12]

It is basic to the right understanding of justification that it is an act of God as our *judge*. And it is fundamental to our understanding of justification that we consider ourselves as standing before the awesome majesty and righteousness of God. According to Calvin, "the basis of this whole discussion" is that in justification we are "concerned with the justice not of a human court but of a heavenly tribunal."[13]

Calvin does not mean that this heavenly tribunal is where we are going to stand *some day* at the moment of our death, and also on the *last day*, when all of us stand before the judgment seat of Christ, but he means that this is where we stand *every day* in the matter of justification. There, before this heavenly tribunal, in which judgment the judge has awesome majesty and righteousness, not even the righteousness of the holiest saint can stand the test of the awesome righteousness of God. Calvin quotes Job 15:15, 16: "Behold, among his saints none is faithful, and the heavens are not pure in his sight. How much more abominable and unprofitable is man, who drinks iniquity like water?" Calvin also quotes Psalm 130:3: "If thou, O Lord shouldest mark iniquities, Lord, who shall stand?" Calvin warns against trusting in "the integrity of works... to satisfy the divine judgment."[14]

"Now, this is the basis of the whole discussion," Calvin is saying to his readers. "As we discuss justification, consciously place yourself before God the judge whose majesty is awesome and whose righteousness is perfect! This will make a difference as to what justification means to you and a difference with regard to the temptation to bring your own works to satisfy the divine judgment." Those who bring their own works into the judgment are not standing before the "heavenly tribunal"; they have some earthly tribunal in mind. An earthly judge can be put off with man's works. God cannot.

Consciousness of the divine righteousness, Calvin thinks, will effect humility. This humility will utterly renounce all one's own righteousness. This is Calvin's application to justification of the all-important knowledge of God, a great theme of the *Institutes*. Two things are necessary to know: knowledge of God and knowledge of ourselves. This is true for the doctrine of justification. We must know ourselves as devoid of any righteousness before God. If we are going to know ourselves thus in this matter of justification, we must have a living knowledge of God as the righteous judge.

The biblical basis of the doctrine of justification as a legal act includes Galatians 3:8, "And the scripture, foreseeing that God would justify the heathen through faith, preached before the gospel unto Abraham," and Romans 3:26, according to Calvin's translation: "God justifies the impious person who has faith in Christ."[15]

Justification is not at all an act of God that *makes* a sinner righteous or good in the sense of making him a better person. It is fundamental to the truth of justification that justification is sharply distinguished from sanctification.

Already in the original, 1536 *Institutes*, in his treatment of Christian freedom, Calvin wrote, "The question [in justification] is not how we may *become* righteous, but how...we may be *reckoned* righteous."[16]

Calvin acknowledges that justification and sanctification are inseparable; nevertheless, they are distinct saving works of God. Calvin uses an apt analogy to illustrate that two important things may be inseparable but nevertheless distinct from each other. He speaks of the heat of the sun and the light of the sun. They are inseparable, but they are quite distinct. "But if the brightness of the sun cannot be separated from its heat, shall we therefore say that the earth is warmed by its light, or lighted by its heat?"[17]

This sharp distinction between justification and sanctification, between declaring the believing sinner righteous by imputation and making the believing sinner holy by the inner renewing of the Spirit, is biblical. Contending with the Lutheran theologian Osiander, who "mixes that gift of regeneration [sanctification] with this free acceptance [justification]," Calvin writes,

> Yet Scripture, even though it joins them, still lists them separately in order that God's manifold grace may better appear to

us. For Paul's statement is not redundant: that Christ was given to us for our righteousness and sanctification [1 Cor. 1:30]. And whenever he reasons—from the salvation purchased for us, from God's fatherly love, and from Christ's grace—that we are called to holiness and cleanness, he clearly indicates that to be justified means something different from being made new creatures.[18]

The distinction between justification and sanctification is necessary in order to expose, condemn, and keep out the heresy of justification by faith and works. The Roman Catholic doctrine of justification by faith and works depends on an explanation of justification as partly forgiveness and partly inner renewal unto holiness of life. So also does the contemporary heresy of the federal vision in Reformed and Presbyterian churches promote itself by confusing justification and sanctification.

That the legal act of justification is "by faith" does not mean that the faith of the sinner is a work that merits righteousness. Rather, faith is the "instrument"[19] by which the sinner receives the righteousness of another, even Jesus Christ. The believing sinner receives Christ's righteousness by way of "imputation."[20]

Already in Calvin's day the subtle error had to be combated that made faith—faith that is so important in justification—a work of the sinner that deserves righteousness, a work of the sinner upon which the sinner's righteousness depends.

Fifty years after Calvin this would be the clever error by which the Arminian party in the Reformed churches in the Netherlands corrupted justification by faith alone, which error the Canons of Dordt explicitly condemn:

> The Synod *rejects* the errors of those... who teach that the new covenant of grace, which God the Father, through the mediation of the death of Christ, made with man, does not herein consist that we by faith, inasmuch as it accepts the merits of Christ, are justified before God and saved, but in the fact that God having revoked the demand of perfect obedience of the law, regards faith itself and the obedience of faith, although imperfect, as the perfect obedience of the law, and does esteem it worthy of the reward of eternal life through grace.[21]

Calvin inveighs against the corruption of the fundamental doctrine of justification by faith that makes faith a work of the sinner that earns righteousness or makes the sinner worthy of righteousness. He denies that faith justifies by "some intrinsic power." Rather, faith is only "a kind of vessel" to receive the righteousness of Christ: a vessel, an empty vessel that receives something from Christ. He continues, "Faith...is only the instrument for receiving righteousness."[22]

Later Calvin declares, "We say that faith justifies, not because it merits righteousness for us by its own worth, but because it is an instrument whereby we obtain free the righteousness of Christ."[23] The instrumental function of faith in justification, Calvin expresses when he insists that in the matter of justification faith is "merely passive."[24]

François Wendel, the astute expositor of Calvin's thought, remarks correctly that for Calvin, "faith is nothing in itself. It acquires its value only by its content; that is, by Jesus Christ."[25] The object of faith is the word of God, and more particularly, the promise of mercy in the word of God, and more particularly still, Jesus Christ. Faith attaches to Jesus Christ. This is what gives faith its value.

The Belgic Confession confesses that faith is merely an instrument in justification: "However, to speak more clearly, we do not mean that faith itself justifies us, for it is only an instrument with which we embrace Christ our Righteousness."[26]

Justification by faith alone

Not only is Calvin one with Luther in viewing justification as a strictly legal act of God, but he is also in full agreement with Luther that justification is by faith *alone*.

The little word *alone* in the phrase "justification by faith alone" expressed the heart of the controversy of the sixteenth-century Reformation with the Roman Catholic Church, as it expresses the essential controversy of a genuinely Protestant church with Rome still today. The word *alone* also conveys the biblical doctrine of justification and safeguards the doctrine against all misunderstanding and corruption of the truth of it.

The word *alone* in the phrase "justification by faith alone" affirms, clearly but simply, that sinners are, and can only be, justified by means exclusively of faith in Jesus Christ. *Alone* denies that the good works of the sinner are the means of the sinner's becoming righteous with God, whether in whole or in part.

In the sixteenth century, Rome denied justification by faith by denying that justification is by faith *alone*. This is the heresy—the *fundamental* heresy—of Rome still in the twenty-first century. Rome taught then, as it teaches still today, that sinners are, must be, and can only be justified partly by faith and partly by their own good works.

Calvin recognizes the importance of the word *alone* in the controversy over justification:

> They [the Roman Catholic theologians] dare not deny that man is justified by faith because it recurs so often in Scripture. But since the word "alone" is nowhere expressed, they do not allow this addition to be made.[27]

With appeal to Romans 3:28, "Therefore we conclude that a man is justified by faith without the deeds of the law," Calvin confesses, "We say that man is justified by faith alone."[28] Calvin's appeal at the decisive point in the controversy over justification to Romans 3:28 is highly significant. This text is conclusive regarding justification. By its explicit exclusion of human works from God's act of justifying in connection with its affirmation that justification is by means of faith, the text plainly teaches that justification is by faith alone.

Romans 3:28 was also controversial in Calvin's day. In his rendering of the Bible into German, Luther had translated the text, "*Der Mensch gerecht werde ohne des Gesetzes Werke, allein durch den Glauben*" ("Man is justified without the works of the law, only by faith"). Luther perfectly captured the thought of the text by use of the word *allein* (only), although the word does not occur in the original Greek. Rome, of course, charged that Luther illegitimately added to Scripture, a charge that Luther vehemently denied.

By his deliberate appeal to Romans 3:28 as the basis of the word *alone* in his confession of justification by faith *alone*, Calvin completely aligns himself with Luther in the truth of justification. At the same time, Calvin confesses the fundamental doctrine of the sixteenth-century Reformation in the form of the expression of the doctrine that conveys the truth of it and safeguards it against the Roman Catholic corruption, and thus rejection, of it.

Also today, Romans 3:28, rightly understood as teaching justification by faith *alone*, is the crucial text in the controversy over justification, including the controversy that now is found within Reformed and Presbyterian churches. When Reformed theologian Norman Shepherd, a proponent of the covenant theology of the federal vision, writes that Luther erred in inserting the word *alone* in his translation of Romans 3:28 and that the word *alone* distorts Paul's meaning, he indicates his embrace of the Roman Catholic heresy of justification by faith and works and his apostasy from the Reformation gospel of salvation by grace alone.

> Luther inserted the word "alone" into his translation of Romans 3:28 to make it read "For we hold that one is justified by faith *alone* apart from works of the law." This is the origin of the dogmatic formula, justification by faith alone. However, his insertion actually distorts Paul's meaning.[29]

Calvin vigorously defends justification by faith alone against attacks on the doctrine by the Roman Catholic opponents of the doctrine. "We say ... that man ... stripped of all help from works ... is justified by faith alone."[30] As the phrase "stripped of all help from works" expresses, justification by faith alone means, negatively, that all works of the justified sinner are excluded from consideration in the divine act of justifying. Already in the 1536 *Institutes*, Calvin had written, "Utterly no account is taken of works [in justification]."[31]

The biblical basis of the teaching of justification from which all works of the sinner are excluded is, first, the passages that teach that justification is by faith and, second, the passages that deny that justification is by the works of the law. Romans 3:28 and Galatians 2:16 do both: affirm faith and deny works.

The works of the justified sinner that are excluded from justification, according to Calvin, are not only ceremonial works, but also the good works that faith produces by the Spirit of Jesus Christ. Rome argued in Calvin's time, as it does still today, that the "works of the law" excluded by Paul from justification, for example in Romans 3:28, are only ceremonial works, such as circumcision. Rome's position was, as it is still today, that truly good works of love for God and the neighbor are included in justification of the sinner. The men of the federal vision in the Reformed community today take the same position, although they also exclude from justification works performed with the purpose of meriting by them.

Calvin calls Rome's contention that the works of the law excluded from justification are only ceremonial works an "ingenious subterfuge." "Here they have an ingenious subterfuge... it is still utterly silly. They prate that the ceremonial works of the law are excluded, not the moral works."[32] So foolish an explanation of Paul's exclusion of works from justification is this that "even schoolboys would hoot at such impudence."[33] Calvin adds, "When the ability to justify is denied to the law, these works refer to the whole law."[34]

Calvin's refutation of the attempt to negate the Bible's teaching of justification by faith alone by restricting "works of the law" to ceremonial works is devastating. Calvin points out that Romans 3:20, 31 and Galatians 3:10, 12 attribute such powers and qualities to the law as cannot possibly be restricted to the ceremonial law, but obviously refer to the entire law of God, especially the moral law. "By the law is knowledge of sin" (Rom. 3:20). Galatians 3:10 speaks of "the works of the law" and declares that "as many as are of the works of the law are under the curse." Paul is not teaching that only those who do not continue in all the ceremonial laws are cursed.[35]

Calvin teaches that also the good works of the regenerated children of God, which are the fruits of faith, are excluded in justification. He takes note of the evasion of the "Sophists":

> The Sophists... explain "works" as meaning those which men not yet reborn do only according to the letter by the effort of their own free will, apart from Christ's grace. But they deny that these refer to spiritual works. For, according to them, man is justified by both faith and works provided they are not his own works but the gifts of Christ and the fruit of regeneration.[36]

Calvin responds to this evasion: "All works are excluded, whatever title may grace them [Gal. 3:11, 12]."[37] He adds, "Not even spiritual works come into account when the power of justifying is ascribed to faith."[38]

There are especially two reasons why the truly good works of the regenerated child of God are, and must be, excluded from justification. First, even one sinful deed among many good works would damn a man, if justification were by good works. Calvin maintains that in the judgment of justification the man himself and his whole life are judged as a single unit. If the judgment is based on works, one evil work—just one—would result in condemnation. Calvin questions "whether [a man] is reckoned righteous even on account of many good works if he is in some part indeed found guilty of transgression."[39]

Second, all the good works of the believer are imperfect and, therefore, incapable of satisfying the demand of the divine righteousness. "I shall inquire still further—whether there be any work that does not deserve to be censured for some impurity or imperfection."[40] In this connection Calvin teaches that in the justification of the believer not only the believer himself but also all his good works are justified. "We can deservedly say that by faith alone not only we ourselves but our works as well are justified."[41] This is devastating to every doctrine of the justifying of sinners by their own works. So far is it from being true that good works justify that, on the contrary, good works themselves need to be justified.

If the good works of the believer cannot justify, the works of the unbeliever are certainly condemnable. In the course of his consideration of justification by faith alone apart from works, Calvin takes note of, and passes judgment on, the seeming good works of unregenerated, unbelieving persons. Calvin recognizes the difference between decent unbelievers and profligate unbelievers, between a Titus, on the one hand, and a Caligula and a Nero, on the other hand. But this difference is only "the dead image" of the difference between true righteousness and unrighteousness.[42] The difference between the decent deeds of a Titus and the dastardly deeds of a Nero is not the difference between good works and sinful works but, as the Westminster Confession of Faith explains, the difference between sinful works and works that are even "more sinful."[43]

The seeming good works of unbelievers are only an "outward image of virtue" and "external and feigned righteousness."[44] The apparent good works of the ungodly are "no more to be reckoned among virtues than the vices that commonly deceive on account of their affinity and likeness to virtue."[45] All the seeming good works of unregenerated persons are "sin" because "they do not look to the goal that God's wisdom prescribes."[46] These deeds are "not at all good."[47] "Whatever a man thinks, plans, or carries out before he is reconciled to God through faith is accursed...surely deserving condemnation."[48]

In his condemnation of all the seeming good works of unbelievers, Calvin is, in fact, honoring Christ and proclaiming the necessity of union with Christ. At bottom, the explanation of the condemnation of the seeming good done by unbelievers is that "there is no sanctification apart from communion with Christ." Apart from Christ, men, whether decent or debauched, "are evil trees; they can bear fruit beautiful and comely to the sight, and even sweet to the taste, but not at all good."[49]

Those Calvinists who are committed to the notion that unbelievers are able to perform good works by a common grace of God and who are quick to brand those who hold that the seeming good done by unbelievers is sin as hyper-Calvinists would do well to study this passage of the *Institutes* very carefully.

In his defense of justification by faith alone, Calvin contends against two enemies of the truth. One is the Roman Catholic Church. Calvin refers to the Roman Catholic teachers variously as the "Scholastics," "Sophists," "Sorbonnists," and "papists." Through its apologists Rome violently assailed the doctrine of justification by faith alone, contending that the sinner is justified also by his own good works, so that his righteousness before God is partly what he himself has done in obedience to the law of God. Significantly, Calvin insists that the controversy over justification is "the principal point of dispute that we have with the papists."[50] On Calvin's judgment, those Protestants today who have resolved their difference with Rome regarding justification no longer have any "principal" dispute with Rome. They can, and should, return to the Roman Catholic Church.

Calvin also opposes a Protestant, indeed a Lutheran, heretic in the matter of justification. Andreas Osiander (d. 1552) was an ill-tempered Lutheran theologian whom Calvin met (and disliked for his crude talk at table) at the Diet at Worms, which was intended to reunite Rome and the churches of the Reformation, during Calvin's exile in Strasbourg (1538–1541). Osiander went astray on a number of doctrines, including limiting Christ's work in justification to his divine nature and the teaching that believers receive the "essence" of God. Calvin concentrates on Osiander's erroneous teaching of justification by the infusion of renewing grace.

Osiander taught that in justification not only is the sinner forgiven, but he also becomes righteous actually by the infusion of grace. For the Lutheran theologian—already at that early date an apostate from the gospel proclaimed by Luther—"to be justified is not only to be reconciled to God through free pardon but also to be made righteous, and righteousness is not a free imputation but the holiness and uprightness that the essence of God, dwelling in us, inspires."[51] Justification for Osiander is a mixture of forgiveness and sanctification: "Osiander mixes that gift of regeneration with this free acceptance and contends that they are one and the same."[52]

Against Osiander, as against Rome, Calvin maintains, "There is in justification no place for works."[53]

Also Osiander's doctrine of justification destroys assurance of salvation: "For faith totters if it pays attention to works, since no one, even of the most holy, will find there anything on which to rely."[54]

For Calvin, all those who introduce works into justification are present-day "Pharisees": "the Pharisees of our day."[55] Such are all Roman Catholics. Such are all Protestants today who teach justification by faith and works, as well as those who rely on their works, even in part, for their righteousness with God. And on the testimony of the Lord Jesus Christ, Pharisees are not justified. In the parable of the Pharisee and the publican, the publican returns home "justified *rather than the other*" (Luke 18:14, emphasis added).

Refutation of arguments against justification by faith alone

Calvin refutes the arguments that the Roman Catholic Church has always raised against justification by faith alone. These are the same arguments brought against the doctrine by adversaries of justification by faith alone within the Reformed churches in the twenty-first century. The basic objection to justification by faith alone by the Roman

Catholic Church, as by the doctrine's Protestant foes today, is that the doctrine of justification by faith alone weakens zeal for the performance of good works, if it does not lead to carelessness and sheer licentiousness. Rome's objection to justification by faith alone is exactly that which Paul envisions as raised against the doctrine in Romans 6:1: "What shall we say then? Shall we continue in sin, that grace may abound?" It is the objection considered and rejected by the Heidelberg Catechism: "But does not this doctrine make men careless and profane? No; for it is impossible that those who are implanted into Christ by true faith should not bring forth fruits of righteousness."[56]

To the objection that justification by faith alone is destructive of a life of good works, Calvin responds, "Christ justifies no one whom he does not at the same time sanctify."[57] Therefore, "we are justified not without works yet not through works."[58]

This objection that the truth of justification cuts the nerve of zeal for godliness of life is so far from being true that, on the contrary, the Scriptures "derive their most powerful exhortations from the thought that our salvation stands upon no merit of ours but solely upon God's mercy."[59] Calvin appeals to Romans 12:1: "I beseech you therefore ... by the mercies of God, that ye present your bodies a living sacrifice, holy, acceptable unto God, which is your reasonable service."

Rome contends that the doctrine of justification by faith alone is disproved by the fact that especially the Old Testament extends God's promises to those who obey the law. "If ye hearken to these judgments, and keep, and do them ... the LORD thy God shall keep unto thee the covenant and the mercy which he sware unto thy fathers" (Deut. 7:12).

Calvin's response to this contention is twofold. First, no one keeps the law, for the required obedience is perfection. Therefore, justification is, and must be, by faith alone. Having justified the elect sinner, God also sanctifies him, so that he begins to obey the law, albeit imperfectly. God then rewards the good works of his child in his grace.

> The promises also that are offered us in the law would all be ineffectual and void, had God's goodness not helped us through the gospel. For this condition, that we should carry out the law—upon which the promises depend and by which alone they are to be performed—will never be fulfilled.[60]

Second, the promises especially in the Old Testament that have a conditional form do not express the "reason" for the promise and its fulfillment, but rather identify the object of the promise. "The fulfillment of the Lord's mercy does not depend upon believers' works. [Doing] righteousness... is not the foundation by which believers stand firm before God... but the means whereby our most merciful Father introduces them into his fellowship."[61]

Especially significant is Rome's appeal, against justification by faith alone, to Romans 2:13: "Not the hearers of the law are just before God, but the doers of the law shall be justified." Rome's interpretation of the passage is that there are men who are, in fact, "doers of the law" and that their obedience to the law is an essential part of their justification. Thus explained, the text contradicts the doctrine of justification by faith alone.

The men of the contemporary heresy of the federal vision, as well as other advocates of justification by faith and works in Reformed and Presbyterian churches, make the same appeal to Romans 2:13, giving it the same interpretation, and for the same purpose.

Calvin responds to Rome's appeal to Romans 2:13 by denying that it teaches that there are humans who, in fact, are "doers of the law."[62]

> [Rather,] here the apostle is casting down the foolish confidence of the Jews, who claimed for themselves the sole knowledge of the law, even while they were its greatest despisers. Lest, then, mere skill in the law should please them so much, he warns that if righteousness be sought from the law, not knowledge but observance of it is sought. We assuredly do not question that the righteousness of the law consists in works, and not even that righteousness consists in the worth and merits of works. But it has not yet been proved that we are justified by works unless they produce some one man who has fulfilled the law.[63]

The strongest biblical case that Rome can make for justification by works and against justification by faith alone is James 2:21, 25: "Abraham... [was] justified by works"; "Rahab... [was] justified by works."

Calvin replies that James cannot contradict Paul, who plainly teaches justification *apart from works*, for "the Spirit is not in conflict with himself."[64] The perfect harmony of James and Paul lies in the fact that James speaks of both faith and justification in different senses than does Paul. The "faith" against which James inveighs is not true faith, but "an empty opinion far removed from true faith."[65]

Also, "if you would make James agree with the rest of Scripture and with himself, you must understand that word 'justify' in another sense than Paul takes it." What is this other sense? "[James] is speaking of the declaration, not the imputation, of righteousness."[66]

To Rome's argument that God's promise that he will reward the good works of his people with eternal life implies justification by works, Calvin replies, "The use of the term 'reward' is no reason for us to suppose that our works are the cause of our salvation."[67] The parable of the householder in Matthew 20:1–16 proves that the promised reward is not a "matter of merit." In that Jesus has the householder pay all the workers the same, regardless how long they labored, the parable teaches that "God's mercy rewards" his people for their works "at the end of their lives, in order to reveal the excellence of his grace."[68] In the words of the Heidelberg Catechism, the reward of good works "comes not of merit, but of grace."[69]

Rome's appeal to the Bible's teaching in Matthew 16:27, 2 Corinthians 5:10, Romans 2:9, 10, and other places that in the final judgment all will be judged according to their works is also picked up by Romanizing enemies of the doctrine of justification by faith alone in Reformed churches in the twenty-first century. The argument is that the good works of the believer enter into his justification—the decisive justification—in the final judgment.

Calvin replies that the order, good works followed by the judgment of acceptance into eternal life, is "an order of sequence rather than the cause."[70] God's purpose in promising the reward of eternal life for our good works is "not to puff up our hearts with vainglory," but to encourage us to persevere in all the difficulties of the Christian life in the world. "Whoever, then, deduces merit of works from this, or weighs works and reward together, wanders very far from God's own plan."[71] Calvin reminds those who explain the Bible's teaching of a final judgment according to works as a form of justification by and on the basis of good works that Ephesians 1:18 teaches "that the Kingdom of Heaven is not servants' wages but sons' inheritance."[72]

Calvin might also have simply called attention to the fact that the Bible does not teach that God will judge his people *on the basis of* their works, but *according to* their works. The final judgment of God's elect, which will be the public manifestation of God's judgment of them in this life by faith alone, will be solidly and exclusively based on the obedience of Christ for them and in their stead. The final judgment will be, and will be displayed as being, in accord with the good works they performed by the grace of the Spirit of sanctification.

Justification by faith alone does not only exclude from justification all the works of the believing sinner. It also has the positive meaning that the only obedience that constitutes the righteousness of the guilty sinner before God is the obedience of Jesus Christ, especially the obedience of his atoning death. Calvin, therefore, charges Osiander, who taught that the good works of the believer are, in part, his righteousness with God, with making "mockery" of Christ. "Whoever wraps up two kinds of righteousness in order that miserable souls may not repose wholly in God's mere mercy, crowns Christ in mockery with a wreath of thorns [Mark 15:17, etc.]."[73]

The righteousness of justification is "Christ's obedience... reckoned to us as if it were our own."[74]

Corresponding to the imputation of Christ's righteousness to us in the act of justification, and the basis of it, is God's imputation to Christ of the guilt of the sins of the elect church in Christ's death on the cross. Commenting on 2 Corinthians 5:21 ("He hath made him to be sin for us, who knew no sin; that we might be made the righteousness of God in him"), Calvin writes,

> Do you observe, that, according to Paul, there is no return to favour with God, except what is founded on the sacrifice of Christ alone?... How are we righteous in the sight of God? It is assuredly in the same respect in which Christ was a sinner. For he assumed in a manner our place, that he might be a criminal in our room, and might be dealt with as a sinner, not for his own offences, but for those of others, inasmuch as he was pure and exempt from every fault, and might endure the punishment that was due to us—not to himself. It is in the same manner, assuredly, that we are now *righteous in him*—not in respect of our rendering satisfaction to the justice of God by our own

works, but because we are judged of in connection with Christ's righteousness, which we have put on by faith, that it might become ours."[75]

The good works of the believer have no part whatever in his justification. Indeed, his good works are not the "cause" of his salvation in any respect. Availing himself of the "four kinds of causes to be observed in the outworking of things" proposed by the "philosophers," Calvin confesses, "The efficient cause of our obtaining eternal life is the mercy of the Heavenly Father... the material cause is Christ, with his obedience... the formal, or instrumental cause [is]... faith... the final cause ... consists both in the proof of divine justice and in the praise of God's goodness." Calvin concludes, "We see that every particle of our salvation stands thus outside of us." He asks, "Why is it that we still trust or glory in works?"[76]

The right relation of good works and justifying faith is that, "as gifts of God" to the believer, good works confirm the believer in the assurance of salvation that is his in justification. "They [the saints] regard them [their good works] solely as gifts of God from which they may recognize his goodness and as signs of the calling by which they realize their election."[77]

Necessity of justification by faith alone

Justification by faith alone is necessary for salvation, and Calvin, therefore, urges the proclamation and defense of the doctrine. Apart from justification, which is by faith alone, "you have neither a foundation on which to establish your salvation nor one on which to build piety toward God."[78]

Only justification by faith alone affords peace of conscience. "If we ask in what way the conscience can be made quiet before God, we shall find the only way to be that unmerited righteousness be conferred upon us as a gift of God."[79] Of the Roman Catholic defenders of justification by works, Calvin says, "They do not much care about imparting their peace to consciences... They indeed gnaw at justification of faith but meantime set no standard of righteousness upon which consciences may rely."[80]

Above all else, the truth of justification by faith alone magnifies the righteousness of God in the obedience of Christ, to the glory of God alone. "[This is] how we ought to glory in the Lord: namely, that we should swear that our righteous acts and our strength are in the Lord [Isa. 45:24]." "To sum up, man cannot without sacrilege claim for himself even a crumb of righteousness, for just so much is plucked and taken away from the glory of God's righteousness."[81]

Christian freedom

"An appendage of justification" is Christian freedom, or liberty. The freedom of the Christian "is a thing of prime necessity."[82] The importance of Christian liberty for Calvin is evident in the prominence of the subject in the 1536 *Institutes*. The whole of the sixth and last chapter of the original edition of the *Institutes* is devoted to Christian freedom. The topics of church power and of civil government are treated as aspects of Christian freedom.

The importance of Christian freedom is, first, the soul's peace with God that is bound up with Christian freedom. This peace is assurance of salvation—*undoubted* assurance of salvation—as the benefit of justification by faith alone, apart from the works of the believer. The "whole force [of Christian freedom] consists in quieting frightened consciences before God."[83] This is genuinely "experiential" religion. The Reformation was concerned with this "experience" and, by the gospel of justification with its "appendage," Christian freedom, gave it to the believing people of God. Any religion, including corrupted forms of the Reformed faith, that withholds assurance of salvation from believers, or grounds assurance elsewhere than in justification by faith alone, sins against genuine "experience."

The second importance of Christian freedom is its cost: the blood and life of Christ. "We should not put a light value upon something that we see cost Christ so dear, since he valued it not with gold or silver but with his own blood [1 Peter 1:18, 19]."[84]

Christian freedom is important, third, in that, rightly exercised, it preserves and promotes peace in the church, as well as the edification of the weaker brother. "We should use our freedom if it results in the edification of our neighbor, but if it does not help our neighbor, then we should forgo it."[85]

"Christian freedom, in my opinion, consists of three parts."[86]

The first part of Christian freedom is assurance of righteousness with God and salvation by gracious justification. Freedom is the consciousness—the experience—of deliverance from the condemnation of the law, as from the law's demand of perfect obedience for righteousness with God. "Christian freedom [is] . . . that the consciences of believers, in seeking assurance of their justification before God, should rise above and advance beyond the law, forgetting all law righteousness."[87]

That the law is excluded in the matter of righteousness before God, regarding both its curse and its demands for obedience, does not imply that "the law is superfluous for believers." It continues to function as the guide of a holy life, "teaching and exhorting and urging them [believers] to good."[88]

The implication of this part of Christian freedom is that all souls who seek justification by their own works are in bondage.

The second part of Christian freedom is the believer's willing, joyful obedience to the law of God. The holy life of the believer is motivated, not by a sense of obligation to the rigorous demands of the law, but by thankful love for God. The believer does not work on behalf of God with the crippling fear that all his works come short of perfection, but in the confidence that, although all his works are "incomplete and half-done and even defective," they will be "accepted" by a gracious heavenly Father.[89]

Calvin expresses this second part of Christian freedom this way: "Consciences observe the law, not as if constrained by the necessity of the law, but that freed from the law's yoke they willingly obey God's will."[90]

The third part of Christian freedom is the believer's liberty to use and enjoy, or to decline to use and enjoy, the "adiaphora," that is, things that are "indifferent." "The third part of Christian freedom lies in this: regarding outward things that are of themselves 'indifferent,' we are not bound before God by any religious obligation preventing us from sometimes using them and other times not using them, indifferently."[91]

Defending the right of the Christian freely to use and enjoy all kinds of earthly things that God neither commands nor forbids, Calvin writes this delightful, penetrating paragraph:

But these matters are more important than is commonly believed. For when consciences once ensnare themselves, they enter a long and inextricable maze, not easy to get out of. If a man begins to doubt whether he may use linen for sheets, shirts, handkerchiefs, and napkins, he will afterward be uncertain also about hemp; finally, doubt will even arise over tow. For he will turn over in his mind whether he can sup without napkins, or go without a handkerchief. If any man should consider daintier food unlawful, in the end he will not be at peace before God, when he eats either black bread or common victuals, while it occurs to him that he could sustain his body on even coarser foods. If he boggles at sweet wine, he will not with clear conscience drink even flat wine, and finally he will not dare touch water if sweeter and cleaner than other water. To sum up, he will come to the point of considering it wrong to step upon a straw across his path, as the saying goes.[92]

Christian freedom must not be abused. A real danger is the misuse of Christian freedom regarding enjoyment of earthly life to indulge in luxury. Calvin is an inveterate enemy of lavish and luxurious living, as were the prophets and the apostles. "Away, then, with uncontrolled desire, away with immoderate prodigality, away with vanity and arrogance—in order that men may with a clean conscience cleanly use God's gifts."[93]

Christian freedom can also be abused by the exercise of it in such a way as offends the weaker brother. The right use of freedom is the edification of the brother. "We should use our freedom if it results in the edification of our neighbor, but if it does not help our neighbor, then we should forgo it."[94]

But there is also the evil of a Pharisaical *taking* of offense. Calvin is as severe against this needless, and even malicious, taking of offense as he is against a thoughtless giving of offense. "An offense is spoken of as received when something, otherwise not wickedly or unseasonably committed, is by ill will or malicious intent of mind wrenched into occasion for offense."[95]

In connection with his admonition that Christian freedom be used rightly, Calvin astutely condemns the evil of appealing to the danger of giving offense in order to excuse one's failure to teach the truth of the word of God. "Things necessary to be done must not be omitted for fear of any offense." Calvin adds, "Suave fellows are they who, whether their neighbor is to be instructed in doctrine or in example of life, say he must be fed with milk while they steep him in the worst and deadliest opinions."[96]

Because the conscience is so intimately involved in Christian freedom, Calvin defines conscience. It is "a sense of divine judgment, as a witness...which does not allow them [men] to hide their sins from being accused before the Judge's tribunal."[97] "A good conscience...is nothing but inward integrity of heart."[98]

In availing himself of his freedom in Christ, the believer must live in the consciousness that he is a citizen of two kingdoms, a "spiritual" kingdom and a "temporal," or "political," kingdom. The freedom that is the Christian's in the spiritual kingdom does not imply that the Christian is "released from all bodily servitude" in the political kingdom of civil government. Christian freedom is not the right to be a political revolutionary. Indeed, Calvin reminds his readers that Romans 13:1, 5 requires the Christian to submit to civil government for conscience' sake.[99]

CHAPTER 14

Prayer

Introduction

The climax of the Christian life in the experience and practice of the believer is prayer. Calvin, therefore, treats prayer at the end of his explanation of the Christian life of holiness, following his consideration of sanctification and justification and immediately preceding his consideration of predestination, the source and cause of the Spirit's work of salvation in a man.

Prayer relates to its context in book three of the *Institutes* in three ways. First, prayer is the gracious work of the Spirit of Christ in the one who prays, and book three sets forth the truth of the Holy Spirit as the Spirit of Christ applying the redemption of the cross to elect men and women. "To pray rightly is a rare gift," says Calvin.[1] With appeal to Romans 8:26, "The Spirit itself maketh intercession for us with groanings which cannot be uttered," Calvin declares, "God gives us the Spirit as our teacher in prayer," who "arouses in us assurance, desires, and sighs" of prayer.[2]

Calvin likewise attributes the prayers of the saints to the working of the Spirit within them when he views faith as the "mother" of prayer and ascribes this faith to the Spirit. "Faith grounded upon the Word is the mother of right prayer."[3] "Faith is the principal work of the Holy Spirit."[4] The heading of chapter twenty, in which Calvin sets forth the Protestant and Reformed doctrine of prayer, is, in part, "Prayer, Which Is the Chief Exercise of Faith."

Second, prayer is simply an important part of the life of holiness by which every Christian praises God. Responding to the objection that prayer is "superfluous" because God knows our needs regardless of our petitions, Calvin states that our prayers attest "that everything men desire and account conducive to their own profit comes from him."[5] When he comes to treat the public prayers of the congregations in the worship services, Calvin declares, "The chief part of his [God's] worship lies in the office of prayer."[6] To fail to pray, especially in trouble, as is the case with all unbelievers, is to "defraud him [God]... of his due honor."[7]

Third, prayer finds its rightful place in book three of the *Institutes* in that book three is devoted, as the heading states, to "The Way in Which We Receive the Grace of Christ," and prayer is the God-ordained means by which "We Daily Receive God's Benefits," as Calvin's heading of chapter twenty reads. "By the benefit of prayer... we reach those riches which are laid up for us with the Heavenly Father."[8]

What prayer is

Prayer, then, for Calvin, is petitionary: the believer's calling upon God for the "happiness" and "heavenly treasures" that God has for us in Christ.[9] "It remains for us to seek in him, and in prayers to ask of him, what we have learned to be in him."[10] To refrain from bringing our petitions to God in prayer, for whatever reasons, would be as foolish as "for a man to neglect a treasure, buried and hidden in the earth, after it had been pointed out to him."[11]

Even though God on his part cares for his people, knows their needs, and is ready liberally to supply these needs, it is necessary that his people bring their needs to God in petitionary prayers. It pleases God to supply their needs in answer to their requests. Receiving God's gifts as answers to their prayers makes the people of God thankful to him. "Those very things which flow to us from his voluntary liberality he would have us recognize as granted to our prayers."[12] Calvin quotes 1 Peter 3:12: "For the eyes of the Lord are over the righteous, and his ears are open unto their prayers."

Calvin is not of the opinion that petitionary prayer renders an uncaring, or even unfavorably disposed, God favorable.

But prayer is by no means only petitionary. Prayer is also "thanksgiving."[13] Every prayer must express thanks to God, including those that are urgently petitionary on account of some pressing need or trouble. By thanksgiving Calvin also has reference to worship and praise of God. "All entreaties not joined with thanksgiving are wicked and vicious."[14] Calvin quotes Philippians 4:6: "Be careful for nothing; but in every thing by prayer and supplication with thanksgiving let your requests be made known unto God." This thanksgiving, which is also praise of God, "flow[s] from [the] sweetness of love."[15]

In the original, 1536 *Institutes*, Calvin expressly states, "There are two parts to prayer...: petition and thanksgiving."[16] Similarly, he states that the "goal of prayer" is to arouse our hearts and carry them to God, "whether to praise him or to beseech his help."[17]

As this last quotation suggests, the spiritual essence of prayer is "communion of men with God,"[18] specifically, "an intimate conversation of the pious with God."[19] A virtual definition of prayer then is "that prayer itself is properly an emotion of the heart within, which is poured out and laid open before God."[20] Thus prayer is the expression and experience of the fundamental nature of salvation, which Calvin has described at the very beginning of book three as "communion with Christ" and, by implication, as communion with God in Christ.[21]

Rules for praying rightly

Calvin lays down four "rules" for rightly praying a proper prayer. The first rule is that we pray with reverence. Included are that we pray "moved by God's majesty"; guarding our mind, "itself a wanderer," from "carnal cares and thoughts" that detract from our contemplation of and communication with God; and not allowing ourselves to ask of God "anything our blind and stupid reason is wont to devise." Concerning this last aspect, Calvin reminds his readers of the instruction of 1 John 5:14 that we are to "ask...according to his will."[22]

The second rule of right prayer is that we pray with a heartfelt sense of our deep need. Although this need extends to material things, regardless that one has plenty of earthly goods as he is asking for bread ("since he cannot enjoy a single morsel of bread apart from God's continuing favor"[23]), Calvin has especially in mind the spiritual need of the guilty sinner for the forgiveness of sins. It is remarkable, and eminently instructive, that the first and great need of the praying believer that comes to Calvin's mind is the "pardon for his sins."[24] Required in every prayer, therefore, is repentance—sincere sorrow over one's sins. "Let each one, therefore, as he prepares to pray be displeased with his own evil deeds, and (something that cannot happen without repentance) let him take the person and disposition of a beggar."[25]

How contrary to the spirit and teaching of Calvin that professing Calvinists today raise many prayers in which there is no mention of sin or request for forgiveness!

The sense of deep need, especially the need of forgiveness, will prevent the evil of "perfunctory" prayers. If "we ever sense our own insufficiency," we will have "an earnest—nay, burning—desire to attain" what we need.[26]

The third rule for praying rightly follows naturally from the second: praying with humility. Humility consists of abandoning all thoughts of one's "own glory," casting off all notions of one's "own worth," and putting away "all self-assurance."[27] The one who prays with humility has no confidence of being heard and answered based on himself. This necessary humility is rooted in the knowledge of oneself as a guilty, depraved sinner. Explaining his third rule for praying, Calvin expressly states what was clearly implied in his exposition of the second rule, that "the beginning, and even the preparation, of proper prayer is the plea for pardon with a humble and sincere confession of guilt."[28]

Calvin points to a number of biblical examples of those who prayed in humility, including Daniel (Dan. 9:18–20), David (Ps. 143:2), Isaiah (Isa. 64:5–9), and Jeremiah (Jer. 14:7). For good measure Calvin adds the apocryphal Baruch (Baruch 2:18, 19; Baruch 3:2).

Calvin guards against an antinomian abuse of the third rule by warning that one who sincerely asks forgiveness of God also desires deliverance from "the cause," that is, the sin itself.[29]

Regarding those passages of Scripture in which "the saints sometimes seem to shout approval of their own righteousness in calling upon God for help," for example, Psalm 86:2 and 2 Kings 20:3, Calvin denies that these passages teach any confidence "according to the merits of works."[30] Rather, in such passages the praying saints express that "by their regeneration itself they are attested as servants and children of

God to whom he promises that he will be gracious."[31] The saints *identify* themselves; they do not ground their being heard and answered. The godly man's "assurance his prayers will be answered rests solely upon God's clemency, apart from all consideration of personal merit."[32]

With these words about assurance, Calvin indicates his fourth rule of prayer: praying with the confidence of being heard and answered. We are to pray "by a sure hope that our prayer will be answered."[33]

Praying with the confidence of being heard and answered by God, who is favorably inclined toward us, is *necessary*. "Without that firm sense of the divine benevolence God could not be rightly called upon."[34] "Only that prayer is acceptable to God which is born, if I may so express it, out of such presumption of faith, and is grounded in unshaken assurance of hope."[35] For Calvin, true faith is "unshaken assurance" that "God is favorable and benevolent" to one who believes on him.[36] Prayer, which rises from and expresses this confident faith, is, in the nature of the case, confident also. Those who think it "absurd" that all right prayer, which alone is heard by God and acceptable to him, is confident are those who have no "experience" of "the power of faith" in their heart.[37]

Among other passages of Scripture, Calvin appeals to Hebrews 4:16 and Ephesians 3:12.

Whoever the "opponents"[38] may be to whom Calvin refers here (and clearly he has certain persons in mind who challenge the necessity, perhaps even the possibility, of praying with confidence), his teaching of the necessity of confidence in praying exposes the grievous error of a certain, definite branch of theological thought and practice in the sphere of Reformed churches. This mentality teaches its adherents either to pray in doubt whether God is favorable to them and will answer; or, though lacking confidence that God is gracious to them as their Father in Christ, to pray regardless of this unbelief; or, since they lack all confidence, despite their claim to be "believers," to refrain from praying altogether.

To this branch of theological thought and corresponding practice belong many Puritans and their contemporary disciples; many in the Dutch Reformed tradition, specifically those who embrace the movement known as the *nadere reformatie* ("further reformation") with its un-Reformed, unbiblical, and unhealthy emphasis on religious feelings and introspection; Scottish Presbyterians who are influenced heavily by the doubtful Puritans; and those German Reformed Christians whose spiritual father is Herman Friedrich Kohlbrugge (1803–1874).

The fundamental error of all of them, which brings them into conflict with Calvin's fourth rule for right prayer and constitutes a radical difference from Calvin, as from the sixteenth-century Reformation of the church, is their denial that faith is essentially confidence, or assurance—assurance that God is gracious to them and will certainly hear them when they pray, despite their unworthiness on account of their sin.

Calvin grants the argument of those who deny that confidence in prayer is possible or who deny that confidence is necessary for praying rightly, namely, "believers... feel pressed down or troubled by a heavy weight of sins."[39] But he responds that this experience of the weight of sin is intended to drive us to God for unburdening ourselves by confession. Further, "according to his incomparable compassion, our most gracious Father" has promised "to be easily entreated and readily accessible" with regard to everyone who comes to him confessing his sins. Calvin quotes Psalm 50:15 and Matthew 7:7.[40]

One who refuses to pray is disobedient to the command, for God commands all those who profess to be his children to pray.

One who declines to pray because of his doubt, like the one who prays while doubting, is "convicted of unbelief because [he] distrust[s] the promises."[41]

Because confidence in prayer applies also to the certainty that the one who prays will receive what he asked of God, Calvin admonishes that in prayer we "not break forth by chance but follow faith as guide."[42]

Regarding petitions for gifts or deliverance "where no certain promise shows itself, we must ask of God conditionally."[43] That is, we subject our request to God's decree.

With respect also to petitions raised in prayer, Calvin condemns all doubting: "Those who are not sure of God's promise and call his truth into question, and so doubting and hesitating whether they are to be answered, invoke God himself, get nothing (as James says)." Calvin is referring to James 1:6, 7.[44]

It is Calvin's doctrine that one who cannot, or does not, pray in the faith that for Christ's sake God loves him—loves *him*—and, therefore, will grant him—grant *him*—whatever he asks in Christ's name cannot pray. Calvin is right.

Calvin acknowledges that no believer observes the four rules of prayer perfectly. Particularly the fourth rule is broken, especially when God tries the believer with "sharp trials." There are times when it seems to the believer that "prayers themselves annoy God." God does not "rigorously" enforce the four rules of praying rightly. Rather, he pardons the defects. Knowledge of this mercy, however, must not encourage carelessness in praying. On the contrary, believers are called "to correct their faults, and each day come nearer to the perfect rule of prayer."[45]

Jesus Christ, the only mediator of the prayers of the saints

Fundamental to the confidence of the saints that God hears and answers their prayers is the truth that Jesus Christ is their mediator in praying. By the truth of Christ's mediation with regard to prayer, Calvin understands that the sacrifice of Christ is the basis of all prayer; that the saints bring their prayers to God through Jesus Christ as the way to the Father; and that Jesus Christ intercedes with God so that God will hear the praying saint and grant his petition.

All of this is comprehended in the biblical injunction that the believer pray in Jesus' name (John 16:24, 26).

Apart from this mediation of Jesus Christ, the "dread majesty" of God must throw the hearts of unworthy sinners into "despair" of being received by God. In a great line, Calvin declares that "Christ comes forward as intermediary, to change the throne of dreadful glory into the throne of grace."[46] Calvin's meaning is not that Christ actually changes a hostile God into a God of grace toward his people. But Calvin describes the effect of the saint's believing knowledge of Christ's mediation upon the saint's thinking and experience.

The intercession of the ascended Christ on behalf of his praying people is an aspect of Christ's high-priestly office, the fulfillment of the function of the Old Testament high priest.

Motivated both by zeal for the honor of Jesus Christ and by concern for the assurance of the praying believers, Calvin carries on a vigorous, sharp polemic against the Roman Catholic teaching and practice of praying to God through the mediatorship of the saints. Calvin is well-read in the Roman Catholic literature advocating prayers to the saints. He is well aware of the labored defenses of the practice of seeking access to God in prayer through dead saints. For example, the "Sophists" babble that, although "Christ is the Mediator of redemption . . . believers are mediators of intercession."[47] Also, a speculative defense against the Protestant charge that the dead saints have "no contact" with the church in the world (as Calvin puts it, the ears of the dead are not "long enough to reach our voices," nor are their "eyes so keen as to watch over our needs") is that the dead see a reflection of "the affairs of men" in the face of God.[48]

But Calvin is also thoroughly familiar with the practical piety of the Roman Catholic faithful. They pray "prostrate before a statue or picture of . . . saints." They call on the saints as "determiners of their salvation." They adopt "a particular saint as a tutelary deity, in whose keeping [they] put [their] trust."[49] Although Rome pays lip service to Christ as the mediator in its theology, especially its defense of the intercession of saints in controversy, its liturgical practice ignores Christ altogether. "In all their litanies, hymns, and proses, where they leave no honor unapplied to dead saints, Christ goes unmentioned."[50]

With appeal to John 14:6, 1 Timothy 2:5, and other passages, Calvin affirms that Christ "is the only way, and the one access, by which it is granted us to come to God."[51] In heaven Christ "alone bears to God the petitions of the people."[52] Living saints certainly do and must pray for each other, but "all intercessions of the whole church" must be directed "to that sole intercession" of Christ.[53]

Rome's doctrine and practice of praying to and through saints are condemned simply by the fact that "there is nothing about it in Scripture."[54]

The wickedness of Roman doctrine and practice of the intercession of saints is great. Roman Catholics "dishonor Christ . . . and make void the cross."[55] "To direct prayer to others [than to God through Jesus Christ] involves manifest sacrilege."[56] "To transfer to the dead what properly belonged to God and Christ" is "devilish insolence."[57]

Calvin concludes his refutation of the Roman Catholic doctrine of prayers, and his own treatment of the biblical truth that Jesus Christ is the only mediator and intercessor of his praying people, with the exhortation to his readers: pray only to God; pray only through Christ.

Private and public prayers

Calvin recognizes two kinds of prayers, private and public, and gives brief instruction concerning both in sections twenty-eight through thirty-three of chapter twenty of book three.

Specifically with regard to private prayers, Calvin teaches that the constant prayers of the believer must consist of both petitions and mingled praise and thanksgiving. The guilt of our transgressions and the many temptations that assail us afford ample reason for petitions. In addition, all the adversities of life drive us to God with petitionary prayers.

God's many benefits to his people naturally evoke in them the love that praises him in prayer. Our "praises... flow from this sweetness of love."[58] Calvin warns that, apart from God's blessing, which we enjoy by our praise and thanksgiving, "neither we nor our possessions prosper."[59]

A great temptation to all saints at one time or another is that their praise of God weakens, or even ceases, because of adversity, or because God does not give them some gift they ardently desire. At best, yielding somewhat to the temptation, they "mumble when praying." Calvin exhorts these "believers so to temper their emotions that while still waiting to obtain what they desire, they nonetheless cheerfully bless God."[60]

Regarding both private and public prayer, Calvin is insistent that all prayer be heartfelt and sincere. He warns against the hypocrisy that likes to impress the audience with a showy public prayer. "Prayer itself," says Calvin, "is properly an emotion of the heart within."[61] Combating the evil forbidden by Christ in Matthew 6:7, namely, "vain repetition," Calvin calls for prayers that are "earnest and come forth from the depths of the heart."[62]

God demands public prayers, as well as the private prayers of each believer. Public prayers are prayers raised by the entire congregation at their regular gatherings of public worship. These "common prayers of the church" and, therefore, the gatherings for public worship "may not be held in contempt."[63] When God called the temple the "house of prayer" (Isa. 56:7; Matt. 21:13), he taught that "the chief part of his worship lies in the office of prayer."[64] The one who refuses "to pray in the holy assembly of the godly knows not what it is to pray individually."[65]

God's ordinance that his people pray together in public gatherings necessitates church buildings, "public temples." Ever vigilant against superstition, Calvin immediately warns that the building itself is not holy. The church building is not "God's proper dwelling place." It is the saints themselves who are "God's true temples."[66]

All public prayers must be in the "language of the people...for the edification of the whole church."[67]

Public prayers include congregational singing. Calvin "strongly commend[s]"[68] congregational singing as part of the public worship of the church. This element of public worship has biblical warrant in 1 Corinthians 14:15 and Colossians 3:16. "Singing [in church]...both lends dignity and grace to sacred actions and has the greatest value in kindling our hearts to a true zeal and eagerness to pray."[69]

Calvin warns against becoming more delighted with the melody of the tunes than with "the spiritual meaning of the words."[70] Songs composed for use at church "only for sweetness and delight of the ear are unbecoming to the majesty of the church and cannot but displease God in the highest degree."[71] In this section of the *Institutes*, Calvin leaves to be inferred what elsewhere he makes explicit concerning his condemnation of all songs whose content is insipid or even heretical.

Calvin expressly approves those "bodily gestures...observed in praying" that incite "a greater reverence for God," specifically "kneeling and uncovering the head."[72]

The model prayer

Calvin concludes his treatment of prayer in the life of the believer and in the worship of the church with an explanation of the model prayer, as taught by Jesus Christ in Matthew 6:9–13 and Luke 11:2–4. This prayer is the "form or rule of prayer" for Christians.[73] It instructs us concerning "all that he [God] allows us to seek of him, all that is of benefit to us, all that we need to ask."[74]

Running through Calvin's entire treatment of prayer is his fear that Christians will regard prayer as the opportunity to ask of God anything they please. This fear is certainly realized in the prayers of many professing Christians and nominally Christian churches at the beginning of the twenty-first century. At the outset of his explanation of the model prayer, Calvin warns against requesting of God in prayer that which is "unacceptable to him."[75] Calvin quotes Plato, the "heathen man" who is, however, "wise," against the evil of seeking from the Lord "what our greed dictates." Plato taught his disciples to pray, "King Jupiter, bestow the best things upon us whether we wish for them or not, but command that evil things be far from us even when we request them."[76] The clear implication is that the heathen thinker was wiser than contemporary, "evangelical" churches whose theory and practice of prayer are that Christians may ask of God any earthly thing their foolish hearts desire and expect to receive it.

The structure of the model prayer is an address ("Our Father who art in heaven"), six petitions, and a conclusion. Of the six petitions, the first three "have been particularly assigned to God's glory." The last three "are concerned with the care of ourselves."[77]

The force of the first three petitions is that we pray for God's name, kingdom, and will without any regard for "our own private good." Calvin points to the examples of Moses and Paul, who "long[ed] for their own destruction with fierce and burning zeal in order that, despite their own loss, they might advance God's glory and Kingdom [Ex. 32:32; Rom. 9:3]."[78]

Such is the significance of the first three petitions for the last three that, although in the last three "we desire what is to our benefit," our seeking of these benefits is strictly subservient to "God's glory."[79]

Having thus introduced the model prayer, Calvin proceeds to a brief explanation of each of its parts. The address at once confronts us with Jesus Christ, for no one can address God as Father apart from Jesus Christ. "We ought to offer all prayer to God only in Christ's name." Not only is it impossible for anyone to call God Father apart from Christ, but also a prayer raised to God apart from Christ Jesus "cannot be agreeable to him [God]."[80]

This first principle of all true prayer demolishes the ecumenical gatherings of Christians, Jews, Muslims, and other religions. They cannot even pray together.

Calling on God as Father, the one who prays is assured of God's love for him and care over him. "'Father' . . . frees us from all distrust, since no greater feeling of love can be found elsewhere than in the Father."[81] In fact, the address requires of all who pray that "[they] should call upon him with assured faith."[82] Nor may the one who prays plead his sinfulness as the reason for doubting God's fatherly love of him. As an earthly father is compassionate to a penitent child, so God is ready to forgive and receive every penitent sinner who calls on him for Christ's sake. It is the Spirit in the believers who witnesses to them of their adoption as children of God, so that they cry, "'Abba, Father' [Gal. 4:6; Rom. 8:15]."[83] "Those who do not feel assured" pray in vain: "in doubt and perplexity turn ever their prayers within their minds."[84]

At the same time, the address admonishes us to have brotherly love and to pray for all of God's children. Calvin emphasizes that Jesus taught his disciples to pray "*our* Father," not my Father.[85]

That our Father is "in heaven" bespeaks his "infinite greatness or loftiness ... incomprehensible essence ... boundless might, and ... everlasting immortality."[86] The knowledge that God is "in heaven" will affect the one who prays in three ways. First, he will, in seeking God, "rise above all perception of body and soul." Second, he will depend upon God as "lifted above all chance of either corruption or change." Third, he will be confident that God can help him, inasmuch as God "holds together the entire universe and controls it by his might."[87]

The first petition, concerning the hallowing of God's name, has to do with God's revelation of himself in his "teaching" and in his "works." The petition desires "God to have the honor he deserves." God gets this honor from the church in that "Scripture will obtain a just authority among us" and in that the church blesses God regarding "the whole course of his governance of the universe."[88]

But the petition also asks that "all impiety which has besmirched this holy name may perish and be wiped out."[89] Answering this petition, God will "finally completely destroy everything that casts a stain upon his holy name."[90]

The second petition requests the coming of God's kingdom. Calvin defines the kingdom of God: "God reigns where men, both by denial of themselves and by contempt of the world and of earthly life, pledge themselves to his righteousness in order to aspire to a heavenly life."[91] This reign of God is the kingdom of Jesus Christ in the power of the

Spirit of Christ. Obviously, for Calvin the kingdom is spiritual in nature, not carnal.

The kingdom of God in Christ comes, progressively, in three ways, according to Calvin. The first is the progressive sanctification of the elect believer: "God by the power of his Spirit correct[s] all the desires of the flesh... [and] shape[s] all our thoughts in obedience to his rule."[92]

The kingdom comes also by the establishing of churches throughout the world: "that God gather churches unto himself from all parts of the earth; that he spread and increase them in number."[93]

Third, the kingdom will come in "its fullness" at "the final coming of Christ."[94] Then, Christ will "slay Antichrist... and destroy all ungodliness."[95]

The prayer for the kingdom of God and its coming implies the request that God destroy all the enemies of his kingdom. These include "all enemies of pure teaching and religion."[96]

It is conclusively evident from Calvin's explanation of the second petition of the model prayer that Calvin rejects the notions of both premillennial dispensationalism and postmillennialism that the kingdom of God is an earthly, political, carnal reign of Christ and that this carnal kingdom will be fully, or well-nigh fully, established for a thousand years prior to the end of all things.

Calvin *defines* the kingdom as "*contempt* of the world and of earthly life."[97] He describes the coming of the kingdom in terms of progressive sanctification in every believer and of the flourishing of the churches. And he "delays" the "fullness" of the kingdom to Christ's second coming and the end of the world.[98]

In addition to all of this, Calvin admonishes all believers that the prayer for the kingdom "instruct[s] us in bearing the cross. For it is in this way that God wills to spread his Kingdom."[99] The way of cross-bearing is not the way of the coming of the kingdom for either premillennialism or postmillennialism.

In the time between the 1536 edition of the *Institutes* and its final form in 1559, Calvin changed his mind about the reference to the will of God in the third petition. In 1536 Calvin thought that the reference is both to the secret counsel and to the precepts of God. "By this petition we ask him... to temper and compose all things according to his will, govern the outcome of all things," etc.[100] But in the 1559 edition, Calvin tells us, "Here it is not a question of his secret will, by which he controls all things and directs them to their end ... But here God's other will is to be noted—namely, that to which voluntary obedience corresponds."[101]

The third petition, therefore, is the heartfelt request that God will work in us by his Spirit "pure agreement with his will." The broader scope of the petition is that "the earth be in like manner [as in heaven] subject to such a rule" as results in willing obedience to God.[102]

Reflecting on the first three petitions before proceeding to the last three, Calvin remarks that the things we request will come to pass "without any thought or desire or petition of ours." The importance of our praying the petition is that we "testify and profess ourselves servants and children of God, zealously, truly, and deeply committed ... to his honor."[103]

With the fourth petition concerning bread, "we descend to our own affairs," without "bid[ding] farewell to God's glory."[104]

"Bread" stands for "all things in general that our bodies have need to use under the elements of this world." The fourth petition, therefore, expresses our reliance on "his providence, that he may feed, nourish, and preserve us." Prayed with sincerity, the fourth petition is "no light exercise of faith," for our wickedness causes us to be anxious about the supply of the needs of the body. Indeed, "the shadow of this fleeting life mean[s more] to us than ... everlasting immortality."[105] In the 1536 *Institutes*, Calvin expresses our worry over our material needs very forcefully: this anxiety "sinks its teeth into the very bones of almost all men."[106]

Both the phrase "this day" and the adjective "daily" require us to be content with the satisfying of our needs and to depend upon God for these needs each day. Those who pray for bread while "panting after countless things with unbridled desire" are "mocking him."[107]

The fact that we ask God for our bread indicates that bread, that is, the supply of our physical needs, is "a simple and free gift of God."[108] He gives us these things, which are his, even if the means is our labor, and he makes these things nourish and prosper us.

The fifth and sixth petitions ask for the two benefits that comprise "all that makes for the heavenly life, as the spiritual covenant that God has made for the salvation of his church rests on these two members alone": justification and sanctification. The fifth petition is a request for justification, that is, "the forgiveness of sins." Sins are "'debts' because we owe penalty for them."[109] Forgiveness releases the praying believer from this penalty.

What the penalty that is cancelled by forgiveness is, Calvin does not state. But he clearly implies that it is the infinite wrath of God when he declares that the judicial ground of forgiveness is the death of Christ. Calvin gives a precise, profound definition of the death of Christ, indicating at the same time his own understanding of the cross. The cross of Christ was God's own "making satisfaction to himself by his own mercy in Christ, who once for all gave himself as a ransom."[110]

Because the sole ground of forgiveness is the satisfaction of the cross, those who plead for forgiveness on the basis of "their own or others' merits... share not at all in this free gift."[111] This is the Reformation's judgment of the Roman Catholic doctrine and practice of justification, that is, forgiveness by good works.

The implication of the prayer for pardon is that Christ's disciples remain sinners as long as they live. Calvin condemns the teachers of perfectionism: "these new doctors, who try to dazzle the eyes of the simple-minded with the specter of perfect innocence."[112]

Calvin does justice to the comparison in the fifth petition: "as we forgive our debtors." "We ought not to seek forgiveness of sins from God unless we ourselves also forgive the offenses against us of all those who do or have done us ill."[113] In the strict sense, we cannot forgive, "for this belongs to God alone." Calvin carefully describes what our forgiveness consists of: "willingly to cast from the mind wrath, hatred, desire for revenge, and willingly to banish to oblivion the remembrance of injustice." It even includes that we "try to get back into our enemies' good graces."[114]

However, our forgiveness of others is not the "cause" of God's forgiveness of us. By our forgiveness we do not "deserve his forgiveness."[115] At every point, Calvin is vigilant to safeguard the gospel of grace. Rather, the comparison between God's forgiveness of us and our forgiveness of others indicates that our forgiveness is "a sign to assure us he has granted forgiveness of sins to us."[116] The comparison also excludes vengeful persons "from the number of his [God's] children" and makes it impossible for them to "call upon him as Father."[117]

In his exposition of the fifth petition, Calvin has said that the sixth petition, "Lead us not into temptation, but deliver us from evil," requests the benefit of salvation that God promised in Jeremiah 31:33: "I will put my law in their inward parts, and write it in their hearts."[118] This is the word of grace that delivers the children of God from the *power* of sin, as justification delivers from the *guilt* of sin. This work of the Spirit makes God's people *holy*, as justification constitutes them *righteous*.

Calvin finds two aspects of sanctification in the sixth petition: "The grace of the Spirit... soften[s] our hearts within... to bend and direct them to obey God... [and] render[s] us invincible against both all the stratagems and all the violent assaults of Satan."[119]

Temptations to sin, against which we pray for aid in the sixth petition, are twofold, "either from the right or from the left." Those from the right use prosperity and success to entice us to "forget [our] God." Those from the left use adversity and suffering to cause us to "become despondent in mind," or bitter against God.[120]

Behind all temptations to sin is Satan. Indeed, Calvin favors the explanation of the word "evil" in the petition that reads the word as "evil *one*," that is, Satan. Against such a "ferocious and well-equipped enemy," only the power of God himself in his tempted children can preserve them. Calvin warns those who trust "in their own capacities and powers of free choice, which they seem to themselves to possess" that they must be destroyed.[121]

Calvin points out that in the sixth petition the children of God do not ask that they not be tempted. Temptation is profitable, indeed necessary, for our spiritual well-being, lest "we grow sluggish." Calvin importantly distinguishes "trial," which God sends, from "temptation" to sin, the author of which is always Satan.[122]

Ever the theologian of holiness, Calvin reminds his readers that the sixth petition is not only the request to be undefeated by Satan in the lifelong spiritual war, but also the request for "victory." And God grants the request. The victory over Satan and sin for the believer consists of "new increases of God's grace [being] continually... showered upon us, until, completely filled therewith, we triumph over all evil."[123] The

Christian life of holiness, according to Calvin and the Reformed faith, although a constant, fierce battle, is dynamic, progressive, and victorious.

This does not imply, however, that there is never for some saints what the Canons of Dordt call a "lamentable fall" into sin.[124] Calvin concludes his explanation of the sixth petition with a solemn warning. The sixth petition implies that it may please God on occasion to lead one of his children into temptation. Then he turns "us over to Satan" and casts us into "foul desires" by a "just but often secret judgment."[125] Although Calvin does not here further explain this severe judgment of God upon one of his children, it is in accord with Calvin's theology that the reason for the judgment is one's pride and willful disregard of God's word and that the outcome will certainly be the repentance and restoration of the sinner.[126]

Calvin recognizes that there is a textual question concerning the conclusion of the model prayer: "For thine is the kingdom, and the power, and the glory, forever! Amen." Some Greek manuscripts of the New Testament omit these words. His judgment is that this ending of the prayer is "appropriate" and "ought not to be omitted." The significance is that the ending is "the reason...we should be so bold to ask and so confident of receiving." "Amen" expresses not only "the warmth of desire to obtain" the petitions, but also the "confidence of being heard."[127]

Both the beginning and the ending of the model prayer, the address and the conclusion, establish that prayer is the activity of *faith* and that faith is *assurance*—assurance of God's fatherly love toward and God's care over the one who prays.

In a parting glance at the model prayer, Calvin observes that it is "perfect," so that nothing "which cannot be related to it" may be added in our prayers. As Tertullian has said, it is "the lawful prayer."[128] This by no means implies, however, that saints are bound to the very words of the model prayer, that is, must restrict their praying to a repetition of it. It is, Calvin reminds us, a "form of prayer."[129]

Pastoral counsel concerning praying

The conclusion of Calvin's treatment of prayer in the life of the Christian consists of several practical exhortations. First, everyone should "set apart certain hours" for prayer.[130] Calvin stipulates the times: on arising; before we take up our work; when we eat our meals, both before and after; and upon retiring for the night.

Second, we must make all our petitions subject to God's will. Calvin is the enemy of those who brazenly impose their will upon God in prayer. So popular has the notion become in the twenty-first century that prayer is the forcing of one's own will upon God, regardless of the content of one's own will, and so ungodly is this notion, that it is worth quoting Calvin at length on this matter.

> Lastly, in all prayer we ought carefully to observe that our intention is not to bind God to particular circumstances, or to prescribe at what time, in what place, or in what way he is to do anything. Accordingly, in this prayer we are taught not to make any law for him, or impose any condition upon him, but to leave to his decision to do what he is to do, in what way, at what time, and in what place it seems good to him. Therefore, before we make any prayer for ourselves, we pray that his will be done [Matt. 6:10]. By these words we subject our will to his in order that, restrained as by a bridle, it may not presume to control God but may make him the arbiter and director of all its entreaties.[131]

Third, Calvin calls for perseverance in praying, when it seems as though God has "ears deaf to [our] prayers."[132] This raises the difficult, spiritually trying matter of petitions for things good in themselves that go seemingly unanswered, even after a long time of patiently waiting on God.

Calvin shows himself a gentle, wise pastor in his counsel of those who find themselves in this situation. First, he recognizes that this may well be the experience of God's believing children; God does not always give them what they desire and ask. Although Calvin does not mention the examples, the biblical proof is that God did not remove the cup of the cross from Jesus, nor did he remove Paul's thorn in the flesh.

Second, God always gives his praying child "what [is] expedient" for the child, as God knows what is good for him.[133]

Third, although God may not give the thing desired, for example, a child to the childless couple, or may not deliver from some affliction, for example, the fatal disease and early death of a young mother, he always gives *himself*: "He alone will be for us in place of all things, since all good things are contained in him."[134]

Fourth, even though God "does not always respond to the exact form of our request," he is "still attentive and kindly to our prayers," so that they are not in "vain."[135]

Fifth, by withholding for a time, even for a *long* time, what his child ardently desires and asks for, God "proves" his child, and he does so "by no light trials, and does not softly exercise them."[136]

Sixth, it is certain that "God has regard for" his distressed people "and will bring an end to their present misfortunes," if not in this life, then in the life to come.[137]

CHAPTER 15

Predestination

Introduction

Although not the central dogma in Calvin's theology (the one dogma out of which all of Calvin's teachings flow, and around which all of his teachings circle, and upon which all of his teachings depend), as has been proposed, predestination is fundamental in the theology of John Calvin. Calvin states this importance of election when he calls it "the foundation of our salvation."[1]

The importance Calvin attributes to predestination is evident from several considerations.

First, Calvin increasingly developed and emphasized the doctrine of predestination throughout his ministry, right up to the very end. This was in contrast to Martin Luther, who stressed predestination more strongly at the beginning of his ministry and backed away from it in his later years, likely under Philip Melanchthon's influence.

Second, the importance of predestination for Calvin is evident from the vigor with which he defended the doctrine throughout his ministry against those who assailed it.

Third, the importance Calvin attributed to predestination is evident from the fact that at one point in his ministry, during the Bolsec affair in the early 1550s, Calvin stood alone, and was willing to stand alone, in his defense of predestination. At that time, almost without exception his fellow reformers throughout Europe, particularly Bullinger, not only refused to support Calvin, but also actively opposed him on the doctrine of predestination, specifically the doctrine of reprobation.

I note here the lesson of history with respect to the essential doctrines of the Christian faith. There is always a time when *one* champion of a doctrine stands alone for the defense of that doctrine. This was true of the doctrine of the deity of Christ and the Trinity. The champion was Athanasius. It was true regarding the truth of justification by faith alone. The champion was Martin Luther. This was also true regarding the doctrine of predestination. The one champion was John Calvin.

Those churches and ministers today who renounce predestination, corrupt predestination, or politely decline to preach predestination are not Calvinists, regardless of their profession. If the doctrine of predestination is, as Calvin thought, "the foundation of salvation," those churches and ministers who renounce it, corrupt it, or are completely silent regarding it are guilty of evil work regarding salvation at its foundation; they are undermining the very foundation of salvation.

Calvin's very brief treatment of predestination in the 1536 *Institutes* occurs in his explanation of the Apostles' Creed as part of his explanation of the holy catholic church.[2] There he defines the church as "the whole number of the elect."[3] This is where the continually expanding treatment of predestination remained in the *Institutes* until the final edition of 1559.

We recognize that this is where the Heidelberg Catechism brings up the doctrine of election:

> What dost thou believe concerning the *Holy Catholic Church*?
> That out of the whole human race, from the beginning to the end of the world, the Son of God, by his Spirit and Word, gathers, defends, and preserves for himself unto everlasting life, a chosen communion in the unity of the true faith; and that I am, and forever shall remain, a living member of the same.[4]

In the final, 1559 edition of the *Institutes*, which Calvin completely restructured according to a trinitarian division of doctrine, he makes predestination the conclusion of his treatment of salvation, following his treatment of justification and immediately following his exposition of prayer, particularly his exposition of the Lord's prayer.

Calvin's placement of predestination differs, of course, from the placement of it in dogmatics by later Reformed theologians, most of whom treat predestination in the first locus, theology. Why Calvin placed predestination where he did in the 1559 *Institutes*, he himself suggests at the beginning of his treatment of predestination: predestination is "the well-spring" whence all salvation flows.[5]

Jacobs made the intriguing suggestion that the placement of predestination at the conclusion of his treatment of salvation reflects Calvin's determination to present predestination from "a Christocentric point of view."[6] According to Jacobs' suggestion, treating predestination after having treated salvation in Christ enables Calvin to put forth the doctrine of predestination as a decree appointing some to salvation in Christ.

Where one places predestination in dogmatics is not important. What is important is the explanation of predestination that one gives and the significance that predestination has in one's theology. Calvin's placement of predestination in book three in connection with salvation rather than in book one as part of the doctrine of God implies absolutely no minimizing of the doctrine or of the fundamental importance of predestination.

The history of Calvin's struggle on behalf of the truth of predestination must not be overlooked. This history is the background to the expansive treatment and defense of the doctrine of predestination in the 1559 *Institutes*.

Throughout his ministry, as Calvin himself tells us, he bore reproach especially for his confession of God's providence and God's predestination.[7] These two related truths are the main aspects of the sovereignty of God. Providence is God's sovereignty in history. Predestination is God's sovereignty in salvation and damnation. So closely are providence and predestination related that prior to the final edition of 1559, Calvin treated the two doctrines together. Only in the 1559 *Institutes* does Calvin separate the two doctrines, treating providence in connection with God the Father and creation and placing predestination in book three as the conclusion to the treatment of salvation.

It was especially the Dutch Roman Catholic theologian Albertus Pighius, in the early 1540s, and the maverick Protestant theologian Jerome Bolsec, in the early 1550s, who put Calvin to the test regarding predestination. In his attack on Calvin's doctrine of predestination,

Pighius also attacked Calvin's doctrine of the bondage of the will of unregenerated men. In 1543 Calvin responded to Pighius' attack on Calvin's doctrine of the bondage of the will,[8] intending to address Pighius' attack on predestination a little later with another book. Because Pighius died soon thereafter, Calvin delayed publishing a defense against Pighius' attack on predestination.

In the early 1550s, Bolsec violently attacked Calvin over Calvin's doctrine of predestination, election and reprobation. This controversy threw Geneva into an uproar.

In 1552 Calvin wrote a treatise, "On the Eternal Predestination of God," known in scholarly circles as *Consensus Genevensis*. Calvin informed his readers that his treatise on predestination was directed against Albertus Pighius, who had attacked the doctrine of predestination some years earlier, and against a certain "George, the Sicilian," who also had taught "that it lies in each one's own liberty, whether he will become a partaker of the grace of adoption or not; and that it does not depend on the counsel and decree of God who are elect and who are reprobate."[9]

At the same time, the treatise on predestination is responding to and refuting Bolsec, even though Calvin does not name him.

Yet another very worthwhile work by Calvin on predestination came out of the Bolsec controversy. This is a short work titled in English, "Congregation on Eternal Election."[10] Calvin wrote the treatise at the request of the Genevan ministers to calm the people who had been disturbed by Bolsec's assault on predestination. Calvin informs the reader that he wrote the treatise against "a master muddler [who] has departed from I know not what order of the Carmelites and monks, and has become at once a quack doctor," that is, Bolsec.[11] Calvin has even less regard for Bolsec as a theologian.

The 1559 *Institutes* reflects these fierce controversies over predestination and contains the fruits of the study of predestination that these controversies forced on Calvin.

Calvin's approach to the doctrine of predestination

Predestination is the explanation why the "covenant of life"— Calvin's description of the gospel at the outset of his treatment of predestination—is preached to some and not to others.[12] The fact that it is not preached to some means that many perish, never having heard the gospel. And predestination is the explanation why the effect of the preaching is the saving of some and the perishing of others. This is Calvin's approach to the doctrine of predestination.

The opening line of his treatment of predestination indicates the approach:

> In actual fact, the covenant of life is not preached equally among all men, and among those to whom it is preached, it does not gain the same acceptance either constantly or in equal degree. In this diversity the wonderful depth of God's judgment is made known. For there is no doubt that this variety also serves the decision of God's eternal election. If it is plain that it comes to pass by God's bidding that salvation is freely offered to some while others are barred from access to it, at once great and difficult questions spring up, explicable only when reverent minds regard as settled what they may suitably hold concerning election and predestination.[13]

This is exactly the approach to predestination of the Canons of Dordt in Head 1. There are two effects of the preaching of the gospel: unbelief and faith.[14] "That some receive the gift of faith from God, and others do not receive it, proceeds from God's eternal decree."[15]

This fact, which cannot be ignored, makes it impossible for a church or a minister to be silent about predestination. No matter how a minister may try to be silent about predestination, in the end this is impossible. The minister has to recognize the two effects of the preaching of the gospel, and he must explain them, and he will explain them. Either he will explain them by God's sovereign will, in which case he teaches predestination; or he will explain them by the sinner's sovereign will, in which case he denies predestination and the grace of salvation.

It is the confession of the grace of salvation that is Calvin's special concern in his approach to predestination as the explanation of the faith and salvation of some and also of the unbelief and damnation of others:

> We shall never be clearly persuaded, as we ought to be, that our salvation flows from the wellspring of God's free mercy until

we come to know his eternal election, which illumines God's grace by this contrast: that he does not indiscriminately adopt all into the hope of salvation but gives to some what he denies to others.[16]

We must be persuaded, we whom the preaching of the covenant of life has saved, both so that we may rest assured of our present and everlasting salvation and so that we may glorify God for our salvation. This persuasion that the wellspring of salvation is God's election always takes into account that others are not adopted into the hope of salvation because God denies to them, according to reprobation, what he gives to us.

What predestination is

What is this predestination upon which our salvation depends as "foundation," and that also determines that others perish in unbelief? Calvin defines predestination very briefly: "God's eternal decree, by which he compacted with himself what he willed to become of each man ... eternal life ... for some, eternal damnation for others."[17] There is a similar definition in the treatise "On the Eternal Predestination of God":

> Now, if we are not really ashamed of the Gospel, we must of necessity acknowledge what is therein openly declared: that God by His eternal goodwill (for which there was no other cause than His own purpose), appointed those whom he pleased unto salvation, rejecting all the rest; and that those whom he blessed with this free adoption to be His sons He illumines by His Holy Spirit, that they may receive the life that is offered to them in Christ; while others, continuing of their own will in unbelief, are left destitute of the light of faith, in total darkness.[18]

In the light of these definitions and Calvin's explanation of predestination overall, it is clear that for Calvin predestination is one eternal decree consisting of both election and reprobation. Calvin insists on what is called today the double decree.

Even though he knows and experiences that reprobation stirs up the most tumultuous opposition, he boldly and uncompromisingly confesses reprobation. With regard to reprobation, Calvin remarks, "Now when human understanding hears these things, its insolence is so irrepressible that it breaks forth into random and immoderate tumult as if at the blast of a battle trumpet."[19]

Calvin says that some, whether to avoid this tumult or for other reasons, including their own abhorrence of reprobation, try to maintain election while rejecting reprobation. Calvin has especially the Lutherans, except Luther, in view, particularly Philip Melanchthon. During the Bolsec controversy, also Bullinger went in this direction. His response to Calvin's request for support against Bolsec was, in essence, that Calvin was wrong in teaching reprobation; he should teach election but not reprobation. This is highly popular today with many who profess to be Calvinists.

To maintain election while rejecting reprobation is impossible, says Calvin. Not only is it not right to ignore the Bible's teaching about eternal reprobation, but also it is impossible to deny reprobation and still maintain election: "Election itself could not stand except as set over against reprobation... Those whom God passes over, he condemns; and this he does for no other reason than that he wills to exclude them from the inheritance which he predestines for his own children."[20]

Calvin says much the same thing in a significant paragraph in his treatise "On the Eternal Predestination of God":

> There is, most certainly and evidently, an inseparable connection between the elect and the reprobate. So that the election, of which the apostle speaks [in Ephesians 1:3, 4], cannot consist unless we confess that God separated from all others certain persons whom it pleased Him thus to separate. Now, this act of God is expressed by the term *predestinating*, which the apostle afterwards twice repeats [vv. 5, 11].[21]

God is equally sovereign in the damnation of the wicked as in the salvation of those who are righteous by his grace.

In support of the truth of reprobation, Calvin appeals to Matthew 15:13: "Every plant, which my heavenly Father hath not planted, shall be rooted up," and to Romans 9:17, 18, 22, 23:

> For the scripture saith unto Pharaoh, Even for this same purpose have I raised thee up, that I might shew my power in thee, and that my name might be declared throughout all the earth. Therefore hath he mercy on whom he will have mercy, and whom he will he hardeneth. What if God, willing to shew his wrath, and to make his power known, endured with much longsuffering the vessels of wrath fitted to destruction: And that he might make known the riches of his glory on the vessels of mercy, which he had afore prepared unto glory.

That Calvin insists on the teaching of reprobation does not imply that he supposes that he or any other human being can comprehend predestination, particularly the doctrine of reprobation; nor does confession of reprobation imply that the doctrine of reprobation leaves Calvin cold and unmoved.

With respect to the fact that Calvin acknowledges that we cannot comprehend reprobation, again and again when his enemies are pressing him with the charge, "How can it be right of God to decree the damnation of men and women before they are born and have done any good or evil?" Calvin falls back on the confession that God is the righteous one. Indeed, he is the ultimate and only standard of righteousness, so that we believe reprobation and God's righteousness in reprobation, although we are not able to comprehend it. Calvin also exclaims again and again that God's ways are higher than our ways. He confronts the objectors with Paul's response to the same objection: "Nay but, O man, who art thou that repliest against God?" (Rom. 9:20).

That Calvin's confession of reprobation does not leave him unmoved means, not that Calvin opposes the doctrine, but that the doctrine of reprobation causes Calvin to tremble. This is evident from his well-known statement "*decretum quidem horribile, fateor*," that is, "The decree is dreadful indeed, I confess."[22] Calvin is actually referring to God's decree of the fall of Adam, but Calvin refers to God's decree of Adam's fall as entailing the eternal death of many members of the human race; therefore, in reality, the statement, "The decree, I admit, is dreadful," is a description of the decree of reprobation. It hardly needs to be noted here that the word *horribile* (dreadful) has the sense of "awesome," not "horrible" in the sense of being bad.

For Calvin, God's purposes in reprobation are to glorify himself in the demonstration of his justice and, especially, to illustrate to the elect the grace of their election. Elect believers must always see and be thankful for their own election against the background of God's reprobation of others. Both of these purposes of the decree of reprobation are expressed in the Canons of Dordt:

> What peculiarly tends to illustrate and recommend to us the eternal and unmerited grace of election is the express testimony of sacred Scripture, that not all, but some only, are elected, while others are passed by in the eternal decree... at last, for the declaration of his justice, to condemn and punish them forever.[23]

Predestination is one eternal plan in God, consisting of two inseparable aspects; as such it must be confessed with both its aspects. Calvin states the oneness of the plan of predestination:

> As Scripture, then, clearly shows, we say that God once established by his eternal and unchangeable plan those whom he long before determined once for all to receive into salvation, and those whom, on the other hand, he would devote to destruction. We assert that, with respect to the elect, this plan was founded upon his freely given mercy, without regard to human worth; but by his just and irreprehensible but incomprehensible judgment he has barred the door of life to those whom he has given over to damnation.[24]

As this quotation points out with respect to both aspects of predestination, predestination has as its sole cause God's good pleasure. For Calvin, both election and reprobation are unconditional. Even though Calvin acknowledges that objects of reprobation are worthy of reprobation,[25] that which alone accounts for God's rejection of them is his good pleasure: "If, then, we cannot determine a reason why he vouchsafes mercy to his own, except that it so pleases him, neither shall we have any reason for rejecting others, other than his will."[26] Calvin appeals to Paul's teaching concerning the reprobation of Esau in Romans 9 as proof that both aspects of predestination are due to the sovereign good pleasure of God:

When as yet they had done nothing good or evil, one was chosen, the other rejected. This is to prove that the foundation of divine predestination is not in works. Then when he raised the objection, whether God is unjust, he does not make use of what would have been the surest and clearest defense of his righteousness: that God recompensed Esau according to his own evil intention. Instead, he contents himself with a different solution, that the reprobate are raised up to the end that through them God's glory may be revealed. Finally, he adds the conclusion that "God has mercy upon whomever he wills, and he hardens whomever he wills" [Rom. 9:18]. Do you see how Paul attributes both to God's decision alone?[27]

Election is preeminent

Although Calvin insists upon reprobation and the teaching of reprobation, election certainly is preeminent in Calvin's theology of predestination. It is preeminent in his doctrine of predestination because it is preeminent in the estimation of God, as he makes known in Scripture.

Election is the choice unto salvation of individuals.

With regard to Old Testament Israel, Calvin speaks of a "general election" of the nation,[28] adding, "We must now add a second, more limited degree of election, or one in which God's more special grace was evident, that is, when from the same race of Abraham God rejected some but showed that he kept others among his sons by cherishing them in the church."[29] Henry Beveridge's translation is significantly different: "We must add a second step of a more limited nature, or one in which the grace of God was displayed in a more special form, when of the same family of Abraham God rejected some, and by keeping others within his Church showed that he retained them among his sons."[30] Beveridge's translation makes clear that God's election of individuals is a second step in the reality of election and that this second step *displays* the grace of God in a special way, rather than being a special grace in distinction from a non-special grace.

Calvin distinguishes the election of Israel as a nation from God's election of individuals, including individual descendants of Abraham in the Old Testament, unto salvation. Mention of the election of Israel as a nation leaves the truth of election "only half explained." The full truth of election is God's election of individuals unto salvation.[31] Also, the election of the nation did not appoint all the members of the nation unto salvation. In sharp contrast, God's election of individuals "not only offers salvation but so assigns it that the certainty of its effect is not in suspense or doubt."[32] The election of the nation involved only "the outward change [of the nation], without the working of inner grace." The election of Israel was "intermediate between the rejection of mankind and the election of a meager number of the godly."[33]

However Calvin may conceive the relation of God's national election of Israel, which Calvin describes as "the general election of a people," and God's election of individuals unto salvation, Calvin is at pains to insist that "the general election of a people" is qualitatively different from God's election of individuals unto salvation. The national election of Israel was not "effectual and truly enduring"; did not involve the gift of "the spirit of regeneration" to all the members of the nation "that would enable them to persevere in the covenant to the very end"; and certainly cannot, and must not, be explained in such a way that God "with indiscriminate grace effectually elect[s] all."[34]

The truth of the election of Israel is that God chose that nation *organically*, that is, not each and every physical descendant of Abraham, but the nation as an organism—an organism at the heart of which, determining the organism, is Jesus Christ and the "remnant according to the election of grace" (Rom. 11:5).

Romans 9:6–33 is the inspired explanation of God's election of Old Testament Israel, especially in view of the perishing of many Israelites. "They are not all Israel, which are of Israel" (v. 6). The seed of Abraham, who are the true Israel of God, are not all the physical descendants of Abraham but "the children of the promise" (v. 8). The children of the promise, in distinction from "the children of the flesh" (v. 8), are determined by God's election of individuals: "that the purpose of God according to election might stand" (v. 11). And the election of individuals, Jacob in distinction from Esau, depends finally on God's election of the man Jesus Christ, who is the seed of Abraham (Gal. 3:16, 29).

There is very definitely in Calvin at least the beginning of this understanding of God's election of Old Testament Israel. With specific reference to the reality that many descendants of Abraham "were cut off as rotten members," Calvin explains that "we must, in order that election may be effectual and truly enduring, ascend to the Head, in whom the Heavenly Father has gathered his elect together, and has joined them to himself by an indissoluble bond."[35]

It is noteworthy that Calvin links election tightly with the covenant. Although election and covenant are not identical, the one implies the other: "Where God has made a covenant of eternal life and calls any people to himself, a special mode of election is employed for a part of them."[36] If Calvin teaches that, in some sense, God established his covenant with all the physical descendants of Abraham in the Old Testament, he also teaches that God did not establish the covenant with all in the same way. "For the fact that God was continually gathering his church from Abraham's children rather than from profane nations had its reason in his covenant, which, when violated by that multitude, he confined to a few that it might not utterly cease."[37]

The election of individuals is the preeminent aspect of the decree of predestination. This choice of individuals is always effectual to save the one who is elected: the "free election" of God's "secret plan" is a choice of "individual persons, to whom God not only offers salvation, but so assigns it that the certainty of its effect is not in suspense or doubt."[38]

Calvin's emphasis on individual election must not obscure the fact that at the same time the decree of individuals unto salvation forms the one church. Already in the 1536 *Institutes*, Calvin has defined "the holy catholic church" as "the whole number of the elect."[39]

This election of individual human beings unto salvation is "in . . . Christ." Calvin does not mean that their *salvation* is in Christ, which is certainly true, but that their eternal *election* in the decree of predestination is "in . . . Christ."[40] This is an important insight of Calvin into the biblical truth of election, which demands more development than Calvin gives it in the *Institutes*. With reference to Ephesians 1:4, "According as he hath chosen us in him [Christ] before the foundation of the world," Calvin writes, "Those whom God has adopted as his sons are said to have been chosen not in themselves but in his Christ."[41] That we are chosen in Christ points out the way, the *only* way, the *all-important* way, in which the believers can have "assurance of our election."[42]

We can and should have assurance of election. In this context of assurance, Calvin raises the subject of election in Christ: "Christ... is the mirror wherein we must, and without self-deception may, contemplate our own election... If we are in communion with Christ... we have a sufficiently clear and firm testimony that we have been inscribed in the book of life."[43] Calvin warns against attempting to find assurance of election in any other way than faith in Christ as he is found in the gospel. "If we have been chosen in him [Christ], we shall not find assurance of our election in ourselves; and not even in God the Father, if we conceive him as severed from his Son."[44] Implied is the truth that communion with Christ, which is the essence of salvation, does not begin in time but in eternity: by electing grace, the believer has eternally been in communion with Christ.

Election is effectual and sure, so that the elect believer will persevere in faith and holiness to the end, so as to inherit eternal life. By faith in Christ, the believer has both assurance of election and assurance of perseverance unto eternal life. Calvin marshals a number of biblical passages, including John 6:37, 39, John 17:6, 12, John 10:27–29, Matthew 15:13, and Romans 8:38, in support of the truth that "the gift of perseverance... applies... to all the elect."[45]

Concerning those who seem to be believers but fall away, Calvin says that they never were true believers; they "never cleaved to Christ with the heartfelt trust in which certainty of election has... been established for us."[46] Calvin quotes 1 John 2:19: "They went out from us, but they were not of us; for if they had been of us, they would no doubt have continued with us: but they went out, that they might be made manifest that they were not all of us."[47]

Election and faith

The important relation between election and faith is that election is the cause of faith; faith depends upon election, not election upon faith.

Calvin carries on a running battle with Rome, specifically with Pighius, over Rome's denial of biblical election by its teaching of foreseen faith. An aspect of Rome's error was, and still is, its doctrine of foreknowledge as God's foreseeing who would believe and persevere and choosing persons for this reason. Calvin says, "These persons consider that God distinguishes among men according as he foresees what the merits of each will be."[48]

Although Calvin describes Rome's erroneous doctrine as teaching that God foresees men's "merits," Calvin, in fact, is condemning every form of the teaching that some worthiness of the sinner himself is the cause and explanation of God's election of him. One may vehemently reject the Roman Catholic doctrine of merit but still be guilty of teaching that election unto eternal life is due to, and depends upon, foreseen faith, that is, a worthiness of the sinner to be chosen and saved. Calvin condemns every form of the false doctrine that election is *conditional*.

Calvin refutes the teaching that election depends on foreseen faith. First, he appeals to Ephesians 1:4, which teaches that God chose his people "in Christ," thus ruling out all worthiness as the cause of election. "When Paul teaches that we were chosen in Christ 'before the creation of the world' [Eph. 1:4a], he takes away all consideration of real worth on our part."[49] God did not elect his people in themselves or by themselves, which might leave some room for the notion that election was based on some worth in those chosen.

Calvin notes that verse 5 adds that God's election was "according to the purpose [good pleasure] of his will," not according to the worthiness of the elect. Calvin adds that Ephesians 1:4 teaches that holiness is not the *cause* of election, but the *effect*: "that we should be holy." "If he chose us that we should be holy, he did not choose us because he foresaw that we would be so. For these two notions disagree: that the godly have their holiness from election, and that they arrive at election by reason of works."[50]

Ephesians 1:6 teaches the purpose of election: "the praise of the glory of his [God's] grace," which cannot be the case if election is based on faith or any other worthiness in the elect.

Especially important to Calvin for the doctrine of unconditional election is Romans 9–11, "where Paul both reiterates this argument more profoundly and pursues it more at length."[51] On the basis of the apostle's teaching concerning Jacob and Esau in Romans 9:10–16, Calvin exposes the error of conditional election:

Here is the sum of their facile argument: in the person of Jacob, God showed that he chooses those worthy of his grace; in the person of Esau, that he repudiates those whom he foresees as unworthy. So, indeed, they boldly argue. But what does Paul say? "Though they were not yet born and had done nothing either good or bad, in order that God's purpose of election might continue, not because of works but because of his call, it was said, 'The elder will serve the younger.' As it is written, 'Jacob I loved, but Esau I hated'" [Rom. 9:11–13; cf. Gen. 25:23]. If foreknowledge had any bearing upon this distinction between the brothers, the mention of time would surely have been inopportune.[52]

Asserting that he could construct his entire argument from Augustine, Calvin quotes Augustine: "God's grace does not find but makes those fit to be chosen."[53]

Basic to the controversy over the relation between election and faith is the question whether faith is the gift of God or a condition of election that lies in the ability of the sinner. Calvin maintains that faith is the gift of God to the elect, not only regarding "the ability to believe," but also regarding "faith itself."[54] Election is the "cause" of faith; faith is the "effect" of election.[55]

In the Bolsec controversy, Calvin declares, the fundamental issue was Bolsec's perversion of the right order between God's predestination and the faith of the child of God: "By overthrowing God's order of predestination or election and putting it after faith, he [Bolsec] brought faith into the power of every single person."[56] In the "Congregation on Eternal Election," which was written to settle the people who had been disturbed by Bolsec's attack on predestination, Calvin states flatly, "Election precedes faith."[57]

In light of Calvin's refutation of the heresy of election based on foreseen faith, it is almost incredible that only thirty or forty years later Reformed theologians could introduce this very doctrine into the Reformed churches in the Netherlands. It is similarly astounding that contemporary Reformed theologians are teaching that the election of children of believers in the covenant follows, and depends upon, the faith (and obedience) of the children.

The popularity of the message that faith precedes election, Calvin accounts for, as he takes note of the embrace of Bolsec's teaching by some in Geneva: "Although the error of his doctrine was evident... this doctrine was still plausible to our fallen nature."[58]

Calvin rejects as "absurd" the teaching that God's election of some is subject to his foreknowledge, which is understood as God's awareness beforehand of some worth or merit in those whom he chose.[59]

God's foreknowing, which lies behind his eternal election, as taught in Romans 8:29 and other places, is his sovereign, discriminating love of those whom he chose.

Election and the call of the gospel

Of great importance to the Reformed community today is the relation between election and the gracious, effectual call of the gospel by the preaching of the word. Calvin takes up this truth in book three, chapter twenty-four, which he titles, "Election is Confirmed by God's Call."

Earlier Calvin recognized an objection to election based on "the universality of God's invitation" in the gospel.[60] The objection was that there could not be election accompanied by reprobation founded on God's good pleasure, because in the preaching of the gospel there are universal invitations. "Some object that God would be contrary to himself if he should universally invite all men to him but admit only a few as elect."[61] This objection in Calvin's day was probably from Philip Melanchthon. Calvin replies that, although the preaching comes to all, God "directs the promises of salvation specifically to the elect." He adds, "Hence it is clear that the doctrine of salvation, which is said to be reserved solely and individually for the sons of the church, is falsely debased when presented as effectually profitable to all."[62]

Regarding the relation between election and the call of the gospel, Calvin teaches, "God by his call manifests election."[63] Again, "the preaching of the gospel streams forth from the wellspring of election."[64] Therefore, from the call, that is, the preaching accompanied by the inner illumination of the Holy Spirit, a believer can and will be sure of his election. "The call... consists not only in the preaching of the Word but also in the illumination of the Spirit... This inner call, then, is a pledge of salvation that cannot deceive us."[65] Exactly because the call "manifests... election,"[66] Calvin adds that the believer is certain that his calling is "according to his [God's] election."[67] "The fact that... the firmness of our election is joined to our calling is another means of establishing our assurance."[68]

That the call is particular and discriminatory, Calvin proves from the following passages of Scripture: "As many as were ordained to eternal life believed" (Acts 13:48); "Moreover whom he did predestinate, them he also called" (Rom. 8:30); "No man can come to me, except the Father which hath sent me draw him... Every man therefore that hath heard, and hath learned of the Father, cometh unto me" (John 6:44, 45); "[Salvation] is not of him that willeth, nor of him that runneth, but of God that sheweth mercy" (Rom. 9:16).

Calvin sharply distinguishes "the general call," which consists only of the "outward preaching of the word," to the reprobate wicked from the gracious, effectual, saving call to the elect. Explaining Matthew 22:14 ("For many are called, but few are chosen"), Calvin writes,

> There are two kinds of call. There is the general call, by which God invites all equally to himself through the outward preaching of the word—even those to whom he holds it out as a savor of death [cf. 2 Cor. 2:16], and as the occasion for severer condemnation. The other kind of call is special, which he deigns for the most part to give to the believers alone, while by the inward illumination of his Spirit he causes the preached Word to dwell in their hearts.[69]

The "two kinds of call" are strictly controlled by, and serve, God's predestination, the election of some and the reprobation of the others.

> Why, then, does he bestow grace upon these but pass over the others? Of the former, Luke gives the reason: because they "were ordained to life" [Acts 13:48]. Of the latter, what shall we think except that "they are the vessels of wrath for dishonor" [Rom. 9:21, 22]?[70]
>
> As God by the effectual working of his call to the elect perfects the salvation to which by his eternal plan he has destined them, so he has his judgments against the reprobate, by which he executes his plan for them.[71]

In the line with which he opens his treatment of election's relation to the call of the gospel, Calvin expresses his conviction (and Scripture's teaching) that the preaching of the gospel is the gracious, saving calling of the elect and the non-gracious hardening of the reprobate wicked: "We must deal with both the calling of the elect and the blinding and hardening of the wicked."[72]

Calvin was the sworn foe of the doctrine of the "well-meant offer" of the gospel that reigns supreme in contemporary Reformed Christianity as the explanation of the call of the gospel. This is the theory, not simply that the gospel must be preached to all humans promiscuously, with the urgent command to repent and believe, but that God is gracious to all who hear the preaching of the gospel, sincerely desires the salvation of all—those who perish, as well as those who are saved—and, in this grace, offers them Christ and salvation.

Again and again in his treatise "On the Eternal Predestination of God," Calvin excoriates Pighius for teaching that God is gracious to all alike in the preaching of the gospel, offering grace equally to all.

> The fiction of Pighius is puerile and absurd, when he interprets grace to be God's goodness in inviting all men to salvation, though all were lost in Adam...Pighius will himself confess that there is need of illumination to bring unto Christ those who were adversaries to God; but he, at the same time, holds fast the fiction that grace is offered equally to all, but that it is ultimately rendered effectual by the will of man, just as each one is willing to receive it.[73]

The doctrine that God is gracious in the preaching of the gospel to all hearers alike cuts the call of the gospel loose from eternal election and attributes the saving effect of the call to the acceptance, that is, the will, of those sinners who are saved by the call. Calvin opposed this doctrine. He opposed it because he was determined to honor the eternal election of God as the source and cause of salvation, for election magnifies, and safeguards, divine mercy.

> But when the call is coupled with election, in this way Scripture sufficiently suggests that in it nothing but God's free mercy is

to be sought. For if we ask whom he calls, and the reason why, he answers: whom he had chosen. Moreover, when one comes to election, there mercy alone appears on every side.[74]

Defense of predestination against objections

Calvin defends the doctrine of predestination against various objections to it. Those who object are "venomous dogs [who] spew out more than one kind of venom against God."[75]

These objections (which are the same in every age) are to be distinguished from the two dangers attending the right treatment of the doctrine that Calvin has noted earlier. One danger is curious, speculative investigation of predestination that "exceed[s] the bounds of the Word."[76] Against this danger, Calvin admonishes believers, including theologians, to restrict their thinking about predestination within the limits of Scripture, in which God has set forth "the secrets of his will that he has decided to reveal to us."[77]

The other danger is that especially preachers and theologians are silent concerning predestination. These "all but require that every mention of predestination be buried; indeed, they teach us to avoid any question of it, as we would a reef."[78] Silence is wrong. "[Predestination] ought to have been gloriously and vociferously proclaimed."[79]

The very first attack on biblical predestination, indeed on election, considered by Calvin is a professed acceptance of the doctrine of election, while at the same time rejecting reprobation. That Calvin takes up this attack on predestination first is significant. Always, the enemies of predestination first couch their assault on God's sovereignty in salvation as opposition to reprobation. Calvin responds, "Election itself could not stand except as set over against reprobation."[80] As biblical proof of reprobation, Calvin adduces Matthew 15:13 and Romans 9:17, 18, 22, and 23.

A second objection is that predestination presents God as a "tyrant."[81] The charge is that God capriciously assigns men to heaven or hell. Repudiating the philosophical notion of "absolute might," which holds that the supreme being cannot be challenged or questioned, even though he is lawless, Calvin affirms that "the will of God ... is the highest rule of perfection."[82] Calvin denies that God is "liable to render an account [of his predestinating will]" and that "we are competent judges to pronounce judgment in this cause."⁸³

Regarding God's justice in the decree of reprobation, "if all whom the Lord predestines to death are by condition of nature subject to the judgment of death, of what injustice toward themselves may they complain?" "If all are drawn from a corrupt mass, no wonder they are subject to condemnation!"⁸⁴ Evidently, Calvin holds that the objects of the decree of predestination appeared to God's mind as fallen and guilty. Calvin does not, of course, pronounce on the debate within the Reformed camp concerning the order of the eternal decree, whether supralapsarian (the decree of predestination preceding the decree of the fall) or infralapsarian (the decree of predestination following the decree of the fall). This debate developed after Calvin's death. But Calvin does express himself clearly on two important truths that bear on the later debate.

First, the objects of the electing and reprobating decree appear to the mind of the predestinating God as fallen into sin. This truth establishes that election is gracious and that reprobation is just. That this was Calvin's view of the decree of predestination is evident from the citation just given.

Second, Calvin taught that the triune God decrees Jesus Christ first, prior to the decree of the fall of the human race in Adam. Jesus Christ is first in the counsel of God, as the apostle teaches in Colossians 1:13–20. All the rest of the counsel serves Jesus Christ. Specifically, the decree of the fall serves God's purpose to glorify himself in Jesus Christ. Calvin expresses in the *Institutes* this primacy of Jesus Christ in the eternal counsel when he calls attention to the fact that, according to Ephesians 1:4, God elects his people in Christ. Calvin also teaches the primacy of the decree of Jesus Christ in his great work on the providence of God. "Wherefore, as God, from the beginning, predestinated Christ to succour those who were lost, so by His inconceivable and inestimable *counsel* He decreed a way by which He might manifest forth His glory by the Fall of Adam."⁸⁵

One aspect of the accusation of divine tyranny is that men were "previously predestined by God's ordinance to that corruption which is now claimed as the cause of condemnation."⁸⁶ Calvin admits, "All of Adam's children have fallen by God's will."⁸⁷ With Paul in Romans

9:20, Calvin responds to the charge, "Nay but, O man, who art thou that repliest against God?"

Yet another objection is that predestination denies the responsibility of the sinner: "Why should God impute those things to men as sin, the necessity of which he has imposed by his predestination?"[88] Worthy of note are the defenses against this objection that Calvin deliberately declines to give. He will not have recourse to divine foreknowledge (God merely foresaw the sins men would commit), "since he foresees future events only by reason of the fact that he decreed that they take place."[89]

Neither will Calvin fall back on a permissive will of God (God merely permits the wicked to sin and to perish), for, as Augustine said, "The will of God is the necessity of things."[90]

Calvin confesses that Adam and all his posterity fell into sin and death, including "eternal death" for many, by God's decree: "He [God] so ordained by his decree." Here occurs the statement, "The decree is dreadful indeed, I confess."[91]

Why God decreed the rebellion of Adam and the fall of the race "is hidden from us. Yet it is certain that he so judged because he saw that thereby the glory of his name is duly revealed."[92]

Man's falling into sin "according as God's providence ordains" does not rule out, or minimize, that man "falls by his own fault."[93]

Another objection against predestination is that it represents God as showing "partiality toward persons," contrary to the teaching of Scripture.[94] Calvin acknowledges that Scripture everywhere denies that God is a respecter of persons, that is, shows partiality toward persons. But the meaning is that God has no regard, particularly in election and saving sinners, for anything in those whom he elects and saves, for example, riches, power, physical beauty, or race. "The fact that God therefore chooses one man but rejects another arises not out of regard to the man but solely from his mercy, which ought to be free to manifest and express itself where and when he pleases."[95]

A perennial charge against predestination is that it destroys "all carefulness and zeal for well-doing."[96] Calvin acknowledges that some do, in fact, abuse the doctrine of predestination by making it the pretext for a wicked life. "There are many swine that pollute the doctrine of predestination with their foul blasphemies, and by this pretext evade all admonitions and reproofs."[97] "But the foul grunting of these swine is duly silenced" by Ephesians 1:4, which teaches that "we have been chosen to this end: that we may lead a holy and blameless life."[98]

Regarding the argument that, according to predestination, a reprobate might lead an "innocent and upright life" in vain, Calvin replies that such a life is the effect of election: "Whence could such [a life] arise, but from election?" All reprobate persons will lead ungodly lives, for "they are vessels made for dishonor [cf. Rom. 9:21]."[99]

Closely related to the preceding objection is the charge that predestination must weaken, if not preclude, the preaching of exhortations and admonitions unto a holy life: "as if it [predestination] overthrew all exhortations to godly living."[100] Calvin's response to this "malicious" and "shameless" charge is, first, to recommend a book by Augustine on this very issue, *Rebuke and Grace*, and then to point out that that "plain and outspoken preacher of free election Paul" was also fervent "in admonition and exhortation."[101] Quoting Augustine, Calvin affirms that both piety and predestination must be preached, piety "that ... God may be rightly worshiped" and predestination "that he who has ears to hear of God's grace may glory, not in himself but in God."[102]

Émile Doumergue commented on Calvin's uncompromising insistence on both God's sovereignty and man's responsibility.

> Alongside the fact of the sovereignty of God, Calvin establishes the *fact* of human responsibility. No theologian ever emphasized the sovereignty of God and applied to it such a rigorous logic as did Calvin. But also no theologian laid such strong emphasis on the responsibility of man and carried through the implications of responsibility further than did Calvin.[103]

One front of the war on predestination in Calvin's day consisted of an appeal to a few passages of Scripture that seem to teach that God wills, or desires, to save all men without exception and, therefore, that God has ordained no one to damnation. "Our opponents are in the habit of quoting in opposition a few Scripture passages in which God seems to deny that the wicked perish by his ordination."[104] This small battery of supposed anti-predestinarian texts, brought to bear against

Calvin by Bolsec and Pighius, are the very same as the texts raised by Pelagius against Augustine, by Erasmus against Luther, by the Remonstrants (Arminians) against the Synod of Dordt, and by the contemporary advocates of universal, resistible grace in the preaching of the gospel (the "well-meant offer") against the doctrine that God is gracious in the preaching only to the elect.

The texts are Ezekiel 33:1, 1 Timothy 2:3, 4, 2 Peter 3:9, and Matthew 23:37.

Whether one fully agrees with Calvin's explanation of the texts or not, one thing is unmistakably clear: Calvin's interpretation does not allow the texts "paradoxically" to contradict the doctrine of predestination. What Calvin says of Ezekiel 33:11, "I have no pleasure in the death of the wicked," is typical: "This passage is violently twisted if the will of God, mentioned by the prophet, is opposed to his eternal plan, by which he has distinguished the elect from the reprobate."[105] Calvin's sound explanation of the much-abused text is "that God is without doubt ready to forgive, as soon as the sinner is converted." Calvin reminds his readers, "Ezekiel himself," as well as all the rest of Scripture, "clearly teach to whom repentance [conversion] is given," namely, the elect.[106]

Benefits of the knowledge of election

Knowledge of election, which, of course, demands the regular preaching of the doctrine as well as the strong defense of it, bestows "three benefits."[107] The benefits are the glorifying of God by those who know "that our salvation flows from the wellspring of God's free mercy ... [in] his eternal election"; a deep humility inasmuch as believers ascribe all their salvation to the grace of election; and a firm "confidence" on the part of believers that they are "victorious" and "safe" amid many dangers, their salvation depending upon God's election.[108]

Election is simply "the foundation of our salvation."[109]

Those who silence the doctrine of election, corrupt it, or deny it are guilty, therefore, of robbing God of his glory; of rendering the congregation arrogant; and of casting all souls into "constant fear" concerning their salvation.[110]

Preaching predestination wisely

Predestination must be preached, but it must be preached "fittingly," as well as "truly."[111] There is a foolish and destructive way of preaching the doctrine. Calvin warns against such foolish preaching of predestination. He gives an example, which he borrows from Augustine: "If you do not believe, the reason is that you have already been divinely destined for destruction."[112]

Preachers will avoid such unwise preaching of predestination, which gives unwarranted offense, if they are motivated by "zeal for edification" of their flock.[113]

Calvin adds, again quoting Augustine with approval, "For as we [preachers] know not who belongs to the number of the predestined or who does not belong, we ought to be so minded as to wish that all men be saved."[114]

CHAPTER 16

The Final Resurrection: Calvin's Eschatology

Introduction

Fittingly, Calvin closes book three, which treats the benefits that come to the elect of God from the grace of Jesus Christ, with a stirring proclamation of the resurrection of the dead bodies of those who have fallen asleep in Jesus, in the day of Christ. Since "the ungodly and accursed of God have a common resurrection" with the "pious worshipers of God," Calvin also describes the resurrection of the wicked.[1] But he concentrates on the resurrection of the godly, for "Scripture more often sets forth resurrection, along with heavenly glory, to the children of God alone." The reason is that "Christ came properly not for the destruction of the world but for its salvation."[2]

Nature of the resurrection body

Calvin is deliberately restrained in his description of the resurrection body of the believer, because Paul, in 1 Corinthians 15:51, calls the "manner of resurrection" a "mystery."[3] Calvin emphasizes two truths about the resurrection body. First, it will be the very same body that was buried and that decayed in the grave. "As to substance we shall be raised again in the same flesh we now bear."[4] Calvin rejects the error that teaches that the resurrection body will be a new creation of a "different" body.[5] This teaching does not do justice to the biblical doctrine that the body of the dead believer will "rise," that is, from the grave, or to the biblical doctrine that, in his body, the believer now "sleep[s]" in the grave to be awakened in the resurrection.[6] Calvin refers to John 6:39 and 1 Thessalonians 4:15, 16. In addition, the resurrection of Christ, which is the pattern of our own, was the restoration to life of the "same flesh of Christ which had been offered as a sacrifice."[7] In the Christology section of the *Institutes*, Calvin has already explained the bodily resurrection of Jesus himself. There Calvin affirms that Christ "received immortality in the same flesh that, in the mortal state, he had taken upon himself."[8]

The second truth about the resurrection body that Calvin stresses is "that the quality [of the body] will be different." Calvin adduces as proof 1 Corinthians 15:51–54. The "change" of the quality of the body will be that the resurrection body will be "far more excellent" than the form of the body in earthly life.[9] Calvin mentions the incorruptibility of the resurrection body.

Again, the pattern is the resurrection body of Jesus Christ. So surpassingly excellent is the resurrection body of Christ that it is "as if it had become utterly different."[10]

Raised into union with God

With regard to the very essence of the resurrection as the "full fruition" of "man's highest good" and of "the sole and perfect happiness," it is "union with God" as a "sacred bond."[11] Although Calvin does not expressly mention the covenant in this context, "union with God" and "the sacred bond of that union" are the language of the covenant. Indeed, the phrases express the nature of the covenant of grace. The resurrection of the body, therefore, will be "the full fruition" of the covenant.

That Calvin's understanding of the perfecting of salvation and the enjoyment of the greatest happiness is that of communion with God in Christ is confirmed by Calvin's analysis of the eternal life into which the resurrection of the body will usher elect believers: "[The Lord] will somehow make them to become one with himself."[12]

Grounds of belief of the resurrection

Calvin recognizes the difficulty of believing the resurrection of the body in view of the seeming impossibility of it. "It is difficult to believe that bodies, when consumed with rottenness, will at length be raised up in their season."[13] There are "two helps" to faith's difficulty: the resurrection of Jesus Christ as the head of his body, the church, and "the omnipotence of God."[14]

By virtue of Christ's union with us as our head, his resurrection is "the pledge of our coming resurrection."[15] Calvin proves our "fellowship with Christ in the blessed resurrection" from Philippians 3:20, 21, Colossians 3:4, and Romans 8:11.[16] So solid and so close is our union with Christ with specific regard to bodily resurrection that, as Paul argues in 1 Corinthians 15:16, "If the dead do not rise up again, then Christ did not rise up again."[17]

The importance of Christ's resurrection for our hope of resurrection, as well as for the entire gospel, requires that Calvin demonstrate the grounds of our belief that Christ arose from the dead. This is all the more necessary because already in Calvin's day "scorners…treat as a fairy tale what the Evangelists relate as history."[18] The grounds are the many, intrinsically convincing testimonies of Scripture to Jesus' resurrection, the eyewitness accounts of those who on their part were inclined to doubt the resurrection. "To discredit so many authentic evidences is not only disbelief but [also] a depraved and even insane obstinacy."[19]

The other "help" to faith's hope in the resurrection of the body is "God's boundless might."[20] In the face of the objections of our senses to the raising of bodies that have rotted, turned to dust, been swallowed by the sea, or been burned with fire, Scripture sets "before us an incalculable miracle, which by its greatness overwhelms our senses."[21] God's almighty power to raise the dead was prophesied by Isaiah (Isa. 26:19); sustained David in deep distress (Ps. 68:20); was the hope of Job, who was "more like a corpse than a man" (Job 19:25–27); was figuratively taught by Ezekiel's vision of the field of dry bones (Ezek. 37:1–10); and was plainly declared by Jesus (John 5:28, 29).[22]

To the confounding of unbelief, even nature witnesses to a bodily resurrection. As Paul exclaims to foolish doubters in 1 Corinthians 15:36, "That which thou sowest is not quickened, except it die."

Eschatological errors

Carrying out his policy of defending the truth by exposing the errors opposed to the truth, Calvin examines a number of arguments against the resurrection of the body raised by men and movements within the church. There is the argument of "chiliasts," false teachers who take their name from the Greek word for "a thousand years," in Revelation 20. The "chiliasts," or "millenarians" (the Latin equivalent of "chiliasts"), jeopardize the truth of the resurrection by limiting the glorious "reign of Christ to a thousand years."[23] Calvin rejects their explanation of the thousand-year period of Revelation 20 and insists that "there will be no end to the blessedness of the elect" in the glorious kingdom of Christ.[24]

One aspect of the error of the chiliasts is their denial of "eternal punishment" for the wicked. They argue that as sin is "temporal," so also must punishment be temporal.[25] Calvin responds that eternal punishment is just inasmuch as sins are a transgression of the eternal majesty of God.

An error related to the denial of the resurrection of the body, evidently inasmuch as the error concerns the believer's hope with regard to death, is the teaching that the soul dies with the body, to be resurrected with the body in the day of Christ. This is the error commonly referred to as "soul sleep." Calvin contends that souls "still retain their essence" when death divests them of their bodies.[26] On the basis of 2 Corinthians 5:1ff., Hebrews 12:23, Luke 23:43, 46, Acts 7:58, and 1 Peter 2:25, Calvin teaches that "the souls of the pious... enter into blessed rest" at death, "where in glad expectation they await the enjoyment of promised glory," and that "the souls of the reprobates suffer... torments."[27]

Calvin speaks of the "immortality" of the soul.[28] It is clear, however, that he uses the word *immortality* loosely, indeed inaccurately. *Immortality* means "not capable of dying." The fact is that the soul of the unregenerated man is dead spiritually, and the soul of the reprobate passes at death into eternal death. What Calvin means by the "immortality of the soul," as he makes plain, is that the soul is an indestructible essence, or substance.

The argument of the Manichees against the resurrection of the body was twofold: the body is corrupted by sin, and the body is inherently vile as a creation of the devil. Calvin responds that God can and does cleanse the body from sin, as well as the soul, and that the body has been created by God. Indeed, the admittedly sinful body of the believer is a temple of God, according to 1 Corinthians 6:19, and "it would be utterly absurd that the bodies which God has dedicated to himself as temples ...should fall away into filth without hope of resurrection!"[29]

Calvin's doctrine of the last things

Even though Calvin did not write a commentary on Revelation, his thorough treatment of the doctrine of the resurrection of the body with the accompanying refutation of related errors gives us a complete overview of Calvin's eschatology. His doctrine of the last things includes the intermediate state of elect and reprobate; the rejection of millennialism, which always plays with the thousand years of Revelation 20 as a description of a carnal kingdom of Christ in the world; the resurrection of both believers and unbelievers in one general resurrection; and an eternal destiny both of the righteous and of the wicked. The foundation of Calvin's eschatology is the bodily resurrection of Jesus Christ.

The resurrection: our hope

The intensely practical purpose of the gospel of the resurrection of the body of the child of God is that this truth is, and must be, the hope that keeps and encourages him throughout his entire life in the world. With this, Calvin begins his treatment of the resurrection. It belongs to Calvin's eschatology, which is the eschatology of the Bible, as Calvin points out by referring to 1 Corinthians 15:19 and Romans 8:35–39, that the life of the believer in this world is one of a "huge mass of miseries," the "jests of profane men," and "violent temptations."[30] The danger is that "in our weariness" we "reverse our course or desert our post."[31] One thing holds and holds up the Christian: the sure hope of the future resurrection of the body. "He alone has fully profited in the gospel who has accustomed himself to continual meditation upon the blessed resurrection."[32]

Our hope is not only expectation. It is also intense longing. Calvin notes that nonhuman creatures are "naturally long[ing] for the undamaged condition whence they have fallen," as Paul has written in Romans 8:19–23. Should not the believer "at least... imitate the dead elements"? Here Calvin teaches the coming "renewal" of "everything in heaven and on earth."[33]

Eternal punishment

That Calvin does not include reprobate, ungodly men (and by implication the devils) in the renewed creation is evident from his teaching that the "ungodly and accursed of God" will be raised in the body, in an "incidental resurrection," in order to be "punished for their obstinacy."[34]

In the theological thinking of Calvin, Jesus Christ's resurrection is the foundation of all resurrection, indeed of all eschatology. This raises a "difficult question": "By what right do the ungodly and accursed of God have a common resurrection, which is a singular benefit of Christ?"[35] Calvin's intriguing answer seems not only to relate the resurrection of the ungodly to the resurrection of Christ, but also to make their resurrection an "incidental" aspect of his. "The things proper to Christ and his members also pour forth abundantly upon the wicked, not to become their lawful possession, but rather to render them inexcusable."[36]

The punishment of the wicked will be dreadful. Calvin speaks of the inexpressible "gravity of God's vengeance against the wicked." All of Scripture's descriptions of the "torments and tortures" of the wicked, for example, "darkness, weeping,... gnashing of teeth,... unquenchable fire,... [and] an undying worm" bring home to us "how wretched it is to be cut off from all fellowship with God."[37]

For Calvin, as the bliss of heaven is fellowship with God, so the misery of hell is separation from God.

But the agony of hell is not only negative: separation from God. It is also positive: "so to feel his sovereign power against you that you cannot escape being pressed by it."[38] God will be present in hell.

And the punishment of the wicked, in soul and body, will be everlasting: "to be eternally and unceasingly besieged by him."[39] Faithful to Scripture, for example, 2 Thessalonians 1:9, which speaks of "everlasting destruction," Calvin does not countenance annihilationism. He has already argued that sin against God's eternal majesty deserves eternal punishment.

Eternal bliss

In contrast, the everlasting destiny of the elect children of God in their resurrection bodies will be "eternal happiness."[40] Just as the misery of the punishment of the wicked defies description, so also the bliss of the righteous "would scarce be told," even in the "minutest part," "if all were said that the tongues of all men can say." Only the event will reveal the "splendor, joy, happiness, and glory"[41] of eternal life with Christ in a restored world.[42] In the 1536 *Institutes* Calvin speaks of a blessedness "crammed with all brightness, joy, power, happiness."[43]

Nevertheless, it would be a serious mistake for the believer to look forward only, or even primarily, to the great good that God has in store for those who love and fear him. Their future bliss will be God himself. "Nothing beyond him is to be sought by those who strive after the highest good," for "God contains the fullness of all good things in himself."[44]

There will be a "special reward for each [believer]," according to the gifts and work of grace in each in this life. Although all will receive eternal life, "there will not be an equal measure of glory in heaven."[45]

With regard to the tendency of many to ask all kinds of curious questions about the nature of heaven and its life, Calvin thinks that people are "titillated by an immoderate desire to know more than is lawful."[46] With obvious allusion to the Greek myth of Icarus, who flew too near the sun with the wings that his father, Daedalus, had constructed for him and perished, Calvin warns against "soar[ing] aloft with the greater boldness, and be[ing] overcome by the brightness of the heavenly glory."[47] Calvin makes the shrewd observation that "few out of a huge multitude care how they are to go to heaven, but all long to know beforehand what takes place there."[48]

Calvin's very last word on the hope of the children of God is highly appropriate. It is an implicit exhortation to the struggling and hardly beset believers in the world to press on to the end, motivated above all by the prospect of the full manifestation of the glory of God. "He urges his own worshipers on, the more because they are timid in this world, that he may inspire them, burdened with the cross, to press forward ... until he himself is 'all in all' [1 Cor. 15:28]."[49]

His mention of the "timid" makes unmistakably plain that Calvin was encouraging himself, as well as us.

BOOK FOUR

The External Means or Aids by Which God
Invites Us into the Society of Christ
and Holds Us Therein

CHAPTER 17

The Doctrine of the Church

Introduction

Calvin concludes his explanation and defense of the Christian faith in the 1559 *Institutes* with the doctrine of the church. It is true that the specific topic treated at the very end is that of civil government. But Calvin views civil government, though distinct from the church as a separate "kind of government" pertaining to "civil justice and outward morality," as a definite, powerful aid to the church in the protection and promotion of the true religion.[1] In Calvin's thinking, civil government is called "to cherish and protect the outward worship of God [and] to defend sound doctrine of piety and the position of the church."[2]

Calvin's doctrine of the church—ecclesiology—is related to his doctrine of salvation—soteriology— in these ways: the work of salvation *forms* the church as a bride and body of Christ; and in the church and by means of the church, the elect of God receive and enjoy the benefits of salvation. Concerning the latter, God has "deposited" the preaching of the gospel and the sacraments, by which he "beget[s] and increase[s] faith," in the church.[3]

The section of the *Institutes* on the church is also related to the preceding section on salvation in that both set forth the work of the Holy Spirit. The Spirit of Christ unites the elect sinner to Jesus Christ and thus gives him Christ and all the blessings of salvation, obtained for him by Christ's redeeming death. The Spirit of Christ creates the church and works through the means of grace in the church to save the members.

The doctrine of the church in book four is an important aspect of the third main division of the *Institutes*, that concerning the Christian's faith in the Holy Spirit. The division of the *Institutes* is trinitarian.

The section of the *Institutes* devoted to the doctrine of the church is the largest section of the entire *Institutes*, even excluding the treatment of civil government. In the McNeill/Battles edition the exposition of the doctrine of the church in book four, chapters one through nineteen, runs to four hundred seventy-six pages. If Calvin's treatment of civil government is included, as Calvin intended, the exposition is significantly longer.

One reason for the lengthy treatment is the richness itself of the biblical truth of the church. Another reason is the importance of the church for Calvin, as for all the Protestant reformers. The Reformation, after all, was not only, or even primarily, the recovery of the pure gospel of grace (fundamental as that was), but also the *reformation of the church* by that recovered gospel.

The importance of the church for Calvin is indicated by his well-known affirmation that God has so closely joined the church to himself that "for those to whom he is Father the church may also be Mother."[4]

Still another reason for the bulk of Calvin's doctrine of the church is that he sets forth the truth of the church *antithetically*. That is, his positive explanation of the truth of the church is accompanied, and sharpened, by the exposure and condemnation of the false teachings and practices of the Roman Catholic Church, the Lutherans, and the Anabaptists. Often, Calvin weaves his polemic against ecclesiastical errors into his positive exposition. At other times, he devotes an entire chapter, or even a number of chapters, to the criticism of heretical teachings and wicked practices concerning the church. For example, chapters five through seven of book four are an examination and condemnation of the papacy of Rome. The heading of chapter eighteen is, "The Papal Mass, a Sacrilege by Which Christ's Supper Was Not Only Profaned but Annihilated." Chapter nineteen treats the five sacraments that Rome has added to the two instituted by Christ.

Not a page of Calvin's long and careful explanation of the church is superfluous at the beginning of the twenty-first century. No teaching of Calvin is more urgent for Protestant Christianity, indeed *Reformed* Christianity, today. For the most part the church lies in shambles, like Jerusalem after its destruction by Babylon.

So-called "evangelical Christianity," of which Willow Creek Community Church in Illinois (USA), Calvary Church and Mars Hill Bible Church in Grand Rapids, Michigan (USA), and other "mega-churches" are the bright and shining manifestations, has no ecclesiology—no doctrine and corresponding practice of the marks of the true church; of pure worship regulated by the word of God; of the proper administration of the sacraments; of right church government; of Christian discipline of those walking impenitently and publicly in gross sins; or of the chief calling of the church, namely, the preaching of the pure gospel of salvation by sovereign grace, which was recovered by the sixteenth-century Reformation.

The ecclesiology of most of evangelical Christianity, such as it is, consists of the practice of the entertaining running of the "show" by a charismatic leader/pastor and of the doctrine that all who attend shall feel good and have a "ministry."

If this is the fruit of the Protestant Reformation, that great religious movement was in vain, indeed, a disaster. Protestants could better return to Rome, which, in fact, the more thoughtful evangelicals are now doing.

The charismatic churches share in the debacle of evangelical Christianity, except that the charismatic churches add to the general ruin the heresy of the Anabaptist "enthusiasm," that is, the mysticism that was condemned by John Calvin, as by all the reformers.

Reformed and Presbyterian churches likewise display serious weaknesses regarding both the doctrine and practice of the church. Some are so bold as openly to reject the teaching of the "invisible church" of all the elect—the doctrine that was fundamental to the ecclesiology of the Reformation, as it is fundamental to the teaching of Scripture concerning the church.

There is blatant disregard of the doctrine of the marks of the true church, determining church membership, as authoritatively laid down in the Reformed creeds, for example, Article 29 of the Belgic Confession. Expressly by the members (at least, by virtue of their membership) and tacitly by the office bearers, the genuine marks of the true church are replaced by such "marks" as a friendly, likeable minister; a congregation that "shows love"; one's feeling comfortable or good there; zeal for missions and evangelism; and the possibility of having a "ministry" in the ecclesiastical organization.

"Progressive worship," that is, worship regulated by the whims of a "worship leader" and by the pleasure of the audience rather than by the word of God, makes powerful inroads. So far have these inroads gone in reputedly conservative Presbyterian churches that their theologians advocate, and presumably the churches practice, "liturgical dance" in the worship services of the congregations.

The inevitable result of progressive worship, if it is not the avowed purpose, is the minimizing of the preaching of the word of God. Preaching, which was the central activity of public worship for the Reformation, is marginalized, severely shortened, and even, at times, excluded from worship altogether.

With regard to church government, women are ordained to the offices of minister, elder, and deacon, in defiance of the clear prohibition of Holy Scripture (and of John Calvin).

Christian discipline is relaxed, because of the failure of the churches to withstand the admittedly powerful pressures upon their members from the ungodly society in which they live. An outstanding, exceedingly shameful, and utterly destructive instance is the widespread refusal of the churches to discipline those who are guilty of unbiblical divorce and remarriage after divorce. Adulterers and adulteresses are permitted church membership, indeed, occupy pulpits, sit in the elders' bench, and have access to both baptism and the Lord's supper. Thus the covenant of God with the church is violated, and the sacraments are profaned.

Then there is the essential matter of the church's belief and confession of the authority of the word of God, Holy Scripture. As Calvin demonstrates in book four of the *Institutes*, Scripture, received and confessed by the church as the inspired word of God, is both the foundation on which the church is built and the message that the church proclaims.

How is the inspiration and, therefore, the authority of Scripture doubted, questioned, challenged, and openly rejected by Reformed and

Presbyterian churches today, especially by seminary professors—the teachers of the churches' pastors and preachers!

The seriousness of all this ecclesiastical error, confusion, and disorder is the implication of Calvin's dictum: whoever lacks the (true) church as his mother cannot have God as his father.

Protestants, particularly Reformed Protestants, must attend to the instruction of John Calvin concerning the church, not as an informative academic exercise, but as an urgent, spiritual necessity.

What the church is

One of the great themes of the *Institutes*, especially in books three and four—union with Christ—is on the foreground in Calvin's doctrine of the church. The heading of book four, in Allen's translation of the *Institutes*, is "On the External Means or Aids by Which God Calls Us into Communion with Christ, and Retains Us in It."[5] Living membership in the church, by faith, is participation in the communion, or society, of Christ, inasmuch as the church is Christ's own body and bride. To this communion with Christ, God calls the elect by the church's ministry of word and sacraments.

So important it is that there be the church, that visible churches remain faithful to Christ, and that believers and their children are lively members of the visible church!

Essentially, for Calvin, the church taught by Scripture and confessed in the Apostles' Creed is the whole number and entire company of those whom God has chosen in Christ unto eternal life, that is, all the elect. "The article in the Creed in which we profess to 'believe the church' refers not only to the visible church (our present topic) but also to all God's elect, in whose number are also included the dead."[6] Calvin discerns that "Holy Scripture speaks of the church in two ways." The first is "that which is actually in God's presence, into which no persons are received but those who are children of God." In this first, fundamental sense, the church "includes...all the elect from the beginning of the world," and them only.[7]

"[The] foundation [of the church] is his [God's] secret election."[8]

In the 1536 edition of the *Institutes*, Calvin began his treatment of the church with this definition: "We believe the holy catholic church—that is the whole number of the elect, whether angels or men [Eph. 1:9, 10; Col. 1:16]."[9] It was there, in his doctrine of the church, that Calvin had the most to say about election in the first edition of the *Institutes*. Among those teachings was the truth that all the blessings of salvation that God bestows on certain persons by the ministry of the church have their source in, are determined by, and are intended to extol election: "When he calls his own, justifies and glorifies his own, [the Lord] is declaring nothing but his eternal election, by which he had destined them to this end before they were born."[10] Another grand truth implied by the church's being the company of the elect was, for Calvin in the 1536 *Institutes*, that of the preservation of the saints. "Since the church is the people of God's elect [John 10:28], it cannot happen that those who are truly its members will ultimately perish [John 10:28], or come to a bad end."[11]

As the company of the elect, the church, in the first and basic sense of the word, is invisible: "The former church, invisible to us, is visible to the eyes of God alone."[12] Calvin notes that the Apostles' Creed confesses, "I *believe* an holy, catholic church." The church is "beyond our ken." "It belongs to the realm of faith."[13]

The unity and catholicity, or universality, of the church are the attributes primarily of the church as the invisible body of Christ, made up of all the elect. "The church is called 'catholic,' or 'universal,' because there could not be two or three churches unless Christ be torn asunder... But all the elect are so united in Christ... that... they also grow together into one body."[14]

To the unity of the church belongs the communion of saints. Although Calvin explains the communion of saints as a "keep[ing] in brotherly agreement" and as a sharing of benefits with each other on the part of the members of "the outward church," that is, the visible, instituted church, he recognizes that also this characteristic of the church applies, first of all, to the invisible society of the elect. "This article of the Creed [the communion of saints] *also applies to some extent* to the outward church."[15]

For Calvin, just as the church is essentially the spiritual body and bride of Christ, consisting of all those given to Christ in the eternal decree of election and joined to him as head and husband by the Holy Spirit, so the unity and universality of the church are spiritual in nature, not exclusively, or even primarily, organizational and "outward."

In the 1536 *Institutes*, Calvin wrote that the oneness of the church consists of "liv[ing] together in one faith, hope, and love, and in the same Spirit of God."[16] True unity is not merely, or even primarily—much less exclusively—organizational.

The other outstanding perfections of the church, holiness and apostolicity, Calvin treats later in the 1559 *Institutes*, as part of his description of the visible, instituted church. Intriguingly, Calvin brings up the holiness of the church in the context of his sharp rebuke of those who are quick to leave a church on account of that church's lack of holiness, to some extent. The holiness of the church, which is certainly taught in such a passage as Ephesians 5:25–27 (quoted by Calvin), refers to a progressive work of Christ in the church in history of "smoothing out wrinkles and cleansing spots" of sin in the members. "The church is holy, then, in the sense that it is daily advancing and is not yet perfect."[17]

The apostolicity of the church Calvin explains in his comparison of the true church and the false church of Rome. Calvin rejects Rome's claim to, and explanation of, apostolicity: "The church exists wherever bishops succeed one another."[18] The truth of apostolicity, which also identifies the true church, is that "the church was founded... upon the teaching of apostles and prophets."[19] Calvin appeals here, as he does again and again on behalf of his insistence that the reformed church of the Reformation is the true church, to Ephesians 2:20: "built upon the foundation of the apostles and prophets, Jesus Christ himself being the chief corner stone."

Those theologians and churches that reject the doctrine of the invisible church of all the elect with the purpose, evidently, of conceiving the church as exclusively institutional and organizational contradict Calvin, betray the Reformation, and play into the hands of Rome. Rome burned John Hus for his teaching that the church is the company of the predestinated. One of the foremost controversies that the entire Reformation and every leading reformer had with Rome concerned Rome's teaching that the catholic church of Christ is as organizational and visible as any earthly kingdom (and that this visible organization is the Roman Catholic Church).

Regardless of the intentions of those Reformed and Presbyterian theologians who reject the doctrine of the church invisible, that is, the doctrine that the church is the spiritual body of Christ made up of all those whom God elected in eternity, this rejection is, in fact, a veiled attack on election.

The church of Ephesians 5:25–27 ("Christ also loved the church, and gave himself for it . . . that he might present it to himself a glorious church") is not this or that congregation or denomination, but the total number of persons God gave Christ in the decree of election, *as* they were given to him in the decree. The foundation and source of this church are election: "According as he hath chosen us in him before the foundation of the world" (Eph. 1:4).

In this fundamental sense, the Apostles' Creed confesses the reality of the church in the article on the one, holy, catholic church. As the Heidelberg Catechism explains, the church of the Christian confession is essentially the body, or "communion," made up of all those humans whom God has "chosen" and whom, therefore, the Son of God gathers, defends, and preserves "from the beginning to the end of the world."[20]

It is one thing to teach that the company of the elect, which is presently invisible, always takes visible form in institutes. It is another thing to dissolve the one, universal, holy, and apostolic church into this or that institute, whether Roman Catholic or Reformed.

Calvin makes two important, practical observations concerning membership in the catholic church of the elect. The first is that one can know the truth of the church only if he knows himself to be a member of it, that is, one of God's elect, united to Jesus Christ by the Holy Spirit. "The basis on which we believe the church is that we are fully convinced we are members of it."[21] In the 1536 edition of the *Institutes*, Calvin had expressed the necessity of knowing oneself a member of the church negatively, and more sharply: "If each one of us did not believe himself to be a member of it, we would vainly and fruitlessly believe there to be a church catholic."[22]

Right knowledge of the church, for Calvin, although intellectual and doctrinal, is the unique knowledge of *faith*. And faith—*true* faith—is always certainty of one's own participation in the saving reality that is believed. In the genuine, sixteenth-century Reformation sense, the knowledge of faith is "experiential." Without this experiential knowledge of the church as the body of the elect that includes *me* as a member, I am ignorant of the church.

In the language of the Heidelberg Catechism, one who cannot say, "And . . . I am, and forever shall remain, a living member of the same [the one, holy, catholic church]," can say nothing about the church.[23]

Calvin's second practical observation about church membership concerns our judgment of the membership of others. Regarding those who "by confession of faith, by example of life, and by partaking of the sacraments, profess the same God and Christ with us," we make a "certain charitable judgment" that they are "members of the church" of the elect.[24]

Calvin recognizes that this judgment is not certainty. No human can be certain of the election and salvation of another. Certain knowledge of the salvation of humans, grounded in election, is "a prerogative belonging solely to God [2 Tim. 2:19]."[25] Often, in fact, those whom we thought to be saved show themselves unbelieving and lost, whereas some whom we regarded as incorrigibly wicked repent and manifest themselves as regenerated children of God.

Calvin expressly contrasts our "charitable judgment" of others with the "assurance of faith" that the believer has of his own membership in the church and salvation. Whereas assurance of our own salvation is necessary, such assurance of the salvation of others is not necessary: "Assurance of faith [concerning the membership in the church of the elect of others] was not necessary."[26] For our life together in the visible church, as in the covenant home, it is sufficient, and "of some value," that we make this judgment of love.[27]

The "visible church"

That the church is essentially the invisible communion of the elect does not mean any disparagement of what Calvin calls the "visible church" or the "outward church."[28] In fact, the visible church is the main subject of book four: "The visible church [is] (our present topic)."[29] If Calvin treats the invisible church in chapter one, sections one through three, all of the rest of book four (1.4–19.37), exclusive of the last chapter on civil government, is devoted to the visible church. Barely five pages in the McNeill/Battles edition of the *Institutes* explain the invisible church; some four hundred sixty-eight pages concern the visible church.

So much for the fear that the doctrine of the invisible church of the elect results in disregard of the visible, instituted church!

Calvin indicates from the outset that his main concern is the visible church, not the invisible church. Already in the opening section of book four, he refers to the church in which God has put aids to our faith, namely, "the preaching of the gospel" and "sacraments."[30] These, of course, belong to the visible church.

By the "visible" or "outward" church, Calvin has in mind the local congregation, organized in the offices of pastor, elder, and deacon, which gathers regularly in her "holy assemblies,"[31] especially on the first day of the week, in order to preach and hear the word of God and in order to administer and use the sacraments.

> The face of the church comes forth and becomes visible to our eyes. Wherever we see the Word of God purely preached and heard, and the sacraments administered according to Christ's institution, there, it is not to be doubted, a church of God exists [cf. Eph. 2:20]. For his promise cannot fail: "Wherever two or three are gathered in my name, there I am in the midst of them" [Matt. 18:20].[32]

But Calvin's conception of the full reality of the visible church is broader than only individual congregations, important as they are. In the first instance, the visible church is "the church universal [as] a multitude gathered from all nations; it is divided and dispersed in separate places, but agrees on the one truth of divine doctrine, and is bound by the bond of the same religion." Only "under it are thus included individual churches, disposed in towns and villages."[33]

This "church universal" is not the invisible church of all the elect, for it is visible, dispersed in separate places, and confessing the truth.[34] Neither is it a particular denomination in one country, or even an ecumenical organization over all the world, although denominational, and even ecumenical, organization is implied. But the visible church is the number of all those men and women who believe and confess the truth everywhere in the world at any given time, with their children. No doubt, they are members of congregations; Calvin insists on it. But in its broadest extension, the visible church is the "whole multitude itself," throughout the whole world, that "has the ministry of the Word and honors it," as well as having "the administration of the sacraments." Thus Calvin "preserve[s] for the universal [visible] church its unity," despite geographical separation and institutional differences.[35]

Is not Calvin thinking here of those persons preaching, believing, and confessing the restored gospel of the Reformation in Cranmer's Church of England and in Luther's evangelical churches throughout Germany, as well as in Reformed and Presbyterian churches in continental Europe, Great Britain, and more distant places?

The Westminster Confession of Faith captures Calvin's ecclesiology when, having first described the church as "the whole number of the elect," which is "invisible,"[36] it goes on to affirm, "The visible Church, which is also catholic or universal under the gospel...consists of all those, throughout the world, that profess the true religion, and of their children."[37]

Without detracting at all from the importance, indeed, the necessity, of instituted congregations or minimizing whatsoever the seriousness of doctrinal differences between congregations and denominations, this doctrine of the visible church recognizes the work of Jesus Christ of gathering, defending, and preserving his church everywhere in the world.

"Under it," that is, "under" the visible church universal of the multitude in all nations that confess the gospel, "are thus included individual churches, disposed in towns and villages according to human need."[38] The visible church in all nations does not exist as an unorganized, "spiritual" mass. Rather, it exists and takes form as instituted congregations in every town or locality where believers and their children are found.

It is these instituted congregations that Calvin intends "to discuss" in book four, that he mainly has in mind when he refers to "the visible church," and that he explains at great length in by far the largest part of book four.[39]

It is of the greatest importance for the right understanding of Calvin's doctrine of the church to apprehend that each one of the "individual churches, disposed in towns and villages...rightly has the name and authority of the church."[40] For Calvin, the local congregation is "the church," not merely a part of the instituted church, as is the ecclesiology of Rome. Reformed church polity has come to express this aspect of Calvin's (and of the Bible's) doctrine of the church as the *autonomy of the local congregation*. The local congregation governs itself (by the Spirit of Christ and according to the word of God) inasmuch as it is a complete (though not, of course, exhaustive) manifestation of the universal body of Christ.

Just as Calvin has defined the invisible church as to its very essence (the complete number of the elect as the body and bride of Jesus Christ), so also he defines the visible church, that is, the local congregation. The visible church is the regular gathering of believers and their children in holy assemblies, for the preaching and hearing of the word of God.

Before Calvin explains the marks of the true, visible church, which include the pure preaching of the word of God as chief, Calvin calls attention to "the preaching of the heavenly doctrine" and extols its power and worth.[41] In this section (4.1.4–6) is Calvin's virtual definition of the visible church: the preaching assembly.

Later, taking up explicitly the subject of the means by which faith is aided, the subject that Reformed theology calls "the means of grace," Calvin limits himself to an explanation of the sacraments. It might seem that he neglects the first and fundamental means, namely, the preaching of the word. But Calvin considers himself to have adequately explained the preaching in the exposition that precedes, particularly in the treatment of the marks of the church, the keys of the church, the government of the church, and especially the virtual definition of the visible church.

Calvin has the highest regard for the preaching of the gospel by the human minister of the word. In and by the preaching, God himself speaks, thus working the salvation of his own children. In the preaching, by the ministry exercised by "a mortal and despised man, . . . God himself appears in our midst."[42] God himself speaks in the preaching: "He deigns to consecrate to himself the mouths and tongues of men in order that his voice may resound in them."[43] The preacher of the doctrine of salvation is "his [God's] own mouth."[44]

Calvin returns to the doctrine of the preaching in his consideration of the "jurisdiction" of the church.[45] The first of the "keys" by which the church exercises divine judgment is the preaching of the gospel.

With appeal to Matthew 16:19 ("I will give unto thee [Peter] the keys of the kingdom"), Calvin declares, "Christ has testified that in the preaching of the gospel... it was he himself who would speak and promise all things through their [the apostles'] lips as his instruments."[46]

Because the preaching is the living voice of God in Jesus Christ, "the church is built up solely by outward preaching." "God breathes faith into us only by the instrument of his gospel, as Paul points out ... [in] Romans 10:17." "The power to save... God... displays and unfolds... in the preaching of the gospel." Calvin appeals to Romans 1:16.[47] In the preaching God himself "come[s] down to us, in order to be near us... [and by this earthly means] to bear us up as if in chariots to his heavenly glory."[48]

Calvin recognizes that some object to this high view of preaching, as though it attributes to preachers what "belongs to the Holy Spirit." Calvin lists many passages from both the Old and New Testaments to prove that the Spirit does indeed work salvation by means of preaching. One such text is 1 Corinthians 4:15, where "Paul... boasts that he 'begat' the Corinthians 'through the gospel.'"[49]

Nothing is attributed to the human preacher, however, for it is God who freely joins his Spirit with the preaching, and he alone accomplishes all the salvation worked by the preaching. The same Paul who "boasted" in 1 Corinthians 4:15 acknowledges in 1 Corinthians 15:10 that all his work was "the grace of God which was with me."[50]

That the preaching of the gospel by a mere man is indeed the voice of Jesus Christ, without any implication that the preacher therefore possesses any credit for or power over the saving work of the preaching, Calvin explains more fully in his treatment of the keys of the kingdom. "The power of the keys is simply the preaching of the gospel, and... with regard to men it is not so much power as ministry. For Christ has not given this power actually to men, but to his Word, of which he has made men ministers."[51]

Calvin recognizes that in distinction from the invisible church, the visible church contains "many hypocrites."[52] Nevertheless, in view of the presence of God in the visible church, Christ's own speaking, and the saving work of the Spirit by the preaching of the gospel, Christians must honor the visible church. The visible church is the "mother" of believers and their children. Calvin is expressly referring to the visible church when he states, "There is no other way to enter into life unless this mother conceive us in her womb, give us birth, nourish us at her breast, and lastly, unless she keep us under her care and guidance until, putting off mortal flesh, we become like the angels [Matt. 22:30]."[53] Likewise, "God's fatherly favor and the especial witness of spiritual life are limited" to the visible church.[54]

For anyone to leave this church (which is, of course, impossible with regard to the invisible church of all the elect) "is always disastrous."[55]

Although Calvin does not make this explicit, it is clear that he regards the invisible church and the visible church as one and the same. Only then can he write, "The article in the [Apostles'] Creed in which we profess 'to believe the church' refers *not only to the visible church... but also to all God's elect*."[56] Similarly, concerning the following line in the creed regarding the communion of saints, Calvin states, "This article of the Creed *also* applies *to some extent* to the outward church."[57] The implication is that both lines of the creed apply both to the invisible church of the elect and to the visible church of the preaching assembly, because they are one and the selfsame *one* church of the Apostles' Creed (and of Scripture).

The invisible church of the elect manifests itself and takes visible form in each and every (true) visible congregation. Each (true) congregation is a visible manifestation and instituted form of the invisible church of the elect, which Jesus Christ is gathering, defending, preserving, and edifying by means of the visible church.

Calvin gives a broad outline of the order of his treatment of the doctrine of the church at the outset. "Our plan of instruction now requires us to discuss the [visible] church, its government, orders, and power; then the sacraments; and lastly the civil order."[58]

The marks of the visible church

The marks of the true, visible, instituted church of Christ are two: the pure preaching of the word of God and the right administration of the sacraments. "Wherever we see the Word of God purely preached and heard, and the sacraments administered, according to Christ's institution, there it is not to be doubted, a church of God exists."[59]

Here and elsewhere throughout his discussion of the identification of the true visible church, Calvin bases his teaching that the chief mark of the true church (clearly distinguishing her from the false church) is the pure preaching of the word of God on Ephesians 2:20: "[The church is] built upon the foundation of the apostles and prophets, Jesus Christ himself being the chief corner stone."

Calvin makes his explanation of the keys of the kingdom part of his exposition of the marks of the church (thus showing that, for Calvin, as for Christ himself in Matthew 16:17–19 and in Matthew 18:15–20, the kingdom of God is the visible church). The keys are the same as the marks: preaching and sacraments. The distinction is only that whereas the marks identify the church, the keys dispense the forgiveness of sins to believers. "[The forgiveness of sins] is dispensed to us through the ministers and pastors of the church, either by the preaching of the gospel or by the administration of the sacraments; and herein chiefly stands out the power of the keys, which the Lord has conferred upon the society of believers."[60]

The omission of discipline, or excommunication, from the list of the marks of the church does not indicate any minimizing of the importance of discipline in Calvin's teaching. Of course, the history of Calvin's own ministry in Geneva is proof to the contrary. But Calvin affirms the importance of discipline, exercised by the elders of the church, later in book four, under the rubric of the jurisdiction of the church. There he insists that discipline is one of the keys of the kingdom—the key referred to in Matthew 18:15–18. Such is the importance of discipline that "as the saving doctrine of Christ is the soul of the church, so does discipline serve as its sinews, through which the members of the body hold together."[61] Indeed, discipline is necessary: "Those who trust that without this bond of discipline the church can long stand are . . . mistaken."[62] "Therefore, all who desire to remove discipline or to hinder its restoration . . . are surely contributing to the ultimate dissolution of the church."[63]

This is a warning that "evangelical" and even Reformed churches in the twenty-first century very much need to hear and heed. One critic has observed that there is more discipline in the average American country club than in most "evangelical" churches.

The Belgic Confession is true to the spirit of Calvin, if not the letter, when Article 29 makes church discipline one of the marks of the true church, as a lack of discipline or a persecuting discipline of the orthodox and godly is a mark of a false church.

Nevertheless, it is significant that Calvin does not mention discipline as one of the marks of the (true) visible church. Undoubtedly, discipline is not as important as the preaching of the gospel, to which are attached the sacraments.

For all his insistence on the necessity of discipline, Calvin recognizes that there can be circumstances that hinder elders from exercising discipline as they desire. In addition, he warns against leaving a church because of some weakness or lack in the exercise of discipline.

> Individual laymen, if they see vices not diligently enough corrected by the council of elders, should not therefore at once depart from the church; and ... pastors themselves, if they cannot cleanse all that needs correction according to their hearts' desire, should not for that reason resign their ministry or disturb the entire church with unaccustomed vigor.[64]

There is also, Calvin thinks, a real danger of severity, harshness, and rigor in the exercise of discipline. Calvin calls for a "moderation of discipline."[65] Although he is referring directly to the church's treatment of excommunicated persons, he has in mind the beginning of the process of discipline as well. He commends a "prudence" that reckons with the Lord's warning against uprooting tares to the harm of the grain (Matt. 13:29). He quotes Cyprian approvingly: "Let a man mercifully correct what he can; let him patiently bear what he cannot correct, and groan and sorrow over it with love."[66]

Surely, by his counsel of "prudence," Calvin has in mind a situation in the congregation with which every pastor and elder is familiar. There is a member, or even a clique, that is opposed to the truth of the word of God or behaving wickedly. Nevertheless, because of the cleverness of the member or clique there is not sufficient evidence to warrant discipline. In fact, the exercise of discipline would disturb the congregation. In such a case, although the minister must certainly preach pointedly and the elders may privately admonish, the consistory must let the tares grow together with the grain. Only when members make their departure from the truth or their sinful conduct clearly manifest (as invariably they will do) should the ruling elders act in formal discipline.

If there can, and should, be a certain bearing with a temporary weakness regarding discipline, this is not the case with regard to the preaching of sound doctrine and the right administration of the sacraments. "As soon as falsehood breaks into the citadel of religion and the sum of necessary doctrine is overturned and the use of the sacraments is destroyed, surely the death of the church follows—just as a man's life is ended when his throat is pierced or his heart mortally wounded."[67] Once again, Calvin adduces Ephesians 2:20.

Obviously, the purpose of the marks of the church is to "be to us a perpetual token by which to distinguish the church."[68] The marks must determine church membership—which visible church we join, which we remain a member of, and which we leave if it does not have, or loses, the marks. "In order that the title 'church' may not deceive us, every congregation that claims the name 'church' must be tested by this standard as by a touchstone."[69]

The church with the marks is "the pillar and ground of the truth," according to 1 Timothy 3:15. This "means that the church is the faithful keeper of God's truth in order that it may not perish in the world."[70] By the "preaching of his Word" in this church, God "feeds us with spiritual food and provides everything that makes for our salvation."[71] Since this church is Christ's bride and body (Calvin applies Ephesians 5:27 and Ephesians 1:23 to the visible church, that is, the local congregation that preaches the word of God), believers and their children enjoy communion with Christ by their membership in the church. Their membership in a church with the marks is "the marriage that the only-begotten Son of God deigned to contract with us."[72]

For these reasons, "the Lord esteems the communion of his church so highly," and so ought every believer.[73] The believer esteems the church highly by joining it and never leaving it (so long, of course, as it displays the marks).

With a warning that ought to terrify vast numbers of nominal Protestants, Calvin inveighs against the sin of "deserting" the church that has the marks and, by implication, the sin of refusing to join her. "Where the preaching of the gospel is reverently heard and the sacraments are not neglected... no one is permitted... to desert it and break its unity." Whoever leaves this "Christian society," God "counts as a traitor and apostate from Christianity." Separation from the church, which is pillar and ground of God's own truth, would be "sacrilegious disloyalty" and a violation of Christ's marriage with us.[74]

"How dangerous," Calvin exclaims, "nay how deadly... a temptation is it, when one is prompted to withdraw from that congregation wherein are seen the signs and tokens with which the Lord thought his church sufficiently marked."[75]

Believers are called to remain members of the church that displays the marks (and exercises the keys) even though the church has weaknesses. Calvin warns against being overly critical in our judgment of the visible church. He condemns those who leave a church because the lives of the members are not sufficiently holy. Such would include men and women in our day who are quick to leave the church because the members are not "loving" and "friendly." Calvin calls these deserters "airy spirits." "There have always been those who, imbued with a false conviction of their own perfect sanctity, as if they had already become a sort of airy spirits, spurned association with all men in whom they discern any remnant of human nature."[76]

Taking up the charge of the "airy spirits" (Calvin informs us that he has in mind "certain Anabaptists"[77]) that the church is not sufficiently holy, Calvin considers the holiness of the church. Once again, it is evident that he views the visible church of the local congregation as the instituted form of the invisible church of the Apostles' Creed, for he applies the holiness confessed in the creed to the visible church.

The holiness of the church is the work of the Lord in his bride (Calvin quotes Ephesians 5:25–27) cleansing her from sin and devoting her to himself. But this work is progressive and imperfect. "The church is holy, then, in the sense that it is daily advancing and is not yet perfect: it makes progress from day to day but has not yet reached its goal of holiness."[78]

Calvin points to the sinful imperfections of the church in the Old Testament and to the grave weaknesses regarding holiness in the New Testament churches in Galatia and at Corinth.

That there will always be bad men in the church is proved from Jesus' parables of the net that gathers every kind of fish and of the tares of the field (Matt. 13:24–30, 36–43, 47–50).

Even the good men in the church, although "they zealously aspire to holiness and perfect purity," are never in this life "without blemish."[79]

Calvin acknowledges that, not only certain members, but also entire churches—the institute itself—can be markedly and seriously unholy: "The most heinous sins have sometimes possessed entire churches."[80] Calvin mentions the Galatian churches and the church at Corinth. Paul did not at once call "airy spirits" to leave those churches, but he called the churches to repentance.

For a church to allow "the openly wicked" to be members is a "fault" that Calvin, like Paul, "sharply rebukes."[81] Nevertheless, it is nothing but "surliness and arrogance," an "overscrupulousness... born ... of pride and arrogance and false opinion of holiness," that motivate some to leave the church because the church is insufficiently holy.[82]

Shrewdly, Calvin observes that the article in the Apostles' Creed that confesses the holiness of the church is immediately followed by the article that confesses the forgiveness of sins. The implication is that both the holiest of God's children and the visible church herself "remain unable to stand before God without forgiveness of sins."[83]

Here Calvin brings up the truth of the keys of the kingdom with particular reference to the preaching of the gospel and the sacraments. Discipline, he informs us, he will treat elsewhere. Since only imperfectly holy, all the children of God need forgiveness. God dispenses this benefit "through the ministers and pastors of the church, either by the preaching of the gospel or by the administration of the sacraments."[84] Calvin's high view of preaching is again in evidence. He applies the truth that God forgives sins by means of preaching to the inclination of "airy spirits" to leave the church for insubstantial, and even trivial, reasons. "This benefit [of forgiveness] so belongs to the church that we cannot enjoy it unless we abide in communion with the church."[85]

Not even every doctrinal error is ground for leaving a church. "For not all the articles of true doctrine are of the same sort... Nonessential matters should in no wise be the basis of schism among Christians."[86] Calvin is quick to assure his audience that he does "not support even the slightest errors." But he intends to guard against forsaking, or splitting, the visible church "because of any petty dissensions."[87]

Instructive, almost amusing in fact, is the one example Calvin gives of a "nonessential" teaching. He refers to a difference in eschatology, specifically the intermediate state. Churches, and presumably believers, should not separate over the question whether the souls of believers at the moment of death "fly to heaven" or "live to the Lord" in some other place.[88] To be sure, this is a minor doctrinal disagreement. It should be noted that Calvin does *not* allow for disagreement over the question whether souls live to the Lord (in either heaven or some other place) or sleep. His first theological treatise was a vigorous refutation of the error that the souls of believers sleep in the interim between death and the resurrection of the body.[89]

Examples of doctrine that are "so necessary to know that they should be certain and unquestioned by all men as the proper principles of religion" include the truths that "God is one; Christ is God and the Son of God; [and] our salvation rests in God's mercy."[90] Errors concerning these and other fundamental doctrines of the Christian faith warrant, indeed demand, uncompromising struggle, separation, and split. These errors efface the marks and corrode the keys.

It is worthy of note that among the three examples Calvin gives of necessary "principles of religion" is the doctrine of salvation by the mercy of God alone.[91] This is the great Reformation gospel of salvation by the sovereign, particular grace of God in Jesus Christ alone. The heart and center of this gospel for Calvin, as for all the reformers, was justification by faith alone. In describing the gospel as the message of God's mercy, Calvin has his eye on such passages as Romans 9:16, which contrasts the false gospels of salvation by the will of the sinner and by the works of the sinner with the one, true gospel of salvation "of God that sheweth mercy."

The denial of the doctrine of salvation by God's mercy alone, whether by the Roman Catholic Church; by Arminianism; by the contemporary movement that calls itself the federal (covenant) vision; or by any church that teaches a grace of God in Jesus Christ that is wider than election and, therefore, conditioned by the response of the sinner and resistible, is, in Calvin's reckoning, fundamental departure from the Christian faith, the loss of the mark of the true church, and if the church does not repent, ground for a believer's leaving.

Calvin's fervent plea that believers bear with many faults in the church will surprise many. Repeatedly, Calvin insists that no one should tolerate or excuse the faults. But his love of Christ's bride and body in the world, his ardor for her peace, and his keen awareness of the ever-present reality of sin in the church and her members move him to warn that "so long as it [the visible church] retains them [the marks]," one "must not reject it [the church]...even if it otherwise swarms with many faults."[92]

Calvin was a genuine "churchman"—an exemplary churchman.

Rome: the false church

The truth of the marks of the church, chiefly the "unmistakable sign" of "God's Word," exposes the Roman Catholic Church as the false church.[93] In Rome, "doctrine...has been entirely buried and driven out. Public assemblies have become schools of idolatry and ungodliness."[94] "Their chief bond of communion is in the Mass, which we abominate as the greatest sacrilege."[95] The papacy, which Calvin judges to be the "Antichrist" predicted in 2 Thessalonians 2:4, has already in Calvin's day "corrupted and well-nigh killed by his evil and deadly doctrines [the churches under his tyranny]."[96]

Calvin's judgment of Rome is that "every one of their congregations and their whole body lack the lawful form of the church."[97]

"If anyone recognizes the present [Roman Catholic] congregations ...as churches (in full communion of which a Christian man must stand)...he will gravely err."[98] For anyone to remain in the Roman communion would be a "deadly participation in so many misdeeds."[99] Writing during the time that the Reformation is ongoing, Calvin calls all to "withdraw."[100]

In his day, Calvin does allow that "the Lord wonderfully preserves in them [Roman Catholic churches] a remnant of his people," adding that they are "woefully dispersed and scattered."[101] Also, some "traces of the church" remain in Rome. One is "baptism,...a witness to [the] covenant."[102] But "those marks...to which we should pay particular regard," namely, the preaching of the pure word of God and the proper administration of the sacraments, "have been erased."[103]

To Rome's most powerful defense of herself as the catholic church, namely, her external unity, and to Rome's most potent accusation against the Reformation, namely, that it is schismatic, Calvin responds that genuine unity and communion are in Jesus Christ, that is, in the truth of the word of God. Unity is the "unity of faith." With appeal to Ephesians 4:5, Philippians 2:1, 5, and Romans 15:5, Calvin declares, "Apart from the Lord's Word there is not an agreement of believers but a faction of wicked men."[104]

The separation of Protestants from Rome (many of whom, in fact, were "expelled...with anathemas and curses") is not schism. "It behooved us to withdraw from them that we might come to Christ."[105]

In the history of the Reformed churches after the Reformation, it has repeatedly happened that apostatizing or false churches have vilified those whom they cast out, or those who were compelled to leave, as schismatic and sectarian. But Calvin's response to Rome's charge expresses the truth of the matter. Not those unjustly expelled or those compelled to leave are guilty of schism, but the church that corrupts and buries essential truths of the Christian and Reformed faith. Those cast out or leaving are cast out or leave unto Jesus Christ. With him is the unity of the church.

It may surprise us that in setting forth the marks of the visible church, Calvin does not mention Scripture and its authority. Calvin has already established in book one the nature of Scripture as the inspired word of God and insisted on its authority over the church. He will return to the subject of the sole authority of Scripture in the church in his treatment of the "government, orders, and power" of the church, which immediately follows his explanation of the marks. There he will make plain that when, in his exposition of the marks, he speaks of the preaching of the word of God or of the administration of the sacraments according to the word of God, he refers to the holy writings of the Old and New Testaments.

Submission to the sole, unique authority of Holy Scripture as the inspired word of God is indeed the mark of the church. The church acknowledges the authority of Scripture by preaching the gospel of God's grace in Jesus Christ that is Scripture's content and by governing herself in all aspects as Scripture regulates.

Church government

The aspect of the visible church that Calvin treats, at great length, between his explanation of the marks and his consideration of the sacraments is church government. Calvin distinguishes this broad subject as "government, orders, power."[106] Included are the special offices in the church, certain ecclesiastical assemblies, the authority of the church to establish doctrines, and the discipline of sinners, especially excommunication.

The length and detail of the treatment (the exposition of church government runs from chapter three of book four through chapter thirteen, taking up more than two hundred pages in the McNeill/Battles edition) indicate the importance of the right and orderly government of the church in Calvin's judgment. In Calvin's biblical and theological thinking, the church—the visible, instituted church—is the kingdom of Christ. Over and in his kingdom, Christ the king rules, and *must* rule, sovereignly, wisely, and justly. Subversion of church government is rebellion against Christ the king and imminent peril to the citizens. "Since the church is Christ's Kingdom, and he reigns by his Word alone, will it not be clear to any man that those are lying words [cf. Jer. 7:4] by which the Kingdom of Christ is imagined to exist apart from his scepter (that is, his most holy Word)?"[107] In the 1536 *Institutes*, Calvin charges that by the imposition of unbiblical laws (by the Roman Catholic Church) "the Kingdom of Christ is invaded."[108]

As this last quotation indicates, Calvin's concern for right church government is heightened by his, and the entire Reformation's, awareness of the utter devastation of the church by the Roman Catholic tyranny.

Calvin states the basic principle, and really the whole truth, of the government of the church in his opening line: "Now we must speak of the order by which the Lord willed his church to be governed. He alone should rule and reign in the church as well as have authority or pre-eminence in it, and this authority should be exercised and administered by his Word alone."[109]

Calvin teaches, not only the "regulative principle of worship," but also the regulative principle of all the life of the church. That is, Christ regulates, or governs, all the life of the church by his scepter, which is the word of God. And the word of God is Holy Scripture.

It pleases Christ to govern his church by means of men. The nature of this mediate government is not that Christ transfers to the men "his right and honor," but that Christ speaks, rules, and administers mercy through them.[110]

On the basis of his understanding of Ephesians 4:11, "some, pastors and teachers," Calvin distinguishes the special work of the pastor from the special work of the teacher. The pastor preaches, administers the sacraments, exhorts and warns the congregations, privately as well as publicly, and, with the elders, exercises discipline. The teacher's work is limited "only [to] Scriptural interpretation—to keep doctrine whole and pure among believers."[111] Calvin's "teachers" resemble the contemporary professors of theology.

Calvin seizes the opportunity, once again, to emphasize the necessity of the pastor and his work of preaching for the church. Light, heat, food, and drink are not "so necessary to nourish and sustain the present life as the apostolic and pastoral office is necessary to preserve the church on earth."[112] "There is nothing more notable or glorious in the church than the ministry of the gospel, since it is the administration of the Spirit and of righteousness and of eternal life [2 Cor. 4:6; 3:9]."[113]

The pastor of the post-apostolic church takes "the place of the apostles" with regard to the duty of preaching the gospel and administering the sacraments. This work Christ imposes upon every pastor by a "holy, inviolable, and perpetual law."[114] One claiming to be a pastor and a successor of the apostles who does not preach is an impostor.

Every pastor, Calvin insists, is assigned by Christ to a church. God himself has ordained this in Acts 14:22, 23 and Titus 1:5. God does not want pastors "dashing about aimlessly without an assignment" or "break[ing] over into another man's province."[115] A pastor may "transfer . . . to another place" only by "public authority."[116]

Calvin regards the offices of apostle, evangelist, and prophet in Ephesians 4:11 as temporary and "extraordinary," having "no place" in "duly constituted churches."[117] Surprisingly, he supposes that "apostles, or at least evangelists," have been raised up by Christ in his own day, in order to reform the church.[118]

Certainly, Calvin has Luther in mind. Does he also refer to himself?

The Doctrine of the Church 325

Basic to Calvin's church government is his conviction, solidly based on Scripture, that the terms "bishops," "presbyters," "pastors," and "ministers" all refer to the same office. "Scriptural usage... interchanges these terms."[119] Calvin appeals to Titus 1:5, 7, 1 Timothy 3:1, and a comparison of Acts 20:17 and Acts 20:28. Scripture does not know of a hierarchy of ministers of the word.

Scripture does know of two other permanent (special) offices in addition to those of pastor and of teacher: "government and caring for the poor."[120] Governors, or elders, are "charged with the censure of morals and the exercise of discipline along with the bishops [or, pastors]."[121] Calvin points to 1 Corinthians 12:28 and Romans 12:8.

"The care of the poor was entrusted to the deacons."[122] Calvin finds the New Testament origin of this office in Acts 6. He thinks that Scripture teaches "two distinct grades" of deacons, one bestowing alms on the poor, the other devoting "themselves to the care of the poor and sick."[123] To this second "grade" belonged the widows of 1 Timothy 5:9, 10, according to Calvin.

In the twenty-first century, when Reformed churches are installing women into the office of deacon under the influence of the antichristian feminist movement and with the purpose of thus opening the way to the future installation of women into the offices of ruling elder and minister of the word and sacraments, Calvin would have distinguished the work of the widows in 1 Timothy 5:9–13 more sharply from the office of deacon as described in 1 Timothy 3:8–13.

Those who appeal to Calvin's putting women into the second "grade" of deacons must reckon with two facts. First, "women could fill no other public office" than the second "grade" of deacons.[124] Second, in his commentary on 1 Timothy 5:9–13, Calvin is insistent that the women who are admitted to the second "grade" of deacons must meet the strict requirements laid down by the apostle. The women must be widows; sixty or older; prior to their widowhood the wife of one man; well reported of for good works; etc.[125]

The importance of the offices for the decency and order that 1 Corinthians 14:40 demands in the church requires that "no one should assume public office in the church without being called."[126] Regarding the necessity of the call, Hebrews 5:4, 5 is decisive for Calvin: "And no man taketh this honour unto himself, but he that is called of God, as was Aaron. So also Christ glorified not himself to be made an high priest; but he that said unto him, Thou art my Son, to-day have I begotten thee."

Call to one of the (special) offices in the church has two aspects: the "secret call, of which each minister is conscious before God," and "the outward and solemn call, which has to do with the public order of the church."[127]

Concerning the secret, or internal, call, Calvin warns that a man must come to the office "not with ambition or avarice, not with any other selfish desire, but with a sincere fear of God and desire to build up the church."[128] With regard particularly to the office of pastor, Calvin holds that "learning joined with piety," as well as "the other gifts of the good pastor," is "preparation" for the office.[129]

All the men called outwardly by the church must have demonstrated two fundamental qualifications: "Only those are to be chosen who are of sound doctrine and of holy life."[130] Calvin appeals to 1 Timothy 3:1–7 and Titus 1:7, 8. No one who is "notorious in any fault" may hold office in the church, for this would both "deprive them of authority and disgrace the ministry."[131]

The entire church must choose its office bearers, not the elders only, much less one man. Here Calvin translates Acts 14:23, "presbyters elected by show of hands in every church."[132] But it is essential, in view of the fact that in choosing office bearers the congregation is "doing the most serious thing of all," that the church conduct the election "with the highest reverence and care."[133]

As must be the case with every aspect of the life of the church, the call to office is strictly governed "according to the Word of God."[134] The word of God pronounces a call "lawful . . . when those who seemed fit are created by the consent and approval of the people."[135]

Implied is the warning—to twenty-first-century Reformed churches—that the calling of men known to be weak or ignorant doctrinally and suspect concerning their godly life because they are rich, or popular, or supporters of some "party line" or other, in a frivolous or political manner, is not "lawful"—legal, but not lawful. Christ does not call weak men—the consistory and congregation may call, but not Christ. Then the blessing of Christ is withdrawn from the church—withdrawn in this "most serious thing of all."[136]

The call ends in the public ceremony of the laying on of hands, "the rite of ordination" into the privileges and duties of the office. Calvin observes that this rite was used in the New Testament for ordination to all the offices and that only the pastors laid their hands on the office bearers. The meaning, Calvin thinks, is that those who lay their hands on office bearers are "offering to God him whom they [receive] into the ministry."[137]

The Roman Catholic hierarchy

Calvin leads into his searching examination and scathing denunciation of Roman Catholic church government, with specific reference to the offices, by a study of the church government of the early, post-apostolic church. He intends to show how that government differed from Rome's and how the government of the early church gradually developed into the Roman hierarchy, as illicit authority was increasingly ascribed to, and eagerly sought by, the bishop of Rome.

Calvin shows that he has read widely in the church fathers and theologians and, therefore, has broad knowledge of the history of the early church.

He is charitable in his reading of that history. For example, the appointment of archbishops and patriarchs was "an extremely rare practice" and "connected with the maintenance of discipline."[138] But he condemns the use of the term "hierarchy" to describe this government in the early church: "an improper term... certainly one unused in Scripture. For the Holy Spirit willed men to beware of dreaming of a principality or lordship as far as the government of the church is concerned."[139]

As time went on, the theologians of the early church erred also in going beyond the biblical requirements of a bishop in 1 Timothy 3 by demanding "celibacy."[140]

One basic aspect of office in the early church, Calvin emphasizes: "Both bishops and presbyters had to devote themselves to the dispensing of Word and sacraments." Quoting Gregory the Great in support of his assertion, Calvin notes that "even in Gregory's time [Gregory was pope from AD 589–604], when the church had well-nigh collapsed ..., it was not tolerable for any bishop to refrain from preaching."[141]

Calvin's brief survey of the history of the church government of the early church and particularly his observation that in the early church a bishop preached introduce Calvin's critical examination of the Roman hierarchy. "Now it behooves us to turn our attention to the order of church government adhered to today by the Roman see and all its satellites."[142]

Thus at the outset of his critique does Calvin issue a damning indictment of Roman Catholic church government and, therefore, of the Roman Catholic Church itself.

For as Calvin has demonstrated earlier, according to biblical church polity every true, visible, instituted congregation is a complete church of Christ. But according to Rome, the papacy—"the Roman see"—is the church. The various congregations, or parishes, are nothing but "satellites."

Calvin's fundamental criticism of the offices in the Roman church is that they do not function, nor are they required to function, as the word of God requires. The worst evil is that the bishops and priests do not preach. "Almost none of the bishops, or at least very few, and of the other clergy scarcely one man in a hundred... once in his whole life mounted any pulpit[.] For men have become so insane as to consider it beneath the bishop's dignity to preach to the people."[143] As for Rome's presbyters, or priests, rather than "feed[ing] the church, and administer[ing] the spiritual Kingdom of Christ [by preaching the gospel],... they sacrifice Christ" on "the altar."[144]

To the boasting of bishops and priests that they are the successors of the apostle, Calvin responds that they, and therefore the Roman church, have nothing "in common with the apostles." For the apostolic office was chiefly "the office of preaching, from which they so strenuously flee."[145]

Inasmuch as preaching the gospel is not the all-important work of bishops and priests, in electing these men to office Rome ignores the basic qualification. "For a hundred years scarcely one man in a hundred has been elected who has comprehended anything of sacred learning."[146]

Closely related to the gross sin of ordaining bishops and priests "to perform sacrifice," rather than to preach, is the evil of ordaining these men "to whom you assign no place."[147] Calvin insists on the biblical injunction that a pastor (the biblical bishop or teaching "presbyter") is called by Christ to labor in a particular congregation: "that is, that a place be assigned to the person ordained where he is to exercise his office." One reason is "that the church may not be burdened with needless expense."[148] Countless bishops, priests, and monks, most of whom are not assigned to one congregation to preach to it and govern it, but rather float freely about doing nothing more than sacrificing Christ anew on the altar, are an enormous and useless expense to the people.

Calvin's criticism applies to many of the larger Protestant denominations in the twenty-first century. They are bloated with a bureaucracy of ordained men, who are paid handsomely to do everything but preach the gospel to and govern a local congregation.

To these reverend bureaucrats, as much as to the Roman bishops, applies Calvin's sarcasm: "He who has never seen a sheep of his flock is the shepherd of it."[149]

The other offices in the Roman Catholic hierarchy likewise completely ignore the work assigned to the office by the word of God. Rome's deacons, for instance, minister at the altar and busy themselves with "other trifles."[150] "There is nothing of alms, nothing of the care of the poor, nothing of that whole function which they once performed."[151]

Yet another fundamental criticism of the offices in the Roman Catholic Church is that "the people's right in electing a bishop has been taken away," despite the example of the early post-apostolic church and the teaching of Scripture. Thus the church has been "despoiled... of its right."[152]

Rome's hierarchy does not consist only of a gradation of authority of the ranks of its office bearers, but it also consists of the office bearers' lording it "over God's heritage... the flock," in the language of 1 Peter 5:3. This aspect of Roman Catholic hierarchy, which is by no means the least expression of the evil, manifests itself, Calvin charges, when Roman Catholic officialdom imposes bishops on the people. "The whole power [of electing a bishop] has been transferred to the canons alone. They confer the episcopate on whom they please; they introduce him directly before the people, but to be adored, not to be examined."[153]

With regard to the marks of bishops and priests, godliness of life is neither a qualification for office in Rome, nor the "abiding standard of life" of that order. Calvin is certain that the Roman Catholic Church itself "cannot deny [that] there is scarcely a bishop, and not one in a hundred parish priests, who, if his conduct were to be judged according to the ancient canons, would not be subject either to excommunication or at least to deposition from office."[154]

Calvin's response to Rome's attempt to ward off his scathing denunciation of the wealth of their bishops and the magnificence of their church buildings is of great importance for indicating the Reformed, indeed, Christian, interpretation of Old Testament prophecy of the coming glory of the church. Rome argued that by their earthly riches, pomp, and splendor "the dignity of the church is decently sustained." Rome added that this earthly magnificence fulfilled those prophecies "with which the ancient prophets describe the splendor of Christ's Kingdom."[155] Rome appealed to Psalm 72, Isaiah 52, and Isaiah 60.

Premillennial dispensational Protestants and postmillennialists in the Reformed camp appeal to the same prophecies in support of an earthly kingdom of Christ of carnal riches, power, and splendor in the future. They share with Rome the same mistaken, literalistic interpretation of Old Testament prophecy, asserting an earthly fulfillment of prophecy that was couched in the language of earthly riches and splendor.

Calvin's interpretation of Old Testament prophecy is radically different. Rome's literalistic, carnal conception of Old Testament prophecy is both "Jew[ish]" and "stupid."[156] Those Old Testament prophecies of the coming glory of the Messianic kingdom were "things spiritually spoken of Christ's spiritual Kingdom. For we know that the prophets sketched for us under the image of earthly things God's heavenly glory, which ought to shine in the church."[157]

In contrast to the wealth and splendor of Roman Catholic bishops, Calvin calls for bishops, that is, ministers of the word, to live as "example[s] of frugality, modesty, continence, and humility." He thinks the bishop "should have a little house not far from his church, with inexpensive fare and furnishings."[158]

Calvin practiced what he preached. His utter disinterest in riches, his contentment with the bare necessities of earthly life, and his dedication to preaching the word of God make him the model of a godly bishop in the church of Christ.

The papacy

"The capstone of the whole structure [of the government of the Roman Catholic Church is] ... the primacy of the Roman see," that is, the papacy.[159]

The claim of Rome is that "the Roman pontiff (as the vicar of Christ, who is Head of the church) presides over the whole church in Christ's place."[160]

Such is the essential importance of the papacy for Rome that "from [the papacy] they strive to prove that the church catholic is their exclusive possession." Rome contends that "the chief and almost sole bond of church unity is that we cleave to the Roman see and remain in obedience to it."[161]

Calvin lived before the meeting of the Roman Catholic council Vatican I (AD 1870), which decreed as official Roman dogma that Christ "fixed in [Peter and his successors, the bishop of Rome] the abiding principle of this twofold unity [of bishops and of the church] and its visible foundation" and that "the Roman Pontiff, when he speaks *ex cathedra* ... defin[ing] a doctrine regarding faith or morals, ... is possessed of ... infallibility."[162]

But Calvin is well aware of the extravagant claims being made on behalf of the papacy in his day: "that the pope cannot err, that the pope is above councils, that the pope is the universal bishop of all churches and the supreme head of the church on earth."[163]

Calvin rejects the papacy and refutes all Roman Catholic arguments for it, defenses of it, and claims on its behalf by his declaration that the papacy "originated neither in Christ's institution, nor in the practice of the ancient church."[164] The papacy was not "established by Christ" in "God's Word."[165]

In a powerful argument against the papacy, Calvin calls attention to the fact that when Paul in Ephesians 4:11 lists the offices Christ uses for the edifying and unity of his church, he does not mention the pope. "Why does Paul not say that Christ has set one over all to act as his vicegerent?"[166] In addition, in Ephesians 4, the apostle is commending the unity of the church. If the pope is the principle and foundation of the oneness of the church, why did the apostle "not immediately also add, one supreme pontiff, to keep the church in unity?"[167]

Regarding Matthew 16:17–19, the chief biblical basis of Rome's doctrine of the papacy, Calvin explains that the "keys of the kingdom" are especially the preaching of the gospel. By the preaching of the gospel, the kingdom is opened to believers and closed against unbelievers. The office is not to be separated from the work belonging to the office. Since the pope does not preach the gospel, he cannot be thought to hold the office referred to in Matthew 16:17–19.

In addition, Matthew 18:18 and John 20:23 prove that Christ gave the keys to *all* the apostles, not to Peter only. "If the same right was granted to all that was promised to one, in what respect will Peter be superior to his colleagues?"[168]

As for the "rock" upon which Christ will build his church, it is not the person of Peter in the unbiblical office of pope. Rather, the rock is Peter's confession "that Christ was the Son of God" and, thus, Christ himself, "for there is but one foundation . . . apart from which no other can be laid [1 Cor. 3:11]."[169]

Again demonstrating his wide reading and thorough study of his subject, Calvin exposes the illegitimacy of the Roman papacy by a review of the history of the development of the papacy in the early post-apostolic and medieval church. It is a history fraught with folly, deception, fraud, and naked, carnal power-grabbing.

Calvin allows himself a little humor at one point in his historical survey of what is really a ridiculous, as well as wicked, reality.

> As robbers are accustomed to divide up the common spoil, so these good gentlemen arranged between themselves that Pepin should be allowed the earthly and civil lordship after the true king had been deprived, while Zacharias should become the head of all the bishops and hold the spiritual power.[170]

The ultimate, and devastating, refutation of papal claims is Calvin's denial that Rome is a church, that is, a true church: "What is not a church cannot be the mother of churches."[171] The pope cannot be head of the church, since the religious organization of which he is head is no church. Calvin tests Rome by the three marks of the true church, which he has earlier listed, and concludes that Rome shows none of them. "Surely a church is recognized by its own clear marks."[172]

Not only is the pope not the head of the church and "vicar of Christ," but on the contrary, he is the "Antichrist" prophesied in 2 Thessalonians 2:4 and symbolically represented in Revelation 13:5. "Since, therefore, it is clear that the Roman pontiff has shamelessly transferred to himself what belonged to God alone and especially to Christ, we should have no doubt that he is the leader and standard-bearer of that impious and hateful kingdom."[173]

A Reformed man or woman may differ with Calvin in thus identifying the antichrist of Daniel 7:25 and 2 Thessalonians 2:4 as the papacy. The antichrist of Daniel's prophecy and 2 Thessalonians 2:4 is an individual, not an institution or office. In addition, Daniel 11:36–38 and 2 Thessalonians 2:4 describe an individual who will be openly and avowedly irreligious, anti-supernatural, and hostile to "all that is called God, or that is worshipped"—a pure naturalist, or secularist (2 Thess. 2:4). Daniel's prophecy and Revelation 13 clearly depict the antichrist as a political figure, a head of state, the sovereign of the coming world kingdom.

But no Reformed man or woman will, or may, differ with Calvin regarding his condemnation of the papacy as a usurpation of the office and honor of Jesus Christ and as a tyrannical government, marking the Roman Catholic Church as the false church.

As the false church, Rome will cooperate with and serve the personal antichrist, as Revelation 13:11–18 and Revelation 17 foretell. For this reason, one's difference with Calvin over his identification of the antichrist of Daniel and 2 Thessalonians 2:4 is not fundamental.

So far is it from being true that "Rome ... [is] ... the head of churches" that, in fact, "it is not worthy of being regarded among the smallest toes of the church's feet."[174]

One reason that Rome is not even the little toe of the church's foot is the pope's toleration of wicked behavior on the part of clergy and people at Rome. Indeed, the popes "themselves together with their household, with almost the whole college of cardinals, and with the whole flock of their clergy, have been prostituted to all wickedness, filthiness, and uncleanness, and to all kinds of crimes and misdeeds, so that they resemble monsters rather than men."[175] Calvin restrains himself in order to "spare chaste ears."[176] But he knows the immorality that is rampant in the highest levels of the Roman hierarchy.

The great positive truth at stake in the controversy over the papacy is Christ's headship over his church and high priesthood in the church. "Christ...alone keeps that office without vicar or successor...[He] resigns that honor to no one else."[177]

Here, very emphatically, with regard to the government of the church, sounds the Reformation confession, "Christ alone!"

Church power

The genuine "power of the church [is] spiritual power...[and] consists either in doctrine or in jurisdiction or in making laws."[178] Fundamental to all understanding and exercise of church power is that its purpose must be "for upbuilding and not for destruction [2 Cor. 10:8; 13:10]."[179] This will be the case if Christ "alone is the schoolmaster of the church."[180] If men exercise power in the church according to their own "whim," the result will necessarily be "tyranny."[181]

Whether laying down and explaining doctrine, or disciplining impenitent sinners, or making laws, "the power of the church...is not infinite but subject to the Lord's Word and, as it were, enclosed within it."[182]

By "the Lord's Word," Calvin means Holy Scripture. Significantly, in his treatment of church power, in the exercise of which, not only Roman Catholic popes and councils, but also Protestant theologians and synods are wont to add to, stray from, and contradict Scripture, Calvin confesses the Reformation's (and the Bible's own) doctrine of Scripture. The entire Old Testament was "composed under the Holy Spirit's dictation." "That whole body, put together out of law, prophecies, psalms, and histories, was the Lord's Word for the ancient people."[183]

Likewise, the New Testament: the apostles wrote "with Christ's Spirit as precursor in a certain measure dictating the words."[184] Beveridge's translation of this important statement is, "The Spirit of Christ went before, and in a manner dictated words to them."[185] The apostles, says Calvin, "were sure and genuine scribes of the Holy Spirit, and their writings are therefore to be considered oracles of God."[186] Beveridge translates, "sure and authentic *amanuenses* of the Holy Spirit."[187]

Calvin speaks the same language in his commentary on 2 Timothy 3:16, "All scripture is given by inspiration of God," or, as is the literal translation of the Greek, "all scripture is God-breathed." The Old Testament, Calvin explains, is "not a doctrine delivered according to the will and pleasure of men, but dictated by the Holy Spirit." God is "the Author of the Scripture." Therefore, "we owe to the Scripture the same reverence which we owe to God; because it has proceeded from him alone, and has nothing belonging to man mixed with it."[188]

Calvin did not suppose that the Spirit actually dictated Scripture. No one has ever supposed this. But Calvin *did* believe and teach that the Spirit dictated Scripture "*in a certain measure*" or "*in a manner.*" By the mysterious, marvelous, inexplicable wonder of inspiration, Scripture is as truly, completely, and exclusively the word of God, having "nothing belonging to man mixed with it," as if the Spirit had, in fact, dictated the book to perfectly faithful and accurate scribes.

Contemporary scholarship, professedly "conservative" as well as openly (and honestly) "liberal," does not believe this about the Bible. It may not, then, claim to represent the faith of Calvin, and of the entire sixteenth-century Reformation of the church, with regard to one of Calvin's (and the Reformation's) fundamental doctrines: "Scripture alone." And those who do share Calvin's (and the Reformation's) faith concerning Holy Scripture observe two deadly consequences of contemporary scholarship's skepticism concerning Scripture in the churches influenced by this doubt and criticism. The first is that the churches do not exercise church power, whether in doctrine, laws, or discipline, strictly according to Scripture. The second consequence is that they turn toward Rome.

The implication of Calvin's believing acceptance of "all Scripture" as the inspired word of God is the full and sole authority of Scripture regarding church power. And this principle is forever the impassable gulf between the true church of Christ and the Roman Catholic Church.

Hear Calvin.

> Let this be a firm principle: No other word is to be held as the Word of God, and given place as such in the church, than what is contained first in the Law and the Prophets, then in the writings of the apostles; and the only authorized way of teaching in the church is by the prescription and standard of his Word.[189]

It is the inspired and "in a manner" dictated Scripture that is the full and final revelation of God in Jesus Christ to the church. In and through Scripture, Jesus Christ authoritatively teaches the church, as her schoolmaster, when pastors rightly explain and apply those Scriptures.

Calvin vehemently rejects the notion that Jesus Christ reveals God and teaches the churches apart from and even contrary to Scripture, as is the Roman Catholic position.

According to Rome, "the church has the power to frame new articles of faith," apart from Scripture.[190] Rome has such power, it claims, by virtue of its possessing a living "tradition" alongside Scripture. By "tradition," Rome means doctrine "that the church needed to add ... to the writings of the apostles, or that the apostles themselves afterward properly supplied through a living voice" to the content of the Bible.[191]

To this Calvin responds, "Every schoolboy knows that in the writings of the apostles, which these [Roman Catholic] fellows ... maim and halve, there abides the fruit of that revelation which the Lord then promised to the apostles."[192]

Later, when contending against Rome's imposition of man-made laws upon the consciences of the members of the church, "this tyranny of human tradition," Calvin declares that "to trace the origin of these traditions ... back to the apostles is pure deceit ... The apostles not only were ignorant of what the Romanists attribute to them but [also] never even heard of it."[193]

Rome also claims the power to decree authoritative doctrine and interpretation of doctrine by virtue of her allegedly infallible church councils. In Calvin's day, the Roman church had not yet officially declared the infallibility of the pope. But Calvin sees this coming: "They so stubbornly contend over the power of the church to no other purpose but to bestow all they can extort upon the Roman pontiff and his entourage."[194] In AD 1870, Rome would validate Calvin's analysis by the decision of Vatican I.

Against Rome's insistence on the infallibility and unquestioned, and unquestionable, authority of its councils, Calvin shows from Scripture that councils of pastors and elders can err and often have erred, grievously. Calvin points to "the council convened by Ahab [1 Kings 22:6, 22]." Not that council of four hundred lying, flattering prophets, but the lone prophet Micaiah, who was "condemned as a heretic," spoke the infallible word of God.[195] The council of the Sanhedrin that condemned Jesus is another instance of an evil assembly of the church, whose decision was wrong and wicked.

The fact is, says Calvin, "Christ and his apostles [often did] foretell that pastors would pose the greatest dangers to the church [Matt. 24:11, 24; Acts 20:29, 30; 1 Tim. 4:1; 2 Tim. 3:1ff.; 4:3]."[196]

Even though God has certainly used such councils as Nicea, Constantinople, Ephesus I, and Chalcedon (which Calvin expressly "embrace[s] and reverence[s] as holy") for the development and defense of "the teachings of faith," other councils, especially the later ones, erred and were contradictory.[197]

One sharp criticism of councils applies all too often to church assemblies in our own day: "So long as opinions are counted, not weighed, the better part had often to be overcome by the greater."[198]

All decisions of church councils, therefore, are to be tested by Scripture. The decisions are authoritative only if they are in accordance with Scripture, and for this reason.

On the basis of Matthew 18:20, Calvin demands that authoritative councils assemble and decide "in his [Christ's] name." And no council gathers in Christ's name that "not content with the oracles of Scripture... concoct some novelty out of their own heads."[199]

Positively, at all councils "Scripture [must] stand out in the higher place, with everything subject to its standard."[200]

Calvin specifies the decisions of church councils to which he objects as heretical, harmful novelties: "purgatory... intercession of saints... auricular confession... [withholding of the] cup [of the Lord's supper, and]... prohibition of marriage to priests." "Not one syllable" of all these decisions "will be found in Scripture."[201]

The Reformed faith recognizes the power of the true church authoritatively to declare sound doctrine, explain sound doctrine, and settle doctrinal controversies. But the "difference" between the Reformed conception of church power and Rome's is this: "Our opponents locate the authority of the church outside God's Word; but we insist that it be attached to the Word, and do not allow it to be separated from it."[202]

Calvin's response to Rome's appeal to the Spirit on behalf of the authority of its councils applies as well to the claims of the neo-Pentecostal movement in the twenty-first century:

> How wrongly our opponents act when they boast of the Holy Spirit solely to commend with his name strange doctrines foreign to God's Word—while the Spirit wills to be conjoined with God's Word by an indissoluble bond, and Christ professes this concerning him when he promises the Spirit to his church.[203]

No one should suppose that Calvin denies the authority of the church. "Men must listen to the church." But "the reason is that the church makes no pronouncement except from the Lord's Word."[204]

The issue in the controversy over church power between Calvin and the Reformation, on the one hand, and the Roman Catholic Church, on the other hand, is simply that Rome claims power in itself as an inherent right, apart from the word of God, Holy Scripture. Therefore, the power of the Roman Catholic Church is not the authority of Jesus Christ, who teaches and governs only by Scripture. The power of Rome is an unchristian and antichristian tyranny.

Nowhere is Rome's tyranny more evident, more dishonoring of Christ, and more destructive of the peace of the member of the church than in its making of laws, a second aspect of church power.

Rome claims, and vigorously exercises, the right to make extrabiblical laws and to bind these man-made laws upon the consciences of the members of the church. Rome calls these laws "ecclesiastical constitutions."[205] These laws are of two kinds: ceremonies and rites, and discipline. Calvin concentrates his criticism on the laws prescribing ceremonies and rites, reserving his examination of Roman Catholic discipline for later treatment.

Calvin mentions a number of these laws: "auricular confessions";

abstaining from "meat on Friday"; special observances of "a day consecrated to some saintlet"; forbidding priests to marry; keeping vows concerning pilgrimages; honoring images of Mary and other saints; murmuring "long senseless words at certain hours"; and worshiping according to "the theatrical props that the papists use in their sacred rites, where nothing appears but the mask of useless elegance and fruitless extravagance."[206]

With these and many other such laws, Rome binds the consciences of the members of the church. They "bind souls inwardly before God and ... lay scruples on them, as if enjoining things necessary to salvation."[207]

Since Rome's laws oppress the conscience, Calvin defines conscience: "an awareness of divine judgment adjoined to [men] as a witness which does not let them hide their sins but arraigns them as guilty before the judgment seat."[208]

Calvin's condemnation of Rome's law-making is penetrating and thorough. Fundamentally, the evil is that men, though they be bishops in the church, "have no right to command the church to observe as obligatory what they have themselves conceived apart from God's Word."[209]

Once again, the basic Reformation doctrine: Scripture alone.

By these laws the freedom of the conscience of the believer "is utterly oppressed and cast down," for Christ, the only king of the conscience of his people, has freed the conscience of the believer from all laws other than those of the "one law of freedom, the holy Word of the gospel."[210] By the making and enforcing of its laws, Rome is the "most savage butcher" of the members of the church.[211]

Also, the man-made, conscience-binding laws of Rome are an open assault upon the kingship of Christ, sole lord of the conscience of his citizens. "Thus the Kingdom of Christ ... is invaded."[212]

In addition, the Roman Catholic faithful are taught to find their righteousness in the keeping of the laws. "They let the poor folk seek in those outward trifles a righteousness which they may offer to God."[213]

Nor does it escape Calvin's attention that the decreed ceremonies are moneymakers for Rome. "Many ceremonies have been invented by greedy priestlings as snares to catch money."[214]

The true church, the church reformed by the Spirit of Christ according to the word of God, recognizes that she has no power to make laws binding the consciences of believers and their children. Her calling is simply to teach and exhort the laws that God has commanded in Scripture. "In his law the Lord has included everything applicable to the perfect rule of the good life, so that nothing is left to men to add to that summary."[215] God has two important reasons for restricting the church to his law as revealed in Scripture. One is that the church and every member of the church "acknowledge God as sole ruler of souls," as "the master and guide of our life."[216] The second is that "there is nothing he requires of us more than obedience," since "his will [is] the perfect rule of all righteousness and holiness."[217]

The calling of the church is not to play God by creating laws, but to submit to God by obeying his law.

Calvin applies the truth that the church is bound to the laws God has revealed in Scripture particularly to the church's public worship. With explicit appeal to Isaiah 29:13, 14, Matthew 15:9, Colossians 2:4, Colossians 2:22, 23 ("will worship"), and other passages, Calvin affirms that "a part of the reverence that is paid to him [God] consists simply in worshiping him as he commands, mingling no invention of our own."[218]

This rule governing the public worship of the congregation has come to be known in the Reformed tradition as the regulative principle of worship. It has confessional authority for all churches bound by the Three Forms of Unity. The Heidelberg Catechism explains the second commandment of the moral law as requiring that we "worship him [God] in [no] other way than he has commanded in his Word."[219] The Belgic Confession rejects "all human inventions, and all laws which man would introduce into the worship of God, thereby to bind and compel the conscience in any manner whatever."[220] Well aware of the allure of "will worship," Calvin deliberately turns from his denunciation of Roman Catholic worship to warn the church of "all ages":

> Whenever this superstition creeps in, that men wish to worship God with their fictions, all laws enacted for this purpose immediately degenerate to these gross abuses [viewing empty ceremonies as appeasing God; the display in worship of ceremonies

that are not understood; using ceremonies as moneymakers; and the like]. For God threatens not one age or another but all ages with this curse, that he will strike with blindness and amazement those who worship him with the doctrines of men [Isa. 29:13, 14].[221]

This is a warning that reputedly conservative Reformed and Presbyterian churches are disdaining in the twenty-first century. They mandate their creative "worship leaders" and "worship committees" to invent new elements of public worship and to devise novel ways of worshiping God. Thus they bring down on themselves the same judgments Calvin saw falling on the Roman Catholic Church. Thus they also "embrace every kind of absurdity."[222]

One of the reasons for the spreading "will worship" (euphemistically called "progressive worship" by its proponents) is the same as that which explains the extravagant ritual and lush ceremony of Rome. People "puffed up with worldly wisdom [are] marvelously captivated by ceremonial pomp."[223] These are especially "hypocrites and lighthearted women."[224]

In contrast to this "empty pomp,"[225] the worship of the true church is characterized by "simplicity."[226] The "spiritual worship of God" consists of "a few ceremonies" that "God has given us, ... ease in observance, [and] dignity in representation, which also includes clarity."[227]

Calvin acknowledges that God gives the New Testament church liberty to adopt "laws by which the order of the church is shaped."[228] These are rules that have in view that "in the sacred assembly of believers all things be done decently and with becoming dignity; and that the human community itself be kept in order with certain bonds of humanity and moderation."[229] Calvin mentions rules that set the "hours ... for public prayers, sermons, and sacraments,"[230] fix the date of the celebration of the Lord's supper, have to do with the exercise of discipline, and the like. Calvin warns extremists ("unlettered persons"[231]) not to react against Rome's tyranny by rejecting the legitimate rules of a church order.

But these lawful and necessary "observances," as Calvin refers to them, must be useful to the church; few in number; "not ... considered necessary for salvation," nor "associated with the worship of God [so that] piety [is] thus...lodged in them."[232] These laws may be changed, as the time and circumstances of the church require.[233]

"The third part of ecclesiastical power" is "jurisdiction."[234] By "jurisdiction" Calvin means church discipline, or censure, or excommunication: "The whole jurisdiction of the church pertains to the discipline of morals."[235]

To discipline, Christ referred when he gave the keys of binding and loosing to the church in Matthew 18:15–18, whereas in Matthew 16:19 the reference was to the ministry of the gospel.

Calvin sharply distinguishes the spiritual discipline of the church, essentially excommunication, from the physical punishments inflicted by the civil state. Neither church nor state may intrude upon the domain of the other. The church's "spiritual power [must] be completely separated from the [state's] right of the sword."[236] Nor is it "fitting for us to accuse to the magistrate those who do not obey our admonitions."[237]

Had Calvin observed these, his own and Scripture's principles, he would not have delivered the heretic Servetus over to the magistrates for execution or called upon the civil authorities in Geneva many times to jail or fine church members charged with sins by the eldership.

But there is more to Calvin's view of the relation between the power of the church and the power of civil government than only the separation of the two jurisdictions. Just as the spiritual discipline of the church "greatly helps and furthers" the "civil polity,"[238] so "it is the duty of godly kings and princes to sustain religion by laws, edicts, and judgments."[239] Calvin enlarges on this supposed duty and competency of the civil state, and vehemently defends it, in book four, chapter twenty. Thus the heretic Servetus, condemned by the elders in the consistory room, is handed over by the consistory to the civil authorities to be burned to death for the sin of false doctrine.

As has already been pointed out, Calvin regards discipline as necessary.

The discipline enjoined by Christ in Matthew 18 has "three ends in view."[240] The first end, or purpose, significantly, is the maintenance of God's honor: "They who lead a filthy and infamous life may not be called Christians, to the dishonor of God."[241] The second end is the preservation of the church from being corrupted by the wickedness of the impenitent sinner. Calvin quotes 1 Corinthians 5:6, "A little leaven ...ferments the whole lump." "The third purpose is that those overcome by shame for their baseness begin to repent."[242] The purpose of all discipline, including excommunication, which Calvin calls "the final thunderbolt,"[243] is the repentance and salvation of the sinner.

Calvin distinguishes "public" sins from "others, private or somewhat secret." Private sins must be dealt with in "the steps," or stages, laid out by Christ in Matthew 18. Public sins, those "committed openly and to the offense of the entire church," must be dealt with by the church forthwith: "When any such sin appears, the church ought to do its duty in summoning the sinner and correcting him."[244]

Although pastors and presbyters are called to admonish sinners privately, as Paul did according to Acts 20:20, 31, the discipline of formal excommunication must be carried out by an assembly of pastors and elders, not by one man as is the case with Roman Catholic discipline.[245] Indeed, the church must carry out excommunication in such a way that "the elders do not do it by themselves alone, but with the knowledge and approval of the church." Thus Christ "himself presides at his own tribunal."[246]

In excommunication, besides aiming at the repentance and restoration of the as yet impenitent sinner (as Paul teaches in 1 Corinthians 5:5: "that the spirit may be saved"), the church is not judging the one excommunicated to be a reprobate, but is only judging his works.[247]

Members of the church may not have fellowship with the one who has been cut off from the Lord's supper and the church. "Ecclesiastical discipline does not permit us to live familiarly or have intimate contact with excommunicated persons." Nevertheless, members of the church must speak with them "in order that they may turn to a more virtuous life and may return to the society and unity of the church," God being gracious.[248]

Calvin's warnings against members leaving a church in disgust over weaknesses regarding the exercise of discipline are appropriate. He appeals to the bad example of the Donatists, the fourth-century, largely African movement that separated from the church because of the church's alleged unholiness and lack of discipline.[249] But one may wonder whether Calvin's warnings do full justice to the concerns of those whom he admonishes.

Calvin had adopted the Constantinian state church idea or, at least, the city church idea. All citizens of Geneva were, by virtue of that fact, members also of the church. Many were unconverted Roman Catholics. Others were outright unbelievers. In the nature of the case, gross iniquities of belief and behavior abounded (which kept Calvin and his consistory busy day and night).

The records of the consistory meetings of the Genevan church during Calvin's pastorate indicate the volume and nature of the consistory's labor with the sinful lives of the Roman Catholic and outright ungodly citizens of the city. A random selection of a typical week of consistory meetings reveals that on Thursday, March 15, 1543, the consistory called to its meeting Angellinaz "because of idolatrous superstitions"; Piaget "because of superstition" (worshiping images of the saints and saying the rosary); Rugoz "because of his faith and creed" (Roman Catholic); Jaquemetaz because of her observance of Roman rituals; Pollet "because of the evil course he follows and what is said about his maid" (Pollet "spoke insolently" to Calvin and the elders); Thibauda "because of papistic ceremonies, rosaries and other things"; and Nycolardaz, a maid, because of suspicion that she was sleeping with her married master.

On Tuesday, March 20, 1543—a mere five days later—the consistory dealt with twenty-three more citizens of Geneva. Most of these were summoned before the consistory "because of papal superstitions."

Cowed by Calvin, the consistory, and the threatening officials of the civil government who were present at the consistory meetings, most of the defendants denied the charges of adhering to the Roman Catholic faith. They obviously lied. "Nobel Jane Pertennaz" had the courage of her convictions. She admitted that "sometimes she says her rosary." She informed the consistory that "she believes that which the holy church believes...and...in good works." And then, with some daring, she "asked whether Monsieur Calvin is God."[250] Criticism of the unholiness of the church of Geneva, whether by Anabaptists or by sound Reformed men and women, was then well founded. Christ's church in the world is, and must be, holy. The proper response to the criticism was not simply to warn against a Donatist rigor. Rather, it was the recognition that the state church idea is erroneous and fatal to the holiness of the church. The members of the church are not all the citizens of a nation, or even of a city. The members of the church are believers and their children. These Christ sanctifies, not all the citizens of a nation or of a city. The Apostles' Creed confesses "an holy catholic church," not a holy earthly nation or city.

In a surprising conclusion to his treatment of the discipline of all the members of the church, Calvin recommends fasting as "the remaining part of discipline," although he admits that fasting "is not properly contained within the power of the keys."[251]

"Pastors... should exhort" the members of the church "to fasting" at times of special spiritual need, for example, religious controversy, the choosing of a pastor, or such divine judgments as "pestilence, war, and famine."[252]

Fasting, Calvin thinks, serves three good purposes: to "weaken and subdue [sinful]... flesh"; help in praying and meditating; and to testify to self-abasement before God, "when we wish to confess our guilt before him."[253]

Although the reformer regards fasting as "an excellent aid for believers today,"[254] he is aware of the corruptions to which the practice is prone: "hypocritical fasting," which is merely external and formal; viewing fasting as a meritorious work or "a form of divine worship"; and an emphasis on abstinence from food and drink as though it were "one of the chief duties" of a Christian. If fasting succumbs to such "superstition," it would be better "if fasting were not practiced at all."[255]

A special aspect of church discipline (Calvin calls it "the second part of discipline"[256]) is the ministers' censure of their own behavior. Calvin refers to the minister's carefulness to be godly and utterly devoted to his office in his personal life. The evils against which the minister must guard, Calvin indicates: "No cleric [minister of the word and sacraments] should devote himself to hunting, gambling, or reveling. No cleric should practice usury or commerce; no cleric should be present at wanton dances."[257] "The clergy [must] practice harsher censures among themselves and be far less indulgent toward themselves than toward others."[258]

Elsewhere in his writings Calvin states the reason for this severe self-discipline on the part of ministers. By it, they commend their office and bring honor to him whom they preach.

Calvin himself modeled this "harsher" censure of oneself.

In the early post-apostolic church, a bishop had the oversight of the lives of the clergy. In the Reformed system of church government, the body of elders is charged with this important responsibility. The Reformed "Form for Ordination of Elders and Deacons" charges the elders with "the duty particularly to have regard unto the doctrine and conversation [conduct] of the ministers of the Word."[259]

The Roman Catholic Church, Calvin observes, is a stickler for one requirement concerning the life of the clergy: the unbiblical demand that the clergy be celibate. "In one thing they are extremely rigid and inexorable—in not permitting marriage to priests."[260]

The Roman prohibition of marriage to its clergy plainly contradicts the word of God in 1 Timothy 3 and Titus 1, where God explicitly *permits* bishops to be married, indeed expects, as the rule, that they *will be* married.

Since the Roman law contravenes "all equity," as well as Scripture, it "has also brought in a sink of iniquities" in the sexually scandalous lives of the Roman Catholic clergy.[261] The widespread buggery of Roman Catholic bishops and priests uncovered and publicized at the turn of the twenty-first century demonstrates the truth of Calvin's charge.

A little later in the *Institutes*, when he is critiquing the monastic vow of celibacy, Calvin notes shrewdly that "celibacy is one thing, virginity another!"[262]

Those who "disgrace[d] . . . the ancient church" by introducing the celibacy of the clergy were "superstitious little fellows who dream[ed] up something new to win admiration for themselves."[263]

To the Roman Catholic prohibition of marriage for its clergy, Calvin rightly applies the searing condemnation of 1 Timothy 4:1–5: "doctrine of devils."[264]

Calvin exposes the evil of Rome's law forbidding marriage to its clergy, and indicates the judgment of God on this foolish and wicked law, in detail in his commentary on 1 Corinthians 7:7:

> After celibacy had begun to be so much esteemed, many, vying with each other, rashly vowed perpetual continency, while scarcely the hundredth part of them were endowed with the

power and gift. Hence, too, a *third* [error] sprung up—that the ministers of the church were forbidden to enter into marriage, as a kind of life unbecoming the holiness of their order. As for those who, despising marriage, rashly vowed perpetual continency, God punished their presumption, first, by the secret flames of lust, and then afterwards, by horrible acts of filthiness. The ministers of the Churches being prohibited from lawful marriage, the consequence of this tyranny was, that the Church was robbed of very many good and faithful ministers; for pious and prudent men would not insnare themselves in this way. At length, after a long course of time, lusts, which had been previously kept under, gave forth their abominable odour. It was reckoned a small matter for those, in whom it would have been a capital crime to have a wife, to maintain with impunity concubines, that is, prostitutes; but no house was safe from the impurities of the priests. Even that was reckoned a small matter; for there sprung up monstrous enormities, which it were better to bury in eternal oblivion than to make mention of them by way of examples.[265]

In response to the disparagement of marriage implied in the prohibition of marriage to the clergy, Calvin praises marriage highly. It is "an image of his [Christ's] sacred union with the church [Eph. 5:23, 24, 32]."[266]

The subject of vows comes up in Calvin's treatment of church power in that members of the Roman Catholic Church, already burdened by the extrabiblical laws of their church, "further...seek [their] own burdens" for themselves by making rash vows.[267] Adding to and departing from the "simple obedience of his [God's] will"[268] as fully revealed in Scripture, the making of and attempting to keep rash vows is another instance of "feigned acts of worship, which we ourselves invent to deceive God's favor," and which "are not at all acceptable to him, no matter how well they may please us."[269]

A vow is a "promise...with respect to God."[270]

A rash, superstitious, or unlawful vow is such a promise either made apart from God's word; or made contrary to one's ability to keep it or to one's God-given calling; or made with a sinful intention, for example, to merit salvation.

Calvin thinks that Jephthah's vow in Judges 11 was "rash."[271]

Although the Roman Catholic Church is full of unlawful vows, including a vow to abstain from meat on certain days and vows regarding pilgrimages—"counterfeit worship"[272]—Calvin singles out the vows of the monks for particular and damning criticism.

With their vows, the monks intend "to establish a new and forged worship to merit God's favor."[273] The vows of the monks "invent any mode of life they please without regard to God's call, and without his approval."[274] Here Calvin has in mind the monks' promise of "perpetual virginity to God," in contempt of God's revelation in 1 Corinthians 7:9 that those who do not have the special gift of continence should marry—a continence not only of the body, but also of the mind.[275] The judgment of God upon this monkish disregard of both Scripture and created human nature is that "you will scarcely find one in ten [monasteries] which is not a brothel rather than a sanctuary of chastity."[276]

Calvin has also in mind another gross evil of monasticism, an evil that is seldom noted but that is every bit as grievous a rebellion against "God's call" as the willful vow of celibacy. Indeed, by this criticism Calvin strikes at the heart of monasticism. Monasticism is schismatic. The monks and nuns separate themselves from the life of the church, which is the communion of saints. "All those who enter into the monastic community break with the church. Why? Do they not separate themselves from the lawful society of believers, in adopting a peculiar ministry and a private administration of the sacraments? If this is not to break the communion of the church, what is?"[277]

By his vows the monk not only separates himself from the church, but he also shrugs off God's calling of his people that they serve him *in* the everyday life and work of this world, not by fleeing out of the world.

> God prefers devoted care in ruling a household, where the devout householder, clear and free of all greed, ambition, and other lusts of the flesh, keeps before him the purpose of serving God in a definite calling. It is a beautiful thing to philosophize

in retirement, far from intercourse with men. But it is not the part of Christian meekness, as if in hatred of the human race, to flee to the desert and the wilderness and at the same time to forsake those duties which the Lord has especially commanded.[278]

In this criticism of monasticism, Calvin proclaims the important Reformation doctrine that all believers are called of God to his service and that this service takes place in all the ordinances and spheres of earthly life.

Adding to the wickedness of the vows of the monks (to say nothing of their folly) is that the monks suppose that their way of life is "more perfect...than the common one committed by God to the whole church."[279] Regarding Christ's commands in Matthew 5, which they call "the evangelical counsels,"[280] as law only for themselves, not for the common people, the monks "dignify their order alone with the title of perfection."[281] Calvin exposes this arrogance by pointing out that all Christians "must of necessity obey every little word uttered by Christ."[282]

In the light of all these evils, by their rash and unlawful vows the monks "are consecrated not to God but to an evil spirit."[283]

By no means, however, does Calvin exclude (lawful) vows from the Christian life.

With penetrating insight into Scripture, as well as into the nature of the Christian life, Calvin teaches that "all believers have one common vow...made in baptism." This is the promise of "obedience." This vow is then "sanction[ed] by catechism and receiving the Lord's Supper."[284]

There is also place in the life of the Christian for particular, special vows, if only the Christian makes his vow with the right intention, according to the word of God, and having due regard for his ability and calling. Calvin gives several examples, including promising God some "votive offering" for a past deliverance and promising more diligent exercise of piety.[285]

All "unlawful or improperly conceived vows...are...invalid for us." They may and ought to be rescinded.[286]

The sacraments

Calvin's explanation and defense of that aspect of the doctrine of the church consisting of the truth of the sacraments are lengthy. The treatment of the sacraments takes up six chapters and, in the McNeill/Battles edition of the *Institutes*, some two hundred pages.

Calvin was followed in this lengthy, thorough treatment of the sacraments by the Heidelberg Catechism, which devotes six long Lord's Days and eighteen questions and answers to the subject.

One should be cautious about criticizing this lengthy treatment as "inordinate" and dismissing it as explicable only in view of the ecclesiastical circumstances and doctrinal controversies in Calvin's day. One should be cautious about such criticism and dismissal especially in the twenty-first century.

For, first, Calvin's long and thorough explanation of the sacraments expresses the high view that the Reformed faith has always had of the sacraments. By no means does the Reformed emphasis on the word, particularly the word preached, imply any disparagement of the sacraments.

Second, the doctrinal controversies over the sacraments that Calvin necessarily engaged in for the sake of maintaining one of the marks of the true church—"pure administration of the sacraments as instituted by Christ"[287]—continue unresolved, unchanged, and unabated for Reformed churches, pastors, and theologians in the twenty-first century. There are the controversies of the Reformed faith with the fundamentalists (mostly Baptists), the modern Anabaptists; with Lutheran doctrine; and with the Roman Catholic sacramental doctrine.

In the third place, what makes a serious study of Calvin's long and detailed treatment of the sacraments worthwhile, if not necessary, for Reformed people in the twenty-first century are the weaknesses, ignorance, and errors concerning the sacraments in the Reformed churches themselves. Under the influence of a false ecumenical spirit, some Reformed churches minimize the seriousness of the Baptist condemnation of infant baptism; tolerate the Lutheran doctrine of the sacraments; or deny that the Roman Catholic teaching on the sacraments, particularly its doctrine of the mass, is heresy.

Weakness is especially severe with regard to the meaning of the sacrament of baptism in its application to the infants of believers. Reformed churches and theologians sharply disagree among themselves. Some deny that infant baptism signifies the salvation of the baptized children in their infancy. They regard all baptized children as unregenerated and unsaved, regardless of their baptism, until some grow up and confess their faith in Christ. Inconsistently, these usually make an exception of the infants who die in infancy and early childhood, regarding these children as regenerated and saved.

Other Reformed churches and theologians teach that the meaning of infant baptism is that all the baptized children without exception are alike savingly united to Christ in the spiritual bond of the covenant of grace, if not by the efficacy of the sacrament of baptism, then in closest connection with the sacrament. All alike begin to share in Christ and his salvation. This doctrine of infant baptism implies, indeed strongly emphasizes, the possibility of the falling away to damnation of many of the children who were once united to Christ and were once the recipients of his covenantal grace. This is the doctrine of the theological movement that calls itself the federal (covenant) vision. The doctrine is the development of the teaching of God's gracious establishment of a conditional covenant with all the children of believers alike.

Still other Reformed churches so belittle the sacrament of baptism in its administration to the children of godly parents that they permit professing and practicing Baptists to be members in good standing of the congregations and denomination. These churches then aggravate their violation of the "pure administration of the sacrament as instituted by Christ" by replacing Christ's sacrament of baptism with a man-made ceremony of "dedication" in the case of the infants of the Baptist members. This is an audacious move on the part of a Reformed church. It comes perilously close to being the sin of Rome of adding sacraments to those instituted by Christ, if, in fact, it is not this sin. This is nothing less than rebellion against the lordship of Christ in and over his church. Indeed, in one respect it is worse than Rome's sin. Not only does it add a ceremony—a quasi-sacrament—that has no basis in Scripture, but it also replaces Christ's sacrament of baptism administered to the infant members of the church with the man-made substitute. This, even Rome does not dare to do.

Reformed theologians, ministers, ruling elders, and members do well to read carefully, study intently, and take to heart Calvin's long treatment of the sacraments.

One might correct Calvin's arrangement of the treatment of related subjects at the point at which Calvin explains the sacraments. There is no separate, concentrated explanation of the preaching of the word of God, which, with the sacraments, makes up the important subject of the means of grace in the church. Both the Heidelberg Catechism and the Belgic Confession of Faith show the same lack. There are Lord's Days and chapters devoted to the sacraments, but none devoted to the preaching of the gospel.

That Calvin chooses not to explain the preaching in a separate chapter is no indication of any lack of treatment of the preaching in the *Institutes* or of any minimizing of the importance of preaching in comparison with the sacraments.

Calvin chooses to explain the preaching of the word in connection with his exposition of all the aspects of the truth and reality of the church, especially the marks of the church and the power of the church. In his explanation of preaching, scattered throughout the fourth book of the *Institutes*, Calvin makes plain that he has the highest estimation of preaching as the very voice of Christ and that he regards the preaching of the pure doctrine of the gospel as the chief mark of the true church and the main means by which Christ gathers and builds up his church and bestows faith and salvation upon the elect members of the church.

The importance of preaching for Calvin was evident in the man's own ministry. It was a ministry of preaching.

That the sacraments are secondary (after the preaching), that the sacraments depend upon the preaching for their meaning and power, and that the sacraments function only in connection with preaching, Calvin expresses in the line with which he opens his explanation of the sacraments: "We have in the sacraments another aid to our faith related to the preaching of the gospel."[288]

Almost at once in his explanation of a sacrament, Calvin affirms that it is the "preached" word that alone makes "us understand what the visible sign [of the sacraments] means."[289] Such is the dependency of the sacrament on the preaching that "the sacrament requires preaching to beget faith."²⁹⁰ The "sacramental word" is "the promise, proclaimed in a clear voice by the minister [in contrast to the foreign language and mumbling of the Roman Catholic priest]." This proclamation "lead[s] the people... wherever the sign tends and directs us."²⁹¹

The Reformed Church Order of Dordt is certainly faithful to Calvin, therefore, when, in Article 56 concerning the administration of baptism, it requires that "the covenant of God shall be sealed unto the children of Christians by baptism, as soon as the administration thereof is feasible, in the public assembly when the Word of God is preached" and when, in Article 64 concerning the administration of the Lord's supper, it requires that "the administration of the Lord's Supper shall take place only there where there is supervision of elders, according to the ecclesiastical order, and in a public gathering of the congregation."²⁹²

The order of Calvin's consideration of the sacraments is, first, the nature of sacraments generally; next, the sacrament of baptism, with particular attention paid to infant baptism; then, the Lord's supper; next, a separate critique of Rome's doctrine of the papal mass; and, finally, an examination of the five ceremonies of the Roman Catholic Church, falsely termed sacraments.

Calvin begins his explanation of the Reformed doctrine of the sacraments with a definition.

Calvin's "simple and proper definition" of a sacrament is this: "an outward sign by which the Lord seals on our consciences the promises of his good will toward us in order to sustain the weakness of our faith; and we in turn attest our piety toward him in the presence of the Lord and of his angels and before men."²⁹³ In the 1536 *Institutes* Calvin had proposed two briefer definitions with the longer definition that would find its way into the final edition. One was "a testimony of God's grace, declared to us by an outward sign."²⁹⁴ The other was "ceremonies by which the Lord wills to exercise and confirm the faith of his people."²⁹⁵

In his insistence that the true church is clearly marked by the word and sacraments instituted by Christ, Calvin has earlier intimated that the church's sacraments must have been ordained as such by Christ, as revealed by Scripture. In his subsequent treatment of each of the two sacraments of the New Testament separately, Calvin affirms that a ceremony in the church is a sacrament by virtue of Christ's having instituted it. Especially in his controversy with Rome over their five spurious "sacraments," Calvin emphasizes the necessity of the ordaining of a sacrament by the Lord Christ. "The decision to establish a sacrament rests with God alone... Man cannot establish a sacrament... the Word of God must precede, to make a sacrament a sacrament."[296]

In his introductory treatment of sacraments in general, Calvin only states that at the coming of Christ, "two sacraments were instituted which the Christian church now uses, Baptism and the Lord's Supper [Matt. 28:19; 26:26–28]."[297]

Sacraments add nothing to the promise of the gospel. They "have the same office as the Word of God: to offer and set forth Christ to us, and in him the treasures of heavenly grace."[298] Christ is the "matter or (if you prefer) the substance of all the sacraments; for in him they have all their firmness, and they do not promise anything apart from him."[299] But "the sacraments... have this characteristic over and above the word because they represent them [the promises of the gospel] for us as painted in a picture from life."[300] A sacrament is "Augustine['s] ... 'visible word.'"[301]

Sacraments are also seals in that, like government stamps on official documents, they confirm "and in a sense ratify" to us the promise of the word of God. "Properly speaking," sacraments do not confirm the promise, for the word of God is "firm and sure enough," but our "slight and feeble" faith.[302]

This is the saving function of the sacraments: to strengthen the weak faith of the believing child of God. Calvin "assign[s] this particular ministry to the sacraments": "the confirmation and increase of faith."[303]

The sacraments, therefore, are means, or instruments, of the grace of God.

Calvin rejects the Anabaptist doctrine that the sacraments are merely signs of the confession of Christ by the one who is baptized. The chief function of the sacraments is not to express "our confession before men," but to be a means by which the grace of God in Christ "serve[s] our faith before God."[304]

The power of the grace that works by means of the sacraments, however, is not inherent in the sacraments themselves. As he opposes the error that reduces the sacraments to empty signs, particularly of our confession of Christ, so Calvin also opposes the error "on the opposite side" that "attach[es] to the sacraments some sort of secret powers."[305] This latter error is the Roman Catholic doctrine of the sacraments. According to Rome, the sacraments "justify and confer grace" simply by virtue of the performance of the ceremony by the Roman clergy, "provided we do not set up a barrier of mortal sin."[306] Calvin quotes the Latin phrase by which Rome describes its doctrine of the working of sacramental grace: "*opus operatum*," that is, by the performance of the work (ceremony).[307]

This Roman Catholic doctrine of the sacraments is "deadly and pestilential... Of a certainty it is diabolical."[308] It promises righteousness apart from faith and causes "men's pitiable minds" to trust for righteousness and salvation in outward ceremonies and a "physical thing rather than in God himself."[309]

In this preliminary criticism, Calvin exposes and lays waste the whole of Roman Catholic sacramental theology and, since its sacramental theology is fundamental to that church, the Roman Catholic Church itself. Rome's doctrine of the sacraments remains unchanged to the present.

The power of the saving operation of the sacraments, as also of the preaching of the gospel, is the sovereign, free Spirit of Jesus Christ. Here, Calvin again shows himself to be "the theologian of the Holy Spirit." Recognition of the agency of the Spirit is especially significant in Calvin's, and the Reformed faith's, doctrine of the sacraments. "The sacraments properly fulfill their office only when the Spirit, that inward teacher, comes to them, by whose power alone hearts are penetrated and affections moved and our souls opened for the sacraments to enter in."[310] The sacraments are of no "benefit unless the Holy Spirit accompanies them."[311]

The work of grace by means of the sacraments must be viewed in the light of the whole of the truth of the saving work of God in Christ. This truth is that "the Holy Spirit... is he who brings the graces of God with him." Accordingly, it is the Holy Spirit who "gives a place for the sacraments among us and makes them bear fruit."[312]

And the Spirit's work by means of the sacraments is emphatically a saving work. Sacraments are means of grace. The Spirit convinces us that it is God speaking to us in the word of the gospel and the word of the sacraments, so that we give God "that obedience" which is his due, namely, faith. Also, "the Spirit transmits those outward words and sacraments from our ears to our soul."[313] The Spirit gives us Christ himself, who is the "matter," or "substance," of the sacraments: "They [the benefits of salvation, which the sacraments signify] are conferred through the Holy Spirit, who makes us partakers in Christ; conferred, indeed, with the help of outward signs, if they allure us to Christ."[314]

"If they allure us to Christ"! Calvin is emphatic that the sacraments do not bestow grace on all who use them. Calvin quotes Augustine approvingly: "The sacraments [are] common to all, [but] grace [is] not common—which is the power of the sacraments."[315] The sacraments "avail and profit nothing unless received in faith."[316]

It is of vital importance in this connection, writes Calvin, sharply to distinguish the "matter" of the sacrament from the "sign." The translation of the *Institutes* by John Allen has, "The thing signified ought always to be distinguished from the sign."[317] Although the sign—the water of baptism and the bread and wine of the Lord's supper—and the "matter" or "thing signified"—Christ and his spiritual salvation—are "linked" in the sacrament, they can be, and in the case of many who use the sacraments often are, "separated."[318] Many receive the sign who do not receive Christ and his salvation.

Ultimately, the Spirit's giving of grace by means of the sacraments is determined by God's eternal election. Calvin quotes Augustine: "In the elect alone the sacraments effect what they represent."[319] Contending against the Roman Catholic doctrine that teaches that the sacraments bestow grace on all by virtue of the performance of the ceremony, Calvin declares that the Lord Jesus "exclusively bestows" the Holy Spirit, who is the one who "brings the graces of God with him," "on his own people." "The sacraments do not bring [the Holy Spirit] indiscriminately to all men."[320]

It is the Reformed faith of John Calvin that the grace of God in Christ in both the preaching of the gospel and the sacraments is particular and that the particularity of grace is determined by God's eternal election.

Although the sacraments are primarily testimonies and means of God's good will toward elect believers, they are also, secondarily, "marks of profession, by which we openly swear allegiance to God, binding ourselves in fealty to him."[321] Thus sacraments are signs of the covenant. By the sacraments "God leagues himself with us, and we pledge ourselves to [God in] purity and holiness of life."[322]

The sacrament of baptism

In his explanation of the sacraments generally, Calvin succinctly describes the significance of baptism as cleansing: "Baptism attests to us that we have been cleansed and washed."[323]

When he comes to treat baptism in particular, Calvin describes the significance of the sacrament more fully: "Baptism is the sign of the initiation by which we are received into the society of the church, in order that, engrafted in Christ, we may be reckoned among God's children."[324]

Fundamental to Calvin's theology, as to the confessional Reformed faith, is union with Christ.

As Calvin has already established concerning both sacraments, baptism is primarily a means by which God gives grace to believers. As Calvin expresses it, baptism "serve[s] our faith."[325] Those (the Anabaptists of Calvin's day and the Baptists of ours) who regard baptism as nothing but a sign of one's confession of Christ "have not weighed what was the chief point of baptism."[326] Calvin appeals to Mark 16:16: "He that believeth and is baptized shall be saved."

Calvin distinguishes three outstanding benefits of salvation that baptism both shows us and "brings...to our faith," and brings to our faith by showing us.[327]

On the basis of Ephesians 5:26, Titus 3:5, and 1 Peter 3:21, Calvin identifies the first benefit as the forgiveness of sins. Baptism is a sign and seal of the washing away of sins, first of all, as the remission of sins. By means of this sacrament, attached to the promise of the gospel, we have "the knowledge and certainty" of forgiveness.[328]

Nor does baptism avail for the forgiveness only of those sins committed before baptism, an error that caused some in the early church to postpone baptism to "their last gasp." Rather, it signifies, and "serves faith" regarding, the forgiveness of sins throughout one's entire life. "At whatever time we are baptized, we are once for all washed and purged for our whole life."[329]

The practical implication of this lifelong significance and use of baptism is that we should always be remembering our baptism. "As often as we fall away, we ought to recall the memory of our baptism and fortify our mind with it, that we may always be sure and confident of the forgiveness of sins."[330] Indeed, whenever we are "troubled by a consciousness of [our] faults, [we] may venture to remind [ourselves] of [our] baptism."[331] Thus we are assured of forgiveness.

Calvin repudiates the Roman Catholic sacrament of "penance," which purports to forgive sins committed after baptism—something to which he will return when he criticizes Rome's spurious sacraments. "As if baptism itself were not the sacrament of penance."[332]

With regard to this benefit of baptism, Calvin expresses the truth that the grace of the sacraments is particular in a pastoral, practical way. The cleansing of forgiveness, testified and bestowed by baptism, "is only given to sinners who groan, wearied and oppressed by their own sins... To them the mercy of God is offered."[333]

The second benefit brought by baptism is "our mortification in Christ, and new life in him."[334] Calvin bases his teaching on Romans 6:3, 4. This is "the grace of the Holy Spirit to reform us to newness of life." Calvin is referring to the Christian life of holiness as a life of resisting sin and of consecrating oneself to God. Like the gospel itself, baptism signifies, and is a means to realize, both forgiveness and holiness.

The high Calvinistic doctrine of the sacraments is indicated when Calvin declares that baptism does not only admonish us to a holy life. In light of the apostle's teaching in Romans 6, something "far higher" is true of baptism. "Through baptism Christ makes us sharers in his death, that we may be engrafted in it."[335] In baptism is a mighty, saving power. By baptism, the Lord "does not feed our eyes with a mere appearance only, but leads us to the present reality and effectively performs what it symbolizes."[336]

Lest one suppose that this power is inherent in the sacrament and that it therefore works the saving work in all who use the sacrament, Calvin immediately adds, "So those who receive baptism with right faith truly feel the effective working of Christ's death in the mortification of their flesh, together with the working of his resurrection in the vivification of the Spirit."[337] A little later Calvin will say, "From this sacrament, as from all others, we obtain only as much as we receive in faith."[338]

In the 1536 *Institutes*, Calvin freely admits that his own baptism as a child in the Roman Catholic Church "benefited [him] not at all" as long as he was unbelieving. It only began to benefit him, by means of the promise made to him in baptism, when God fulfilled this promise by giving him faith.[339]

The third distinct benefit of baptism is that we are "so united to Christ himself that we become sharers in all his blessings." The idea is that we are assured of union with Christ and experience this union by believing reception of baptism's "sure testimony" to us of this union.[340]

Because Christ is "the proper object of baptism," the book of Acts (for example, Acts 8:16 and Acts 19:5) mentions that the apostles baptized in Christ's name. They did not disobey Christ's own instruction to baptize in the name of the triune God, but because Christ is the revelation of the triune God in his covenant mercy and salvation, baptizing in the name of the triune God amounts to baptizing in the name of Jesus Christ.[341]

Convinced as he is of the unity of the covenant in the Old and New Testaments, as of the fundamental importance of this unity, Calvin is at pains to instruct his readers that baptism was foreshadowed in the Old Testament. As Paul teaches in 1 Corinthians 10:1, 2, God's people were baptized in the cloud and in the Red Sea. The significance was the same as that of baptism—a spiritual significance. The meaning of the cloud's covering Israel, and giving coolness from "the merciless heat of the sun," was, in reality, being "covered and protected by Christ's blood, that God's severity, which is truly an unbearable flame, should not assail us."[342]

This explanation of Old Testament events and things, which Paul calls "types" in 1 Corinthians 10:6 (AV: "examples"), expresses Calvin's, and the Reformed faith's, understanding of the relation between the Old Testament and the New Testament, as well as his, and the Reformed faith's, theory of the right interpretation of Old Testament history and prophecy. Calvin has described this understanding and interpretation earlier, with specific reference to the ceremonies of the Old Testament. With appeal to Colossians 2:17 and to Hebrews 7–9, Calvin says,

The whole matter comes to this: first, all the pomp of ceremonies which was in the law of Moses, unless it be directed to Christ, is a fleeting and worthless thing; secondly, they looked to Christ in such a way that, when he was at length revealed in the flesh, they had their fulfillment; lastly, it was fitting that they should be abrogated by his coming, just as shadows vanish in the clear light of the sun.[343]

The Old Testament is fulfilled spiritually in Jesus Christ—in his spiritual kingdom and covenant; in his spiritual people, the church; and in his spiritual salvation.

Contrary to the teaching of Rome, baptism does not deliver God's people from original sin. That is, the sacrament does not abolish in them "the corruption that descended from Adam into all his posterity" and restore to them "the same righteousness and purity of nature" that Adam had before the fall.[344]

Such is the sinful corruption of the old human nature that remains in the regenerated, baptized, believing child of God all his earthly life that "the whole man is of himself nothing but [sinful] concupiscence."[345] This corrupt nature is "properly called 'sin' in the Scriptures."[346] All sinful works originate from this source, like sparks from a "glowing furnace,"[347] and should be called "fruits of sin."[348]

Baptism does indeed signify and give assurance of the forgiveness of original sin, as of all one's other guilt. But baptism does not promise that our inherited perversity of nature "no longer exists or gives us trouble" in this life, any more than the gospel promises this. Rather, baptism promises that the power of sin in us will "not overcome us," will not "dominate or rule."[349] In proof of his assertion that baptism promises, not the eradication of sin, but that sin will not rule, Calvin adduces Romans 6:12, 14.

The Belgic Confession follows Calvin closely regarding original sin:

> Nor is it [original sin] by any means abolished or done away by baptism; since sin always issues forth from this woful [should be woeful] source, as water from a fountain: notwithstanding it is not imputed to the children of God unto condemnation, but by his grace and mercy is forgiven them.[350]

That a regenerated, baptized believer retains his "depravity of nature" as long as he lives, Calvin proves from Romans 7:14–25. In this passage, which climaxes in the lament, "O wretched man that I am!" (v. 24), Paul is describing the spiritual experience of a "regenerated man, that is, [Paul] himself."[351] It is the regenerated believer, not the unregenerated unbeliever, who has a "perpetual conflict with the vestiges of his flesh."[352] This conflict causes the believer to humble himself, confessing his "weakness and misery." This conflict also sends him to Christ for "consolation": "Who shall deliver me from the body of this death?" (v. 24). Calvin is certainly right when he analyzes his explanation of Romans 7 as "the simple and genuine interpretation of Paul."[353]

Those professing Calvinists today who deny that Paul in Romans 7 describes the spiritual condition of all regenerated believers throughout their earthly life break with Calvin; necessarily embrace the Arminian heresy (the man of Romans 7 wills the good and delights in the law of God); oppress the believer whose experience is that of Romans 7 (with the implicit charge that he is not regenerated); and virtually adopt the Roman Catholic heresy that baptism *does*, in fact, eradicate the "depravity of nature" that presses from the soul of a godly man, "O wretched man that I am."

Although this is not the main end of baptism, much less the only purpose of God with the sacrament, baptism also "serves as our confession before men." By baptism "we openly affirm our faith" in Christ.[354]

Our thinking on our baptism all our life long, therefore, is not only a constant assurance of the washing away of our sins and our union with Christ, but also a daily reminder that we can "no longer confess any other but Christ alone."[355]

Against the "Donatists" and the "Catabaptists" (Calvin's name for the Anabaptists), Calvin holds that "the force and value" of baptism do not depend on "the worth of the minister." The institution of baptism is "of God."[356] We are baptized into the name of the triune God, not into the name of any man.

Because the "authority of Christ alone" must govern the sacraments and their proper observance, Calvin condemns all man-made additions to the ceremony.[357] The ceremony, "which came from God, its author," must not be "buried in outlandish pollutions."[358] Calvin is taking dead aim at the "theatrical pomp" with which Rome "dazzles the eyes of the simple and deadens their minds."[359]

The mode of baptism is "of no importance," whether immersion, sprinkling, or some other manner of applying water.[360]

In condemning the practice of permitting laymen, and even women, to baptize one who is in danger of dying unbaptized, usually a little child, Calvin contends that only ordained ministers may baptize. In Matthew 28:19, Christ "ordained the same men as heralds of the gospel and ministers of baptism."[361] Calvin approves the position that "it is a mockery to give women the right to baptize." Baptism by women is a "corrupt practice... [and] inexcusable under any pretext."[362] Calvin's "any pretext" includes the extraordinarily daring modern one of putting women in the office of minister of the word and sacraments in flagrant disobedience of the Lord's prohibition in 1 Timothy 2 and 3 and other passages of Scripture.

A hasty baptism of a baby in danger of dying is completely unnecessary. That which renders a hasty baptism unnecessary is God's covenant promise in Genesis 17:7 "that he adopts our babies as his own before they are born... Their salvation is embraced in this word. No one will dare be so insolent toward God as to deny that his promise of itself suffices for its effect."[363] The sacrament of baptism is not necessary for salvation, particularly regarding infants who die unbaptized. "The grace of regeneration" is not dependent upon the sacrament.[364]

In this way, Calvin's treatment of baptism leads naturally to a defense of infant baptism, as an "appendix."[365]

Infant baptism

Calvin's defense of the Reformed doctrine and practice of infant baptism is occasioned by the vehement attack on the doctrine by the Anabaptists. Insisting on the exclusive baptism of adults, upon their confession of faith, the Anabaptists charge that infant baptism "is not founded upon any institution of God."[366] Inasmuch as Calvin teaches that a sacrament must "rest upon the sure foundation of God's Word," Calvin must, and does, take seriously the attack of the Anabaptists upon infant baptism.[367]

Calvin names one of his Anabaptist adversaries: "Servetus... the great glory of that tribe."[368] The rest of the Anabaptists, Calvin dismisses as Servetus' "little Anabaptist brothers."[369]

It is evident, both from their rejection of infant baptism and from the arguments they use against infant baptism, that all contemporary Baptists, whether Arminian or "Calvinistic" (as some like to call themselves), are the true spiritual descendants of the Anabaptists with regard to the fundamental truth of infant baptism. Calvin's refutation and condemnation of the Anabaptists of his day, in this regard, apply with equal validity and force to the Baptists of our day.

Calvin mentions two truths that are basic to the issue. One is that baptism has its full significance when applied to infants. It signifies God's work of grace in his elect people: cleansing from sin, rebirth unto holiness, and union with Christ. It also signifies, secondarily, "bearing witness to our religion before men."[370]

Infant baptism may not be reduced to a mere sign of the parents' dedication of their child to God or of the child's belonging formally and outwardly to God. This would be utterly to impoverish the sign and seal of baptism and, thus, to annihilate the sacrament.

The second basic truth is that only infant children of believing parents may, and must, be baptized. Calvin makes this explicit: "Those infants who derive their origin from Christians... are thus to be received into baptism." A child "sprung from impious parents" is not to be baptized until he believes. The child of unbelieving parents "is reckoned an alien to the fellowship of the covenant." To baptize such a child would be completely contrary to the sign of baptism itself since "what is signified would be fallacious and empty in him."[371]

The practice in certain Reformed churches of baptizing the infants of admitted unbelievers disregards the instruction of John Calvin and, as Calvin warns, grossly violates the covenant of God, which is not established with unbelievers' children, but with the children of believers.

Calvin gives one great ground for the baptism of the infant children of believers or, in keeping with 1 Corinthians 7:14, the children of one believer. All of the other arguments for infant baptism are aspects or implications of this one ground. This one ground is the unity of the covenant of God with his people in both the Old and New Testaments. "The covenant is common, and the reason for confirming it is common."[372] "If the covenant still remains firm and steadfast, it applies no less today to the children of Christians than under the Old Testament it pertained to the infants of the Jews."[373]

To the one covenant belongs the oneness of the Old Testament sign and seal of circumcision and the New Testament sacrament of baptism with regard to the all-important promise and meaning of both. Calvin demonstrates from Genesis 17, Luke 10:38, Matthew 22:32, Ephesians 2:12, Deuteronomy 10:15, 16, Deuteronomy 30:6, Jeremiah 4:4, Ezekiel 16:30, and Genesis 12:2, 3 that the promise and meaning of circumcision were the same as the promise and meaning of baptism. His conclusion is that, in one and the same covenant, if the sign of the covenant and its spiritual blessings were given to infants in the Old Testament, the sign of the same covenant and spiritual blessings ought to be given to infants in the New Testament. "A right consideration of signs does not rest solely in external ceremonies, but depends chiefly upon the promise and the spiritual mysteries, which the Lord ordains the ceremonies themselves to represent."[374]

When he refutes the arguments of the Anabaptists against infant baptism, Calvin appeals to Colossians 2:12 in support of the truth "that baptism is for the Christians what circumcision previously was for the Jews." "[Baptism and circumcision] signify one and the same thing."[375]

Calvin observes in this connection that to debar infants from the covenant in the New Testament, when they were included in the Old Testament, would mean that Christ "lessened or curtailed the grace of the Father"—something Calvin regards as "execrable blasphemy!"[376]

That this, in fact, is not the case, Calvin proves from an incident in the ministry of Jesus and from the common practice of the apostles. According to Matthew 19:13–15 and the parallel passage in Luke 18:15, Jesus called to himself and blessed infant children as citizens of the kingdom of heaven. "If it is right for infants to be brought to Christ, why not also to be received into baptism, the symbol of our communion and fellowship with Christ?"[377]

And the apostles regularly baptized households, as the book of Acts records. This answers the "silly objection" that there is no evidence of the apostles' baptizing infants.[378]

A powerful argument, drawn from the unity of the covenant, to which Calvin returns again and again, is that, since infant children have the spiritual reality signified by the sign of baptism (just as circumcised children had the same reality in the Old Testament), they may, and should, have the sign also. "If they are participants in the thing signified, why shall they be debarred from the sign?"[379]

Basic to this argument is Calvin's firm conviction that God gives the infant children of believers the "matter," or "substance," of the sacrament, namely, Jesus Christ and with him the blessings of salvation. God promises Christ and salvation to them. God realizes this promise to them and in them in its "effect," namely, their regeneration by the Spirit of Christ.

This was true of God's dealings with the children of believers in the Old Testament. "The Lord did not deign to have them circumcised without making them participants in all those things which were then signified by circumcision [cf. Gen. 17:12]. Otherwise, he would have mocked his people with mere trickery if he had nursed them on meaningless symbols, which is a dreadful thing even to hear of."[380]

It is no less true in the New Testament.

This argument is rejected today, not only by the Baptists, but also by many Reformed and Presbyterian churches and theologians. They deny the regeneration and salvation of infant children. They insist that parents and church must regard the children as unregenerated and lost until they grow up and confess their faith, that is, when they are no longer children, much less infants. The children themselves are taught to regard themselves as apart from, and without, Christ in the world.

Whereas Calvin argues from the reality of union with Christ, that is, salvation, to the right and necessity of the infants' receiving the sign, this popular, contemporary Reformed doctrine of the children of believers grants the sign but denies the thing signified by the sign. Calvin's response would be that these Reformed churches and theologians have God mocking his people "with mere trickery" by nursing them "on meaningless symbols."

Calvin teaches the regeneration and inner sanctification of infant covenant children by the Holy Spirit—in these children's infancy, before they attain consciousness.

He expressly denies the popular, contemporary Reformed notion that "children are to be considered solely as children of Adam until they reach an appropriate age for the second birth" as Anabaptist error.[381]

Calvin affirms that the infants are alive in Christ, by "communion with him." Against the characteristic Anabaptist position that regeneration requires knowledge, Calvin responds, "Those infants who are to be saved (as some are surely saved from that early age) are previously regenerated by the Lord."[382] A "proof" of this is God's sanctification of John the Baptist in his mother's womb, as revealed by Luke 1:15.[383] Also, "Christ was sanctified from earliest infancy in order that he might sanctify in himself his elect from every age without distinction." Christ's sanctification in infancy is "a proof that the age of infancy is not utterly averse to sanctification."[384]

In the infant children of the covenant, "the seed of both [repentance and faith] lies hidden within them by the secret working of the Spirit."[385]

Calvin explains the holiness of children spoken of in 1 Corinthians 7:14 as "newness of spiritual life...by supernatural grace," that is, as regeneration of the heart.[386]

Calvin considers himself to have established the truth of "the regeneration of infants."[387]

Only this doctrine accounts for the salvation of those infants who die in their infancy, something Calvin heartily believes and teaches.

In the light of Calvin's teaching that the one covenant promise in both testaments, that God will be the God of the children of believers, expresses that as a rule God will actually save the children in their infancy, we can better understand a statement Calvin makes at the end of his earlier treatment of the sacrament of baptism. Calvin is contending with those who think that unbaptized babies are certainly lost and that, therefore, even women should be permitted to baptize babies who are in danger of dying. Calvin then quotes the covenant promise of Genesis 17:7: "I will establish my covenant between me and thee and thy seed after thee in their generations for an everlasting covenant to be a God unto thee, and to thy seed after thee." Calvin gives this explanation of the covenant promise: "Their [our babies'] salvation is embraced in this word. No one will dare be so insolent toward God as to deny that his promise of itself suffices for its effect."[388]

Two vitally important truths are expressed, to which attention must be paid not only by Roman Catholics who suppose that "without baptism [dying babies are] deprived of the grace of regeneration," but also by Reformed churches and theologians who differ sharply with Calvin on these truths.

The first is that God's promise, "I will be the God of your children," "suffices for," that is, by itself certainly and efficaciously realizes, its effect, namely, the covenant salvation of the children in union with Christ. Of extraordinary importance, especially regarding God's covenant promise to the children of believers, is the truth that the promise of God does not consist merely of a willingness on God's part to save, but consists also of the "effect"—the realization—of the promise. And this "effect" is not conditioned by the work or will of the infant child, but depends solely upon the will and work of the promising God.

The second truth is that the covenant promise to infants "suffices for its effect" in the salvation of these infants, *as infants*.

To the objection that many physical children of believers, like many physical children of Abraham in the Old Testament, are not regenerated and saved, whether in infancy or adulthood, the answer is, first, that Calvin has already established, in the section of the *Institutes* that treats predestination, that all of God's saving work in Christ has its source in, and is governed by, election. Many of the texts that Calvin adduces in proof of election, particularly the passages in Romans 9–11, apply specifically to the covenant promise and covenant salvation.

In addition, Calvin makes clear in his treatment of infant baptism that the children of the covenant promise, whose regeneration in infancy or early childhood, as a rule, is implied by the promise and by the sign of baptism, are not all the physical children of believers, but the elect among them.

> If those whom the Lord has deigned to elect received the sign of regeneration but depart from the present life before they grow up, he renews them by the power, incomprehensible to us, of his Spirit, in whatever way he alone foresees will be expedient. If they happen to grow to an age at which they can be taught the truth of baptism, they shall be fired with greater zeal for renewal, from learning that they were given the token of it in their first infancy in order that they might meditate upon it throughout life.[389]

This one ground for infant baptism—the unity of the covenant including the replacement of circumcision by baptism—is conclusive against the Anabaptists. "This one reason...would be quite enough to refute all those who would speak in opposition" to infant baptism.[390]

The Anabaptist arguments against infant baptism, Calvin refutes, one by one. To the argument that circumcision had a different meaning than the spiritual meaning of baptism, Calvin replies that this argument implies two different covenants, which is to "dissipate and corrupt Scripture." In this case, the Jews were "carnal." God gave them merely earthly benefits "as men fatten a herd of swine in a sty."[391]

To the argument that infants cannot repent and believe, Calvin responds by affirming that infants are "baptized into future repentance and faith."[392]

Against the Anabaptist argument that Matthew 28:19 and the book of Acts require faith prior to baptism, Calvin responds that Christ prescribed, and the apostles followed, the rule in the case of adults. "Infants," however, "ought to be put in another category."[393]

Yet another Anabaptist argument is of special interest to Reformed churches in the twenty-first century in view of the promotion by some Reformed theologians of child, and even infant, communion, that is, the participation in the sacrament of the Lord's supper by little children ("paedo-communion"). The Anabaptists argued from the exclusion of infants from the supper to their exclusion also from baptism. The present-day advocates of child-communion argue from the inclusion of infants in the sacrament of baptism to their inclusion also in the Lord's supper. Both make the same mistake: they do not take into account the difference between the two sacraments.

Calvin's refutation of the Anabaptists in this regard is also the refutation of paedo-communion. He insists on a "wide difference" between the two sacraments. One signifies spiritual birth, in which one is passive; the other signifies nourishment with "solid food," which is fitting for "older persons." Calvin shows from 1 Corinthians 11:23–29 that participation in the supper requires discernment of the body and blood of the Lord, self-examination, and the understanding necessary to proclaim the Lord's death. In light of the sharp warning against an unworthy partaking in 1 Corinthians 11:29, those who give small children the bread and wine of the supper "offer poison instead of life-giving food to our tender children."[394]

Calvin's sharp indictment of the Anabaptists for ignoring the obvious difference between the sacraments passes upon the present-day advocates of paedo-communion as well: "If these men had a particle of sound brain left, would they be blind to a thing so clear and obvious?"[395]

Calvin does not view the denial of infant baptism with the tolerant attitude of many Reformed theologians today. He opens his defense of infant baptism by describing those who deny the doctrine as "frantic spirits" who "grievously disturb...the church."[396] Deniers of infant baptism are "mad beasts [who] ceaselessly assail this holy institution of God."[397] From their denial of baptism to children, it really follows that children who die in infancy and childhood are condemned to eternal death.[398] Calvin reminds those who refuse to administer the sign of the covenant to children of God's warning in Genesis 17:14: "God will wreak vengeance upon any man who disdains to mark his child with the symbol of the covenant."[399] The reason is that "infants cannot be deprived of it [baptism] without open violation of the will of God its author."[400]

In the denial of infant baptism, "Satan...is trying to take away from us the singular fruit of assurance and spiritual joy which is to be gathered from it, and also to diminish somewhat the glory of the divine goodness."[401]

Infant baptism is the cause of thanksgiving and joy to godly parents, "that their offspring are within his care." It is the incentive to parents to "instruct...our children in piety."[402]

Their baptism as infants is also of "benefit" to the children:

> Engrafted into the body of the church, they are somewhat more commended to the other members. Then, when they have grown up, they are greatly spurred to an earnest zeal for worshiping God, by whom they were received as children through a solemn symbol of adoption before they were old enough to recognize him as Father.[403]

Calvin concludes his defense of infant baptism with an urgent exhortation: "Accordingly, unless we wish spitefully to obscure God's goodness, let us offer our infants to him, for he gives them a place among those of his family and household, that is, the members of the church."[404]

The sacrament of the Lord's supper

In his explanation of the sacraments generally, Calvin succinctly describes the significance of the Lord's supper as redemption. "The Eucharistic Supper [attests to us] that we have been redeemed." Whereas the water of baptism represents washing, the blood signified in the supper represents "satisfaction."[405]

When he comes to treat the Lord's supper in particular, Calvin describes the sacrament as a "spiritual banquet wherein Christ attests himself to be the life-giving bread, upon which our souls feed unto true and blessed immortality."[406]

On the basis of Christ's words instituting the sacrament of the supper, Matthew 26:26–28, Mark 14:22–24, Luke 22:19, 20, and 1 Corinthians 11:23–25, and in light of the important passage bearing on the truth of the supper, John 6:43–65, Calvin distinguishes "two things" of which "the Supper consists": the "physical signs" and the "spiritual truth" represented by the signs. Calvin also calls the "spiritual truth" of the supper the "matter," or substance, of the sacrament, as he did in describing the sacrament of baptism.[407]

The signs are the broken bread and the wine, representing and displaying the crucified body and shed blood of Jesus Christ. The "spiritual truth," or "matter," or reality, is Jesus Christ himself (just as is the case with baptism), but Jesus Christ now risen into new, spiritual life, as the one who was crucified for the redemption of his sinful people.

In his explanation of "the sacred mystery of the Supper"[408] "in a way intelligible to the unlearned,"[409] which is the first part of his exposition of the supper, Calvin usually adds a third thing: "the power or effect that follows from" the signs and the "matter." This third thing is "redemption, righteousness, sanctification, and eternal life, and all the other benefits Christ gives to us" by means of the supper.[410]

Although these three aspects of the supper are not to be separated in the believing use of the sacrament, including the preaching that explains the sacrament, neither are they to be confused and thus denied.

The Roman Catholic Church is guilty of this confusion by its teaching that the physical signs become the "matter," or spiritual reality. In this case, no signs remain. And this would simply mean the annihilation of the sacrament, for the sacrament consists essentially in the signs, as well as in the spiritual reality. "The nature of the Sacrament is therefore canceled, unless... the earthly sign corresponds to the heavenly thing. And the truth of this mystery accordingly perishes for us unless true bread represents the true body of Christ."[411]

As a sign, the Lord's supper impresses upon our physical senses, especially sight, the promise of the gospel, namely, that by his death the now risen Lord Jesus Christ has become our "invisible," spiritual food and drink unto life eternal. "The signs are bread and wine, which represent for us the invisible food that we receive from the flesh and blood of Christ."[412]

The sacrament is meaningless and powerless apart from the promise of the gospel, to which it is attached and by which it is explained. Calvin insists regarding the supper, as he has done regarding baptism, that it "cannot stand apart from the Word," that is, the preaching of the gospel. "For whatever benefit may come to us from the Supper requires the Word."[413] Nor does the supper bestow benefits that are not given by means of the preaching. The application to us of the benefits of the death and resurrection of Christ "is done through the gospel but more clearly through the Sacred Supper."[414]

Inasmuch as the sacrament signifies that "Christ is the only food of our soul," the meaning of the supper is "Christ's secret union with the devout."[415] Just as is true of baptism, so also the meaning of the supper is union with Christ. Union with Christ, mysteriously intimate union with Christ, is the essence of salvation.

The supper is also a seal. As a seal, the supper functions to "confirm that promise by which he [Christ] testifies that his flesh is food indeed and his blood is drink [John 6:56], which feed us unto eternal life [John 6:55]."[416] Here already, Calvin indicates that the supper is much more than a mere memorial feast, or even only "a mark of outward profession."[417] The supper is a means of grace. It strengthens faith. The sacrament "assures us that all that Christ did or suffered was done to quicken us; and again, that this quickening is eternal, we being ceaselessly nourished, sustained, and preserved throughout life by it."[418]

As a means of divine grace, the supper truly bestows the spiritual reality—Christ himself and the benefits of his cross—that the signs represent.

At this crucial juncture in his explanation, Calvin warns against "two faults" regarding the doctrine of the Lord's supper. One fault "divorce[s]" the signs—bread and wine—"from their mysteries," that is, the body and blood of Christ. The other fault so "immoderately" extols the signs that it "obscure[s] somewhat the mysteries themselves."[419] Thus by implication does Calvin describe negatively his own, and the Reformed, doctrine of the Lord's supper. It neither wrenches apart the signs and the spiritual reality, nor collapses the spiritual reality into the signs.

The first "fault" hesitates to confess that in the supper one eats Christ's flesh and drinks Christ's blood. According to this error, eating and drinking are simply believing in Christ. Similarly, this error is content to explain that in the supper we are "partakers of the Spirit only, omitting mention of flesh and blood." This fault holds that worthy partakers can and do receive only the signs, without receiving the body and blood of Christ.[420]

Calvin, perhaps surprisingly to some, is at pains to take issue with this doctrine of the supper. Likely, he has Zwingli and his followers in view. However this may be, Zwingli has disciples today, some of whom may suppose that they embrace the Calvinistic doctrine of the supper. By no means does Calvin intend to deny that the manner of eating Christ is "that of faith, as no other can be imagined."[421] In the course of his explanation of the supper, Calvin makes abundantly clear that it is the Holy Spirit who feeds the believer with Christ's body and gives him Christ's blood to drink. But simply to speak of believing, or of partaking of the Spirit, does not do justice to Jesus' words in John 6 and in the instituting of the supper, that "his flesh is truly food, [and] that his blood is truly drink." This explanation does not rise to the "sublimity" of "so great a mystery" as the supper is.[422] Such is the loftiness of the "secret" of the supper that Calvin "rather experience[s] than understand[s] it."[423]

Nevertheless, he has some profound understanding of the mystery of the supper and, therefore, proceeds to explain it. The Reformed churches are immeasurably the richer because of Calvin's God-given understanding.

Christ, who as the Word of God has life in himself and who as the incarnate savior made his flesh and blood the life of his people by his crucifixion and resurrection, does truly feed us unto immortal life "by [our] partaking of him" in the supper.[424] In the supper "Christ truly grows into one with us, and refreshes us by the eating of his flesh and the drinking of his blood," as if by this "sacred partaking of his flesh and blood" the life of Christ "penetrated into our bones and marrow."[425] In the supper, according to Calvin (and the Reformed faith), there is a "true and substantial partaking of the body and blood of the Lord, which is shown to believers under the sacred symbols of the Supper." Correspondingly, believers receive the body and blood of Christ, not "solely by imagination or understanding of mind," but by enjoying "the thing itself as nourishment of eternal life."[426]

By no means, therefore, is the breaking of bread "an empty symbol."[427]

Calvin summarizes the truth of the supper, which he insists is not the doctrine of "common sense" but the doctrine of faith: "Christ descends to us both by outward symbol and by his Spirit, that he may truly quicken our souls by the substance of his flesh and of his blood."[428]

"And by his Spirit"! By these words Calvin both indicates that the mode of partaking of Christ's flesh and blood is spiritual and sharply distinguishes the truth of the supper from the false doctrine of the Roman Catholic Church and Lutheranism.

The fundamental truth regarding the partaking of Christ in the supper, as it is the fundamental issue in the controversy between the Reformed, on the one hand, and the Roman Catholic Church and Lutheranism, on the other hand, is "the *mode* of partaking of him."[429] In his sharp controversy with the Lutheran doctrine of the supper, Calvin insists that the issue between the Lutherans and the Reformed is not the real "presence of flesh in the Supper." The Reformed teach the real presence of Christ—his body and blood—in the sacrament. But "the question is . . . only of the *manner*" of his presence.[430]

The "mode" of Christ's presence in the supper and of the partaking of him is the Holy Spirit. "Christ's flesh, separated from us by such great distance [in heaven, at God's right hand] penetrates to us, so that it becomes our food [in the supper by] . . . the secret power of the Holy

Spirit."[431] "The Lord bestows this benefit [participation in his body] upon us through his Spirit so that we may be made one in body, spirit, and soul with him. The bond of this connection is therefore the Spirit of Christ, with whom we are joined in unity, and is like a channel through which all that Christ himself is and has is conveyed to us."[432] Calvin appeals to Romans 8:9: "But ye are not in the flesh, but in the Spirit, if so be that the Spirit of God dwell in you. Now if any man have not the Spirit of Christ, he is none of his."

In short, "it is through his [the Holy Spirit's] incomprehensible power that we come to partake of Christ's flesh and blood."[433]

The manner of the Christian's eating and drinking Christ's body and blood, therefore, is spiritual, not physical or carnal. "For us the manner [of eating Christ in the supper] is spiritual because the secret power of the Spirit is the bond of our union with Christ."[434] "I say that we eat Christ's flesh in believing, because it is made ours by faith, and that this eating is the result and effect of faith."[435] Lacking the Spirit of Christ, the unbeliever is incapable of eating and drinking Christ. "All those who are devoid of Christ's Spirit can no more eat Christ's flesh than drink wine that has no taste."[436]

This spiritual manner of partaking is in harmony with the human nature of the risen and glorified Christ. "Christ's flesh itself in the mystery of the Supper is a thing no less spiritual than our eternal salvation."[437]

In his controversy with the teaching of both Roman Catholicism and Lutheranism that unbelievers partake of the body and blood of Christ, Calvin declares that the Spirit's gift of Christ's body and blood and the believer's partaking of that body and blood unto life eternal are determined and limited by God's eternal decree of election. He quotes Augustine with approval: "In the elect alone do the sacraments effect what they symbolize."[438]

To unbelievers who do partake of the symbols and, therefore, make themselves guilty of Christ's body and blood (though they never receive the body and blood, but only trample them under foot), the supper is "deadly poison."[439] There is no grace in the sacraments for unbelievers.

Although the chief "use" of the sacrament is to "serve our faith before God" by the Spirit's nourishing and strengthening our faith with

Christ's body and blood, there is also a "second use." This is the congregation's and the believer's "outward confession." Calvin refers to Paul's declaration in 1 Corinthians 11:26 that in administering and celebrating the supper, the church "shew[s] the Lord's death till he come."[440]

There is also a third use of the sacrament, so important in Calvin's judgment that he makes it a third element of the sacrament with the signs and the spiritual reality. This is the sacrament's "exhortation" to those who partake to live in "purity and holiness of life" and in "love, peace, and concord" with each other. The supper makes this exhortation "more forcefully than any other means."[441] Testifying and realizing that those who partake are one body with Christ, and therefore with each other, the supper warns "that none of the brethren can be injured, despised, rejected, abused, or in any way offended by us, without at the same time, injuring, despising, and abusing Christ by the wrongs we do." The supper is, as Augustine said, "the bond of love."[442]

Because Christ is present in the supper with his blessed body and blood and in view of the dreadful judgments threatened upon those who partake of the bread and wine unworthily, self-examination is required of those who will partake worthily, as Paul commands in 1 Corinthians 11:28–34. This examination of oneself concerns whether one trusts confidently upon the salvation purchased by Christ, whether one aspires to holiness, and whether one is resolved to love the brothers and sisters.

Calvin is quick to add (thus again showing his pastoral heart and indeed his pastoral purpose with his instruction in the *Institutes*) that Christ's purpose with self-examination is not the requirement of sinless perfection. In this case, no one may come to the table of the Lord. Calvin condemns those teachers who "torture and harass pitiable consciences" by leaving the impression that a worthy partaker is a perfect, or nearly perfect, church member.[443]

The fact is that the supper is "medicine for the sick, solace for sinners, alms to the poor." The best worthiness to partake is "to offer our vileness and ... our unworthiness to him [God] so that his mercy may make us worthy of him."[444]

True worthiness to partake of the supper "consists chiefly in faith" and "secondly, in love," although also this faith and love are far from perfect. The supper, after all, is not "ordained... for the perfect, but for the weak and feeble," to "exercise" both faith and love.[445]

So far is it from being true that church members who are of age to discern the Lord's body and to conduct requisite self-examination may absent themselves from the supper on the ground of their unworthiness that, on the contrary, they must be disciplined and, thus, cut off from the church. Referring to decisions of assemblies of the early Christian church, Calvin declares that those who "never... communicate [by partaking of the supper] are to be warned; if, after warning, they still abstain, they are to be excluded."[446]

This proper instruction of Calvin (and of the Christian church) to ruling elders applies both to confessing members who, for one reason or another, stubbornly refuse to partake of the supper and to members by baptism who, when they come to years, refuse to confess faith in Christ and in this way disobey Christ's command to the members of his church, "Take, eat!... drink!" (Matt. 26:26, 27).

With regard to the details of the "outward ceremony" of the supper, for example, whether the people handle the bread, whether the bread is leavened or unleavened, and whether the wine is red or white, "these things are indifferent, and left at the church's discretion."[447]

Calvin does condemn Rome's addition of a "great pile of ceremonies" to the simple ceremony instituted by Christ in Scripture. These are nothing but "lifeless and theatrical trifles" intended to stupefy the people.[448]

And he strongly condemns Rome's withholding of the wine from the people. Rome "has either stolen or snatched half the Supper from the greater part of God's people," contrary to the express command of God in Matthew 26:27 and other places.[449] The explanation of Rome's brazen disregard of Christ's will is a fundamental sin of the Roman Catholic Church. "These Antichrists... so readily trample, scatter, and abolish the teaching and ordinances of Christ."[450] Scripture does not rule in Rome.

Calvin urges a weekly celebration of the sacrament of the supper in the Reformed churches. The supper would be "administered most becomingly if it were set before the church very often, and at least once a week."[451] In this matter most Reformed churches have not heeded the reformer, although they have not restricted the administration of the sacrament to once a year—the practice to which Calvin most strenuously objected.[452] It is difficult to escape the impression that, even though they share fully Calvin's doctrine of the sacrament, the Reformed churches that administer the supper only four times a year may lack something of Calvin's high regard for the supper.

The reformer proposes a biblically based liturgy of the worship service at which the supper is administered and the proper order of the elements of the liturgy: public prayer; the sermon; display of the bread and wine with the words of Christ's institution of the supper and the recitation of the promises; barring of the unworthy; a prayer for the Lord's blessing of the administration and use of the sacrament; the singing of psalms or reading of Scripture, evidently as the church partakes; the partaking; an exhortation to faith and love; thanksgiving and praise; the dismissal of the church in peace.[453]

Divorcing the signs of the supper from their spiritual realties is one grave "fault." The second, Calvin tells the reader, is the immoderate "extolling" of the signs, to the obscuring of the spiritual realities.[454] Calvin describes this "error" as "imagining that Christ is attached to the element of bread."[455] Calvin refers to the false doctrine concerning the supper of both the Roman Catholic Church and the Lutherans. Although their doctrines of the supper differ in important respects, both Roman Catholicism and Lutheranism teach a "local presence" of Christ in the sacrament; a physical, or "carnal," eating and drinking of Christ's body and blood; and the eating and drinking of Christ's body and blood by unbelievers.

And Roman Catholicism and Lutheranism are one in their hatred of and ferocious attack on the Reformed doctrine of the supper, with the Lutherans outdoing the Roman Catholics.[456]

Reserving his examination of that aspect of the Roman Catholic doctrine of the supper consisting of the mass for separate treatment, Calvin first subjects Rome's doctrine to critique in the light of Scripture. He establishes that it is the doctrine of Rome that the body of Christ is present in the supper in such a way that it is "touched by the hands...chewed by the teeth, and...swallowed by the mouth." Pope Nicholas dictated these "monstrous" words to Berengarius as the form of his recantation.[457]

Rome's explanation of this "local presence" and carnal partaking is its "fictitious [doctrine of] transubstantiation," which is of such fundamental importance to Rome that "they fight more bitterly [for it] than for all the other articles of their faith."[458] This is the doctrine that by the words of the priest, a "magic incantation"[459] as Calvin views it, there is a "conversion of the bread into the body [of Christ]," as well as a conversion of the wine into Christ's blood. The substance of the bread and wine is "annihilated," to become the substance of the body and blood of Christ.[460]

Everything Calvin has taught about the presence of Christ by the Spirit, a spiritual partaking, the impossibility of the eating of Christ by unbelievers, and a spiritual Christ condemns the doctrine of Rome.

In addition, Calvin points out that the body of Christ, according to Acts 3:21, is in heaven until the second coming, so that the doctrine of a "local presence" in the supper is a denial of Christ's humanity.[461]

In response to Rome's appeal to the words of institution, "This is my body," and demand for a "literal" interpretation, Calvin responds that "is" [*est* in Latin] does not mean "to be converted into something else" in any language.[462] The expression "this [bread] is my body" in Matthew 26:26 is the well-known figure of "metonymy." Because the sign—bread—is consecrated to represent "the thing signified"—the body of Christ—and "also truly exhibits it," the sign (which is always only "physical and visible") may rightly be called by the name of the spiritual reality that it symbolizes (which spiritual reality is "spiritual and heavenly").[463]

This explanation of the words of the institution of the supper holds against the Lutheran interpretation as well.

The effects of the Roman Catholic doctrine are disastrous. The people suppose that a physical presence of Christ and thus physical eating of him are sufficient for salvation, apart from faith in Christ that depends on his word.[464]

The inevitable result of transubstantiation is the worship of the consecrated bread as God and the adoration of Christ in that bread. This is "superstitious worship" and "idolatry."[465]

The Lutheran doctrine likewise attaches Christ's body (which is in heaven) to the bread of the supper; rejects a spiritual presence of Christ and a spiritual partaking by faith; insists on a physical eating and drinking of the body and blood of Christ; and holds that Christ's body and blood are eaten and drunk by unbelievers.

Although the Lutherans reject the Roman Catholic doctrine of the conversion of the bread into the body of Christ (transubstantiation), they too teach a "local presence" of the body of Christ in the bread in the sense that the body of Christ itself is "enclosed underneath" the substance of the bread or is "in the bread."[466] It is characteristic of Lutheran theologians, Calvin notes, to describe the local presence of the body of Christ for a physical eating this way: "The body of Christ is with the bread, in the bread, and under the bread."[467]

Lutheranism's explanation of its teaching that Christ's body can be, and is, present on earth in the bread of the supper wherever the sacrament is administered over all the world is its "monstrous notion of ubiquity." This is the doctrine that Christ's body and, therefore, the human nature of Christ can be "everywhere [present] at once, without limitation of place."[468]

But the doctrine of ubiquity is necessarily a heretical doctrine of Christ.

With reference specifically to Lutheranism's heretical Christology, Calvin remarks that the papists' doctrine of the supper "is more tolerable or at least more modest" than that of the Lutherans.[469] For the Lutheran doctrine of ubiquity of Christ's body implies that Christ is no longer a genuine human, since it is the essential quality of humanity to be limited, including being limited to one place at one time. "Such is the condition of flesh that it must subsist in one definite place, with its own size and form."[470]

By attributing a divine perfection—omnipresence—to the human nature of Jesus, Lutheranism has fallen into the heresy of ancient Eutyches and of modern (in Calvin's day) Servetus. They explain the union of the two natures of Christ as though "that union had compounded from two natures some sort of intermediate being which was neither God nor man."[471]

Lutheranism makes itself guilty of corrupting the Chalcedonian definition of AD 451: "one and the same Christ, Son, Lord, Only-begotten, to be acknowledged in two natures, *inconfusedly, unchangeably, indivisibly, inseparably*; the distinction of natures being by no means taken away by the union, but rather the property of each nature being preserved, and concurring in one Person."[472]

In contrast, Calvin (and the Reformed faith) maintain a clear, clean Chalcedonian orthodoxy: "The one person of Christ so consists of two natures that each nevertheless retains unimpaired its own distinctive character."[473] Christ's human nature, although glorified in the resurrection, remains truly human. Body and soul, it is now in heaven, not on the earth. Christ's real presence in the supper is not a "local presence," as though enclosed in the bread and wine of the supper, but a presence by the secret, mysterious, and wonderful work of the Spirit.

Basic to this Reformed orthodoxy concerning the nature of Christ is the Reformed explanation of the ascension of Christ. In the ascension the man Christ literally went up from the earth to another place, heaven, as Acts 1:9–11 and Acts 3:21 teach. Lutheranism, in the interest of its doctrine of the supper, denies the historical event of the ascension. "Does it [the ascension] not imply moving from one place to another? They deny this."[474]

It is apparent that Calvin is deeply grieved by the bitter attacks on his and the Reformed faith's doctrine of the supper. He laments the slanders of his enemies against him to the effect that he "discredit[s] Christ's words [instituting the supper]," when, in fact, Calvin embraces them no less obediently than they and "treat[s them] with greater reverence."[475] Employing "stubbornness and insults," both the Roman Catholic and Lutheran adversaries of the Reformed doctrine of the Lord's supper "say that to seek any explanation of the words [of the institution of the supper] is to accuse Christ of lying."[476]

Regardless of the slanders of the theological and ecclesiastical enemies of the doctrine of the supper that Calvin marvelously unfolds and vigorously defends, he is confident that "with this partaking of the body, which we have declared, we feed faith just as sumptuously and elegantly as those who draw Christ himself away from heaven."[477]

The papal mass

Because the "papal Mass" is "the height of frightful abomination" with regard to Rome's corruption of the sacrament of the Lord's supper, Calvin treats this aspect of the Roman Catholic doctrine and practice of the supper separately.[478]

The "whole world" knows what the mass is according to Rome: "a work by which the priest who offers up Christ, and the others who participate in the oblation, merit God's favor, or it is an expiatory victim, by which they reconcile God to themselves."[479] The officiating priest sacrifices Christ anew, in an unbloody manner, "to be a kind of appeasement to make satisfaction to God for the expiation of the living and the dead."[480]

Such is the essential importance of the mass to the Roman Catholic Church that "they have steered the whole vessel of their salvation into this one deadly whirlpool."[481]

The wickedness of the mass, and, therefore, of the Roman Catholic Church, is egregious. "Surely, Satan never prepared a stronger engine to besiege and capture Christ's Kingdom."[482]

The mass is "unbearable blasphemy and dishonor... inflicted upon Christ, who... [being] immortal, is the sole and eternal Priest [Heb. 7:17–19]."[483]

The mass "suppresses and buries the cross and Passion of Christ." With appeal to the plain language of Hebrews 9 and 10 and John 19:30, Calvin proclaims the fundamental truth of the gospel that Christ's one sacrifice of himself on the cross for the forgiveness of sins was perfect. "This one [sacrifice] was offered only once and is never to be repeated." The benefits of the one sacrifice are communicated to us, not by repeating that sacrifice, but "by the preaching of the gospel and the administration of the Sacred Supper."[484]

The mass robs believers of the assurance of redemption by Christ's death. The trust of the people is rather directed to the daily mass, when it ought to be the case that "our faith may be made fast to his cross."[485] The mass destroys the sacrament of the Lord's supper. Whereas the supper is "a gift of God, which ought to have been received with thanksgiving, the sacrifice of the Mass is represented as paying a price to God, which he should receive by way of satisfaction."[486]

Inasmuch as the doctrine of the mass is based on the Roman dogma of transubstantiation, Calvin repeats the charge of idolatry: "It is idolatry when they display bread in their masses to be worshiped in place of Christ."[487] With the strong language that the exceeding evil of the mass deserves, Calvin damns the doctrine and practice. Sacrificing Jesus Christ anew, the Roman Catholic priests are "butchers of Christ."[488] The mass is "a most wicked infamy and unbearable blasphemy, both against Christ and against the sacrifice which he made for us through his death on the cross."[489]

Question and Answer 80 of the Heidelberg Catechism, the official Reformed condemnation of the mass, is in harmony with Calvin's and the entire Reformation's biblical judgment of the mass—and of the Roman Catholic Church, whose heart is the mass.

> What difference is there between the Lord's Supper and the Popish Mass?
>
> The Lord's Supper testifies to us that we have full forgiveness of all our sins by the one sacrifice of Jesus Christ, which he himself has once accomplished on the cross; [and that by the Holy Ghost we are ingrafted into Christ, who with his true body is now in heaven at the right hand of the Father, and is to be there worshiped]. But the Mass teaches that the living and the dead have not forgiveness of sins through the sufferings of Christ unless Christ is still daily offered for them by the priests; [and that Christ is bodily under the form of bread and wine, and is therefore to be worshiped in them]. And thus the Mass at bottom is nothing else than a denial of the one sacrifice and passion of Jesus Christ [and an accursed idolatry].[490]

Five false sacraments of Rome

Calvin's concluding criticism of the mass, that it is an invention of Rome, apart from the word of God, effectively condemns as well the five additional ceremonies that Rome has raised up as sacraments, contrary to the word of God. Calvin makes this observation at the very beginning of his brief examination of what he describes as "the five other ceremonies, falsely termed sacraments." "Our previous discussion of the sacraments would have been enough to persuade teachable and sober folk not to carry their curiosity any farther, or to accept any sacraments apart from God's Word, except those two which they knew to be ordained by the Lord."[491]

Nevertheless, because these five ceremonies are popularly regarded as sacraments, Calvin examines them "individually and more closely" at the end of his treatment of the doctrine of the church. The five ceremonies are confirmation, penance, extreme unction, holy orders, and marriage.

All alike are exposed as false by the truth that "the decision to establish a sacrament rests with God alone." "Man cannot establish a sacrament."[492]

Each also has its own particular errors.

Confirmation is the ceremony performed by bishops upon baptized members of the Roman Catholic Church that supposedly increases grace in the baptized and thus "completes" their baptism. Calvin charges that the ceremony is "an overt outrage against baptism," since it denies the lifelong power of Christ's sacrament of baptism.[493]

In place of confirmation, Calvin pleads for the worthwhile custom of catechizing the baptized children by means of a good catechism book so that "a child of ten would present himself to the church to declare his confession of faith."[494]

Penance is Rome's carefully worked out and elaborate ceremony of forgiving sins committed after baptism. The ceremony is threefold: the sinner's contrition, or sorrow over sin; confession of sins to the priest; and satisfaction demanded by the priest and made by the sinner to God in payment for his sins.

Calvin can be brief in his treatment of the Roman Catholic ceremony of penance at this point because he has subjected penance to a lengthy examination earlier, in chapters four and five of book three, in connection with his exposition of repentance. There he also exposed the related evils of indulgences and purgatory.

At this point, Calvin concentrates on Rome's description of penance as "'the second plank after shipwreck'" for delivering the sinner from sins committed after baptism.[495] Calvin charges that this claim for penance "wipes out" Christ's sacrament of baptism. "Baptism [is] the [real] sacrament of penance."[496] Rather than to have recourse to Rome's penance, the baptized sinner must think on his baptism all his life long.

Extreme unction is the ceremony that consists of the priest's anointing one who is nigh unto death with oil consecrated by a bishop. It bestows forgiveness of sins and "easing of bodily sickness, if such be expedient."[497] Rome bases this ceremony on James 5:14, 25.

Calvin contends that oil in apostolic times was only a "symbol" of the Holy Spirit, not "an instrument of healing." In an important statement, he declares that, in any case, "that gift of healing, like the rest of the miracles... has vanished away in order to make the new preaching of the gospel marvelous forever."[498]

He observes that the appeal to James 5 is groundless. James wants "all sick persons to be anointed," whereas Rome "smear[s] with their grease" only "half-dead corpses."[499] James attributes forgiveness to God's answer of the prayers of believers; Rome teaches that "sins are wiped out with grease."[500]

Holy orders is the ceremony of ordaining various Roman Catholic officials (seven in all) into their offices. Calvin exposes the absurdity of this ceremony regarding the number of different ordaining rites (amounting to seven different sacraments); the rituals themselves, including pouring oil, shaving the head, and breathing on the officials; and the offices themselves, which either ignore or corrupt the work assigned to the offices that do have biblical basis. Calvin confesses that he cannot keep from laughing at Rome's folly in the matter of holy orders. "These things cannot be heard without such laughter that I marvel at their being written without laughter."[501]

With regard to the office of priest, however, Rome's ceremony is more wicked than foolish. For Rome ordains priests, Calvin reminds the reader, "to offer a sacrifice of expiation." This wrongs Christ, who was ordained priest by God to offer the one "sacrifice of eternal expiation and reconciliation." Rome's priesthood and, therefore, its ceremony of holy orders are "impious and sacrilegious."[502]

"The true [biblical] office of presbyter," that is, teaching elder or minister of the word, is entered into by a "special rite," which is not a sacrament. This ordaining ceremony calls the men to preach the gospel, feed the flock, and engage in the government of the church.[503]

The fifth and last false sacrament is Rome's doctrine and practice of marriage. Roman Catholic marriage confers grace on the married couple.

Calvin acknowledges that God instituted marriage and that it is a sign "of the spiritual joining of Christ and the church." But he denies that marriage is "an outward ceremony appointed by God to confirm a promise," which is what a sacrament is.[504]

Calvin points out that the Roman error concerning marriage rests, in large part, on the mistranslation of the word "mystery" in Ephesians 5:32 (which refers to the "spiritual marriage of Christ and the church") in the Latin Bible as "sacrament."[505]

He exposes the pronounced inconsistency of Rome with regard to its view of marriage. On the one hand, Rome exalts it as an institution that confers grace. On the other hand, debarring priests from this sacrament, Rome calls marriage "uncleanness and pollution and carnal filth."[506]

Rome's error regarding marriage has not failed to produce its consequences: "A long train of errors, lies, frauds, and misdeeds have they attached to this one error."[507]

At the conclusion of Calvin's examination of the mass and of Rome's five false sacraments, indeed the conclusion of his entire study of the truth of the church, it is evident that Calvin has successfully accomplished the purpose he set for himself at the very beginning of his doctrine of the church: "to call back godly readers from those corruptions by which Satan, in the papacy, has polluted everything God had appointed for our salvation."[508]

CHAPTER 18

Civil Government

Introduction

In Calvin's thinking the truth of civil government is not simply one, final, biblical doctrine to be explained in the last chapter of the *Institutes*. Rather, civil government is an institution of God, which, although distinct from the church, shares with the church the calling and privilege of promoting and protecting the true religion and of helping, in its own way, the faith of God's children. Therefore, civil government is, or should be, closely allied with the church, and the treatment of civil government properly concludes the treatment of the church in a book that sets forth the Christian faith.

Calvin indicates his conception of civil government as a help to faith in the remarks with which he introduces his explanation of the church. "Since... we need outward helps to beget and increase faith within us, and advance it to its goal, God has also added these aids that he may provide for our weakness." Immediately outlining his treatment of these "outward helps," Calvin informs his readers that he will "discuss the church, its government, orders, and power; then the sacraments; and lastly, the civil order."[1]

Basic to this conception of the state as an outward help to faith is Calvin's conviction that the "appointed end" of the state is "to cherish and protect the outward worship of God, [and] to defend sound doctrine of piety and the position of the church." Thus civil government is a help to believers on their pilgrimage through this present world: "The pilgrimage requires such helps."[2]

Calvin relates what he says about civil government to what he has written earlier about Christian freedom. Toward the end of his explanation of Christian freedom, which truth is "an appendage of justification,"[3] Calvin observed that "there is a twofold government in man: one aspect is spiritual...the second is political."[4] With regard to what he called "the political kingdom," Calvin advised his readers, "Of civil government we shall speak in another place."[5] Chapter twenty of book four of the *Institutes* is the other place where civil government is explained, as Calvin promised. "Since we have established above that man is under a twofold government, and since we have elsewhere discussed at sufficient length the kind that resides in the soul or inner man and pertains to eternal life, this is the place to say something also about the other kind, which pertains only to the establishment of civil justice and outward morality."[6]

There is good reason for Calvin's reminder that he links his treatment of civil government closely to the earlier exposition of Christian freedom. Calvin is concerned to show, not only that Christian freedom does not imply licentiousness in the realm of the spiritual kingdom, but also that it may not become the pretext for revolution and disorder in the realm of the political kingdom. "We are not to misapply to the political order the gospel teaching on spiritual freedom, as if Christians were less subject, as concerns outward government, to human laws, because their consciences have been set free in God's sight."[7]

Scholars have unnecessarily complicated Calvin's doctrine of the two kingdoms in which every Christian lives. Others have wrongly criticized Calvin for this teaching, as though he denied the unity of the Christian life of the elect believer or removed life in the political kingdom from the calling of the spiritual kingdom, that he do all to the glory of God.

Essentially like Luther before him, Calvin simply taught the biblical truth that, with regard to eternal life, the Christian man knows one lord—the crucified and risen Jesus Christ; is under no law—being justified by faith alone; and is perfectly free—by the liberating gospel of grace and the renewing Spirit of Christ.

At the same time, with regard to his earthly life as a citizen of this or that nation, the Christian man acknowledges many earthly lords, whose authority over his earthly life he reverences—the officials of civil government; is under a host of laws, which he must obey—all the laws of the land, with the exception of those that require disobedience to God; and is severely restricted in his life and behavior—by the multitude of binding laws.

The distinction between the two kingdoms is necessary, if for no other reason than that the Christian must not suppose that spiritual freedom in the one kingdom may, or even must, be applied to a revolutionary rejection of the rulers in the other kingdom and a refusal to obey, or even recognize, the laws of the other kingdom. This was Calvin's great concern, and as history has demonstrated, and demonstrates yet today, not without reason.

Thus to distinguish the life of the Christian is by no means to divide his life. The Christian lives submissively and orderly in the political kingdom because Christ his lord calls him to do so. The Christian man works out the spiritual freedom of his soul in the submission and obedience that characterize his political life. And in this way he displays true Christian freedom before a revolutionary, disobedient world, to the glory of Christ his lord.

Making it urgent, Calvin thinks, to set forth the biblical truth concerning civil government are two dangers. One danger is revolution against the civil authority. Calvin has particularly in mind the Anabaptists, who shortly before the publishing of the original edition of the *Institutes* had alarmed all of Europe with their insurrectionary antics in the Peasants' War (AD 1525) and in the madness of Münster (AD 1535). One of the main purposes of Calvin with the original edition of the *Institutes* was to distance Reformed Christianity from the revolutionary sects, as Calvin expresses in the prefatory address to King Francis. The other danger that renders a sound explanation of civil government necessary is the deification of the state and its supreme ruler.

Calvin describes the two dangers that make it necessary for him to teach the life of the Christian with regard to civil government. "From one side, insane and barbarous men furiously strive to overturn this divinely established order; while, on the other side, the flatterers of princes, immoderately praising their power, do not hesitate to set them against the rule of God himself."[8]

Civil government ordained of God

Civil government—the authoritative rule of a nation and its citizens by one man or a body of men—has been ordained of God. Like the church, it is an institution of God, having its existence, and right to existence, from him; exercising his authority; and carrying out his purpose.

Romans 13:1–7 is decisive for Calvin's doctrine of the state: "Let every soul be subject unto the higher powers. For there is no power but of God: the powers that be are ordained of God" (v. 1). Regardless of the different forms of civil government, "we must regard all of them as ordained of God. For Paul also lumps them all together when he says that there is no power except from God [Rom. 13:1]."[9]

The divine institution of civil government implies that the "office" of every magistrate is "a jurisdiction bestowed by God."[10]

Calvin denies that civil government is "only…a kind of necessary evil" among men, invented by humans.[11] "It has not come about by human perversity that the authority over all things on earth is in the hands of kings and other rulers, but by divine providence and holy ordinance."[12]

Although Calvin does not express himself concerning the origin of this divine ordinance among humans, whether God's requirement of the death penalty for murder in his word to Noah after the flood (Gen. 9:6) or the authority of the husband and father in the family (Gen. 2:18–25), Calvin does describe civil government as a creature of God's providence, not an institution of grace. "It is the providence of God's wisdom that kings reign."[13] "That various countries should be ruled by various kinds of government" is the work of "divine providence."[14]

The attribution of civil government to providence—God's power in creation and history upholding and governing all things—underlies the sharp distinction Calvin makes between civil government and "Christ's spiritual Kingdom," which is, of course, the institution of grace. "Christ's spiritual Kingdom and the civil jurisdiction are things completely distinct."[15]

By no means does this imply that civil government is not a great good among men. "The magistrate's office is the highest gift of his [the

Lord's] beneficence to preserve the safety of men."[16] Inasmuch as civil government "provides for their [men's] living together," "its function among men is no less than that of bread, water, sun, and air; indeed, its place of honor is far more excellent."[17]

It is only "fanatics" who "consider the whole nature of government a thing polluted."[18]

Calvin's explanation of the origin of civil government as the ordinance of God the creator in his providential government of nations and peoples contradicts the modern historical fiction that government is the result of a purely human contract between rulers and ruled. The practical implication of the contract theory of civil government is that the submission and obedience of those who are governed are conditioned by the faithfulness of the governors to their end of the bargain. Accordingly, the contract theory of government legitimizes revolution.

Calvin's doctrine of civil government, which is that of Scripture, especially (but by no means exclusively) in Romans 13:1–7, is a fundamentally anti-revolutionary doctrine. Calvin spells this out when he condemns and forbids all revolution on the part of private citizens and when he expressly calls upon Christians to honor and submit to unjust, immoral, and even persecuting rulers. "We are not only subject to the authority of princes who perform their office toward us uprightly and faithfully as they ought, but also to the authority of all who, by whatever means, have got control of affairs, even though they perform not a whit of the princes' office."[19]

As with all his institutions, God has a purpose with his creature, the state. This purpose Calvin indicates when he states that civil government "pertains only to the establishment of civil justice and outward morality."[20] The sphere and extent of political power, therefore, are strictly limited: *only* civil justice and outward morality. When he discusses the duty of the magistrate, Calvin states, "Magistrates... are ordained protectors and vindicators of public innocence, modesty, decency, and tranquility, and... their sole endeavor should be to provide for the common safety and peace of all."[21] Calvin is the foe of the totalitarian and the welfare state.

What Calvin has in view with "civil justice and outward morality," he makes clear: "defend good men from the wrongs of the wicked, and give aid and protection to the oppressed." In order to accomplish these things, the magistrates "have also been armed with power with which severely to coerce the open malefactors and criminals by whose wickedness the public peace is troubled or disturbed."[22]

Order by means of justice is the great purpose of Calvin, as it is the great purpose of God, with civil government. Without civil government there would be "anarchy"—the worst of all possible political and social evils.[23]

Calvin does not so much as hint at a utopian, postmillennial purpose of God with civil government—not even civil government in the hands of a Christian magistrate. If it is erroneous to suppose that the purpose of "Christ's spiritual Kingdom" is that "the whole world [will be] reshaped to a new form," it is certainly a mistake to look to civil government for the realization of this dream. "It is a Jewish vanity to seek and enclose Christ's Kingdom within the elements of this world."[24]

"The whole subject of civil government" consists of three parts: "the magistrate, who is the protector and guardian of the laws; the laws, according to which he governs; the people, who are governed by the laws and obey the magistrate."[25] Calvin explains the three parts of the subject in order.

The magistracy

Because civil government is ordained of God, the magistrates, that is, all officials of the civil government, "have a mandate from God, have been invested with divine authority, and are wholly God's representatives, in a manner, acting as his vicegerents."[26] The office itself "is a calling, not only holy and lawful before God, but also the most sacred and by far the most honorable of all callings in the whole life of mortal men."[27] The Christian man, therefore, may certainly seek and hold political office. Calvin points to Obadiah and Daniel as biblical examples of God-fearing men who served as officials in godless regimes.

Although all forms of government are ordained of God, since "divine providence has wisely arranged that various countries should be ruled by various kinds of government,"[28] Calvin judges that certain forms of government are better than others. "The least pleasant of all ... is the power of one," that is, kingship, dictatorship, or rule by an emperor, because rule by one man "brings with it the common bondage of all."[29] "The fall from kingdom to tyranny is easy."[30]

Nor is Calvin favorable toward pure democracy, for "it is easiest of all to fall from popular rule [democracy] to sedition."[31]

Even aristocracy has its weakness: "It is not much more difficult to fall from the rule of the best men to the faction of a few."[32]

The system of government that "far excels all others" is one "compounded of aristocracy and democracy."[33]

Calvin's keen, realistic sense of man's depravity, particularly the depravity of men in office, demands a form of civil government characterized by a multitude of counselors and by checks and balances. "Men's fault or failing causes it to be safer and more bearable for a number to exercise government, so that they may help one another, teach and admonish one another; and, if one asserts himself unfairly, there may be a number of censors and masters to restrain his willfulness."[34]

Whether the founding fathers of the United States were consciously indebted to Calvin for the system of government they created is a question for historians. But the system itself with its three branches certainly answers to Calvin's political theory. There is no doubt that Reformed, or Presbyterian, church polity, with regard both to the government of the congregation and to the government of the denomination, is a marvelously wise and effective implementation of Calvin's theory of government in the life and work of the church.

Calvin desires a government that safeguards freedom—*earthly* freedom regarding *natural, physical* life. "No kind of government is more happy than one where freedom is regulated with becoming moderation and is properly established on a durable basis."[35] Even though one can be spiritually free in a condition of sheer political bondage—and Calvin insists on it—spiritual freedom in Christ yearns for political liberty. Tyrants have always feared Reformed Christians, as lovers of liberty, and hated the Reformed faith as promoting political freedom. Spiritual slaves, in contrast, whether pagans, Roman Catholics, or unbelievers, are content with, indeed, long and vote for, political bondage.

The task of the magistrate of establishing "civil justice and outward morality" in the nation, which Calvin identifies as concern for "the Second Table"[36] of the law, that is, commandments six through ten of the decalogue, consists of "judgment and justice." "Justice, indeed, is to receive into safekeeping, to embrace, to protect, vindicate, and free the innocent. But judgment is to withstand the boldness of the impious, to repress their violence, to punish their misdeeds."[37] Basically, this amounts to protecting and rewarding those whose behavior is outwardly law-abiding and punishing "open malefactors and criminals by whose wickedness the public peace is troubled or disturbed."[38]

In carrying out this aspect of his task, the magistrate may, indeed, is required of God to, kill. It is simply wrongheaded for professing Christians to appeal to the Bible's prohibition against murder, in Exodus 20:13, in support of their opposition to capital punishment on the part of the state. "The Lawgiver himself puts into the hand of his ministers a sword to be drawn against all murderers."[39] Calvin appeals to Romans 13:4: "He beareth not the sword in vain."

Calvin does recommend clemency in judgment: "clemency, that best counselor of kings." He criticizes "abrupt and savage harshness" and "undue cruelty."[40]

Calvin approves the proverb coming down from the history of the rulers of old Rome: "It is indeed bad to live under a prince with whom nothing is permitted; but much worse under one by whom everything is allowed."[41]

Just as it is right for civil government to execute certain evildoers, particularly murderers, so also is it right, and necessary, that governments wage wars. Wars are "lawful" that defend a nation against invasion or attack. "Both natural equity and the nature of the office dictate that princes must be armed... to defend by war the dominions entrusted to their safekeeping, if at any time they are under enemy attack."[42]

The appeals of pacifists to New Testament admonitions to Christians, that they not retaliate against those who injure them but bear the evil, are mistaken. "An express declaration of this matter [namely, that the civil state may make war] is not to be sought in the writings of the apostles; for their purpose is not to fashion a civil government, but to establish the spiritual Kingdom of Christ."[43] The mistake of the pacifists is due to a failure to distinguish the two kingdoms.

But Calvin warns against going to war too quickly. With a wisdom derived from Scripture and general equity, and validated by the horrors of war, Calvin counsels rulers to exhaust all other possibilities before having recourse to war. "Surely everything else ought to be tried before recourse is had to arms."[44]

The necessity of war implies the necessity of a standing army "and other civil defenses."[45]

Calvin was no muddleheaded, idealistic theologian, living himself in a dream world and offering advice to magistrates that, if followed, would have met with quick political and national disaster. Calvin was no liberal, twenty-first-century Protestant theologian. Wide awake to the harsh realities of sixteenth-century national perils, he gave sound advice to the rulers of Geneva and other cities and nations. The advice, always in harmony with Scripture, guarded the city or nation, its citizens, and the church of Christ in the city or nation from destruction by hostile nations, which, Calvin notes, are nothing but "armed robber[s]."[46]

In the pursuance of his God-given calling, the magistrate may tax the citizenry. "Tributes and taxes are the lawful revenues of princes." Calvin is not averse to the magistracy's use of taxes for a certain enhancing of the "dignity" of the political office. "They [the magistrates] may chiefly use [taxes] to meet the public expenses of their office; yet they may similarly use them for the magnificence of their household, which is joined, so to speak, with the dignity of the authority they exercise."[47]

At the same time, Calvin warns the rulers against a rapacious taxation, as also against wasting the money obtained by taxation. "[Taxes] are almost the very blood of the people, which it would be the harshest inhumanity not to spare."[48]

The calling of the magistrate, however, is not exclusively, or even primarily, the maintenance of outward order by means of civil justice and judgment. The primary task of civil government, according to Calvin, is promotion of the pure worship of God, promotion of the true religion and piety, and promotion and protection of the true church. "The office of the magistrates... extends to both Tables of the Law." God has "enjoined upon them [Christian princes and magistrates]... that they should labor to protect and assert the honor of him whose representatives they are, and by whose grace they govern." "No government can be happily established unless piety is the first concern; and... those laws are preposterous which neglect God's right and provide only for men."⁴⁹ Already in his statement of God's purpose with civil government, Calvin has taught that in the first place, the "appointed end" of government is "to cherish and protect the outward worship of God, [and] to defend sound doctrine of piety and the position of the church."⁵⁰

Calvin severely criticizes those who limit the calling of government to the maintenance of outward order in the nation or, as Calvin puts it, enforcing only the second table of the decalogue. He speaks of the "folly of those who would neglect the concern for God and would give attention only to rendering justice among men." "Laws... which neglect God's right and provide only for men" are "preposterous."⁵¹

Exactly how a Christian magistrate will enforce the first table of the law on all the citizens of the nation and what such enforcement will mean for those citizens who do not worship God according to the Reformed religion or belong to the Reformed church, Calvin does not inform his readers. But his advice to the magistrates of Geneva in the notorious matter of the burning of the heretic Servetus, as well as his and the Geneva consistory's use of the civil magistrates in the political punishment of those citizens of Geneva who transgressed the first table of the law—dereliction with regard to attendance at the worship services of the church, confession of the Roman Catholic religion, superstitious practices, and Sabbath desecration—makes clear what this aspect of his teaching on civil government entails.

Calvin's theory of the calling of civil government to promote the pure worship of God, sound doctrine, and the true church found its way into the Reformed creeds. Article 36 of the Belgic Confession is representative:

> Their [the magistracy's] office is, not only to have regard unto and watch for the welfare of the civil state, but also that they protect the sacred ministry, and thus may remove and prevent all idolatry and false worship; that the kingdom of antichrist may be thus destroyed, and the kingdom of Christ promoted.⁵²

With this aspect of Calvin's doctrine of the civil state, the Reformed church and the Reformed believer must take sharp issue. Calvin was wrong in ascribing enforcement of the first table of the law of God to civil magistrates, as indeed were virtually all theologians of his time, both Protestant and Roman Catholic.

The New Testament Scripture does not mandate civil government with the task of promoting the pure worship of God, sound doctrine, and the true church. With specific, direct reference to existing governments that were non-Christian, headed by kings and emperors who were ungodly, notably the Roman Empire and its Caesar, Romans 13:1–7, 1 Peter 2:13, 14, and other passages affirm that civil government is the servant of God by being a "terror... to evil works" and by praising good works. The only possible understanding of the task of government in apostolic times, by which all governments served God, is government's keeping order in the nation by civil justice and judgment. No government in apostolic times promoted the worship of God or sound doctrine. No government was *expected* to do this by the apostles. Indeed, very few governments have ever done this in all of New Testament history.

Magistrates do not have the *ability* to enforce the first table of the law. Apart from the fact that God gave the law of the ten commandments, not to modern nations, but to his church, and apart from the fact also that enforcement of the first table of the law requires taking heed to men's *hearts*, not only their outward behavior, magistrates *cannot* determine the pure worship of God, sound doctrine, and the identity of the true church. Consistories and synods of true churches of Christ are able to judge these things, but not presidents, congresses, and supreme courts.

Further, the pure worship of God, sound doctrine, and the true church cannot be promoted by the cold, steel sword of the state. For these spiritual exercises, the sword of the Spirit, that is, the word of God, alone avails.

Let the civil government do its important task of maintaining order in the nation, protecting the outwardly law-abiding citizens and punishing the lawless and criminal, and the church will have the earthly freedom (no small gift of God!) to carry on its spiritual work of worship, preaching, and piety. Thus Caesar serves King Jesus, and the steel sword of the state serves the cross.

It is significant that in the section in which he argues for the duty of the state to promote the pure worship of God, Calvin's only appeal to Scripture is an appeal to the history of the godly kings of Old Testament Israel. "Holy kings are greatly praised in Scripture because they restored the worship of God when it was corrupted or destroyed, or took care of religion that under them it might flourish pure and unblemished."[53] But the fulfillment of Old Testament Israel as a holy nation is no nation in the New Testament era, whether Switzerland, the Netherlands, Scotland, the United States, or the modern state of Israel. The fulfillment of Old Testament Israel *as a nation* is the New Testament, spiritual church of Jesus Christ. To the church, Peter declares, "Ye are a chosen generation, a royal priesthood, an holy nation, a peculiar people" (1 Pet. 2:9). The zeal of the godly kings of Judah and Israel for the right worship of God is fulfilled, not in this or that civil magistrate, but in Jesus Christ, the real king of the real Israel of God—the church—and in godly elders of New Testament congregations, who govern his "holy nation"—the church—in his name.

By assigning to civil government the intensely spiritual work that belongs properly to the spiritual kingdom of Jesus Christ, Calvin deviated from the truths about civil government that he himself laid down at the outset of his treatment of the subject. Civil government "pertains *only* to the establishment of *civil justice* and *outward morality*."[54] We must not, he warned, "unwisely mingle these two [the political kingdom of civil government and the spiritual kingdom of the church], which have a completely different nature." Parenthetically he added, in unwitting prophecy of his own impending fault, "as commonly happens."[55]

Civil laws

The second part of civil government is "the laws, stoutest sinews of the commonwealth."[56] Calvin rejects as "false and foolish," indeed "perilous and seditious," the notion "that a commonwealth is duly framed" only if it adopts "the political system of Moses."[57] This notion is raised today in the Reformed churches by the "theonomists." These men advocate the government of (nonexistent) Christian states by the civil and judicial laws of Old Testament Israel and prophesy a future Christian, carnal kingdom before the coming of Christ that, in fact, will adopt "the political system of Moses." Calvin denies that the Lord gave "that law to be proclaimed among all nations and to be in force everywhere." And the thought of some "that the law of God given through Moses is dishonored when it is abrogated and new laws preferred to it, is utterly vain."[58]

"Surely every nation is left free to make such laws as it foresees to be profitable for itself,"[59] so long as the laws are "framed to that rule, directed to that goal, bound by that limit" of "equity."[60] Equity is the sense of justice that is "a testimony of natural law and of that conscience which God has engraved upon the minds of men."[61]

The calling of the Christian toward civil government

Before Calvin admonishes the duties of the Christian with regard to civil government and its officers, he affirms the right of the Christian to make good, profitable use of civil government. "The magistrate may without impiety be called upon and also appealed to."[62] In Reformed thinking and practice, civil government is not an evil, nor does the Christian life consist of avoiding government.

The Christian may litigate in defense of his person and possessions, if his cause is just and his motives pure. "Lawsuits are permissible if rightly used."[63] This right use includes treating the "adversary with ... love and good will."[64] In 1 Corinthians 6:5–8, Paul does not condemn lawsuits but "an immoderate rage for litigation."[65]

The Reformed Church Order of Dordt applies Calvin's instruction concerning a lawful use of civil government to the church:

> The consistory shall take care that the churches, for the possession of their property and the peace and order of their meetings, can claim the protection of the authorities; it should be well understood, however, that for the sake of peace and material possession they may never suffer the royal government of Christ over His church to be in the least infringed upon.[66]

The duties of the Christian citizen to civil government are two. The first is "to think most honorably of their office, which they recognize as a jurisdiction bestowed by God, and on that account to esteem and reverence them as ministers and representatives of God."[67] Calvin recognizes that many officials of government are personally foolish, lazy, and cruel. Honoring them is no covering of their wickedness, much less a praising of their vices. But the Christian reverences the wicked rulers "out of respect for their lordship."[68] Calvin appeals to Romans 13:5: "Be subject... for conscience sake."

The second duty of the Christian to the magistrate is obedience, "whether by obeying their proclamations, or by paying taxes, or by undertaking public offices and burdens which pertain to the common defense, or by executing any other commands of theirs."[69] Calvin quotes Romans 13:1, 2: "Let every soul be subject unto the higher powers. For there is no power but of God: the powers that be are ordained of God. Whosoever therefore resisteth the power, resisteth the ordinance of God: and they that resist shall receive to themselves damnation." Calvin is insistent that this obedience not be merely outward. It must arise out of "hearts inclined to reverence their rulers."[70]

To rebel against the magistrate is to rebel against God: "The magistrate cannot be resisted without God being resisted at the same time."[71]

Calvin rightly condemns as revolution what many twentieth-century churches and professing Christians approved, and enthusiastically participated in, as lawful, even Christian, civil disobedience on behalf of various civil rights movements. "If anything in a public ordinance requires amendment, let them [private citizens] not raise a tumult, or put their hands to the task—all of them ought to keep their hands bound in this respect—but let them commit the matter to the judgment of the magistrate, whose hand alone here is free."[72]

Obedience is due, not only to the just prince, who shows himself "a father of his country,"[73] but also to "a very wicked man utterly unworthy of all honor, provided he has the public power in his hands."[74] "Whoever they may be," wicked Nebuchadnezzar or righteous David, "they have their authority solely from him [God]."[75] Calvin observes that God often raises up unjust and wicked rulers "to punish the wickedness of the people."[76]

Under no circumstances whatsoever are private citizens of a nation permitted by God to revolt against their government and its rulers. The Christian is not permitted to revolt even when an ungodly ruler persecutes the church. "The correction of unbridled despotism is the

Lord's to avenge." To the Christian citizen "no command has been given except to obey and suffer."[77] Here too, Calvin and the Reformed faith take their calling, difficult and painful though it may be, from Romans 13:1–7. The command is clear and unconditional: "Let every soul be subject unto the higher powers" (v. 1).

The prohibition of revolt to "private individuals" does not rule out all violent overthrow of unjust kings, dictators, and other potentates. Other magistrates in a nation have not only the right, but also the solemn obligation to deliver the oppressed people from the tyranny of the supreme magistrate by force.

> If there are now any magistrates of the people, appointed to restrain the willfulness of kings...I am so far from forbidding them to withstand, in accordance with their duty, the fierce licentiousness of kings, that, if they wink at kings who violently fall upon and assault the lowly common folk, I declare that their dissimulation involves nefarious perfidy, because they dishonestly betray the freedom of the people, of which they know that they have been appointed protectors by God's ordinance.[78]

Theodore Beza, Calvin's successor in Geneva, worked out Calvin's teaching concerning this right and duty of the lesser magistrates, without sacrificing the truth that private individuals may never revolt, in his important treatise, "Concerning the Rights of Rulers over Their Subjects and the Duty of Subjects towards Their Rulers." Beza expressed, as Calvin did not, that private individuals may flock to the standard of the lesser magistrates, when these magistrates have taken up arms against a tyrannical ruler.[79]

The overthrow of unjust, tyrannical, and oppressive rulers by other officials of the state is not revolution but a lawful, though admittedly extraordinary, act of justice. The overthrow of tyrants and despots by Calvinists in history should be carefully examined in light of the rights and duties of lesser magistrates before the overthrow is judged a "revolution."

Submission to the civil government by the private Christian citizen is unconditional. Obedience is not unconditional.

> In that obedience which we have shown to be due the authority of rulers, we are always to make this exception, indeed, to observe it as primary, that such obedience is never to lead us away from obedience to him, to whose will the desires of all kings ought to be subject, to whose decrees all their commands ought to yield, to whose majesty their scepters ought to be submitted.[80]

Calvin quotes Acts 5:29: "We ought to obey God rather than men."

Civil government is an institution of God. The ruler is a mere creature, raised to his admittedly exalted station by God, and vested for a short time with God's authority. The state is not God, no matter how powerful it may be. No king, emperor, führer, or president is God, regardless of his might and charisma.

The deification of the state and its impressive head is antichrist.

To no civil government and its magistrates are due trust, worship, absolute loyalty, or unconditional obedience.

Trust, worship, absolute loyalty, and unconditional obedience are the prerogatives only of the king of the spiritual kingdom of God, Jesus Christ the Lord.

Magistrates are mere servants of God. As servants, they have duties to God and duties to the people over whom God has placed them. Running throughout Calvin's treatment of civil government is his reminder to the magistrates that they too have duties, and what these duties are. One day, Calvin warns them, they will give account to their king of their conduct in office. God will take vengeance on their injustice. Calvin cries out to "arrogant kings and... intolerable governments," with a cry that resounds into the twenty-first century, "Let the princes hear and be afraid."[81]

Refusal to obey the command of the ruler that requires us to disobey God will mean suffering. "Let us comfort ourselves with the thought that we are rendering that obedience which the Lord requires when we suffer anything rather than turn aside from piety."[82]

Piety, that awed love of God in Jesus Christ taking form in obedience—a great theme of the *Institutes*—is Calvin's final word in his grand work.

And that our courage may not grow faint [as we suffer at the hands of the godless state and its antichristian rulers], Paul pricks us with another goad: That we have been redeemed by Christ at so great a price as our redemption cost him, so that we should not enslave ourselves to the wicked desires of men—much less be subject to their impiety.[83]

Almighty God, thou hast deigned to show thyself so intimately to us and also daily deignest to confirm us in thy truth. Grant that we may turn aside neither to the right nor to the left, but depend wholly on thy Word and so cleave to thee that no errors of the world may lead us astray. May we stand firm in that faith which we have learned from thy law, from the prophets and the gospel (wherein thou hast more clearly shown thyself through Christ), that we may finally enjoy thy full and perfect glory, being transfigured into it, at last attaining that inheritance acquired for us by the blood of thine only begotten Son. Amen.

—Prayer of John Calvin at the close of his lectures, in Ford Lewis Battles, *The Piety of John Calvin*

Notes

Chapter 1

1. Bernard Cottret, *Calvin: A Biography*, trans. M. Wallace McDonald (Grand Rapids: Eerdmans, 2000), 66.
2. John Calvin, "The Author's Preface," in *Commentary on the Book of Psalms*, trans. James Anderson, 5 vols. (Grand Rapids: Eerdmans, 1948), 1:xl.
3. Ibid., xli.
4. John T. McNeill, *The History and Character of Calvinism* (New York: Oxford University Press, 1954), 230.
5. See John Calvin, "Reply by John Calvin to Letter by Cardinal Sadolet to the Senate and People of Geneva," in *Tracts*, vol. 1, trans. Henry Beveridge (Edinburgh: Calvin Translation Society, 1844), 25–68.
6. Philip Schaff, *History of the Christian Church*, vol. 7, *The Swiss Reformation* (New York: Charles Scribner's Sons, 1892), 420.
7. Ibid.
8. Ibid., 416.
9. John Calvin, "Letter to Farel," dated March 29, 1540, in *Letters of John Calvin: Selected from the Bonnet Edition* (Edinburgh: Banner of Truth, 1980), 59.
10. Ibid., 66.
11. Colladon, quoted in T. H. L. Parker, *Calvin's Preaching* (Louisville, KY: Westminster John Knox Press, 1992), 62, 63.
12. François Wendel, *Calvin: The Origins and Development of His Religious Thought*, trans. Philip Mairet (New York: Wm. Collins, 1965), 82.
13. For Calvin's controversy with the Nicodemites and his insistence on membership in a true church, see John Calvin, "On Shunning the Unlawful Rites of the Ungodly and Preserving the Purity of the Christian Religion," in *Tracts*, vol. 3, trans. Henry Beveridge (Edinburgh: Calvin Translation Society, 1851), 359–411; and John Calvin, *Come Out from Among Them: 'Anti-Nicodemite' Writings of John Calvin*, trans. Seth Skolnitsky (Dallas: Protestant Heritage Press, 2001).
14. Belgic Confession, Art. 28, in Philip Schaff, ed., *Creeds of Christendom with a History and Critical Notes*, 6th ed., 3 vols. (New York: Harper & Row, 1931; repr., Grand Rapids: Baker Books, 2007), 3:418.
15. Wendel, *Calvin*, 105.
16. Theodore Beza, "Life of John Calvin," in Calvin, *Tracts*, 1:xcvi.
17. Émile Doumergue, *Jean Calvin: les hommes et les choses de son temps*, 7 vols. (Lausanne, Switzerland: G. Bridel, 1899–1917).

18. Émile Doumergue, "Calvin: Epigone or Creator?" trans. Joseph H. Dulles, in *Calvin and the Reformation: Four Studies*, ed. William P. Armstrong (New York: Fleming H. Revell, 1909), 31.
19. McNeill, *The History and Character of Calvinism*, 234.
20. Ibid.
21. William James Bouwsma, *John Calvin: A Sixteenth-Century Portrait* (New York: Oxford University Press, 1988), 214, 215.
22. Cottret, *Calvin: A Biography*, xi, xii.

Chapter 2

1. Benjamin B. Warfield, "Calvin's Doctrine of the Knowledge of God," in *Calvin and Calvinism* (New York: Oxford University Press, 1931), 115.
2. Calvin, "The Author's Preface," in *Commentary on the Book of Psalms*, 1:xlii.
3. John T. McNeill, ed., *Calvin: Institutes of the Christian Religion*, trans. Ford Lewis Battles, 2 vols., Library of Christian Classics 20, 21 (Philadelphia: Westminster Press, 1960), 3.4.1, 1:622.
4. "Subject Matter of the Present Work," in *Calvin: Institutes*, 1:8.
5. Karl Barth, *The Theology of John Calvin,* trans. Geoffrey W. Bromiley (Grand Rapids: Eerdmans, 1995), 158.
6. See Anthony N. S. Lane, *John Calvin: Student of the Church Fathers* (Grand Rapids: Baker, 1999).
7. Johannes Calvijn, *Institutie 1536: Onderwijs in de Christelijke Religie,* trans. W. van't Spijker (Kampen: De Groot Goudriaan, 1992).
8. Jean Daniel Benoit, "The History and Development of the *Institutio:* How Calvin Worked," in *Courtenay Studies in Reformation Theology 1: John Calvin*, ed. G. E. Duffield (Appleford, UK: Sutton Courtenay Press, 1996), 102, 103.
9. *Calvin: Institutes*, 1.2.1, 1:41.
10. For piety in Calvin, see "True Piety according to Calvin," in *The Piety of John Calvin: An Anthology Illustrative of the Spirituality of the Reformer*, trans. and ed. Ford Lewis Battles (Grand Rapids: Baker, 1978), 13–26.
11. Alexandre Ganoczy, *The Young Calvin*, trans. David Foxgrover and Wade Provo (Philadelphia: Westminster Press, 1987), 205.
12. "Introduction," in *Calvin: Institutes,* 1:li.
13. "Inleiding," in Johannes Calvijn, *Institutie ofte onderwijsinghe in de Christelicke religie,* trans. Wilhelmus Corsmannus (Doesburg: J. C. van Schenk Brill, 1889), 11; the translation of the Dutch is mine.
14. Ibid., emphasis added; the translation of the Dutch is mine.
15. Ibid.; the translation of the Dutch is mine.
16. Augustine, *The Enchiridion on Faith, Hope and Love* (Chicago: Henry Regenery Company, 1961), 2.
17. Ibid., 2, 3.
18. Barth, *The Theology of John Calvin*, 159.
19. Calvin, "The Author's Preface," in *Commentary on the Book of Psalms*, 1:xli, xlii.

20. "John Calvin to the Reader," in *Calvin: Institutes*, 1:4, 5.
21. "Prefatory Address to King Francis I of France," in *Calvin: Institutes*, 1:9.
22. John Calvin, *Institutes of the Christian Religion: 1536 Edition*, rev. ed., trans. Ford Lewis Battles (Grand Rapids: Eerdmans and H. H. Meeter Center for Calvin Studies, 1986), 6.B.15, 185.
23. "John Calvin to the Reader," in *Calvin: Institutes*, 1:4.
24. Ibid., 1:5.
25. "Subject Matter of the Present Work," in *Calvin: Institutes*, 1:7.
26. Heiko A. Oberman, *The Two Reformations: The Journey from the Last Days to the New World*, ed. Donald Weinstein (New Haven, CT: Yale University Press, 2003), 127.
27. Will Durant, *The Story of Civilization*, vol. 6, *The Reformation: A History of European Civilization from Wyclif to Calvin, 1300–1564* (New York: Simon and Schuster, 1957), 460. Durant added, "But we shall always find it hard to love this man who darkened the human soul with the most absurd and blasphemous conception of God in all the long and honored history of nonsense" (490).
28. McNeill, *The History and Character of Calvinism*, 119.
29. Ibid., 128.
30. Ibid., 234.
31. Warfield, "John Calvin: The Man and His Work," in *Calvin and Calvinism*, 8.
32. Ibid., 9.
33. William Cunningham, "John Calvin," in *The Reformers and the Theology of the Reformation* (London: Banner of Truth, 1967), 295.

Chapter 3

1. "Introduction," in Calvin, *Institutes: 1536 Edition*, xxii.
2. Wendel, *Calvin*, 145.
3. "John Calvin to the Reader," in *Calvin: Institutes*, 1:4, 5.
4. "Introduction," in *Calvin: Institutes*, 1:xxxv.
5. Ibid., 1:xxxviii.
6. Warfield, "On the Literary History of Calvin's 'Institutes,'" in *Calvin and Calvinism*, 389.
7. See Ford Lewis Battles, *Interpreting John Calvin*, ed. Robert Benedetto (Grand Rapids: Baker, 1996), 140.
8. John Calvin, *The Bondage and Liberation of the Will: A Defence of the Orthodox Doctrine of Human Choice against Pighius*, ed. A. N. S. Lane, trans. G. I. Davies (Grand Rapids: Baker, 1966), 28, 29.
9. Barth, *The Theology of John Calvin*, 158.
10. Benoit, "The History and Development of the *Institutio*," in *Courtenay Studies in Reformation Theology 1: John Calvin*, 102.
11. Warfield, "Literary History," in *Calvin and Calvinism*, 389.
12. For a treatment of election in *Institutes: 1536 Edition*, see 2.B.21–29, 58–63. In the 1559 *Institutes* Calvin treats predestination in 3.21–24, 2:920–87.

13. On Calvin's youth when he wrote the *Institutes*, Scottish writer Alexander Smellie has noted that similarly Melanchthon was twenty-four when he wrote the *Loci Communes*, and Ursinus and Olevianus were under thirty when they wrote the Heidelberg Catechism. He observes: "The young men of the Reformation period were giants in understanding and in grace." (See Alexander Smellie, *The Reformation in Its Literature* [London: Andrew Melrose, 1925], 153.)

14. Warfield, "Literary History," in *Calvin and Calvinism*, 380.

15. Calvin, *Institutes: 1536 Edition*, 373, 374.

16. Wendel, *Calvin*, 117.

17. "John Calvin to the Reader," in *Calvin: Institutes*, 1:3.

18. Ibid.

19. See *Calvin: Institutes*, 1.15.3, 5; 2.12.5–7; 3.11.5–12.

20. "Introduction," in *Calvin: Institutes*, 1:xlv

21. T. H. L. Parker, *Calvin: An Introduction to His Thought* (Louisville: Westminster John Knox Press, 1995), 11.

22. Edmund Bunney, *Institutionis Christianae Religionis* (London: Harrison u. a., 1576).

23. William Delaune, *Institutionis Christianae Religionis* (London: Thomas Vautrollier, 1583).

24. "Introduction," in *Calvin: Institutes,* 1:xlix. For other early translations and abridgments of the *Institutes*, see the "Introduction" in volume 1 of the Battles/McNeill edition, to which I am indebted for much of the information regarding translation and abridgment.

25. "John Calvin to the Reader," in *Calvin: Institutes*, 1:3.

Chapter 4

1. Cited in Warfield, "Literary History," in *Calvin and Calvinism*, 390.

2. McNeill, *The History and Character of Calvinism*, 98.

3. Warfield, "Literary History," in *Calvin and Calvinism,* 399.

4. Ibid., 398.

5. Benoit, in *Courtenay Studies in Reformation Theology 1: John Calvin*, 104.

6. McNeill, *The History and Character of Calvinism*, 126, 127.

7. Calvin, *Institutes: 1536 Edition*, 5.B.16, 133, 134; emphasis added.

8. Warfield, "Literary History," in *Calvin and Calvinism,* 399.

9. Philip Schaff, *History of the Christian Church*, 7:281.

10. "Introduction," in *Calvin: Institutes,* 1:lxii.

11. Ibid., 1:lxv.

12. Ibid., 1:lxxi; emphasis added.

13. Heidelberg Catechism, A 80, in Schaff, *Creeds of Christendom,* 3:336.

14. John Calvin, *Commentary on a Harmony of the Evangelists, Matthew, Mark, and Luke*, trans. William Pringle, 3 vols. (Grand Rapids: Eerdmans, 1948), 1:468.

15. J. I. Packer, "Calvin the Theologian," in Benoit, *Courtenay Studies in Reformation Theology 1: John Calvin*, 154.

16. James Anthony Froude, *Calvinism: An Address Delivered at St. Andrew's March 17, 1871* (New York: Scribner, 1871), 42.

17. John Calvin, "The Consent of the Pastors of the Church of Christ at Geneva," in *Calvin's Calvinism*, trans. Henry Cole (Grand Rapids: Eerdmans, 1956), 15.

18. John Calvin, "An Admonition, Showing the Advantages Which Christendom Might Derive from an Inventory of Relics," in *Tracts*, 1:287–341.

19. Ibid., 1:316.

20. Ibid., 1:317.

21. Schaff, *Creeds of Christendom*, 1:439.

22. "John Calvin to the Reader," in *Calvin: Institutes*, 1:5; emphasis added.

23. Cited in McNeill, *The History and Character of Calvinism*, 128.

24. *Calvin: Institutes*, 1.15.6, 1:192.

25. The titles of the four books and the chapter headings are Calvin's own; the section headings are provided by others, most by Otto Weber (see "Editor's Preface," in *Calvin: Institutes*, 1:xx).

26. "Introduction," in *Calvin: Institutes*, 1:l.

27. John Calvin, "Reply by Calvin to Letter by Cardinal Sadolet to the Senate and People of Geneva," in *Tracts*, 1:37.

28. *Calvin: Institutes*, 3.1.1, 1:538.

29. "Introduction," in *Calvin: Institutes*, 1:li.

30. Ibid., 1:lvi; emphasis added.

31. See Warfield, "Literary History," in *Calvin and Calvinism*, 388.

32. Cited in Hans-Joachim Kraus, "The Contemporary Relevance of Calvin's Theology," in *Toward the Future of Reformed Theology: Tasks, Topics, Traditions*, ed. David Willis and Michael Welker (Grand Rapids: Eerdmans, 1999), 329.

33. "Translator's Note," in *Calvin: Institutes*, 1:xxiv.

34. "Introduction," in Calvin, *Institutes: 1536 Edition*, xxvii.

35. See Smellie, *The Reformation in Its Literature*, 160–63.

Chapter 5

1. Smellie, *The Reformation in Its Literature*, 154.

2. "Prefatory Address," in *Calvin: Institutes*, 1:9, 10.

3. Ganoczy, *The Young Calvin*, 91.

4. Belgic Confession, Art. 36, in Schaff, *Creeds of Christendom*, 3:433.

5. "Prefatory Address," in *Calvin: Institutes*, 1:31.

6. Ibid., 1:30.

7. Ibid., 1:13.

8. Ibid., 1:11, 12.

9. Ibid., 1:16.

10. Ibid.

11. Ibid., 1:17.

12. Ibid.

13. Ibid., 1:18.

14. Ibid., 1:19.
15. Ibid., 1:18.
16. Ibid., 1:19–23.
17. Ibid., 1:23.
18. Ibid.
19. Ibid.
20. Belgic Confession, Art. 7, in Schaff, *Creeds of Christendom*, 3:388.
21. "Prefatory Address," in *Calvin: Institutes*, 1:24.
22. Ibid.
23. Belgic Confession, Art. 27, in Schaff, *Creeds of Christendom*, 3:417.
24. "Prefatory Address," in *Calvin: Institutes*, 1:24, 25.
25. Ibid., 1:27.
26. Ibid., 1:20.
27. Ibid., 1:14.
28. Ibid., 1:27.
29. Ibid., 1:10, 11.
30. Ibid., 1:12.

Chapter 6

1. *Calvin: Institutes*, 1.1.1, 1:35.
2. Calvin, *Institutes: 1536 Edition*, 1.A.1, 15.
3. *Calvin: Institutes*, 1.1.3, 1:39.
4. Ibid., 1.2.1, 1:39; see also all of 1.2, 1:39–43.
5. Ibid., 1.3.1, 1:44.
6. Ibid., 1:43.
7. Ibid., n. 2, 1:43.
8. Ibid., 1.4.3, 1:46.
9. Ibid., 1.5.2, 1:52.
10. Ibid., 1.5.8, 1:61.
11. Ibid., 1.5.7, 1:60.
12. Ibid., 1.5.1, 1:52.
13. Ibid., 1.4.4, 1:51.
14. Ibid., 1.4.1, 1:47.
15. Ibid., 1.5.11, 1:64.
16. Ibid.
17. Ibid., 1.5.12, 1:66.
18. Ibid., 1.6.1, 1:69.
19. Warfield, "Calvin's Doctrine of the Knowledge of God," in *Calvin and Calvinism*, 114.
20. Canons of Dordt, 3, 4, Error 5, in *The Confessions and the Church Order of the Protestant Reformed Churches* (Grandville, MI: Protestant Reformed Churches in America, 2005), 171.
21. See R. C. Sproul, John Gerstner, and Arthur Lindsley, *Classical Apologet-*

ics: A Rational Defense of the Christian Faith and a Critique of Presuppositional Apologetics (Grand Rapids: Zondervan, 1984).

22. See Harry R. Boer, *An Ember Still Glowing: Humankind as the Image of God* (Grand Rapids: Eerdmans, 1990).

23. On these proofs, see Herman Hoeksema, *Reformed Dogmatics* (Grand Rapids: Reformed Free Publishing Association, 1966), 43–47.

24. *Calvin: Institutes*, 1.6.14, 1:68.

25. Canons of Dordt, 3, 4.4, in Schaff, *Creeds of Christendom*, 3:588.

26. Canons of Dordt, 3, 4.6, in Schaff, *Creeds of Christendom*, 3:588.

27. Karl Barth, *Nein! Antwort an Emil Brunner* (Munchen: Chr. Kaiser Verlag, 1934) [Karl Barth, *No! Answer to Emil Brunner*, in *Natural Theology*, trans. Peter Fraenkel (London: Geoffrey Bles: The Centenary Press, 1946)].

28. *Calvin: Institutes*, 1.5.13, 1:67.

29. C. S. Lewis, *The Last Battle* (London: The Bodley Head, 1956), 166.

30. *Calvin: Institutes*, 1.5.13, 1:67.

31. Ibid., 1.6.1, 1:70.

32. Ibid., 1:69, 70.

33. Warfield, "Calvin's Doctrine of the Knowledge of God," in *Calvin and Calvinism*, 83.

34. *Calvin: Institutes*, 1.7.1, 1:74.

35. Ibid., 1.7.4, 1:78.

36. Ibid., 4.8.8, 2:1155.

37. Ibid.

38. Ibid., n. 7, 2:1155, 1156.

39. John Calvin, *Institutes of the Christian Religion*, trans. Henry Beveridge, 2 vols. (Grand Rapids: Eerdmans, 1966), 4.8.8, 2:394.

40. John Calvin, *Institutes of the Christian Religion,* trans. John Allen, 8th ed., 2 vols. (Grand Rapids: Eerdmans, 1949), 2:423.

41. *Calvin: Institutes*, 4.8.9, 2:1157; emphasis added.

42. Calvin, *Institutes*, trans. Henry Beveridge, 4.8.9, 2:395.

43. *Calvin: Institutes*, 4.8.9, n. 9, 2:1157.

44. Ibid., 4.8.9, 2:1157.

45. John Calvin, *Commentaries on the Epistles to Timothy, Titus, and Philemon,* trans. William Pringle (Grand Rapids: Eerdmans, 1948), 249.

46. *Calvin: Institutes*, 1.13.1, 1:121.

47. Ibid., 1.7.1, 1:75.

48. Warfield, "Calvin's Doctrine of the Knowledge of God," in *Calvin and Calvinism*, 70, 71.

49. Ibid.

50. *Calvin: Institutes*, 1.7.5, 1:80, 81.

51. Ibid.

52. Belgic Confession, Art. 5, in Schaff, *Creeds of Christendom*, 3:386, 387.

53. *Calvin: Institutes*, 1.7.4, 1:79.

54. Ibid.
55. Ibid., 1.7.5, 1:80.
56. Ibid., 1.8.1, 13, 1:81, 92.
57. Ibid., 1.7.4, 1:79.
58. Ibid., 1.9.1, 1:93.
59. Ibid., 1.9.3, 1:95.
60. Ibid.
61. Ibid., 1.9.1, 1:93.
62. Ibid., 1.9.3, 1:96.

Chapter 7

1. Calvin, *Institutes: 1536 Edition*, 2.A.9, 48.
2. On Gentile, see Wendel, *Calvin*, 100, 101; *The New Schaff-Herzog Encyclopedia of Religious Knowledge* (New York: Funk and Wagnalls, 1909), 4:453, 454.
3. *Calvin: Institutes*, 1.13.23, 1:149.
4. Ibid., 1.13.10, 1:133.
5. Ibid., 1.13.22, 1:147.
6. On Calvin's conflict with Caroli, see David J. Engelsma, *Trinity and Covenant: God as Holy Family* (Jenison, MI: Reformed Free Publishing Association, 2006), 28–33. For a brief history of the controversy, see Wendel, *Calvin*, 53–55, 165.
7. *Calvin: Institutes*, 1.13.5, 1:126.
8. Ibid., 1:127.
9. Wendel, *Calvin*, 54.
10. See Warfield, "Calvin's Doctrine of the Trinity," in *Calvin and Calvinism*, 239.
11. Wendel, *Calvin*, 54, 55.
12. *Calvin: Institutes*, 1.13.19, 1:144.
13. Ibid., 1.13.29, 1:158.
14. Ibid., 1.13.4, 1:124, 125.
15. Ibid., 1.13.3, 1:123.
16. Ibid., 1.13.5, 1:126.
17. Ibid.
18. Ibid., 1.13.20, 1:144.
19. Ibid., 1.13.6, 1:128.
20. Ibid.
21. Ibid., 1.13.17, 1:141, 142.
22. Ibid., 1:141.
23. Heidelberg Catechism, Q&A 25, in Schaff, *Creeds of Christendom*, 3:315.
24. *Calvin: Institutes*, 1.13.29, 1:159.
25. Ibid.
26. Ibid., 1.13.14, 1:139.
27. Ibid., 1.13.16, 1:140.
28. Ibid., 1.13.20, 1:144.

29. Ibid., 1.13.29, 1:159.
30. Ibid., 1.13.18, 1:142.
31. John Calvin, *Commentaries on the First Book of Moses Called Genesis,* trans. John King, 2 vols. (Grand Rapids: Eerdmans, 1948), 1:93.
32. *Calvin: Institutes,* 1.13.18, 142, 143.
33. Ibid., 1.13.2, 1:122.
34. Ibid., 1.13.21–29, 1:145–59.
35. Ibid., 1.13.21, 1:146.
36. Ibid., 1.13.4, 1:124.
37. Ibid., 1.13.8, 1:130.
38. Ibid., 1.13.22, 1:147.
39. Ibid., 1.13.23, 1:149.
40. Ibid., 1.13.5, 1:127, 128.
41. Ibid., 1.13.22, 1:147.
42. Ibid., 1.13.23, 1:149.
43. Ibid., 1.13.25, 1:154.
44. See Warfield, "Calvin's Doctrine of the Trinity," in *Calvin and Calvinism,* 284.
45. Nicaeno-Constantinopolitan Creed, in Schaff, *Creeds of Christendom,* 2:58.
46. Ibid.
47. For the development of the doctrine of the Trinity, particularly God's threeness, in relation to the doctrine of the covenant, see Herman Hoeksema, *Reformed Dogmatics,* 318–36, and David J. Engelsma, *Trinity and Covenant.*
48. *Calvin: Institutes,* 1.13.29, 1:159.
49. John Calvin, *Commentaries on the Twelve Minor Prophets,* trans. John Owen, 5 vols. (Grand Rapids: Eerdmans, 1950), 3:299.
50. Ibid.

Chapter 8

1. *Calvin: Institutes,* 1.5.14, 1:68.
2. Ibid., 1.14.1, 1:160.
3. Ibid., 1:160, 161.
4. Ibid., 1:160.
5. Ibid., 1.14.21, 1:180.
6. Ibid.
7. Ibid., 1:181.
8. Ibid.
9. Ibid., 1.5.2, 1:53.
10. Ibid., 1:54.
11. Ibid., 1.14.1, 1:160.
12. Ibid., 3.21.4, 2:925.
13. Ibid., 1.5.8, n. 27, 1:61.
14. Ibid., 1.14.2, 1:162.

15. Ibid., 1.16.2, 1:199.
16. See Ibid., 1.14.20–23, 1:179–82.
17. See Ibid., 1.5.1–15, 1:51–69.
18. See Ibid., 1.14.2, 1:162; 1.14.20, 1:179.
19. Ibid., 1.14.20, 1:179, 180.
20. Ibid., 1.5.4, 1:56.
21. Ibid., 1.15.5, 1:191.
22. Ibid., 1.14.20, 1:179.
23. Ibid., 1.14.21, 1:181.
24. Ibid., 1.14.20, 1:180.
25. Belgic Confession, Art. 12, in Schaff, *Creeds of Christendom*, 3:395.
26. *Calvin: Institutes*, 1.14.2, 1:161, 162; see also Calvin, *Institutes*, trans. Henry Beveridge, 1.14.2, 1:142: "the paternal goodness of God toward the human race."
27. *Calvin: Institutes*, 1.14.22, 1:182.
28. Ibid., 1.14.21, 1:181.
29. Ibid., 1.14.22, 1:182.
30. Ibid., 1.14.3, 1:162.
31. Ibid., 1:163.
32. Ibid., 1.14.17, 1:175, 176.
33. Ibid., 1.14.3, 1:163.
34. Ibid., 1.14.16, 1:175.
35. Ibid., 1.14.10, 1:170.
36. Ibid.
37. Ibid., 1.14.9, 1:169.
38. Ibid., 1.14.7, 1:167.
39. Ibid., 1.14.4, 1:164, 165.
40. Ibid., 1.14.16, 1:175.
41. Ibid., 1.14.13, 1:172.
42. Ibid., 1.14.19, 1:178, 179.
43. Ibid., 1.14.15, 1:174.
44. Ibid., 1.14.16, 1:175.
45. Ibid.
46. Ibid., 1.14.17, 1:176.
47. Ibid., 1.14.18, 1:176.
48. Ibid., 1:177.
49. Ibid.
50. Ibid., 1.15.1, 1:183.
51. Ibid., 1.14.3, 1:162.
52. Ibid., 1.15.1, 1:183.
53. Ibid., 1.1.1, 1:35.
54. Ibid., 1.15.1, 1:183.
55. Heidelberg Catechism, Q&A 6, in Schaff, *Creeds of Christendom*, 3:309.
56. See J. Lever and Walter Lagerwey, *Where Are We Headed? A Biologist Talks About Origins, Evolution, and the Future/ by Jan Lever* (Grand Rapids: Eerdmans,

1980). See also J. Lever, *Creation and Evolution* (Grand Rapids: International Publications, 1958). Originally published as *Creatie en evolutie* (Wageningen: Zomer en Keuning, 1956).

57. *Calvin: Institutes*, 1.15.1, 1:183, 184.

58. Ludwig Feuerbach, *Sämtliche Werke* (Leipzig, 1846–1866), X:5. The complete declaration indicates Feuerbach's deliberate attack on the spiritual nature of man: "Food becomes blood, blood becomes heart and brain, thoughts and sentiments. Human fare is the foundation of human culture and mind. Would you improve a nation? Give it better food instead of declamations against sin. Man is what he eats."

59. *Calvin: Institutes*, 1.15.2, 1:184.

60. Belgic Confession, Art. 37, in Schaff, *Creeds of Christendom*, 3:435.

61. *Calvin: Institutes*, 1.15.2, 1:184.

62. Ibid., 1.15.7, 1:194.

63. Ibid., 1.15.3, 1:186.

64. Ibid., 1.15.4, 1:189, 190.

65. Ibid., 1:190.

66. *Calvin: Institutes*, 1.15.8, 1:196.

67. Ibid.

68. John Calvin, *The Bondage and Liberation of the Will*, 72.

69. *Calvin: Institutes*, 1.15.8, 1:195.

70. Ibid.

71. Ibid., 1:196; see also Calvin, *Institutes*, trans. Henry Beveridge, 1.15.8, 1:170: "intermediate" will.

72. *Calvin: Institutes*, 1.15.8, 1:196.

73. Ibid.

74. Ibid.

75. Ibid., 1:195.

76. Calvin, *Commentary on the First Book of Moses Called Genesis*, 1:127.

77. *Calvin: Institutes*, 1.15.8, 1:195.

78. Ibid., 1.16.1, 1:198.

79. Heidelberg Catechism, Q&A 26, in Schaff, *Creeds of Christendom*, 3:315; emphasis added.

80. See Heidelberg Catechism, Q&A 27, in Schaff, *Creeds of Christendom*, 3:316.

81. *Calvin: Institutes*, 1.16.1, 1:198.

82. Ibid., 1.16.2, 1:199.

83. Ibid., 1.16.3, 1:201.

84. Ibid., 1.16.9, 1:208.

85. Ibid., 1.16.8, 1:207.

86. Ibid., 1.16.5, 1:204.

87. Ibid.; see also 1.16.1, 1:198.

88. Ibid., 1.16.3, 1:200, 201.

89. Calvin, "The Author's Preface," in *Commentary on the Book of Psalms*, 1:xlvi.

90. "The Consent of the Pastors of the Church of Christ at Geneva," in *Calvin's Calvinism*, 14.
91. *Calvin: Institutes*, 1.18.1, 1:228–31.
92. Ibid., 1:229.
93. Ibid., 1:228–31.
94. Ibid., 1:230.
95. Ibid., 1.18.2, 1:232.
96. Ibid., 1.18.1, 1:231.
97. Ibid., 1.18.3, 1:233.
98. Ibid.
99. Ibid.
100. Ibid., 1:234.
101. Ibid.
102. Calvin, *Institutes*, trans. Henry Beveridge, 1.18.3, 1:203.
103. *Calvin: Institutes*, 1.18.4, 1:235.
104. Ibid.
105. Ibid., 1.18.3, 1:234.
106. Ibid., 1.18.1, 1:230.
107. Ibid., 1:230; 1.18.3, 1:234.
108. Ibid., 1.18.3, 1:235.
109. Ibid., 1.16.1, 1:197, 198.
110. Ibid., 1.17.11, 1:224.
111. Heidelberg Catechism, Q&A 26, in Schaff, *Creeds of Christendom*, 3:315.
112. *Calvin: Institutes*, 1.5.7, 1:60.
113. Ibid., 1.17.1, 1:210.
114. Ibid., 3.2.28, 1:574.
115. John Calvin, *Commentaries on the Twelve Minor Prophets*, trans. John Owen, vol. 5, *Zechariah and Malachi* (Grand Rapids: Eerdmans, 1950), 49, 50.
116. Ibid., 1.16.9, 1:208.
117. Ibid., 1.16.1, 1:197.
118. Ibid., 1.16.8, 1:207.
119. Ibid.
120. John Calvin, *Concerning Scandals*, trans. John W. Fraser (Grand Rapids: Eerdmans, 1978), 53, 54.
121. *Calvin: Institutes*, 1.17.4, 1:216; 1.17.6, 1:218.
122. Ibid., 1.17.4, 1:216.
123. Ibid., 1.17.12, 1:225, 226.
124. Ibid., 1.17.13, 1:227.
125. Clark Pinnock, ed., *The Grace of God, the Will of Man: A Case for Arminianism* (Grand Rapids: Zondervan, 1989), 15.
126. Richard Rice, "Divine Foreknowledge and Free-will Theism," in Pinnock, *The Grace of God, the Will of Man*, 134.
127. *Calvin: Institutes*, 1.17.7, 1:219.
128. Ibid., 1.17.10, 1:223.

129. Ibid., 1.17.11, 1:225.
130. Ibid.
131. Ibid., 1.17.6, 1:218.
132. Ibid., 1.18.4, 1:237.

Chapter 9

1. *Calvin: Institutes*, 2.1.2, 1:243.
2. Ibid., 2.2.1, 1:256.
3. Ibid., 2.5.15, 1:335.
4. See Ibid., 2.2.10, 1:268.
5. Heidelberg Catechism, Q&A 2, in Schaff, *Creeds of Christendom*, 3:308.
6. *Calvin: Institutes*, 2.1.2, 1:242.
7. Ibid., 2.1.3, 1:244.
8. Henri Rondet, *Original Sin: The Patristic and Theological Background* (New York: Alba House, 1972), 245.
9. See Lever, *Where Are We Headed?*, and Henri Blocher, *Original Sin: Illuminating the Riddle* (Grand Rapids: Eerdmans, 1997). On the similar surrender of the biblical teaching of original sin in order to accommodate modern science by contemporary Roman Catholic theology, see S. Trooster, *Evolution and the Doctrine of Original Sin* (New York: Newman Press, 1968).
10. *Calvin: Institutes*, 2.1.3, 1:243, 244.
11. Ibid., 2.6.1, 1:341.
12. John Calvin, *Commentaries on the Epistle of Paul the Apostle to the Romans*, trans. and ed. John Owen (Grand Rapids: Eerdmans, 1948), 215. Earlier on the same text, Calvin had written, "He indeed teaches us, that it was needful that men's ruin should be more fully discovered to them, in order that a passage might be opened for the favour of God" (214).
13. *Calvin: Institutes*, 2.6.1, 1:341, 342.
14. Ibid., 2.1.8, 1:251.
15. Ibid., 1:251, 252.
16. Ibid., 2.1.5, 1:247.
17. Ibid.
18. Ibid., 2.1.4, 1:245.
19. Heidelberg Catechism, A 95, in Schaff, *Creeds of Christendom*, 3:342.
20. *Calvin: Institutes*, 2.1.6, 1:249.
21. Calvin, *The Bondage and Liberation of the Will*, 145.
22. *Calvin: Institutes*, 2.1.6, 1:249.
23. Belgic Confession, Art. 15, in Schaff, *Creeds of Christendom*, 3:400.
24. *Calvin: Institutes*, 2.1.7, 1:249.
25. Ibid., 2.1.5, 1:246.
26. Ibid., 2.1.8, 1:251.
27. Ibid., 2.5.1, 1:317.
28. Calvin, *Calvin's Calvinism*, 270.
29. Ibid.

30. Calvin, *Commentaries on the Epistle of Paul the Apostle to the Romans*, 200.
31. Ibid., 210.
32. Ibid., 201.
33. Ibid., 207.
34. Ibid., 210.
35. The verb is *kathisteemi*.
36. Again in the second part of verse 19, the verb is *kathisteemi*.
37. Canons of Dordt, 3, 4.2, in Schaff, *Creeds of Christendom*, 3:588.
38. Ibid., 3:564. The Latin original of the words "in consequence of a just judgment of God" is "*justo Dei judicio*." Some editions of the Canons, following the translation of the Reformed Dutch church, omit this phrase—a very serious defect.
39. Heidelberg Catechism, Q&A 6, in Schaff, *Creeds of Christendom*, 3:309.
40. *Calvin: Institutes*, 2.2.6, 1:262.
41. Ibid., 1:263.
42. Ibid., 1:262.
43. Calvin, *Institutes*, trans. Henry Beveridge, 2.2.6, 228. The Latin original is "*Nam phreneticos nihil moror, qui gratiam pariter et promiscue expositam esse garriunt.*" The literal translation is "For I do not delay over the madmen who prattle that grace is offered equally and promiscuously [to all]." See John Calvin, *Christianae Religionis Institutio (1559)*, in *Johannis Calvin Opera Selecta*, vol. 3, ed. P. Barth and W. Niesel (Munich: Kaiser, 1957), 248.
44. *Calvin: Institutes*, 2.5.19, 1:340.
45. Ibid., 2.1.8, 1:252.
46. Ibid., 2.1.5, 1:246.
47. Ibid., 2.2.17, 1:277.
48. Calvin, *Institutes: 1536 Edition*, 1.B.2, 15, 16.
49. Martin Luther also used the figure of a horse ridden by Satan to describe the bondage of the will of the natural man. "So man's will is like a beast standing between two riders. If God rides, it wills and goes where God wills... If Satan rides, it wills and goes where Satan wills. Nor may it choose to which rider it will run, or which it will seek; but the riders themselves fight to decide who shall have and hold it" (Martin Luther, *The Bondage of the Will*, trans. J. I. Packer and O. R. Johnston [London: James Clarke, 1957]; reprint with an introduction by J. I. Packer and O. R. Johnston, Grand Rapids: Fleming H. Revell, 1995, 103, 104).
50. *Calvin: Institutes*, 2.3.5, 1:294.
51. Calvin, *The Bondage and Liberation of the Will*, 69.
52. *Calvin: Institutes*, 2.2.27, 1:287.
53. Anthony A. Hoekema is representative of a number of Reformed theologians who opt for the interpretation of Romans 7:13–25 as a description of the condition of the unregenerated: "I believe that what we have here in Romans 7:13–25 is not a description of the regenerate man, but of the unregenerate man who is trying to fight sin through the law alone, apart from the strength of the Holy Spirit" (Anthony A. Hoekema, *The Christian Looks at Himself* [Grand Rapids: Eerdmans, 1975], 62).

54. *Calvin: Institutes*, 2.3.10, 1:304.
55. Ibid., 1:303.
56. Ibid., 2.2.13, 1:272.
57. Ibid., 2.2.14, 1:273.
58. Ibid., 2.2.17, 1:276.
59. Ibid., 2.3.3, 1:292.
60. For Abraham Kuyper's common grace theory, see *De Gemeene Gratie*, 3 vols. (Amsterdam: Höveker & Wormser, 1902–1904) and *Lectures on Calvinism* (Grand Rapids: Eerdmans, 1981). For Herman Bavinck's common grace theory, see *De Algemeene Genade* (Grand Rapids: Eerdmans-Sevensma, n.d.).
61. *Calvin: Institutes*, 2.3.3, 1:292.
62. Ibid.
63. Ibid.
64. Ibid., 1:293; emphasis added.
65. Ibid., 1:292; emphasis added.
66. Calvin, *The Bondage and Liberation of the Will*, 27.
67. Anthony A. Hoekema, *Created in God's Image* (Grand Rapids: Eerdmans, 1986), 150–52.
68. Pinnock, *The Grace of God, the Will of Man*, 21.
69. *Calvin: Institutes*, 2.5.19, 1:340.

Chapter 10

1. *Calvin: Institutes*, 2.5.19, 1:340.
2. Ibid., 2.6, 1:340–48.
3. Ibid., 2.6.1, 1:341.
4. Ibid., 1:341, 342.
5. Ibid., 1:342.
6. Ibid., 2.6.4, 1:348.
7. Ibid., 2.6.1, 1:341.
8. Ibid.
9. Ibid., 2.6.4, 1:347.
10. Ibid., 2.6.1., 1:341.
11. Ibid., 2.6.2, 1:343.
12. Ibid., 1:343.
13. Ibid.
14. Ibid., 1:344, 345.
15. Ibid., 2.7.1, 1:348.
16. Ibid.
17. Ibid., 1:349.
18. Ibid., 2.7.2, 1:351.
19. Ibid.
20. Ibid.
21. Ibid.
22. Ibid., 2.7.3, 1:351.

23. Ibid., 2.7.5, 1:353.
24. Ibid., 2.7.3, 1:352.
25. Ibid., 2.7.5, 1:353.
26. Ibid.
27. Ibid., 2.7.6, 1:354.
28. Ibid., 1:355.
29. Ibid., 2.7.7, 1:355.
30. Ibid., 1:356.
31. Ibid., 2.7.8, 1:357.
32. Ibid., 2.7.9, 1:358.
33. Ibid.
34. Ibid.
35. Ibid., 2.7.10, 1:359.
36. Ibid., 1:358.
37. Ibid.
38. Ibid., 2.7.11, 1:360.
39. Ibid., 2.7.12, 1:360.
40. Ibid., 1:361.
41. Ibid., 2.7.13, 1:362.
42. Ibid., 2.7.12, 1:361.
43. Ibid.
44. Ibid.
45. Ibid.
46. Ibid., 2.7.13, 1:362.
47. Ibid., 1:361.
48. Ibid., 2.7.14, 1:362.
49. Ibid.
50. Ibid., 1:363.
51. Ibid.
52. Ibid., 2.7.16, 1:364, 365.
53. Belgic Confession, Art. 25, in Schaff, *Creeds of Christendom*, 3:412, 413.
54. *Calvin: Institutes*, 2.8.1, 1:367, 368.
55. Ibid., 1:368.
56. Ibid.
57. Ibid., 2.8.3, 1:369.
58. Ibid., 1:369, 370.
59. Ibid., 1:370.
60. Ibid., 2.8.4, 1:370.
61. Ibid., 2.8.5, 1:371.
62. Ibid., 1:372.
63. Ibid., 1:371.
64. Ibid.
65. Ibid., 2:8.6, 1:372.
66. Ibid.

67. Ibid., 2.8.8, 1:374.
68. Ibid.
69. Ibid., 2.8.10, 1:376.
70. Ibid., 2.8.11, 1:376, 377.
71. Ibid., 1:377.
72. Ibid.
73. Ibid., 2.8.50, 1:414.
74. Ibid., 2.8.52, 1:416.
75. Ibid., 2.8.54, 1:417.
76. Ibid., 2.8.12, 1:378.
77. Ibid., 2.8.13, 1:379.
78. Ibid., 2.8.14, 1:380.
79. Ibid., 2.8.15, 1:381.
80. Ibid., 2.8.14, 1:380.
81. Ibid., 2.8.15, 1:381.
82. Ibid., 2.8.16, 1:382.
83. Ibid., 1:383.
84. Ibid.
85. Ibid., 2.8.17, 1:383.
86. Ibid., 1:384.
87. Ibid., 2.8.18, 1:385.
88. Ibid., 2.8.19, 1:386.
89. Ibid., 2.8.21, 1:387.
90. Ibid.
91. Calvin, *Institutes: 1536 Edition*, I.E.11, 21.
92. Ibid.
93. Ibid.; see also Heidelberg Catechism, A 98, in Schaff, *Creeds of Christendom*, 343.
94. Calvin, *Institutes: 1536 Edition*, I.E.11, 21.
95. *Calvin: Institutes*, 2.8.22, 1:388.
96. Ibid.
97. Ibid., 2.8.23, 1:389.
98. Ibid., 2.8.26, 1:391.
99. Ibid., 2.8.27, 1:394.
100. Ibid., 2.8.24, 1:390.
101. Ibid., 2.8.28, 1:394.
102. Ibid., 1:394, 395.
103. Ibid., 2.8.31, 1:397.
104. Ibid., 2.8.29, 1:396.
105. Ibid., 2.8.28, 1:394, 395.
106. Ibid., 1:395.
107. Ibid., 2.8.32, 1:397, 398.
108. Ibid., 1:398.
109. Ibid., 2.8.28, 1:395.

110. Ibid., 2.8.33, 1:398.
111. Ibid., 2.8.34, 1:399.
112. Ibid., 2.8.33, 1:399.
113. Ibid., 2.3.31, 1:397.
114. Ibid., 2.8.34, 1:400.
115. Ibid., 2.8.33, 1:399.
116. Ibid., 1:398.
117. Heidelberg Catechism, A 103, in Schaff, *Creeds of Christendom*, 3:345.
118. Ibid.
119. *Calvin: Institutes*, 2.8.34, 1:401.
120. Ibid., 2.8.35, 1:401.
121. Ibid., 2.8.35, 36, 1:401, 402.
122. Ibid., 2.8.36, 1:402.
123. Ibid., 2.8.38, 1:404.
124. Ibid., 2.8.37, 1:403.
125. Ibid., 2.8.38, 1:403.
126. Ibid., 2.8.40, 1:404.
127. Ibid., 2.8.41, 1:405.
128. Ibid.
129. Ibid.
130. Ibid., 2.8.42, 1:406.
131. Ibid., 2.8.43, 1:406.
132. Calvin, *Institutes: 1536 Edition*, 1.E.19, 26.
133. *Calvin: Institutes*, 2.8.44, 1:407.
134. Ibid., 1:408.
135. Ibid.
136. Ibid., 2.8.41, 1:405.
137. Ibid., 2.8.44, 1:408.
138. Ibid., 2.8.45, 1:408.
139. Ibid., 1:409.
140. Ibid., 2.8.46, 1:410.
141. Ibid.
142. Ibid., 2.8.47, 1:411.
143. Ibid., 1:412.
144. Ibid., 2.8.48, 1:412.
145. Ibid.
146. Ibid., 1:412, 413.
147. Ibid., 1:412.
148. Ibid., 2.8.49, 1:413.
149. Ibid., 2.8.50, 1:414.
150. Ibid., 2.8.51, 1:415.
151. Ibid.
152. Ibid., 2.8.54, 1:417.
153. Ibid.

154. Ibid., 2.8.55, 1:419.
155. Ibid., 2.8.56, 1:419.
156. Ibid.
157. Ibid.
158. Ibid., 2.8.57, 1:421.
159. Ibid.
160. Ibid., 2.8.58, 1:421.
161. Ibid., 2.8.59, 1:422, 423.
162. Ibid.
163. Ibid., 2.10.1, 1:429.
164. Ibid., 2.13.1, 1:474.
165. Heinrich Heppe, *Reformed Dogmatics* (London: Allen & Unwin, 1950), 371–509.
166. *Calvin: Institutes*, 2.10.1, 1:429.
167. Ibid., 2.10.2, 1:429.
168. Ibid., 2.10.1, 1:428.
169. Ibid., 2.10.2, 1:429, 430.
170. Ibid., 2.10.8, 1:434.
171. Ibid., 1:435.
172. Ibid., 2.10.20, 1:446.
173. Ibid., 2.9.4, 1:427.
174. Ibid., 2.10.1, 1:429.
175. Ibid.
176. Ibid., 2.10.15, 1:441.
177. Ibid., 2.10.19, 1:446.
178. Ibid., 2.10.10, 1:436, 437.
179. Ibid., 2.10.11, 1:437.
180. Ibid., 2.10.12, n. 11, 1:438.
181. Ibid., 2.10.20, 1:447.
182. Ibid., 2.10.23, 1:448.
183. Ibid., 1:449.
184. Ibid., 2.11.1, 1:450.
185. Ibid.
186. Ibid., 1:451.
187. Ibid., 2.11.2, 1:451.
188. Ibid., 2.11.4, 1:453.
189. Ibid., 2.11.7, 8, 1:456, 457.
190. Ibid., 2.11.9, 1:458.
191. Ibid.
192. Ibid.
193. Ibid.
194. Ibid., 2.11.11, 1:460.
195. Ibid., 2.11.12, 1:461.
196. Ibid., 2.12.1, 1:464.

197. Ibid.
198. Ibid.
199. Ibid., 2.12.3, 1:466.
200. Ibid.
201. Ibid., 2.12.1, 1:465.
202. Ibid., 2.12.4, 1:467.
203. Ibid., 2.12.5, 1:469.
204. Ibid., 2.12.7, 1:474.
205. Ibid., 2.12.5, 1:470.
206. Ibid.
207. James B. Jordan, "Merit Versus Maturity: What Did Jesus Do for Us?" in *The Federal Vision*, ed. Steve Wilkins and Duane Garner (Monroe, LA: Athanasius Press, 2004), 51–200.
208. *Calvin: Institutes*, 2.14.4, 1:486.
209. Ibid., 2.12.4, 1:467.
210. See David J. Engelsma, *Common Grace Revisited: A Response to Richard J. Mouw's* He Shines in All That's Fair (Grandville, MI: Reformed Free Publishing Association, 2003) and David J. Engelsma, *The Reformed Worldview on Behalf of a Godly Culture* (Grandville, MI: Grandville Protestant Reformed Evangelism Society, 2005).
211. *Calvin: Institutes*, 2.13.1, 1:474, 475.
212. Ibid., 2.13.3, 1:479.
213. Belgic Confession, Art. 18, in Schaff, *Creeds of Christendom*, 3:403.
214. *Calvin: Institutes*, 2.13.2, 1:477.
215. Ibid., 2.13.3, 1:479.
216. Ibid.
217. Ibid., 1:479, 480.
218. Ibid., 2.13.4, 1:481.
219. Ibid., 2.13.1, 1:475.
220. Ibid., 2.13.2, 1:477, 478.
221. Ibid., 2.13.4, 1:481.
222. Ibid., 2.14.1, 1:482.
223. Ibid., 2.14.5, 1:488.
224. Ibid., 2.14.1, 1:482.
225. Ibid.
226. Ibid., 2.14.4, 1:486, 487.
227. Ibid., 2.14.8, 1:493.
228. Schaff, *History of the Christian Church*, 7:785.
229. *Calvin: Institutes*, 2.14.8, 1:493.
230. "Form for the Installation of Professors of Theology," in *The Confessions and the Church Order of the Protestant Reformed Churches*, 297.
231. *Calvin: Institutes*, 2.14.1, 1:483.
232. Ibid., 1:482.
233. Ibid., 2.14.2, 1:484.

234. Ibid., 2.14.3, 1:485.
235. Ibid.
236. Ibid., 2.25.5, 1:501.
237. Heidelberg Catechism, A 31 and Belgic Confession, Art. 27, in Schaff, *Creeds of Christendom*, 3:318, 417.
238. Calvin: Institutes, 2.15.1, 1:494.
239. Ibid.
240. Ibid.
241. Ibid., 2.15.2, 1:495.
242. Ibid., 2.15.5, 1:500.
243. Ibid., 2.15.2, 1:496.
244. Ibid.
245. Ibid., 2.15.5, 1:500.
246. Ibid., 2.15.2, 1:496.
247. Ibid., 2.15.3, 1:496.
248. Ibid., 2.15.4, 1:499.
249. Ibid., 1:498.
250. Ibid., 1:499.
251. Ibid., 1:498.
252. Ibid., 1:499.
253. Ibid., 2.15.3, 4, 1:498, 499.
254. Ibid., 2.15.3, 1:497.
255. Ibid., 1:498.
257. Ibid., 2.15.5, 1:501.
258. Ibid.
259. Ibid., 2.15.6, 1:501, 502.
260. Ibid., 1:501.
261. Ibid.
262. Ibid., 1:502.
263. Ibid.
264. Ibid.
265. Ibid.
266. Ibid.
267. Ibid., 1:503.
268. Ibid., 2.16.1, 1:504.
269. Ibid., 1:503.
270. Ibid., 2.16.5, 1:508.
271. Ibid., 2.16.8, 1:513.
272. Ibid., 2.16.18, 1:527.
273. Ibid., 2.16.2, 1:504.
274. Ibid., 2.16.2, 3, 1:504–6.
275. Ibid., 2.16.4, 1:507.
276. Ibid., 2.16.3, 1:505, 506.
277. Ibid., 2.16.2, 1:504.

278. Ibid., 1:505; emphasis added.
279. Ibid.
280. Ibid.
281. Ibid., 2.16.4, 1:507.
282. Ibid., 2.16.5, 1:507.
283. Ibid.
284. Ibid.
285. Ibid., 1:508.
286. For the federal vision movement and doctrine, see David J. Engelsma, *The Covenant of God and the Children of Believers: Sovereign Grace in the Covenant* (Jenison, MI: Reformed Free Publishing Association, 2005).
287. *Calvin: Institutes*, 2.16.5, 1:507, 508.
288. Ibid., 1:508.
289. Ibid.
290. Ibid., 1:509.
291. Ibid.
292. Ibid., 1:508.
293. Ibid., 1:509, 510.
294. Ibid., 1:510.
295. Ibid., 2.16.6, 1:510.
296. Ibid.
297. Ibid.
298. Ibid., 3.20.45, 2:910.
299. Ibid., 2.16.6, 1:511.
300. Gustaf Aulén, *Christus Victor: An Historical Study of the Three Main Types of the Idea of Atonement*, trans. A. G. Hebert (New York: Macmillan, 1958). A recent advocacy of *Christus Victor* is Hans Boersma, *Violence, Hospitality, and the Cross: Reappropriating the Atonement Tradition* (Grand Rapids: Baker, 2004).
301. *Calvin: Institutes*, 2.16.6, 1:511.
302. Canons of Dordt, 2.8, in Schaff, *Creeds of Christendom*, 3:587.
303. *Calvin: Institutes*, 2.16.7, 1:511.
304. Ibid.
305. Ibid., 1:512.
306. Ibid.
307. Ibid., 2.16.8, 1:512, 513.
308. Ibid., 2.16.9, 1:514.
309. Ibid., 2.16.10, 1:515, 516.
310. Ibid., 2.16.11, 1:517.
311. Ibid., 2.16.12, 1:519.
312. Ibid., 1:518.
313. Ibid., 1:519.
314. Ibid.
315. Ibid., 1:518.
316. Ibid., 1:520.

317. Ibid., 2.16.11, 1:517.
318. Ibid., 2.16.12, 1:520.
319. Ibid., 2.16.13, 1:521.
320. Ibid.
321. Ibid., 1:522.
322. Ibid., 2.16.14, 1:522, 523.
323. Ibid.
324. Ibid., 1:522.
325. Ibid., 2.16.17, 1:525.
326. Ibid., 2.16.14, 1:523.
327. Ibid., 2.16.15, 1:524.
328. Ibid., 2.16.16, 1:525.
329. Ibid.
330. Ibid.
331. Ibid., 1:524.
332. Ibid., 1:525.
333. Ibid.
334. Ibid., 2.16.17, 1:525.
335. Ibid.
336. Ibid.
337. Ibid., 2.16.18, 1:526.
338. Ibid.
339. Ibid., 2.16.19, 1:527, 528.
340. Ibid., 2.17.1, 1:528.
341. Ibid.
342. Ibid., 1:529.
343. Ibid., 2.17.3, 1:530.
344. Ibid., 1:531.
345. Ibid., 2.17.4, 1:531.
346. Ibid., 2.17.5, 1:533.
347. Ibid., 1:532.
348. Ibid., 2.17.4, 1:532.
349. Ibid., 2.17.6, 1:534.
350. Ibid., 2.17.2, 1:529.
351. For the bold denial of the merit of Christ by the men of the federal (covenant) vision, see Rich Lusk, "A Response to 'The Biblical Plan of Salvation,'" in *The Auburn Avenue Theology, Pros and Cons: Debating the Federal Vision*, ed. E. Calvin Beisner (Fort Lauderdale, FL: Knox Theological Seminary, 2004), 118–48; and James B. Jordan, "Merit Versus Maturity: What Did Jesus Do for Us?" in *The Federal Vision*, 151–200. For a contemporary defense of the meritorious nature of Christ's redemptive work against the denial of his merit by the federal vision, see David J. Engelsma, "The Covenant of Creation with Adam," *Protestant Reformed Theological Journal* 40, no. 1 (November 2006): 3–42.

Chapter 11

1. *Calvin: Institutes*, 3.1.1, 1:537.
2. Ibid., 3.2.24, 1:570, 571.
3. Heidelberg Catechism, Q&A 76, in Schaff, *Creeds of Christendom*, 3:332, 333.
4. *Calvin: Institutes*, 3.3.9, 1:601.
5. Ibid., 3.1.1, 1:537.
6. Heidelberg Catechism, Q&A 20, in Schaff, *Creeds of Christendom*, 3:313.
7. *Calvin: Institutes*, 3.1.3, 1:541.
8. Ibid., 3.1.1, 1:538.
9. Ibid., 1:537.
10. Ibid., 3.2.7, 1:551; emphasis added.
11. Ibid., 3.2.15, 1:560.
12. Ibid., 3.2.16, 1:562.
13. Ibid., 3.2.19, 1:565.
14. Ibid., 3.2.24, 1:569.
15. Ibid., 1:570, 571.
16. Ibid., 3.2.14, 1:560.
17. Ibid., 3.2.15, 1:561.
18. Thomas Brooks, "Heaven on Earth: A Serious Discourse Touching a Well-Grounded Assurance," in *The Works of Thomas Brooks*, ed. Alexander B. Brosart, 6 vols. (Edinburgh: Banner of Truth, 1980), 2:335.
19. Thomas Goodwin, "An Exposition of the First Chapter of the Epistle to the Ephesians," in *The Works of Thomas Goodwin*, vol. 1 (Edinburgh: James Nichol, 1861), 235; the emphasis is Goodwin's.
20. Ibid., 228.
21. William Cunningham, "The Reformers and the Doctrine of Assurance," in *The Reformers and the Theology of the Reformation*, 124.
22. Ibid., 118.
23. Ibid., 113.
24. *Calvin: Institutes*, 3.2.40, 1:587.
25. Heidelberg Catechism, Q&A 21, in Schaff, *Creeds of Christendom*, 3:313.
26. *Calvin: Institutes*, 3.2.2, 1:544, 545.
27. Ibid., 3.2.8, 1:551–53.
28. Ibid., 3.2.10, 1:554.
29. Ibid., 3.2.11, 1:555.
30. Ibid., 3.2.12, 1:556.
31. Canons of Dordt, 3, 4.9, in Schaff, *Creeds of Christendom*, 3:589.
32. Westminster Confession of Faith, 10.4, in Schaff, *Creeds of Christendom*, 3:625.
33. *Calvin: Institutes*, 3.2.11, 1:556.
34. Canons of Dordt, 5, Error 7, in *The Confessions and the Church Order of the Protestant Reformed Churches*, 178.
35. For the statements of the union of all baptized children with Christ and

a Reformed critique, see David J. Engelsma, *The Covenant of God and the Children of Believers*.

36. *Calvin: Institutes*, 3.1.4, 1:541.
37. Ibid., 3.2.33, 1:581.
38. Ibid., 3.2.35, 1:582.
39. Ibid., 3.2.29, 1:575.
40. Ibid., 3.2.31, 1:576.
41. Ibid., 3.2.29, 1:575.
42. Ibid.
43. Ibid., 3.3.33, 1:580.
44. Ibid., 3.2.7, 1:550.
45. Ibid., 1:551.
46. Ibid., 3.2.41, 1:589.
47. Ibid., 3.2.19, 1:565.
48. Ibid., 3.2.28, 1:573.
49. Ibid., 1:574.
50. Ibid., 3.2.41, 1:589.
51. Ibid., 3.2.42, 1:590, 591.
52. Ibid., 3.3.9, 1:601.
53. Ibid., 3.3.6, 1:598.
54. Ibid., 3.3.8, 9, 1:600, 601.
55. Heidelberg Catechism, Q&A 88–90, in Schaff, *Creeds of Christendom*, 3:339.
56. *Calvin: Institutes*, 3.3.16, 1:610.
57. Ibid., 3.3.5, 1:597.
58. Ibid., 3.3.6, 1:598.
59. Ibid., 3.3.7, 1:599.
60. Ibid., 3.3.1, 1:593.
61. Ibid., 3.3.2, 1:594.
62. Ibid.
63. Ibid., 594, 595.
64. Ibid.
65. Ibid., 3.3.21, 1:615.
66. Ibid., 1:616.
67. Ibid., 3.3.20, 1:614.
68. Ibid., 3.4.3, 1:626.
69. Ibid., 3.3.22, 1:617.
70. Ibid., 3.3.21, 1:616.
71. Ibid., 3.3.22, 1:618.
72. Ibid., 3.3.23, 1:619.
73. Ibid., 3.4.1, 1:622.
74. Ibid., 1:622, 623.
75. Ibid., 3.4.2, 1:625.
76. Ibid., 3.4.3, 1:626.

77. Ibid., 3.4.27, 1:653.
78. Ibid., 3.4.2, 1:624, 625.
79. Ibid., 3.5.1, 1:670.
80. Ibid., 3.5.2, 1:671.
81. Ibid., 3.5.6, 1:676.
82. Ibid., 3.5.10, 1:684.

Chapter 12

1. *Calvin: Institutes*, 3.6.1, 1:684.
2. John Calvin, *Golden Booklet of the True Christian Life*, trans. Henry J. VanAndel (Grand Rapids: Baker Books, 1952).
3. *Calvin: Institutes*, 3.6.4, 1:688.
4. Ibid; emphasis added.
5. Ibid., 3.6.1, 1:684.
6. Ibid., 3.7.1, 1:689.
7. Heidelberg Catechism, Q&A 91, in Schaff, *Creeds of Christendom*, 3:339, 340; emphasis added.
8. *Calvin: Institutes*, 3.7.1, 1:689.
9. Ibid., emphasis added.
10. Ibid., 3.7.1, 1:690.
11. Ibid.
12. Ibid., 3.7.6, 1:696.
13. Ibid., 3.7.7, 1:697.
14. Ibid., 3.7.8, 1:698.
15. Ibid., 3.7.10, 1:701.
16. Ibid., 3.8.1, 1:702.
17. Ibid.
18. Ibid.
19. Ibid., 3.8.7, 1:707.
20. Ibid., 3.8.3, 1:704.
21. Ibid., 3.9.1, 1:712.
22. Ibid., 3.9.3, 1:714.
23. Ibid., 3.9.1, 1:712.
24. Ibid., 1:713.
25. Ibid., 3.9.2, 1:713.
26. Ibid., 3.9.1, 1:712.
27. Ibid., 3.9.3, 1:714.
28. Ibid., 3.9.5, 1:717.
29. Ibid., 1:718.
30. Ibid., 3.9.6, 1:718.
31. Ibid., 3.10.1, 1:719, 720.
32. Ford Lewis Battles, "Concerning Luxury," in *Interpreting John Calvin*, 329.
33. *Calvin: Institutes*, 3.10.4, 1:722, 723.

34. Ibid., 1:722.
35. Ibid., 3.10.5, 1:723.
36. Ibid.
37. Ibid.
38. Ibid., 3.10.6, 1:725.

Chapter 13

1. Peter A. Lillback, *The Binding of God: Calvin's Role in the Development of Covenant Theology* (Grand Rapids: Baker, 2001), 125.
2. Ibid., 192, 193.
3. Ibid., 308.
4. *Calvin: Institutes*, 3.3.1, 1:593.
5. Ibid., n. 2, 1:593.
6. Ibid., 3.16.1, 1:798.
7. Ibid., 3.11.1, 1:726.
8. John Calvin, "Reply by John Calvin to Letter by Cardinal Sadolet to the Senate and People of Geneva," in *Tracts*, 1:41.
9. *Calvin: Institutes*, 3.11.3, 1:728.
10. Ibid., 3.11.2, 1:726.
11. Ibid., 1:727.
12. Ibid., 3.17.8, 1:811.
13. Ibid., 3.12.1, 1:754.
14. Ibid., 1:754, 755.
15. Ibid., 3.11.3, 1:727.
16. Calvin, *Institutes: 1536 Edition*, 6.A.2, 177; emphasis added.
17. *Calvin: Institutes*, 3.11.6, 1:732.
18. Ibid.
19. Ibid., 3.11.7, 1:734.
20. Ibid., 3.11.2, 1:727.
21. Canons of Dordt, 2, Error 4, in *The Confessions and the Church Order of the Protestant Reformed Churches*, 165.
22. *Calvin: Institutes*, 3.11.7, 1:733, 734.
23. Ibid., 3.18.8, 1:830.
24. Ibid., 3.13.5, 1:768.
25. Wendel, *Calvin*, 262.
26. Belgic Confession, Art. 22, in Schaff, *Creeds of Christendom*, 3:408.
27. *Calvin: Institutes*, 3.11.19, 1:748.
28. Ibid.
29. Norman Shepherd, "Justification by Faith Alone," *Reformation and Revival Journal* 11, no. 2 (Spring 2002): 87.
30. *Calvin: Institutes*, 3.17.8, 1:811.
31. Calvin, *Institutes: 1536 Edition*, 6.A.2, 176.
32. *Calvin: Institutes*, 3.11.19, 1:749.
33. Ibid.

34. Ibid.
35. Ibid.
36. Ibid., 3.11.14, 1:744.
37. Ibid.
38. Ibid.
39. Ibid., 3.17.9, 1:812.
40. Ibid.
41. Ibid., 3.17.10, 1:813.
42. Ibid., 3.14.2, 1:769.
43. Westminster Confession of Faith, 16.7, in Schaff, *Creeds of Christendom*, 3:636.
44. *Calvin: Institutes*, 3.14.2, 1:770.
45. Ibid., 3.14.3, 1:770.
46. Ibid.
47. Ibid., 3.14.4, 1:771.
48. Ibid.
49. Ibid.
50. Ibid., 3.14.11, 1:778 ("principal point" is the translation of the French text; Battles translates, "pivotal point").
51. Ibid., 3.11.6, 1:731.
52. Ibid., 1:732.
53. Ibid., 1:733.
54. Ibid., 3.11.11, 1:739.
55. Ibid., 3.17.7, 1:810.
56. Heidelberg Catechism, Q&A 64, in Schaff, *Creeds of Christendom*, 3:328.
57. *Calvin: Institutes*, 3.16.1, 1:798.
58. Ibid.
59. Ibid., 3.16.3, 1:800.
60. Ibid., 3.17.2, 1:804.
61. Ibid., 3.17.6, 1:809.
62. Ibid., 3.17.13, 1:817.
63. Ibid.
64. Ibid., 3.17.11, 1:814.
65. Ibid., 1:815.
66. Ibid., 3.17.12, 1:816.
67. Ibid., 3.18.2, 1:822.
68. Ibid., 3.18.3, 1:823, 824.
69. Heidelberg Catechism, A 63, in Schaff, *Creeds of Christendom*, 3:327.
70. *Calvin: Institutes*, 3.18.1, 1:821.
71. Ibid., 3.18.4, 1:825.
72. Ibid., 3.18.2, 1:822.
73. Ibid., 3.11.12, 1:743.
74. Ibid., 3.11.23, 1:753.

75. John Calvin, *The Commentary on Epistles of Paul the Apostle to the Corinthians*, trans. John Pringle, 2 vols. (Grand Rapids: Eerdmans, 1948), 2:241, 242.
76. Ibid., 3.14.17, 1:783, 784.
77. Ibid., 3.14.20, 1:786.
78. Ibid., 3.11.1, 1:726.
79. Ibid., 3.13.3, 1:765.
80. Ibid., 3.17.11, 1:814.
81. Ibid., 3.13.2, 1:764, 765.
82. Ibid., 3.19.1, 1:833.
83. Ibid., 3.19.9, 1:840.
84. Ibid., 3.19.14, 1:846.
85. Ibid., 3.19.12, 1:845.
86. Ibid., 3.19.2, 1:834.
87. Ibid.
88. Ibid., 3.19.2, 1:834, 835.
89. Ibid., 3.19.5, 1:837.
90. Ibid., 3.19.4, 1:836.
91. Ibid., 3.19.7, 1:838.
92. Ibid., 1:839.
93. Ibid., 3.19.9, 1:841.
94. Ibid., 3.19.12, 1:845.
95. Ibid., 3.19.11, 1:843.
96. Ibid., 3.19.13, 1:845.
97. Ibid., 3.19.15, 1:848.
98. Ibid., 1:849.
99. Ibid., 1:847, 848.

Chapter 14

1. *Calvin: Institutes*, 3.20.5, 2:856.
2. Ibid., 2:855.
3. Ibid., 3.20.27, 2:887.
4. Ibid., 3.1.4, 1:541.
5. Ibid., 3.20.3, 2:851, 852.
6. Ibid., 3.20.29, 2:892, 893.
7. Ibid., 3.20.14, 2:869.
8. Ibid., 3.20.2, 2:851.
9. Ibid., 3.20.1, 2:850.
10. Ibid.
11. Ibid.
12. Ibid., 3.20.3, 2:853.
13. Ibid., 3.20.28, 2:888.
14. Ibid., 2:890.
15. Ibid.

16. Calvin, *Institutes: 1536 Edition*, 3.A.8, 72.
17. Ibid., 3.A.10, 73; see also *Calvin: Institutes*, 3.20.29, 2:891.
18. *Calvin: Institutes*, 3.20.2, 2:851.
19. Ibid., 3.20.16, 2:872.
20. Ibid., 3.20.29, 2:891, 892.
21. Ibid., 3.1.1, 1:537.
22. Ibid., 3.20.4, 5, 2:853–55.
23. Ibid., 3.20.7, 2:857.
24. Ibid., 3.20.6, 2:856.
25. Ibid., 3.20.7, 2:859.
26. Ibid., 3.20.6, 2:856.
27. Ibid., 3.20.8, 2:859.
28. Ibid., 3.20.9, 2:860.
29. Ibid., 2:861.
30. Ibid., 3.20.10, 2:861, 862.
31. Ibid., 2:861.
32. Ibid., 2:862.
33. Ibid., 3.20.11, 2:862.
34. Ibid., 3.20.12, 2:864.
35. Ibid., 2:865.
36. Ibid., 2:864, 865.
37. Ibid., 2:864.
38. Ibid.
39. Ibid., 2:865.
40. Ibid., 3.20.12, 13, 2:865, 866.
41. Ibid., 3.20.13, 2:866.
42. Ibid., 3.20.11, 2:863.
43. Ibid., 3.20.15, 2:872.
44. Calvin, *Institutes: 1536 Edition*, 3.A.4, 70.
45. *Calvin: Institutes*, 3.20.16, 2:872–74.
46. Ibid., 3.20.17, 2:875.
47. Ibid., 3.20.20, 2:877.
48. Ibid., 3.20.24, 2:883.
49. Ibid., 3.20.22, 2:880.
50. Ibid., 3.20.21, 2:880.
51. Ibid., 3.20.19, 2:876.
52. Ibid., 3.20.20, 2:878.
53. Ibid., 3.20.19, 2:877.
54. Ibid., 3.20.21, 2:879.
55. Ibid.
56. Ibid., 3.20.27, 2:886.
57. Ibid., 3.20.22, 2:881.
58. Ibid., 3.20.28, 2:890.
59. Ibid., 2:888.

60. Ibid., 2:890.
61. Ibid., 3.20.29, 2:891, 892.
62. Ibid., 2:891.
63. Ibid., 2:892.
64. Ibid., 2:892, 893.
65. Ibid., 2:892.
66. Ibid., 3.20.30, 2:893.
67. Ibid., 3.20.33, 2:896.
68. Ibid., 3.20.31, 2:894.
69. Ibid., 3.20.32, 2:895.
70. Ibid.
71. Ibid., 2:896.
72. Ibid., 3.20.33, 2:897.
73. Ibid., 3.20.35, 2:898.
74. Ibid., 3.20.34, 2:897.
75. Ibid.
76. Ibid.
77. Ibid., 3.20.35, 2:898.
78. Ibid., 2:898, 899.
79. Ibid., 2:899.
80. Ibid., 3.20.36, 2:899.
81. Ibid.
82. Ibid., 3.20.40, 2:903.
83. Ibid., 3.20.37, 2:900.
84. Ibid., 3.20.40, 2:903.
85. Ibid., 3.20.38, 2:901.
86. Ibid., 3.20.40, 2:902, 903.
87. Ibid..
88. Ibid., 3.20.41, 2:904.
89. Ibid.
90. Ibid., 3.20.42, 2:905.
91. Ibid.
92. Ibid.
93. Ibid.
94. Ibid.
95. Ibid., 2:906.
96. Ibid., 2:905.
97. Ibid; emphasis added.
98. Ibid.
99. Ibid., 2:906.
100. Calvin, *Institutes: 1536 Edition*, 3.B.20, 79, 80.
101. *Calvin: Institutes*, 3.20.43, 2:906.
102. Ibid., 2:906, 907.
103. Ibid., 2:907.

104. Ibid., 3.20.44, 2:907.
105. Ibid., 2:908.
106. Calvin, *Institutes: 1536 Edition*, 3.B.23, 81.
107. *Calvin: Institutes*, 3.20.44, 2:910.
108. Ibid.
109. Ibid., 3.20.45, 2:910.
110. Ibid.
111. Ibid., 2:910, 911.
112. Ibid., 2:911.
113. Ibid., 2:912.
114. Ibid.
115. Ibid.
116. Ibid.
117. Ibid.
118. Ibid., 2:910.
119. Ibid., 3.20.46, 2:913.
120. Ibid.
121. Ibid., 2:914.
122. Ibid., 2:913, 914.
123. Ibid., 2:914, 915.
124. Canons of Dordt, 5.4, in Schaff, *Creeds of Christendom*, 3:593.
125. *Calvin: Institutes*, 3.20.46, 2:915.
126. See Canons of Dordt, 5.4–8, in Schaff, *Creeds of Christendom*, 3:593, 594.
127. *Calvin: Institutes*, 3.20.47, 2:915, 916.
128. Ibid., 3.20.48, 2:916, 917.
129. Ibid., 3.20.49, 2:917.
130. Ibid., 3.20.50, 2:917.
131. Ibid., 2:918.
132. Ibid., 3.20.51, 2:918.
133. Ibid., 3.20.52, 2:919.
134. Ibid.
135. Ibid.
136. Ibid.
137. Ibid., 2:920.

Chapter 15

1. *Calvin: Institutes*, 3.21.1, 2:922.
2. See Calvin, *Institutes: 1536 Edition*, 2.B.21–26, 58–61.
3. Ibid., 2.B.21, 58.
4. Heidelberg Catechism, Q&A 54, in Schaff, *Creeds of Christendom*, 324, 325.
5. *Calvin: Institutes*, 3.21.1, 2:921.
6. Wendel, *Calvin*, n. 115, 268.

7. Calvin, "The Author's Preface," in *Commentary on the Book of Psalms*, xliii, xliv.
8. See Calvin, *The Bondage and Liberation of the Will*.
9. Calvin, "On the Eternal Predestination of God," in *Calvin's Calvinism*, 27.
10. See John Calvin, "Congregation on Eternal Election," trans. Philip C. Holtrop, in Philip C. Holtrop, *The Bolsec Controversy on Predestination, from 1551-1555: The Statements of Jerome Bolsec, and the Responses of John Calvin, Theodore Beza and Other Reformed Theologians* (Lewiston, NY: Edwin Mellen Press, 1993), vol. 1, bk. 2, 695–720.
11. Ibid., 697.
12. *Calvin: Institutes*, 3.21.1, 2:920.
13. Ibid.
14. Canons of Dordt, 1.4, in Schaff, *Creeds of Christendom*, 3:581.
15. Ibid., 1.6, 3:582.
16. *Calvin: Institutes*, 3.21.1, 2:921.
17. Ibid., 3.21.5, 2:926.
18. Calvin, "On the Eternal Predestination of God," in *Calvin's Calvinism*, 31.
19. *Calvin: Institutes*, 3.23.1, 2:947.
20. Ibid.
21. Calvin, "On the Eternal Predestination of God," in *Calvin's Calvinism*, 45.
22. *Calvin: Institutes*, 3.23.7, 2:955. See also Calvin, *Institutes*, trans. Henry Beveridge, 3.23.7, 2:232: "The decree, I admit, is dreadful."
23. Canons of Dordt, 1.15, in Schaff, *Creeds of Christendom*, 3:584.
24. *Calvin: Institutes*, 3.21.7, 2:931.
25. Ibid., 3.23.3, 1:950, 951: "If all whom the Lord predestines to death are by condition of nature subject to the judgment of death, of what injustice toward themselves may they complain?"; "If all are drawn from a corrupt mass, no wonder they are subject to condemnation!"
26. Ibid., 3.22.11, 2:947.
27. Ibid., 2:946, 947.
28. Ibid., 3.21.7, 2:930.
29. Ibid., 3.21.6, 2:929.
30. Calvin, *Institutes*, trans. Henry Beveridge, 3.21.6, 2:208.
31. *Calvin: Institutes*, 3.21.7, 2:930.
32. Ibid.
33. Ibid., 2:930, 931.
34. Ibid., 2:930.
35. Ibid.
36. Ibid.
37. Ibid., 2:931.
38. Ibid., 2:930.
39. Calvin, *Institutes: 1536 Edition*, 2.B.21, 58.
40. *Calvin: Institutes*, 3.24.5, 2:970.
41. Ibid.

42. Ibid.
43. Ibid.
44. Ibid.
45. Ibid., 3.24.6, 2:971, 972.
46. Ibid., 3.24.7, 2:973.
47. Ibid.
48. Ibid., 3.22.1, 2:932.
49. Ibid., 2:933.
50. Ibid., 3.22.3, 1:935.
51. Ibid., 3.22.4, 2:936.
52. Ibid., 2:936, 937.
53. Ibid., 3.22.8, 2:943.
54. Ibid., 3.24.3, 2:967.
55. Ibid., 2:968.
56. Calvin, "Congregation on Eternal Election," in *The Bolsec Controversy on Predestination*, vol. 1, bk 2, 697.
57. Ibid., 1:704.
58. Ibid., 1:697
59. *Calvin: Institutes*, 3.21.5, 2:926.
60. Ibid., 3.22.10, 2:943.
61. Ibid.
62. Ibid., 2:944.
63. Ibid., 3.24.1, 2:964.
64. Ibid., 2:965.
65. Ibid., 3.24.2, 2:967.
66. Ibid., 3.24.1, 2:964.
67. Ibid., 3.24.2, 2:967.
68. Ibid., 3.24.6, 2:971.
69. Ibid., 3.24.8, 2:974.
70. Ibid., 3.24.13, 2:979.
71. Ibid., 3.24.12, 2:978.
72. Ibid., 3.24.1, 2:964.
73. Calvin, "On the Eternal Predestination of God," in *Calvin's Calvinism*, 49–51.
74. *Calvin: Institutes*, 3.24.1, 2:966.
75. Ibid., 3.23.2, 2:949.
76. Ibid., 3.21.2, 2:923.
77. Ibid., 3.21.1, 2:923.
78. Ibid., 3.21.3, 2:924.
79. Ibid., 3.21.1, 2:921.
80. Ibid., 3.23.1, 2:947.
81. Ibid., 3.23.2, 2:949.
82. Ibid., 2:950.

83. Ibid.
84. Ibid., 3.23.3, 2:950, 951.
85. Calvin, "Defence of the Secret Providence of God," in *Calvin's Calvinism*, 283.
86. *Calvin: Institutes*, 3.23.4, 2:951.
87. Ibid.
88. Ibid., 3.23.6, 2:953.
89. Ibid., 2:954.
90. Ibid., 3.23.8, 2:956.
91. Ibid., 3.23.7, 2:955.
92. Ibid., 3.23.8, 2:957.
93. Ibid.
94. Ibid., 3.23.10, 2:958.
95. Ibid., 2:958, 959.
96. Ibid., 3.23.12, 2:960.
97. Ibid.
98. Ibid.
99. Ibid., 2:961.
100. Ibid., 3.23.13, 2:961.
101. Ibid.
102. Ibid., 2:963.
103. Émile Doumergue, *Calvijn als Mensch en Hervormer*, trans. Helena C. Pos (Amsterdam: W. tenHave, 1931), 107; the emphasis is Doumergue's; the translation of the Dutch is mine.
104. *Calvin: Institutes*, 3.24.15, 2:982.
105. Ibid., 2:982, 983.
106. Ibid., 2:983.
107. Ibid., 3.21.1, 2:922.
108. Ibid., 2:921, 922.
109. Ibid., 2:922.
110. Ibid.
111. Ibid., 3.23.14, 2:963.
112. Ibid.
113. Ibid.
114. Ibid., 2:964.

Chapter 16

1. *Calvin: Institutes*, 3.25.9, 2:1003, 1004.
2. Ibid., 2:1004.
3. Ibid., 3.25.8, 2:1002.
4. Ibid.
5. Ibid.
6. Ibid., 2:1002, 1003.

7. Ibid., 2:1002.
8. Ibid., 2.16.13, 1:522.
9. Ibid., 3.25.8, 2:1002.
10. Ibid.
11. Ibid., 3.25.2, 2:988, 989.
12. Ibid., 3.25.10, 2:1005.
13. Ibid., 3.25.3, 2:990.
14. Ibid.
15. Ibid.
16. Ibid., 2:991.
17. Ibid., 2:990.
18. Ibid., 2:991.
19. Ibid., 2:993.
20. Ibid., 3.25.4, 2:993.
21. Ibid.
22. Ibid., 2:993, 994.
23. Ibid., 3.25.5, 2:994, 995.
24. Ibid., 2:995.
25. Ibid., 2:996.
26. Ibid., 3.25.6, 2:997.
27. Ibid., 2:997, 998.
28. Ibid., 2:996.
29. Ibid., 3.25.7, 2:998, 999.
30. Ibid., 3.25.1, 2:988.
31. Ibid.
32. Ibid.
33. Ibid., 3.25.2, 2:989.
34. Ibid., 3.25.9, 2:1003, 1004.
35. Ibid., 2:1003.
36. Ibid., 2:1004.
37. Ibid., 3.25.12, 2:1007, 1008.
38. Ibid., 2:1008.
39. Ibid.
40. Ibid., 3.25.10, 2:1004.
41. Ibid.
42. Ibid., 3.25.11, 2:1006.
43. Calvin, *Institutes: 1536 Edition*, 2.B.33, 64.
44. *Calvin: Institutes*, 3.25.10, 2:1005.
45. Ibid., 2:1005, 1006.
46. Ibid., 2:1005.
47. Ibid.
48. Ibid., 3.25.11, 2:1007.
49. Ibid., 3.25.12, 2:1008.

Chapter 17

1. *Calvin: Institutes*, 4.20.2, 2:1487; 4.20.1, 2:1485.
2. Ibid., 4.20.2, 2:1487.
3. Ibid., 4.1.1, 2:1011, 1012.
4. Ibid., 2:1012.
5. John Calvin, *Institutes of the Christian Religion*, trans. John Allen (Grand Rapids: Eerdmans, 1949), 2:267.
6. *Calvin: Institutes*, 4.1.2, 2:1012, 1013.
7. Ibid., 4.1.7, 2:1021.
8. Ibid., 4.1.2, 2:1013.
9. Calvin, *Institutes: 1536 Edition*, 2.B.21, 58.
10. Ibid., 2.B.22, 58.
11. Ibid., 2.B.23, 59.
12. *Calvin: Institutes*, 4.1.7, 2:1022.
13. Ibid., 4.1.3, 2:1015.
14. Ibid., 4.1.2, 2:1014.
15. Ibid., 4.1.3, 2:1014; emphasis added.
16. Calvin, *Institutes: 1536 Edition*, 2.B.21, 58.
17. *Calvin: Institutes*, 4.1.17, 2:1031.
18. Ibid., 4.2.3, 2:1045.
19. Ibid., 4.2.4, 2:1046.
20. Heidelberg Catechism, Q&A 54, in Schaff, *Creeds of Christendom*, 3:324, 325.
21. *Calvin: Institutes*, 4.1.3, 2:1015.
22. Calvin, *Institutes: 1536 Edition*, 2.B.25, 60.
23. See Heidelberg Catechism, A 54, in Schaff, *Creeds of Christendom*, 3:325.
24. *Calvin: Institutes*, 4.1.8, 2:1022, 1023.
25. Ibid., 2:1022.
26. Ibid.
27. Ibid.
28. Ibid., 4.1.2, 2:1013; 4.1.3, 2:1014.
29. Ibid., 4.1.2, 2:1013.
30. Ibid., 4.1.1, 2:1011, 1012.
31. Ibid., 4.1.5, 2:1017.
32. Ibid., 4.1.9, 2:1023.
33. Ibid.
34. Ibid.
35. Ibid., 2:1022, 1023.
36. Westminster Confession of Faith 25.1, in Schaff, *Creeds of Christendom*, 3:657.
37. Westminster Confession of Faith 25.2, in Schaff, *Creeds of Christendom*, 3:657.
38. *Calvin: Institutes*, 4.1.9, 2:1023.

39. Ibid., 4.1.4, 2:1016.
40. Ibid., 4.1.9, 2:1023.
41. Ibid., 4.1.5, 2:1017.
42. Ibid.
43. Ibid., 2:1018.
44. Ibid.
45. Ibid., 4.11.1, 2:1211.
46. Ibid., 2:1212, 1213.
47. Ibid., 4.1.5, 2:1017.
48. Ibid., 2:1020.
49. Ibid., 4.1.6, 2:1020.
50. Ibid., 2:1021.
51. Ibid., 4.11.1, 2:1213.
52. Ibid., 4.1.7, 2:1021.
53. Ibid., 4.1.4, 2:1016.
54. Ibid.
55. Ibid.
56. Ibid., 4.1.2, 2:1012, 13; emphasis added.
57. Ibid., 4.1.3, 2:1014; emphasis added.
58. Ibid., 4.1.1, 2:1012.
59. Ibid., 4.1.9, 2:1023.
60. Ibid., 4.1.22, 2:1036.
61. Ibid., 4.12.1, 2:1230.
62. Ibid., 4.12.4, 2:1232.
63. Ibid., 4.12.1, 2:1230.
64. Ibid., 4.12.11, 2:1238.
65. Ibid.
66. Ibid., 2:1239.
67. Ibid., 4.2.1, 2:1041.
68. Ibid.
69. Ibid., 4.1.11, 2:1025.
70. Ibid., 4.1.10, 2:1024.
71. Ibid.
72. Ibid., 2:1025.
73. Ibid., 2:1024.
74. Ibid., 2:1024, 1025.
75. Ibid., 4.1.11, 2:1025.
76. Ibid., 4.1.13, 2:1026, 1027.
77. Ibid., 4.1.23, 2:1036.
78. Ibid., 4.1.17, 2:1031.
79. Ibid., 2:1032.
80. Ibid., 4.1.27, 2:1039.
81. Ibid., 4.1.15, 2:1029.
82. Ibid., 4.1.20, 2:1033; 4.1.16, 2:1030.

83. Ibid., 4.1.22, 2:1036.
84. Ibid.
85. Ibid.
86. Ibid., 4.1.12, 2:1025, 1026.
87. Ibid., 2:1026.
88. Ibid.
89. See John Calvin, "Psychopannychia," in *Tracts*, 3:413–90.
90. *Calvin: Institutes*, 4.1.12, 2:1026.
91. Ibid.
92. Ibid., 2:1025.
93. Ibid., 4.2.4, 2:1046.
94. Ibid., 4.2.2, 2:1042.
95. Ibid., 4.2.9, 2:1050.
96. Ibid., 4.2.12, 2:1052, 1053.
97. Ibid., 2:1053.
98. Ibid., 4.2.10, 2:1051.
99. Ibid., 4.2.2., 2:1042.
100. Ibid.
101. Ibid., 4.2.12, 2:1053.
102. Ibid., 4.2.11, 2:1051, 1052.
103. Ibid., 4.2.12, 2:1053.
104. Ibid., 4.2.5, 2:1047.
105. Ibid., 4.2.6, 2:1048.
106. Ibid., 4.1.1, 2:1012.
107. Ibid., 4.2.4, 2:1046.
108. Calvin, *Institutes: 1536 Edition*, 6.B.14, 184.
109. *Calvin: Institutes*, 4.3.1, 2:1053.
110. Ibid.
111. Ibid., 4.3.4, 2:1057.
112. Ibid., 4.3.2, 2:1055.
113. Ibid., 4.3.3, 2:1056.
114. Ibid., 4.3.6, 2:1058.
115. Ibid., 4.3.7, 2:1059.
116. Ibid., 2:1060.
117. Ibid., 4.3.4, 2:1057.
118. Ibid.
119. Ibid., 4.3.8, 2:1060.
120. Ibid., 2:1061.
121. Ibid.
122. Ibid., 4.3.9, 2:1061.
123. Ibid.
124. Ibid.
125. See Calvin, *Commentaries on the Epistles to Timothy, Titus, and Philemon*, 128–34.

126. *Calvin: Institutes*, 4.3.10, 2:1062.
127. Ibid., 4.3.11, 2:1062, 1063.
128. Ibid., 2:1063.
129. Ibid.
130. Ibid., 4.3.12, 2:1063.
131. Ibid.
132. Ibid., 4.3.15, 2:1066.
133. Ibid., 4.3.12, 2:1064.
134. Ibid., 4.3.15, 2:1066.
135. Ibid.
136. Ibid., 4.3.12, 2:1064.
137. Ibid., 4.13.16, 2:1066, 1067.
138. Ibid., 4.4.4, 2:1071, 1072.
139. Ibid., 2:1072.
140. Ibid., 4.4.10, 2:1078.
141. Ibid., 4.4.3, 2:1071.
142. Ibid., 4.5.1, 2:1084.
143. Ibid., 4.5.12, 2:1096.
144. Ibid., 4.5.9, 2:1093.
145. Ibid., 4.5.13, 2:1096.
146. Ibid., 4.5.1, 2:1084.
147. Ibid., 4.5.5, 2:1089.
148. Ibid., 4.5.4, 2:1088.
149. Ibid., 4.5.11, 2:1095.
150. Ibid., 4.5.15, 2:1097.
151. Ibid., 2:1097, 1098.
152. Ibid., 4.5.2, 2:1085, 1086.
153. Ibid., 2:1085.
154. Ibid., 4.5.14, 2:1097.
155. Ibid., 4.5.17, 2:1099.
156. Ibid.
157. Ibid.
158. Ibid., 4.5.19, 2:1101.
159. Ibid., 4.6.1, 2:1102.
160. Ibid., 2:1103.
161. Ibid., 2:1102.
162. The Dogmatic Decrees of the Vatican Council concerning the Catholic Faith and the Church of Christ, AD 1870, in Schaff, *Creeds of Christendom*, 2:257, 270.
163. *Calvin: Institutes*, 4.7.20, 2:1140.
164. Ibid., 4.6.1, 2:1102.
165. Ibid., 4.6.2, 2:1103.
166. Ibid., 4.6.10, 2:1111.

167. Ibid.
168. Ibid., 4.6.4, 2:1106.
169. Ibid., 4.6.6, 2:1107.
170. Ibid., 4.7.17, 2:1136.
171. Ibid., 4.7.23, 2:1143.
172. Ibid.
173. Ibid., 4.7.25, 2:1144, 1145.
174. Ibid., 4.7.29, 2:1148.
175. Ibid.
176. Ibid.
177. Ibid., 4.6.2, 2:1104.
178. Ibid., 4.8.1, 2:1149.
179. Ibid., 2:1150.
180. Ibid.
181. Ibid.
182. Ibid., 4.8.4, 2:1152.
183. Ibid., 4.8.6, 2:1154.
184. Ibid., 4.8.8, 2:1155.
185. Calvin, *Institutes*, trans. Henry Beveridge, 4.8.8, 2:394.
186. *Calvin: Institutes*, 4.8.9, 2:1157.
187. Calvin, *Institutes*, trans. Henry Beveridge, 4.8.9, 2:395; emphasis added.
188. Calvin, *Commentaries on the Epistles to Timothy, Titus, and Philemon*, 249.
189. *Calvin: Institutes*, 4.8.8, 2:1155.
190. Ibid., 4.8.10, 2:1159.
191. Ibid., 4.8.14, 2:1163.
192. Ibid., 2:1164.
193. Ibid., 4.10.18, 2:1196, 1197.
194. Ibid., 4.9.1, 2:1166.
195. Ibid., 4.9.6, 2:1170.
196. Ibid., 4.9.4, 2:1168.
197. Ibid., 4.9.8, 9, 2:1171–73.
198. Ibid., 4.9.8, 2:1172.
199. Ibid., 4.9.2, 2:1167.
200. Ibid., 4.9.8, 2:1171.
201. Ibid., 4.9.14, 2:1177, 1178.
202. Ibid., 4.8.13, 2:1162.
203. Ibid., 2:1163.
204. Ibid., 4.8.15, 2:1164.
205. Ibid., 4.10.6, 2:1184.
206. Ibid., 4.10.1, 10, 11, 29, 2:1179, 1188, 1206.
207. Ibid., 4.10.2, 2:1181.
208. Ibid., 4.10.3, 2:1181.

209. Ibid., 4.10.6, 2:1185.
210. Ibid., 4.10.1, 2:1180.
211. Ibid.
212. Ibid.
213. Ibid., 4.10.15, 2:1193.
214. Ibid., 2:1193, 1194.
215. Ibid., 4.10.7, 2:1185.
216. Ibid.
217. Ibid., 4.10.7, 8, 2:1185, 1186.
218. Ibid., 4.10.23, 24, 1201–1203.
219. Heidelberg Catechism, Q&A 96, in Schaff, *Creeds of Christendom*, 3:343.
220. Belgic Confession, Art. 32, in Schaff, *Creeds of Christendom*, 3:423.
221. *Calvin: Institutes*, 4.10.16, 2:1194.
222. Ibid.
223. Ibid., 4.10.12, 2:1190.
224. Ibid.
225. Ibid.
226. Ibid., 4.10.14, 2:1192.
227. Ibid., 2:1192, 1193.
228. Ibid., 4.10.27, 2:1205.
229. Ibid., 4.10.28, 2:1206.
230. Ibid., 4.10.29, 2:1207.
231. Ibid., 4.10.27, 2:1205.
232. Ibid., 2:1205, 1206.
233. Ibid., 4.10.32, 2:1209, 1210.
234. Ibid., 4.11.1, 2:1211.
235. Ibid.
236. Ibid., 4.11.5, 2:1217.
237. Ibid., 4.11.4, 2:1216.
238. Ibid., 4.11.1, 2:1211.
239. Ibid., 4.11.16, 2:1229.
240. Ibid., 4.12.5, 2:1232.
241. Ibid.
242. Ibid., 2:1233.
243. Ibid., 4.11.5, 2:1217.
244. Ibid., 4.12.6, 2:1234.
245. Ibid., 4.12.2, 2:1230; 4.11.5, 2:1217.
246. Ibid., 4.12.7, 2:1235.
247. Ibid., 4.12.9, 2:1237.
248. Ibid., 4.12.10, 2:1238.
249. Ibid., 4.12.8–13, 2:1236–40.
250. *Register of the Consistory of Geneva in the Time of Calvin: Volume 1, 1542–1544*, ed. Robert M. Kingdon, trans. M. Wallace McDonald (Grand Rapids: Eerdmans, 2000), 204–212.

251. *Calvin: Institutes*, 4.12.14, 2:1241.
252. Ibid., 4.12.17, 2:1243.
253. Ibid., 4.12.15, 2:1242.
254. Ibid., 4.12.17, 2:1244.
255. Ibid., 4.12.19, 2:1245.
257. Ibid.
258. Ibid., 2:1249.
259. "Form for Ordination of Elders and Deacons," in *The Confessions and the Church Order of the Protestant Reformed Churches*, 291.
260. *Calvin: Institutes*, 4.12.23, 2:1249.
261. Ibid., 4.12.23, 2:1249.
262. Ibid., 4.13.3, 2:1257.
263. Ibid., 4.12.26, 2:1252.
264. Ibid., 4.12.23, 2:1250.
265. Calvin, *Commentary on the Epistles of Paul the Apostle to the Corinthians*, 1:233.
266. Ibid., 4.12.24, 2:1251.
267. Ibid., 4.13.1, 2:1254.
268. Ibid.
269. Ibid., 2:1254, 1255.
270. Ibid., 2:1255.
271. Ibid., 4.13.3, 2:1257.
272. Ibid., 4.13.7, 2:1260.
273. Ibid., 4.13.17, 2:1271.
274. Ibid.
275. Ibid., 2:1271, 1272.
276. Ibid., 4.13.15, 2:1270.
277. Ibid., 4.13.14, 2:1268, 1269.
278. Ibid., 4.13.16, 2:1271.
279. Ibid., 4.13.12, 2:1266.
280. Ibid.
281. Ibid., 4.13.11, 2:1265.
282. Ibid., 4.13.12, 2:1266.
283. Ibid., 4.13.17, 2:1271.
284. Ibid., 4.13.6, 2:1259.
285. Ibid., 4.13.4, 5, 2:1259.
286. Ibid., 4.13, 20, 21, 2:1274–76.
287. Belgic Confession, Art. 29, in Schaff, *Creeds of Christendom*, 3:419.
288. *Calvin: Institutes*, 4.14.1, 2:1276.
289. Ibid., 4.14.4, 2:1279.
290. Ibid.
291. Ibid., 2:1279, 1280.
292. Church Order, Art. 56 and 64, in *The Confessions and the Church Order of the Protestant Reformed Churches*, 397, 399.

293. *Calvin: Institutes*, 4.14.1, 2:1277.
294. Calvin, *Institutes: 1536 Edition*, 4.A.1, 87.
295. Ibid., 4.A.9, 93.
296. *Calvin: Institutes*, 4.19.2, 2:1450.
297. Ibid., 4.14.20, 2:1296.
298. Ibid., 4.14.17, 2:1292.
299. Ibid., 4.14.16, 2:1291.
300. Ibid., 4.14.5, 2:1280.
301. Ibid., 4.14.6, 2:1281.
302. Ibid., 4.14.3, 2:1278.
303. Ibid., 4.14.9, 2:1284.
304. Ibid., 4.14.13, 2:1288, 1289.
305. Ibid., 4.14.14, 2:1289.
306. Ibid.
307. Ibid., 4.14.26, 2:1303.
308. Ibid., 4.14.14, 2:1289.
309. Ibid.
310. Ibid., 4.14.9, 2:1284.
311. Ibid., 4.14.17, 2:1293.
312. Ibid.
313. Ibid., 4.14.10, 2:1286.
314. Ibid., 4.14.16, 2:1291, 1292.
315. Ibid., 4.14.15, 2:1290.
316. Ibid., 4.14.17, 2:1292.
317. Calvin, *Institutes of the Christian Religion*, trans. John Allen, 4.14.15, 2:569.
318. *Calvin: Institutes*, 4.14.15, 2:1290.
319. Ibid.
320. Ibid., 4.14.17, 2:1293.
321. Ibid., 4.14.19, 2:1296.
322. Ibid.
323. Ibid., 4.14.22, 2:1298.
324. Ibid., 4.15.1, 2:1303.
325. Ibid., 2:1304.
326. Ibid.
327. Ibid.
328. Ibid., 4.15.2, 2:1304.
329. Ibid., 4.15.3, 2:1305.
330. Ibid.
331. Ibid., 4.15.4, 2:1306, 1307.
332. Ibid.
333. Ibid., 4.15.3, 2:1306.
334. Ibid., 4.15.5, 2:1307.
335. Ibid.

336. Ibid., 4.15.14, 2:1314.
337. Ibid., 4.14.5, 2:1307.
338. Ibid., 4.15.15, 2:1315.
339. Calvin, *Institutes: 1536 Edition*, 4.B.22, 100.
340. *Calvin: Institutes*, 4.15.6, 2:1307.
341. Ibid., 2:1308.
342. Ibid., 4.15.9, 2:1310.
343. Ibid., 4.14.25, 2:1301.
344. Ibid., 4.15.10, 2:1311.
345. Calvin, *Institutes: 1536 Edition*, 4.B.17, 97.
346. Ibid., 4.B.16, 97.
347. Ibid., 4.B.17, 97.
348. Ibid., 4.B.16, 97.
349. *Calvin: Institutes*, 4.15.11, 2:1312.
350. Belgic Confession, Art. 15, in Schaff, *Creeds of Christendom*, 3:400, 401.
351. *Calvin: Institutes*, 4.15.12, 2:1313.
352. Ibid.
353. Ibid.
354. Ibid., 4.15.13, 2:1313, 1314.
355. Ibid., 2:1314.
356. Ibid., 4.15.16, 2:1316.
357. Ibid., 4.15.19, 2:1319.
358. Ibid., 2:1320.
359. Ibid., 2:1319.
360. Ibid., 2:1320.
361. Ibid., 4.15.22, 2:1322.
362. Ibid., 4.15.20, 2:1321, 1322.
363. Ibid., 2:1321.
364. Ibid.
365. Ibid., 4.16.1, 2:1324.
366. Ibid.
367. Ibid.
368. Ibid., 4.16.31, 2:1353.
369. Ibid., 2:1358.
370. Ibid., 4.16.2, 2:1325.
371. Ibid., 4.16.24, 2:1347.
372. Ibid., 4.16.6, 2:1329.
373. Ibid., 4.16.5, 2:1328.
374. Ibid., 4.16.2, 2:1325.
375. Ibid., 4.16.11, 2:1333.
376. Ibid., 4.16.6, 2:1328.
377. Ibid., 4.16.7, 2:1330.
378. Ibid., 4.16.8, 2:1331.
379. Ibid., 4.16.5, 2:1328.

380. Ibid.
381. Ibid., 4.16.17, 2:1339.
382. Ibid., 2:1340.
383. Ibid.
384. Ibid., 4.16.18, 2:1341.
385. Ibid., 4.16.20, 2:1343.
386. Ibid., 4.16.31, 2:1354, 1355.
387. Ibid., 4.16.26, 2:1349.
388. Ibid., 4.15.20, 2:1321.
389. Ibid., 4.16.21, 2:1344.
390. Ibid., 4.16.5, 2:1328.
391. Ibid., 4.16.10, 2:1333.
392. Ibid., 4.16.20, 2:1343.
393. Ibid., 4.16.23, 2:1346.
394. Ibid., 4.16.30, 1352, 1353.
395. Ibid.
396. Ibid., 4.16.1, 2:1324.
397. Ibid., 4.16.10, 2:1332, 1333.
398. Ibid., 4.16.26, 2:1349.
399. Ibid., 4.16.9, 2:1332.
400. Ibid., 4.16.8, 2:1331.
401. Ibid., 4.16.32, 2:1358, 1359.
402. Ibid., 2:1359.
403. Ibid., 4.16.9, 2:1332.
404. Ibid., 4.16.32, 2:1359.
405. Ibid., 4.14.22, 2:1298.
406. Ibid., 4.17.1, 2:1360.
407. Ibid., 4.17.11, 2:1371.
408. Ibid.
409. Ibid., 4.17.1, 2:1360.
410. Ibid., 4.17.11, 2:1371, 1372.
411. Ibid., 4.17.14, 2:1376.
412. Ibid., 4.17.1, 2:1360.
413. Ibid., 4.17.39, 2:1416.
414. Ibid., 4.17.5, 2:1364.
415. Ibid., 4.17.1, 2:1360, 1361.
416. Ibid., 4.17.4, 2:1363.
417. Ibid., 4.17.6, 2:1366.
418. Ibid., 4.17.5, 2:1364.
419. Ibid., 2:1364, 1365.
420. Ibid., 4.17.5–7, 2:1364–68.
421. Ibid., 4.17.5, 2:1365.
422. Ibid., 4.17.7, 2:1367.
423. Ibid., 4.17.32, 2:1403.

424. Ibid., 4.17.8, 2:1368.
425. Ibid., 4.17.10, 2:1370.
426. Ibid., 4.17.19, 2:1382.
427. Ibid., 4.17.10, 2:1371.
428. Ibid., 4.17.24, 2:1390.
429. Ibid., 4.17.5, 2:1365; emphasis added.
430. Ibid., 4.17.31, 2:1403; emphasis added.
431. Ibid., 4.17.10, 2:1370.
432. Ibid., 4.17.12, 2:1373.
433. Ibid., 4.17.33, 2:1405.
434. Ibid.
435. Ibid., 4.17.5, 2:1365.
436. Ibid., 4.17.33, 2:1406.
437. Ibid.
438. Ibid., 4.17.34, 2:1410.
439. Ibid., 4.17.40, 2:1417.
440. Ibid., 4.17.37, 2:1414.
441. Ibid., 4.17.38, 2:1414.
442. Ibid., 2:1415.
443. Ibid., 4.17.41, 2:1418.
444. Ibid., 4.17.42, 2:1419.
445. Ibid., 2:1420.
446. Ibid., 4.17.44, 2:1423.
447. Ibid., 4.17.43, 2:1420.
448. Ibid., 2:1420, 1421.
449. Ibid., 4.17.47, 2:1425.
450. Ibid., 4.17.50, 2:1428.
451. Ibid., 4.17.43, 2:1421.
452. Ibid., 4.17.46, 2:1424.
453. Ibid., 4.17.43, 2:1421, 1422.
454. Ibid., 4.17.5, 2:1364, 1365.
455. Ibid., 4.17.12, 2:1372.
456. The hatred of the Lutherans for the Reformed doctrine of the Lord's supper and the ferocity of their attack on those who hold it, specifically Calvin, are evident in Calvin's defense of the Reformed doctrine of the supper against the attacks on it by the Lutheran theologian Joachim Westphal (John Calvin, "Second Defence of the Pious and Orthodox Faith concerning the Sacraments in Answer to the Calumnies of Joachim Westphal" and "Last Admonition of John Calvin to Joachim Westphal," in Calvin, *Tracts*, vol. 2, trans. Henry Beveridge (Edinburgh: Calvin Translation Society, 1849, 245–494). Such was the antipathy of Westphal to the Reformed doctrine of the supper in particular that, as Calvin put it, the Lutheran "would sooner immerse himself in the deepest pools of the Papacy than make any approach to us [Reformed]" (Calvin, "Second Defence," 341).

457. *Calvin: Institutes*, 4.17.12, 2:1372.
458. Ibid., 4.17.14, 2:1374.
459. Ibid., 4.17.15, 2:1377.
460. Ibid., 4.17.14, 2:1374, 1375.
461. Ibid., 4.17.12, 2:1373.
462. Ibid., 4.17.20, 2:1383.
463. Ibid., 4.17.21, 2:1385.
464. Ibid., 4.17.13, 2:1374.
465. Ibid., 4.17.36, 2:1412.
466. Ibid., 4.17.16, 2:1379.
467. Ibid., 4.17.20, 2:1383.
468. Ibid., 4.17.30, 2:1401.
469. Ibid., 2:1402.
470. Ibid., 4.17.24, 2:1391.
471. Ibid., 4.17.30, 2:1402.
472. Symbol of Chalcedon, in Schaff, *Creeds of Christendom*, 2:62.
473. *Calvin: Institutes*, 4.17.30, 2:1402.
474. Ibid., 4.17.27, 2:1394.
475. Ibid., 4.17.22, 2:1387.
476. Ibid., 4.17.23, 2:1389.
477. Ibid., 4.17.32, 2:1404.
478. Ibid., 4.18.1, 2:1429.
479. Ibid.
480. Ibid.
481. Ibid., 4.18.18, 2:1445.
482. Ibid.
483. Ibid., 4.18.2, 2:1430, 1431.
484. Ibid., 4.18.3, 2:1431, 1432.
485. Ibid., 4.18.6, 2:1435.
486. Ibid., 4.18.7, 2:1435.
487. Ibid., 4.18.8, 2:1437.
488. Ibid., 4.18.14, 2:1443.
489. Ibid., 2:1442.
490. Heidelberg Catechism, Q&A 80, in Schaff, *Creeds of Christendom*, 3:335, 336.
491. *Calvin: Institutes*, 4.19.1, 2:1448.
492. Ibid., 4.19.2, 2:1450.
493. Ibid., 4.19.8, 2:1456, 1457.
494. Ibid., 4.19.13, 2:1461.
495. Ibid., 4.19.17, 2:1465.
496. Ibid.
497. Ibid., 4.19.18, 2:1466.
498. Ibid., 2:1466, 1467.
499. Ibid., 4.19.21, 2:1468.

500. Ibid., 2:1469.
501. Ibid., 4.19.23, 2:1471.
502. Ibid., 4.19.28, 2:1476.
503. Ibid.
504. Ibid., 4.19.34, 2:1481.
505. Ibid., 4.19.35, 36, 2:1482, 1483.
506. Ibid., 4.19.36, 2:1483.
507. Ibid., 4.19.37, 2:1483, 1484.
508. Ibid., 4.1.1, 2:1012.

Chapter 18

1. *Calvin: Institutes*, 4.1.1, 2:1011, 1012.
2. Ibid., 4.20.2, 2:1487.
3. Ibid., 3.19.1, 1:833.
4. Ibid., 3.19.15, 1:847.
5. Ibid., 1:847, 848.
6. Ibid., 4.20.1, 2:1485.
7. Ibid., 3.19.15, 1:847.
8. Ibid., 4.20.1, 2:1485, 1486.
9. Ibid., 4.20.7, 2:1492.
10. Ibid., 4.20.22, 2:1509, 1510.
11. Ibid., 2:1510.
12. Ibid., 4.20.4, 2:1489.
13. Ibid., 4.20.7, 2:1492, 1493.
14. Ibid., 4.20.8, 2:1494.
15. Ibid., 4.20.1, 2:1486.
16. Ibid., 4.20.25, 2:1512.
17. Ibid., 4.20.3, 2:1488.
18. Ibid., 4.20.2, 2:1487.
19. Ibid., 4.20.25, 2:1512.
20. Ibid., 4.20.1, 2:1485.
21. Ibid., 4.20.9, 2:1496.
22. Ibid.
23. Ibid., 4.20.5, 2:1490.
24. Ibid., 4.20.1, 2:1486.
25. Ibid., 4.20.3, 2:1488.
26. Ibid., 4.20.4, 2:1489.
27. Ibid., 2:1490.
28. Ibid., 4.20.8, 2:1494.
29. Ibid., 4.20.7, 2:1492.
30. Ibid., 4.20.8, 2:1493.
31. Ibid.
32. Ibid.
33. Ibid.

34. Ibid., 2:1493, 1494.
35. Ibid., 2:1494.
36. Ibid., 4.20.9, 2:1495.
37. Ibid., 2:1497.
38. Ibid., 2:1496.
39. Ibid., 4.20.10, 2:1497.
40. Ibid., 2:1498.
41. Ibid., 2:1499.
42. Ibid., 4.20.11, 2:1499.
43. Ibid., 4.20.12, 2:1500.
44. Ibid., 2:1500, 1501.
45. Ibid., 2:1501.
46. Ibid., 2:1500.
47. Ibid., 4.20.13, 2:1501.
48. Ibid.
49. Ibid., 4.20.9, 2:1495.
50. Ibid., 4.20.2, 2:1487.
51. Ibid., 4.20.9, 2:1495.
52. Belgic Confession, Art. 36, in Schaff, *Creeds of Christendom*, 3:432. Most Reformed churches, including the Protestant Reformed Churches, have relieved their members of the obligation to subscribe to this teaching of their creeds.
53. Calvin: *Institutes*, 4.20.9, 2:1495.
54. Ibid., 4.20.1, 2:1485; emphasis added.
55. Ibid., 2:1486. For a thorough critique of the doctrine that God calls the state to enforce the first table of the law, indeed the entire decalogue, see David J. Engelsma, "The Messianic Kingdom and Civil Government," *Protestant Reformed Theological Journal* 37, no. 2 [April 2004]: 8–44.
56. Calvin: *Institutes*, 4.20.14, 2:1502.
57. Ibid.
58. Ibid., 4.20.16, 2:1505.
59. Ibid., 4.20.15, 2:1503.
60. Ibid., 4.20.16, 2:1504.
61. Ibid.
62. Ibid., 4.20.17, 2:1506.
63. Ibid., 4.20.18, 2:1506.
64. Ibid., 2:1507.
65. Ibid., 4.20.21, 2:1509.
66. Church Order, Art. 28, in *The Confessions and the Church Order of the Protestant Reformed Churches*, 389.
67. Calvin: *Institutes*, 4.20.22, 2:1509, 1510.
68. Ibid., 2:1510.
69. Ibid., 4.20.23, 2:1510.
70. Ibid.

71. Ibid., 2:1511.
72. Ibid.
73. Ibid., 4.20.24, 2:1511.
74. Ibid., 4.20.25, 2:1513.
75. Ibid., 2:1512.
76. Ibid.
77. Ibid., 4.20.31, 2:1518.
78. Ibid., 2:1519.
79. Theodore Beza, "Concerning the Rights of Rulers over Their Subjects and the Duty of Subjects towards Their Rulers," trans. Henri-Louis Gonin (Cape Town, Pretoria, South Africa: H. A. U. M., nd.).
80. *Calvin: Institutes*, 4.20.32, 2:1520.
81. Ibid., 4.20.31, 2:1518.
82. Ibid., 4.20.32, 2:1521.
83. Ibid.